British Theatre Yearbook 1990

Edited by
DAVID LEMMON

CHRISTOPHER HELM
London

© 1990 David Lemmon

Christopher Helm (Publishers) Ltd. Imperial House,
21–25 North Street. Bromley. Kent BR1 1SD

ISBN 0-7470-2016-7

A CIP catalogue record for this book is available from the
British Library.

All rights reserved. No reproduction, copy or transmission of this
publication may be made without written permission.

No paragraph of this publication may be reproduced, copied or
transmitted save with written permission or in accordance with
the provisions of the Copyright Act 1956 (as amended), or under
the terms of any licence permitting limited copying issued by
the Copyright Licensing Agency, 7 Ridgmount Street,
London EC1E 7AE.

Any person who does any unauthorised act in relation to this
publication may be liable to criminal prosecution and civil claims
for damages.

Designed and produced in association with Book Production
Consultants, Cambridge.
Typeset by Cambridge Photosetting Services
Printed and bound in Guildford by Biddles Ltd

Contents

Introduction	iv
Section One THE LONDON THEATRE: THE WEST END	1
Section Two THE NATIONAL THEATRE	83
Section Three THE ROYAL SHAKESPEARE COMPANY with an article by Michael Billington	103
Section Four OUTER LONDON, FRINGE AND THEATRE CLUBS	129
Section Five REGIONAL THEATRE	199
Section Six THE TOURING COMPANIES	339
Index of Plays	373

Introduction

David Lemmon *is the author of more than 35 books which reflect his passions for the theatre and cricket. In the late 1950s he was Professional Director of the American Little Theatre in Ankara, Turkey, and more recently he has been an examiner in theatre studies. He is a freelance reviewer for the national press.*

'The theatrical profession is notorious for its extravagance both in praise and blame.' So said Sir Alec Guinness during his tribute to Lord Olivier at the memorial service for the great actor, who died last year. As Sir Alec pointed out, 'great' is a much abused word, but it is:

> a vastly refreshing one when it can be used with total confidence, as it can of Olivier. I wouldn't be sure how to define it when applied to an actor, but it is easily recognisable when seen. Perhaps it consists of a happy combination of imagination, physical magnetism, a commanding and appealing voice, an expressive eye – and danger. Larry always carried the threat of danger with him.

Olivier's contribution to the theatre is immeasurable. We can only begin to glean its magnitude when we consider that many who have never been within the walls of a theatre to see a professional production were still affected by his death. His legacy is tangible, not least in the quality of the National Theatre which he did so much to help bring into being, but because, as Sir Alec Guinness noted, he showed us that the best theatre must always live with the threat of danger. It is the response to this danger which gives theatre its dynamism. Countless examples will be found in the pages that follow – the courageous and vigorous programmes to be found in theatres at Derby and Watford, Michael Napier Brown's decision to stage *Long Day's Journey Into Night* at Northampton, Alan Cody doubling the parts of Leontes and Autolycus and playing 35 venues in seven weeks for The Orchard Theatre – and there are many more.

Such energy and courage has taken British theatre to the forefront in the world, and 1989 will be remembered not simply and sadly for the death of Olivier – which brought an era to an end – but also for the quality of several productions and performances throughout the country.

Sir Alec Guinness spoke in his tribute to Olivier of the nonsense and unfairness of dubbing an actor a 'second Olivier'. 'If he is of outstanding talent and character, then he will carve out his career in his own right and in his own name.' That is an undeniable truth, and it is a healthy theatre that can boast the talent that was apparent in 1989.

Trevor Nunn illuminated *Othello* in such a way as to make one wonder why there had ever been any ambiguities in interpretation. Ian McKellen's Iago took us to the very heart and soul of the character from the first line, and Zoe Wanamaker and Imogen Stubbs achieved a delicacy of relationship that one has rarely seen equalled; that is, unless one thinks of *The Master Builder* with John Wood and Joanna Pearce in Adrian Noble's haunting production.

Greatness, and one has no hesitation in using the word, was not the monopoly of the RSC, for the National Theatre gave us, in *Ghetto*, a production that will remain stamped indelibly upon the mind and the senses. I have sung the praises of Maria Friedman, John Woodvine, Alex Jennings and the rest most fully in the appropriate section.

Nor would one want to forget, in more humble surroundings, Philip Voss and Annabelle Apsion in *Abingdon Square* at the Soho Poly. There were moments of magic here. And, indeed, there were in many places from Edinburgh to Bristol, and from Perth to Bagnor. The theatre was alive and well.

Its importance in our lives was epitomised by the public reaction to the discovery of the remains of the Rose Theatre. It was not just the theatrical profession that demanded that those remains be preserved; there was a public interest that swayed politicians and developers.

This concern for the traditions of our theatre at last touched the government. In the midst of a most difficult economic crisis, they sensibly made more money available to the arts, realising the reduction that can be made in the horrendous trade deficit by contributions, mighty ones, from the invisible earnings of theatre and the arts through tourism and prestigious exports. We have a theatre of which we should be proud.

There was an excellent response – and much very useful and constructive criticism – to last year's *British Theatre Yearbook*, the first. This second edition is fuller and most, although not all, of the gaps have been filled. This living history of the British theatre will only be complete when, each year, every professional production is recorded with a full cast list and comments. We have come much closer to that ideal, but we still lack one or two theatres of note and several small touring companies. Press and publicity communication is not the strongest point of many companies and theatres.

All information will be welcomed and used, and all letters will be acknowledged.

David Lemmon

All information to:
26 Leigh Road
Leigh-on-Sea
Essex SS9 1LD

Photographic Credits

Cover
Thanks are due to the Soho Poly Theatre and to Peter Thompson (photographer John Haynes) for supplying and granting permission to use the photographs on the cover.

Section One
Thanks are due to the following for supplying and granting permission to use the photographs in this section:

Lynne Kirwin Associates – *M. Butterfly* (photographer Nobby Clarke).

Peter Thompson – *Miss Saigon* (photographer Michael Le Poer Trench); *Lettice and Lovage* (photographer Catherine Ashmore); *The Phantom of the Opera* (photographer Clive Barda); *Les Misérables* (photographer Michael Le Poer Trench); *The Merchant of Venice* (photographer John Haynes); *Exclusive* (photographer John Haynes).

Matthew Freud – *Me and My Girl* (photographer Mike Martin).

Bill Kenwright – *Blood Brothers*.

Sue Hyman – *The Black Prince* (photographer John Haynes).

Lipsey Meade – *Return to the Forbidden Planet* (photographer Nobby Clarke).

Town House Publicity for all photos at The Old Vic Theatre (photographer Simon Annand).

Peter Saunders – *The Mousetrap*.

Theatre of Comedy – *Run For Your Wife*.

Young Vic Theatre – *Two Way Mirror* (photographer John Haynes); *Measure for Measure* (photographer Carol Baugh); *From the Mississippi Delta* (photographer Sheila Burnett).

Section Two
All photographs for this section were supplied by the Royal National Theatre Press Office, with the exception of the picture of Maria Friedman which was supplied by Noel Gay Artists. Our thanks are due to the National Theatre and to Noel Gay for providing photographs and granting permission to publish them. (Photographers: *Ghetto* – Clive Barda; *Fuente Ovejuna* – Robert Workman; *Speed-the-Plow* – Nobby Clark; *Hedda Gabler* and *Hamlet* – John Haynes; *The Voysey Inheritance* – Gerry Murphy; *The Grapes of Wrath* – Michael Brosilau.)

Section Three
All photographs in this section were supplied by the press office of the Royal Shakespeare Company. Our thanks are due to them for supplying the photographs and for granting permission to publish them.

Section Four
Thanks are due to the following for supplying and granting permission to publish photographs:

Soho Poly Theatre – *Below the Belt* (photographer Sarah Ainslie); *State of Play*; *Caving In* (photographer Corneyl Jay); *Abingdon Square* (photographer Sarah Ainslie); *Leaf Storm* (photographer Bob Watkins).

The Bush Theatre – *The Marshalling Yard* (photographer Sarah Ainslie).

The Gate Theatre – *The Infant* (photographer Sheila Burnett); *Getting Nowhere – Again*; *Mercedes*.

King's Head Theatre Club – *Peace in Our Time* (photographer Conrad Blakemore); *The Days of Cavafy* (photographer Nicholas Cook).

Riverside Studios – *Shylock* (photographer of Julie Legrand and Jan Shand, Gordon Rainsford).

Talawa Theatre Company – *The Gods Are Not to Blame*.

Warehouse Theatre Croydon – all production photos from that theatre (photographer Paul Thompson).

Section Five
Thanks are due to the theatres in this section which supplied and granted permission for the publication of all the photographs:

Palace Theatre, Westcliff-on-Sea (photographer John Alexander).

Watermill Theatre, Bagnor – *Pack of Lies*, and *Caste* (photographer Lawrence Burns).

Bristol Old Vic – *In the Ruins* (photographer Allen Daniels).

PHOTOGRAPHIC CREDITS

Chichester Festival Theatre.

Belgrade Theatre, Coventry.

Queen's Theatre, Hornchurch.

Wolsey Theatre, Ipswich – *The Importance of Being Earnest* (photographer Eric Palmer).

Century Theatre, Keswick – *City Sugar* and *Play It Again, Sam* (photographer Phil Cutts); *They're Playing Our Song* (photographer Alan C Balsillie).

Liverpool Playhouse – (photographer Phil Cutts).

Northern Stage Company – *Educating Rita*; Talawa Theatre Company – *The Importance of Being Earnest* (photographer Raissa Page).

Perth Theatre (photographer Louis Flood).

Pitlochry Festival Theatre (photographer Sean Hudson).

Theatre Royal, Plymouth.

Palace Theatre, Watford – *Candle-Light* (photographer Donald Cooper).

Section Six
Thanks are due to the following for supplying and granting permission to publish photographs:

Cheek By Jowl – *The Doctor of Honour* (photographer Alastair Muir); *Lady Betty* (photographer Simon Annand).

The Cambridge Theatre Company – *How The Other Half Loves*.

Cavalcade Theatre Company – *Brer Rabbit*; *Alice in Wonderland*.

Vicky Huntley, The Churchill Theatre – *Towards Zero*.

Julia Clotworthy Bird, Theatre Royal, Bath – *The Royal Hunt of the Sun* (photographer Phil Cutts).

Eastern Angles Theatre Company – *Moll Flanders*; *Waterland*.

Hull Truck Company – *Gargling with Jelly*, *Northern Lights*, *Teechers* (photographer Steve Morgan); *Playing Away* (photographer Keith Wade); *Catwalk* (photographer Sean Hudson).

Orchard Theatre Company – *Cold Comfort Farm*; *Hitler's Whistle*; *The Winter's Tale*.

Red Shift Theatre Company and the Warehouse Croydon – *Frida and Diego*.

SECTION ONE

The London Theatre
The West End

1. *G G Goei and Anthony Hopkins in David Henry Hwang's* M Butterfly *at the Shaftesbury Theatre.*

Adelphi Theatre

STRAND, LONDON WC2E 7NA
01-836-7611

Controller **Christopher Blackburn**

Me and My Girl (1937)

Opened at the Adelphi, 12 February 1985

The Leicester Haymarket production of *Me and My Girl* completes its fifth year at the Adelphi early in 1990. It won two Laurence Olivier Awards in 1985, for Best Musical and Best Actor in a Musical, the latter being Robert Lindsay, the first Bill Snibson in the Leicester Haymarket production. Lindsay also took one of the awards which the show claimed on Broadway. It has since opened in ten other countries. The original production opened at the Victoria Palace in 1937 and ran for a

2. Gary Wilmot and Jessica Martin in Me and My Girl at the Adelphi Theatre.

3. Patrick Cargill (Sir John Tremayne) on bended knee to Eileen Page (The Duchess of Dene) in the Adelphi Theatre's long-running musical success Me and My Girl.

Bill Snibson **Gary Wilmot**
Sally Smith **Jessica Martin**
Maria, Duchess of Dene **Eileen Page**
Sir John Tremayne **Patrick Cargill**
Lady Jaqueline Carstone **Meryl Richardson**
Hon. Gerald Bolingbroke **Andrew Charleson**
Herbert Parchester **Roy Macready**
Sir Jasper Tring **Douglas Anderson**
Charles the Butler **Lloyd Lamble**
Lord Battersby **Stuart Sherwin**
Lady Battersby **Marie Lorraine**
Mrs Brown/Mrs Worthington-Worthington **Joyce Blane**
Bob Barking **Andrew Bradley**
Sophia Stainsley-Asherton **Eileen Bell**
Constable/Pearly King **John Waldon**
Lady Brighton/Cook **Anne Grayson**
Miss Miles **Chris Moppett**
Chauffeur/Jonathan Hareford **James Tear**
Major Domo **David Taegar**
Pearly Queen **Jackie Dunn**
Lady Diss **Taffy Taylor**
Thomas De Hareford/Hall Footman **Robert Rawles**
Lord French **Austin Kent**
Richard Hareford **Richard Mitchell**
Simon De Hareford **Philip Hazelby**
Telegraph Boy **Nigel Garton**
Cockney Tart **Kathy Norcross**
Maids/Guests/Cockneys **Amanda Dyer, Gemma Harding and Hayley Milton**

Footmen/Guests/Cockneys **David Ashley, Jeff Crossland, Ian Davies, Nicholas French and Geoff Steer**

Book and Lyrics **L Arthur Rose and Douglas Furber**
Music **Noel Gay**

Design **Martin Johns**
Costume **Anne Curtis**
Lighting **Chris Ellis**
Sound **Rick Clarke**
Choreographer **Gillian Gregory**
Musical Director **Robert Scott**
Director **Mike Ockrent**

record 1,646 performances, but the current production surpassed that number early in 1989.

Linked tenuously in theme to *Pygmalion*, Me and My Girl tells of a cockney lad, Bill Snibson, who suddenly discovers he is an earl. He is ultimately reunited with his sweetheart, Sally Smith, who, like him, has been groomed to take on her new position in life. The success of the musical is based on the exuberance of its songs, many of which have passed into folklore.

Robert Lindsay and Emma Thompson starred in the show in 1985. They have been followed by Enn Reitel, Su Pollard, Lorraine Chase, Bonnie Langford and David Schofield. In 1989, television star Gary Wilmot and rising star Jessica Martin took over the leading roles.

Albery Theatre

ST MARTIN'S LANE, LONDON WC2
01-867-1115

General Manager **Hugh Hales**

Blood Brothers (1983)
WILLY RUSSELL

Opened 28 July 1988

Mrs Johnstone **Angela Richards**
Narrator **Mark Jefferis**
Mickey **Steve McGann**
Eddie **Robin Hart**
Sammy **Phil Hearne**
Linda **Elizabeth Morton**
Mrs Lyons **Helen Hobson**
Mr Lyons **John Conroy**
Policeman/Teacher **Ian Burns**
Donna Marie/Miss Jones **Dee Robillard**
Perkins **Scott Farrell**
with **Fiona Campbell, Tom Roberts and Alex Harland**

Design **Marty Flood**
Lighting **Jon Swain**
Sound **Jon Miller**
Musical Director **Rod Edwards**
Director **Bob Tomson**

Blood Brothers won the SWET Award as the best musical of 1983. Five years later it returned to the West End and was rapturously received once again. It is currently booking until the end of 1990. The highly talented Willy Russell has produced a musical play which is musically and lyrically engaging, notably through the haunting recurrence of the Marilyn Monroe metaphor. Made wretched by poverty, Mrs Johnstone is forced to sell one of her sons at birth to the lady for whom she cleans.

The lives of the two brothers later cross, with tragic consequences. This is a musical which deserves every success that has come its way. It confronts us with the reality of our 'two nations', disturbs us and yet neither preaches nor fails to entertain.

4. Steve McGann and Robin Hart in Blood Brothers *at the Albery Theatre. A musical of quality and social significance.*

Aldwych Theatre

ALDWYCH, LONDON WC2
01-836-6404

The Black Prince (1989)
IRIS MURDOCH

25 April–30 September 1989

Bradley Pearson **Ian McDiarmid**
Francis **John Fortune**
Arnold Baffin **Simon Williams**
Rachel Baffin **Sarah Badel**
Julian Baffin **Abigail Cruttenden**
Priscilla **Norma West**
Christine **Deborah Norton**
Policemen **Peter Yapp,
Christopher Mitchell**
Policewoman **Norma Streader**

Design **Ultz**
Lighting **Gerry Jenkinson**
Music **Ilona Sekacz**
Director **Stuart Burge**

Iris Murdoch's adaption of her novel succeeded *The Sneeze* at the Aldwych Theatre in April. Bradley Pearson is a retired tax inspector and would-be writer whose literary perfectionism prevents him from actually putting pen to paper. He is emotionally stirred by Julian Baffin, the teenage daughter of his friends, Arnold and Rachel, and from his meeting with her emerges what Michael Ratcliffe in *The Observer* described as 'a convincing and resilient play about love, not to mention art, pain, joy, death and the whole damn thing'. At the heart of the story is, as Michael Billington said, 'the Platonic idea of love as the gateway to knowledge'. The performances of Ian McDiarmid, Abigail Cruttenden, John Fortune, Sarah Badel and the supporting cast were very highly praised.

The Black Prince closed at the end of September and was replaced by *The Cherry Orchard*, with Judi Dench. The latter opened on 24 October and details will be included in the third edition of the *British Theatre Yearbook*.

5. The Black Prince *occupied most of the year at the Aldwych Theatre. Sarah Badel (Rachel Baffin) and Ian McDiarmid (Bradley Pearson) console Francis, played by John Fortune, in this play about love as a gateway to knowledge which Iris Murdoch based on her own novel.*

Ambassadors

WEST STREET, LONDON WC2
01-836-6111

Theatre Manager **Wilfred Blunden**

Les Liaisons Dangereuses (1985)

CHRISTOPHER HAMPTON from the novel by Choderlos de Laclos

Opened 2 October 1986

Major-domo **Julien Ball**
La Marquise de Merteuil **Alison Fiske**
Mme de Volanges **Kate Dyson**
Cecile de Volanges **Leigh Funnelle**
Le Vicomte de Valmont **Pip Miller**
Azolan **Paul Sirr**
Mme de Rosemonde **Irene Sutcliffe**
La Presidente de Tourvel **Joanne Stoner**
Emile **Polly Irvin**
Le Chevalier Danceny **Christopher Hollis**

It is more than four years since the RSC's production of Hampton's adaption of de Laclos's novel opened at The Other Place in Stratford. Frequent changes of cast, a re-direction from Howard Davies's original and the challenge of the film version have done nothing to diminish the elegance, eloquence, charm and poignancy of this beautiful play. It is about love and life and the agony that ensues when a philanderer is confronted by truth of feeling, yet it is about so much more. All is expressed in dialogue of a quality rarely matched on the London stage.

Design **Bob Crowley**
Lighting **Chris Parry**
Music **Ilona Sekacz**

Harpsichord **Jonathan Rutherford**
Director **David Leveaux**

Apollo Theatre

SHAFTESBURY AVENUE, LONDON W1
01-437-2663

Manager **John Causebrook**

Mrs Klein (1988)
NICHOLAS WRIGHT

6 December 1988–22 April 1989

The National Theatre production of *Mrs Klein* played until April. The action revolved around analyst Melanie Klein at the time of the death of her son in an accident on the Continent.

Melanie Klein **Gillian Barge**
Paula **Zoe Wanamaker**
Melitta **Francesca Annis**

Design **John Gunter**
Lighting **Mark Seaman**
Costume **Stephen Brimson-Lewis**
Sound **Nic Jones**
Musical Director **Gabriel Amherst**
Director **Peter Gill**

Essentially the play is about the conflict between Klein and her daughter Paula. Ultimately they clash and separate, and Melitta moves into the position of consoler, analyst and surrogate daughter. Much of the dialogue is laden with the analyst's interpretations of actions and accusations, but it is a compelling play, at times amusing, at others agonising in its portrayal of the mother–daughter relationship. Peter Gill directed with sensitivity and surety, and the performances of the three women were of the highest quality.

Thoughts from a Very Private Diary (1989)

PETER WILSON from material by Victor Spinetti

27 April–11 June 1989

with **Victor Spinetti**

Design **Kevin Knight**
Lighting **Andrew Empson**
Director **Ned Sherrin**

First performed at the Donmar Warehouse in March, Victor Spinetti's one-man show is amusing. It deals with his meetings with the principal show business people of the last 25 years and is full of back-stage anecdotes. He displays great talents as a mimic and tells his tales well.

A Madhouse in Goa (1989)
MARTIN SHERMAN

A Table for a King

David **Rupert Graves**
Mrs Honey **Vanessa Redgrave**
Costos **Ian Sears**
Nikos **Larry Lamb**

Keeps Rainin' All the Time

Daniel Hosani **Arthur Dignam**
Oliver **Larry Lamb**
Heather **Vanessa Redgrave**
Dylna **Ian Sears**

Barnaby Grace **Rupert Graves**
Aliki **Francesca Folan**

Design **Ultz**

Lighting **Gerry Jenkinson**
Music **Richard Sisson**
Sound **Matt McKenzie**
Director **Robert Alan Ackerman**

15 June–2 September 1989

Martin Sherman's double-bill played at the Lyric Hammersmith throughout May before transferring to the Apollo Theatre. The first, and shorter, of the two plays is set on a Greek island in 1966; the second in the same place in 1990. The plays are tenuously linked.

In the first play, an American widow, Mrs Honey, refuses to give up her dinner table to King Constantine. Anecdotes and seductions follow. The second play revolves around a burned-out gay novelist whose one great work was based on the incident we have just seen. He interacts with a multitude of extraordinary people in presenting to us the blights of the modern world – AIDS, radioactivity, urban terrorism *et al*.

Although the actors received commendation, Mr Sherman's plays were not well received.

Thunderbirds FAB (1989)

11 September–14 October 1989

The mime theatre project which was successful enough to be granted an extension. It was succeeded by Keith Waterhouse's new play *Jeffrey Bernard is Unwell*, with Peter O'Toole, which will be covered in the third edition of the *British Theatre Yearbook*.

Apollo Victoria

WILTON ROAD, LONDON SW1
01-828-8665

General Manager **Peter Hancock**

Starlight Express (1984)

Opened 27 March 1984

Starlight Express rolls towards the end of its sixth year. One critic dismissed it as that thing about toy trains; a theatre-goer recommended it as 'the theatre of the future'. It continues to excite audiences and fill the theatre.

The Engines:
Electra **Maynard Williams**
Greaseball **Drue Williams**
Poppa **Lon Satton**
Rusty **Bobby Collins**
The Carriages:
Ashley **Erin Lordan**
Belle **Shezwae Powell**
Buffy **Caron Cardelle**
Dinah **Debbie Wake**

Pearl **Beverley Braybon**
The Trucks:
CB **Peter Rees**
Dustin **Danny Metcalfe**
Flat Top **Eddie Kemp**

Rocky I **Antoni Garfield Henry**
Rocky II **KFTD**
Rocky III **Rory Williams**

National Engines, Greaseball Gang, Components, Marshals etc. **Amanda Abbs, Johnny Amobi, Jan Apel, George Canning, Sergio Covino, John Francis Davies, Bob Lee Dysinger, Shaun Fernandes, Gary Forbes, Sean Garvey, Eamon Geoghegan, Dawn Leigh-Woods, Robert Northwood, Sean O'Sullivan, Richie Pitts, Lee Proud, Mykal Rand, Erique Redd, Elizabeth Renihan, Darren Ridley, Mitch Sebastian, Deborah Leanne Spellman, Samantha Sprackling, Paul Thompson, Carol Walton and Ruth Welby**
Booth Singers **Mary Carewe, Alan Colhoun, Barbara Courtney-King, Anna Devere, Jean Gilbert, Don Greig, Michael Lessiter, Bill McGillivray, Jeremy Taylor and Graham Godfrey**

Music **Andrew Lloyd Webber**
Lyrics **Richard Stilgoe**
Design **John Napier**
Lighting **David Hersey**
Sound **Martin Levan**
Musical Director **David Caddick**
Orchestration **David Cullen and Andrew Lloyd Webber**
Choreographer **Arlene Phillips**
Director **Trevor Nunn**

Arts Theatre Club

6–7 GREAT NEWPORT STREET, LONDON WC2
01-836-3334

Screamers (1987)
ANTHONY DAVISON

10 July–12 August 1989

Rodney Shephard **William Osborne**
Derick Capron **Kevin Elyot**
Trevor Stephens **Stephen Tiller**
Mrs Shepherd **Patricia Heneghan**
Linda Shepherd **Celia White**
Mr Martin **Peter Laird**

Design **Demetra Hersey**
Lighting **Ben Ormerod**
Director **Frith Banbury**

First performed at The Warehouse, Croydon, in 1987, and rewritten since last year's Edinburgh Festival, Anthony Davison's first play is set at the beginning of the 1960s and shows the predicament of the homosexual in the days before Gay Liberation. William Osborne won high praise in the central role as the young man to whom the options seem to be defiant effeminacy or exaggerated masculinity. Peter Kemp in *The Independent* found it 'likeable and occasionally very funny' while 'raising its voice not untellingly against the indignities imposed by prejudice'.

Screamers succeeded Hull Truck Company's marvellously witty and compassionate indictment of the education system, *Teechers*, which closed on 17 June after a run of more than a year.

A Slice of Saturday Night (1989)
NEIL, LEA, JOHN and CHARLES HEATHER

Opened 27 September 1989

Eric 'Rubber Legs' De Vene **Binky Baker**
Gary/Terry **David Easter**
Sue **Claire Parker**
Sharon **Mitch Johnson**
Penny/Shirl **Debi Thomson**
Eddie **Roy Smiles**
Rick **James Powell**
Bridget **Lisa Hollander**

Design **Gillian Daniell**

A Slice of Saturday Night opened at the King's Head Theatre on 1 August and transferred to the Arts in September. A wholesome musical play, 'a pleasurable, lightly satirical revel in Sixties manners', as Nicholas de Jongh called it, *A Slice of Saturday Night* was welcomed by some as a new cult musical destined for the same success as was enjoyed by *The Rocky Horror Show*. Katharine Way in *City Limits*, however, felt it to be a slice of nostalgia for the over-40s which had everything in it but the essentials, 'Social history in a vacuum; sunny, but vacuous.'

Musical Director **Keith Hayman**   Director **Marc Urquhart**

Cambridge Theatre
EARLHAM STREET, LONDON WC2
01-379-5299

Sherlock Holmes – The Musical (1988)
LESLIE BRICUSSE

24 April–8 July 1989

Sherlock Holmes **Ron Moody**
Dr Watson **Derek Waring**
Bella Moriarty **Liz Robertson**
Mrs Moriarty **Eileen Battye**
Inspector Lestrade **Roger Llewellyn**
Mrs Hudson **Julia Sutton**
Boffy Martingdale **John Gower**
Duchess of Monmouth **Sally Mates**
Sir Jevons Jarndyce **Lewis Barber**
Professor Moriarty **Terry Williams**
Fred Wiggins **James Francis-Johnston**
Harry Mossop **Derek Cullen**
Potatoes Clark **Jamie Hinde**
Billy Higgins **Luke Hope**
Lofty Daniel **Paul Loxton**
Mick O'Reilly **Stephen Matthews**
Maria **Erika Vincent**

Directed by George Roman, Artistic Director of the Northcott Theatre, Exeter, where the show originally opened in October 1988, *Sherlock Holmes – The Musical* came to the Cambridge after the early demise of *Budgie*. Sadly, it was to have as brief a life as its predecessor.

Using Conan Doyle's characters, though not his tales, Leslie Bricusse could never decide 'whether to send the whole thing up or take it seriously', according to Martin Hoyle in *The Financial Times*. However, most found it a show impossible to dislike, which made its early closure something of a surprise.

Ensemble **John Alexander, Margaret Bankier, Michael Conran, Bronwen Davies, Bonnie Hassell, Peter Johnston, Gaynor Martine, Terry Mitchell, Jenny Sawyer, Debra Stables, Michael Winsor and Kate-Alice Woodbridge**

Design **Sean Cavanagh**
Costume **Antony Mendleson**
Lighting **Mark Henderson**
Choreographer **Christine Cartwright**
Sound **Andy Pink**
Musical Director **Cyril Ornadel**
Director **George Roman**

Return to the Forbidden Planet (1985)
BOB CARLTON

Opened 18 September 1989

Captain Tempest **John Ashby**
Dr Prospero **Christian Roberts**
Ariel **Kraig Thornber**
Cookie **Matthew Devitt**
The Science Officer **Nicky Furre**
Bosun Arras **Anthony Hunt**
Navigation Officer **Kate Edgar**
Miranda **Allison Harding**
Ensign Mike Rhoechip **Ben Fox**
Ensign Penny Scyllen **Jane Karen**
PO Bud Visor **Tim Barron**
Newsreader (on film) **Patrick Moore**

Design **Rodney Ford**
Costume **Adrian Rees and Adrian Gwillym**
Lighting **Benny Ball**
Sound **Bobby Aitken**
Musical Director **Kate Edgar**
Choreographer **Carole Todd**
Director **Bob Carlton**

First performed at the Kilburn Tricycle Theatre and revamped and resurrected at the Belgrade Theatre, Coventry, in April 1989, *Return to the Forbidden Planet* is a rock-and-roll version of *The Tempest* overladen with echoes of the 1956 film *Forbidden Planet.* The music ranges from Elvis Presley to The Beach Boys. Some critics found it loud drivel; others saw it as irresistible.

6. *A rock* Tempest *at the Cambridge – Matthew Devitt as Cookie is in the custody of the robot Ariel, Kraig Thornber.*

Comedy Theatre

PANTON STREET, LONDON SW1Y 4DN
01-930-2578

A Walk in the Woods (1987)
LEE BLESSING

6 November 1988–20 May 1989

Andrey Botvinnik **Alec Guinness**
John Honeyman **Edward Herrmann**

Design **Robin Don**
Lighting **Rick Fisher**
Music **Jeremy Sands**
Director **Ronald Eyre**

Dealing with the growing friendship between an American and a Russian diplomat during protracted disarmament talks in Switzerland, *A Walk in the Woods* marked the return of Alec Guinness to the London stage after an absence of four years. It was also noted for a fine performance by Edward Herrmann as the American negotiator. Martin Hoyle, in *Plays and Players*, described it as a 'pleasant, insubstantial comedy'.

Frankie and Johnny in the Clair de Lune (1987)
TERRENCE McNALLY

Opened 14 June 1989

Frankie **Julie Walters**
Johnny **Brian Cox**

Design **Sue Plummer**
Lighting **Leonard Tucker**
Director **Paul Benedict**

Having enjoyed a highly successful Off-Broadway run in the United States, Terrence McNally's play is about two lonely people in their 40s who come together for sexual companionship. He, a cook, sees the relationship as a permanent one; she, a waitress, considers it to be a very brief meeting. It is a story of finding love through sex, and although it was a comedy considered thin by the majority of critics, it won praise for the strength of the performances by Julie Walters and Brian Cox.

Donmar Warehouse

41 EARLHAM STREET, LONDON WC2
01-240-8230

Three Guys Naked From the Waist Down (1988)

13 January–26 February 1989

Ted Klausterman **Terence Hillyer**
Phil Kunin **Teddy Kempner**
James Gaddas **Kenny Brewster**

Music **Michael Rupert**
Book and Lyrics **Jerry Colker**
Design **Adrian Rees**
Lighting **Tim Aspeling**
Musical Director **Dominic Barlow**

An Off-Broadway cult musical, *Three Guys Naked From the Waist Down* followed Cheek By Jowl's *Tempest*, which closed on 7 January, at the Donmar. Unfortunately, the musical did not cross the Atlantic well, many of those it lampoons being but shadowy figures to a British audience.

Sound **Rick Clarke**
Orchestration **Michael Starobin**
Choreographer **Lindsay Dolan**

Director **Rob Bettinson**

Lorca (1970)
TRADER FAULKNER

6–22 April 1989

Lorca **Trader Faulkner**
Musician **Tito Heredia**
Dancer **Carmela Romero**

The product of many years' work by former RSC actor Trader Faulkner, *Lorca* is an evocation of the poet–playwright's life and work.

24 April–13 May 1989, Cheek By Jowl presented *The Doctor of Honour* (see Touring Companies section).

Laughing Matters (1989)
MICHAEL DAVIS

7 June–15 July 1989

Michael Davis with Bob Hartman

Michael Davis was seen in London in 1988 – his juggling act in *Sugar Babies* was one of the highlights of that show. He has'

Design **Franne Lee**
Lighting **George Owczarski**

now constructed his own one-man show and was very well received at the Donmar Warehouse by both critics and public, as he deserved to have been.

---

17 July–12 August 1989, Hull Truck Company presented *Twelfth Night* (see Touring Companies section).

The Perrier 'Pick of the Fringe' season ran 25 September–14 October 1989.

In Lambeth (1989)
JACK SHEPHERD

17 August–23 September 1989

William Blake **Michael Maloney**
Catherine Blake **Lesley Clare O'Neill**
Tom Paine **Bob Peck**

Design **Jake Shepherd**
Lighting **Clare Sherer**
Costume **Louise Simpson**
Music **Dave Greenslade**
Director **Jack Shepherd**

Originally presented at the Partisan Theatre in Dulwich, Jack Shepherd's play is based on a true incident in which the poet William Blake sheltered Tom Paine, the author of the *Rights of Man*, from a Tory mob of anti-republicans. The play revolves around the argument about whether society can free itself from tyranny without using a greater tyranny. It was exceptionally well received for its writing, direction and acting. Andrew Calloway played all the parts other than the three principals.

Drury Lane, Theatre Royal

LONDON WC2
01-836-8108

Manager **Christopher Edwards**

Back With a Vengeance (1988)

9 March–15 April 1989

Following the close of the exuberant *42nd Street*, the Theatre Royal remained dark for a month before Barry Humphries returned with his second coming of *Back With a Vengeance*,

Sir Les Patterson/Dame Edna Everage/Sandy Stone **Barry Humphries**
The Lesettes **Lisa Houghton, Carlie Johnson, Hayley M Clarke and Jane Shelton**

Music **Barry Humphries**
Lyrics **Barry Humphries**
Additional Material **Ian Davidson, David Mitchell and Edward Clark**
Musical Director **Victy Silva**
Choreographer **Sam Spencer-Lane**
Design **Nicholas Day**
Lighting **Durham Marenghi**
Costume **Billy Goodwin**
Keyboard **Victy Silva**
Bass **Anthony Merrick**
Drums **Chris Wyles**
Director **Harriet Bowdler**

7. *Our prejudices paraded before us – Barry Humphries as Sir Les Patterson, in theatre of cruelty at Drury Lane Theatre Royal towards the beginning of the year.*

which was originally seen at the Strand Theatre the previous year. Those who have not seen Mr Humphries on the stage have missed one of the most vital and disturbing of experiences. In the character of Les Patterson, in particular, he confronts us with our prejudices and, in buoyant humour, shows us the darker side of our personalities. Gilbert Adair has written of him as being a member of the theatre of cruelty when he embarrasses us with the wisdom of Dame Edna. There is reason in this statement, but it should not be imagined that *Back With a Vengeance* was anything but a highly entertaining, laughter-filled evening. It was enhanced by Victy Silva's dynamic musical accompaniment.

Miss Saigon (1989)
ALAIN BOUBLIL and CLAUDE-MICHEL SCHÖNBERG

Opened 20 September 1989

Kim **Lea Salonga**
Mimi **Monique Wilson**
Gigi **Isay Alvarez**
Yvonne One **Pinky Amador**
Yvette **Jenine Desiderio**
Yvonne Two **Dominique Nobles**
Bar Girls **Ruthie Henshall, Shukubi Yo, Suchitra Sen Sawrattan, Antoinette Lo and Claudia Cadette**
The Engineer **Jonathan Pryce**
John **Peter Polycarpou**
Chris **Simon Bowman**
Marines **Johnny Amobi, Gerard Casey, Mark Carroll, Richard Calkin, Greg Ellis, Andrew Golder, Nick Holder, Glyn Kerslake, James Francis-Johnston, Ray Shell and Michael Strassen**
Reporters **Tash O'Connor and Mark Bond**
Barmen **Robert Sena and Jon Jon Briones**
Officers of the South Vietnamese Army **Chooi Kheng Beh and Junix Inocian**
Vietnamese Customers **Miguel Diaz, Jay Ibot, Cocoy Laurel, Bobby Martino, William Michales and Lyon Roque**
Mama San **Andy Lanai**
Thuy **Keith Burns**
Ellen **Claire Moore**
Tam **David Platt/Waseem Hamdan/Christopher Chalker**
Phan **Junix Inocian**

Long awaited, *Miss Saigon* arrived at Drury Lane in September and was rapturously received. There were a few dissenting voices, notably Michael Ratcliffe in *The Observer*, but the majority of critics applauded the latest offering from Cameron Mackintosh and the *Les Misérables* team. *Miss Saigon* is based on *Madame Butterfly* and on the authors' observations of coverage of the Vietnam War. Not a word is spoken in this drama about a passion that was doomed from the outset. Milton Shulman, in the *Evening Standard*, commented, 'Not often does a popular musical make so potent an ideological point so effectively.'

8. Jonathan Pryce as The Engineer in Miss Saigon, *which would seem destined to run at Drury Lane Theatre Royal for many months to come.*

Huynh **Miguel Diaz**
Assistant Commissar **Cocoy Laurel**
Dragon Acrobat **James Francis-Johnston**
Soldiers of the North Vietnamese Army **Bobby Martino, Jay Ibot, Andy Lanai, Jon Jon Briones, Chooi Kheng Beh, Robert Sena and Lyon Roque**
Hustlers **Junix Inocian, Cocoy Laurel, Lyon Roque and Miguel Diaz**
Owner of Moulin Rouge **Nick Holder**
Go-Go Dancers **Pinky Amador, Suchitra Sen Sawrattan, Monique Wilson and Jenine Desiderio**
Shultz **Mark Bond**
Harrison **Greg Ellis**
Travis **Ray Shell**
Weber **Michael Strassen**
Estevez **Andrew Golder**
Allott **Tash O'Connor**

Music **Claude-Michel Schönberg**
Lyrics **Richard Maltby Jr and Alain Boublil**
Design **John Napier**
Costume **Andreanne Neofitou**
Lighting **David Hersey**
Sound **Andrew Bruce**
Musical Director **Martin Koch**
Orchestration **William D Brown**
Choreographer **Bob Avian**
Director **Nicholas Hytner**

9. Miss Saigon *at Drury Lane Theatre Royal.*

The Duchess Theatre

CATHERINE STREET, LONDON WC2B 5LA
01-839-1134

The Players' Theatre, Artistic Director **Reginald Woolley**

Put Some Clothes On, Clarisse!

GEORGES FEYDEAU – adapted by Reggie Oliver from *Mais N'te Promene Donc Pas Toute Nue!*

21 June – 16 July 1989

with **Ray Martin, James Bree, Pia Henderson, Jim McManus** and **Nigel Williams**
Design **Reginald Woolley**
Director **Reginald Woolley**

The Players' Theatre continued to occupy the Duchess Theatre with their traditional and perpetually fresh *Late Joys*, Victorian music hall. For a month in midsummer they added a one-act Feydeau farce to their programme as their joyful contribution to the celebrations which marked 200 years of the French Republic.

Duke of York's Theatre

ST MARTIN'S LANE, LONDON WC2
01-836-5122

Artist Descending a Staircase (1972)
TOM STOPPARD

7 December 1988–10 June 1989

Beauchamp (Older) **Peter Copley**
Beauchamp (Younger) **Gareth Tudor Price**
Martello (Older) **William Lucas**
Martello (Younger) **Karl James**
Donner (Older) **Alan MacNaughtan**
Donner (Younger) **John Warnaby**
Sophie **Sarah Woodward**

Design **Carl Toms**

Originally conceived as a radio play and staged for the first time at the King's Head Theatre Club in 1988, Tom Stoppard's play examines the changing relationship between three artists and a blind girl, Sophie. The play, well played and well received, begins with the death of Donner, and the death prompts a series of flashbacks.

Costume **Tim Heywood**
Lighting **Leonard Tucker**
Music and Sound **Kevin Malpass**
Director **Tim Luscombe**

Shirley Valentine (1987)
WILLY RUSSELL

Opened 28 June 1989

Shirley Valentine **Hannah Gordon**

Design **Bruno Santini**
Lighting **Leonard Tucker**
Director **Richard Olivier**

Following its outstanding success in 1988 on both sides of the Atlantic and its transition to the cinema, *Shirley Valentine* returned to the West End stage in June 1989. Willy Russell relocated his one-woman play about an unfulfilled housewife from Liverpool to Glasgow, and Hannah Gordon took over the role in which Pauline Collins won so much honour and praise.

Fortune Theatre

RUSSELL STREET, COVENT GARDEN, LONDON WC2B 5HH
01-836-2238

Re: Joyce! (1988)
JAMES ROOSE-EVANS and MAUREEN LIPMAN

9 January–18 February 1989

Joyce Grenfell **Maureen Lipman**
Accompanist **Denis King**

Design **Peter Rice**
Costume **Ben Frow**
Lighting **Adam Grater**
Choreographer **Geraldine Stephenson**

Originally performed at the Redgrave Theatre, Farnham, *Re: Joyce!* returned to the Fortune Theatre for a six-week season early in the year. This affectionate look at the work and humour of the late Joyce Grenfell was staged at the Vaudeville Theatre later in 1989.

Music **Joyce Grenfell and Richard Addinsell**

Director **Alan Strachan**

Forbidden Broadway (1983)
GERARD ALESSANDRINI

2 March–20 May 1989

A parody of the musical which started life as a 15-minute show in a New York club, *Forbidden Broadway* has been running for more than six years in Boston. The English version enjoyed a

with **Rosemary Ashe, Simon Slater, Jenny Michelmore** and **Michael Fenton Stevens**

Design **Randy Benjamin**
Costume **Erika Dyson**
Lighting **Adam Grater**
Pianist **Paul Knight**

three-month run at the Fortune. Four singers, who are also impersonators, and a pianist give amusing and often biting views of current musicals – *Starlight Excess* and *The Phantom of the Musical* – and they sharply attack the glamorisation of poverty in *Les Misérables*.

Musical Director **Colin Sell**
Director **Gerard Alessandrini**

The Woman in Black (1987)
STEPHEN MALLATRATT from the novel by Susan Hill

Opened 7 June 1989

Arthur Kipps **Charles Kay/Mark Kingston**
The Actor **John Duttine/Dominic Letts**
with **Nicola Sloane**

Design **Michael Holt**
Lighting **Kevin Sleep**
Sound **Rod Mean/Jackie Staines**
Director **Robin Herford**

Arthur Kipps, a Victorian lawyer, hires a small theatre in order to read to his friends an account of a terrifying supernatural experience that he had in a lonely house in Yorkshire. He is attempting to exorcise the memory by the retelling of the incident. He engages an actor as a coach for his performance, but all goes frighteningly wrong. This is an immensely effective ghost story which, in 1989, played at the Lyric Hammersmith, the Strand and the Playhouse before moving to the Fortune. Charles Kay and John Duttine left the Fortune and toured with the chilling play during the year. Mark Kingston and Dominic Letts took over their roles.

Garrick Theatre

CHARING CROSS ROAD, LONDON WC2
01-836-4601

The Vortex (1924)
NOEL COWARD

26 January–22 July 1989

Preston **Jill Fenner**
Pauncefoot Quentin **Tristram Jellinek**
Helen Saville **Anne Lambton**

A year after it had opened in Glasgow, the Citizens' production of *The Vortex* reached London, succeeding another Coward play, *Easy Virtue*, which closed on 7 January. Just as Jane How had triumphed in *Easy Virtue*, so Maria Aitken won general

Clara Hibbert **Fidelis Morgan**
Florence Lancaster **Maria Aitken**
Tom Veryan **Martyn Stanbridge**
Nicky Lancaster **Rupert Everett**
David Lancaster **Stephen MacDonald**
Bunty Mainwaring **Yolanda Vazquez**
Bruce Fairlight **Derwent Watson**
with **Jill Damas and Philip Rham**

Design **Philip Prowse**

acclaim in *The Vortex*. Jack Tinker, in the *Daily Mail*, saw her as 'the definitive Coward heroine'. It was unlikely that *The Vortex*, dealing as it does with a cocaine-addicted son and his adulterous mother, would have the impact that it had 65 years ago when the subjects were less common and more taboo than they are today. However, Philip Prowse's production underlined the pain and the emotional bewilderment beneath the froth of the 1920s social whirl. Rupert Everett, as the drug-addicted young man, matched Maria Aitken's performance in this thoroughly worthy revival.

Lighting **Gerry Jenkinson** Director **Philip Prowse**
Choreographer **Imogen Claire**

Paris Match (1984)
JEAN POIRET adapted by Marcel Stellman and Leslie Clack

4 October–28 October 1989

Jacques **Stephen Moore**
Julie **Leslie Ash**
Claire **Siân Phillips**
Marie **Chili Bouchier**
Mme Valtère **Madeleine Newbury**
M Valtère **Terence Longdon**
Frédéric Valtère **Peter Treganna**
Marlene **Sheila Steafel**

Design **Douglas Heap**

First produced at the Theatr Clwyd in October 1988, *Paris Match* arrived in London with only Terence Longdon surviving from the cast of the original British production. The play, the work of the author of *La Cage aux Folles*, ran for more than 2,000 performances in Paris. It is a comedy of mistake, intricacy and would-be adultery, always elegant and tasteful, but it had a very brief life.

Lighting **Jenny Cane** Director **Christopher Renshaw**
Costume **Pierre Balmain**
Additional Costume **Catherine Darcy**

The Globe

SHAFTESBURY AVENUE, LONDON W1
01-437-3667

Manager **Stanley Jarvis**

Lettice and Lovage (1987)
PETER SHAFFER

Opened 27 October 1987

Since its world première at the Theatre Royal, Bath, on 6 October 1987, *Lettice and Lovage* has continued to delight.

Lettice Douffet **Carole Shelley**
Surly Man **Bruce Bennett**
Lotte Schoen **Helen Ryan**
Miss Framer/Visitor **Jennifer Lautrec**
Mr Bardolph **Moray Watson**
Visitors to Fustian House **Hattie Arkwright, Judy Harris, Corinna Marlowe, Rosemary Macvie, Harry Perscy, Michael Sherwin and Sheila Vivian**
Cat **Felina, Queen of Sorrows**

Design **Alan Tagg**
Lighting **Robert Bryan**
Costume **Susan Yelland**
Director **Michael Blakemore**

Carole Shelley and Helen Ryan now fill the parts originally played by Maggie Smith and Margaret Tyzack and later by Geraldine McEwan and Sarah Kestleman. Daughter of an eccentric actress who carried out 'missionary' work on the French with her Shakespeare recitals, Lettice Douffet is guide at Fustian House, a stately home whose unromantic history is not to her taste. Her embellishments bring her into conflict with authority, Lotte Schoen, but she sways 'Lovage', and the two women unite in shaping life more to what they would like it to be. It is a tilt at the lies of politicians and the barbarisms of modern architecture. It is a play of hope.

10. *Carole Shelley and Felina, Queen of Sorrows, in Peter Shaffer's* Lettice and Lovage *at The Globe. A play of wit and pertinence.*

Haymarket Theatre Royal

HAYMARKET, LONDON SW1Y 4HT
01-930-9832

General Manager **Nigel P Everett**

Orpheus Descending (1957)
TENNESSEE WILLIAMS

13 December 1988–18 February 1989

Dolly Hamma **Carol Macready**
Beulah Binnings **Mary MacLeod**
Pee Wee Binnings **Jon Rumney**
Dog Hamma **Mitch Webb**
Carol Cutrere **Julie Covington**
Eva Temple **Margery Mason**
Sister Temple **Amanda Walker**
Uncle Pleasant **Doyle Richmond**
Val Xavier **Jean-Marc Barr**
Vee Talbott **Miriam Margolyes**
Lady Torrance **Vanessa Redgrave**
Jabe Torrance **Paul Freeman**
Sheriff Talbott **Manning Redwood**
Mr Dubinsky/Second Man **Brian Poyser**
Woman **Judith Eindsor**
David Cutrere **Richard Vanstone**
Nurse Porter **Carol Gillies**
First Man **Charles Baillie**

Design **Alison Chitty**
Lighting **Paul Pyant**
Sound **Paul Arditti**
Director **Peter Hall**

Tennessee Williams's first commercially produced play, *Battle of Angels*, was greeted with great hostility when it opened in Boston in 1940. Over the next 17 years he reworked the play, brought it closer to the Greek legend from which it sprang and re-presented it as *Orpheus Descending* in 1957. In spite of the reworking, it remains a flawed play, and the themes he explores in it he explored to greater theatrical effect in works like *Camino Real* and *Sweet Bird of Youth*.

Orpheus Descending works on two levels. Val, a young itinerant guitar player dressed in a leather jacket, wanders into a town in the American South and gets work in a dry-goods store. It is run by Jabe Torrance, a sick and bigoted man, and his wife Lady. She is the daughter of an Italian immigrant whose wine garden was burned down, with him inside it, when he sold alcohol to negroes. Lady learns later that she is married to the man who led the Ku Klux Klan band that murdered her father. She welcomes Val as her liberator, spiritually and sexually, but in persuading him to stay when the warnings are clear that he should leave, she brings about the awful destruction of both him and herself.

This is the realistic level, and on the symbolic level are the flashes of light, never so effective as in *Camino Real*, which reveal the poetic universality of Williams's statement.

The universality of Williams's play is in its cry against conformity and bigotry. Carol, wonderfully played by Julie Covington – the finest performance in the play – declaims 'This country used to be wild, the men and women were wild and there was a sweetness in their hearts for each other, but now it's sick with neon, it's broken out sick, with neon, like most other places.'

This corruption of the South, and by implication of America, is the crux of the play. It is inescapable, and the failure of the play to sustain this in poetical terms is its weakness.

Yet, having emphasised these weaknesses, one must admit that Peter Hall's first venture into the commercial theatre after leaving the National was a towering success. Vanessa Redgrave, in spite of a heavy Italian accent which seemed unnecessary in a character who had been raised in the South and had lived there for more than 20 years, gave a performance of great emotional power and dignity. Julie Covington, as we have mentioned, confirmed her standing as an actress of the highest quality. She gave a sensitive and forceful performance as the young woman who has turned to sex and alcohol in despair at the evil she recognises in the society in which she has been raised. There were splendid supporting performances from Miriam Margolyes, Mary MacLeod, Paul Freeman and others in what was, undoubtedly, a major theatrical event.

The Royal Baccarat Scandal (1988)

ROYCE RYTON from the book by Michael Havers and Edward Grayson

23 February–17 July 1989

Sir William Gordon Cumming **Keith Michell**
Mrs Gibbs **Jackie Smith-Wood**
HRH the Prince of Wales **Rowland Davies**
General Williams **John McCallum**
Ethel Lycett Green **Fiona Fullerton**
Mr Lycett Green **Gary Bond**
Mrs Wilson **Jeannette Sterke**
Stanley Wilson **Laurence Kennedy**
Mrs Williams **Marianne Morley**
Mr Levett **Paul M Meston**
Sir Edward Clarke, QC **Gerald Harper**
Sir Charles Russell, QC **Philip Stone**

Originally presented at Chichester Festival Theatre, *The Royal Baccarat Scandal* is the re-enactment of a Victorian court case in which a soldier and friend of the Prince of Wales was accused of cheating at cards by the husband of his mistress. Keith Michell played the philandering officer and gentleman; Gary Bond and Fiona Fullerton were the couple involved.

The French Chef **Christopher Leaver**
Jarvis **Michael Fleming**
Housekeeper **Jacqueline Lacey**
The Prince's Mistress **Andrea Wray**
Miss Naylor **Harriet Benson**
Court Officials **Simon Packham, Sean Patterson and Stanley Page**

Design **Tim Goodchild**
Lighting **Robert Ornbo**
Sound **Paul Arditti**
Director **Val May**

Veterans Day (1989)
DONALD FREED

22 August–28 October 1989

John MacCormick Butts **Jack Lemmon**
Walter Kercelik **Michael Gambon**

Using veterans from three wars, Donald Freed offered an anti-war play, but the reception to this work and to Jack Lemmon's return to the London stage was generally very cool.

Leslie R Holloway **Robert Flemyng**
CIA Man **Michael Higgs**

Design **Eileen Diss**
Costume **Jane Robinson**
Lighting **Mick Hughes**

Jane Edwardes, in *Time Out*, was not alone in wondering how the play had managed to reach the West End stage.

Sound **Dominic Muldowney**
Director **Kevin Billington**

Her Majesty's

HAYMARKET, LONDON SW1Y 4QL
01-839-2244

Manager **Mark Hayward**

The Phantom of the Opera (1986)

Opened 9 October 1986

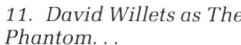

11. David Willets as The Phantom...

The Phantom of the Opera **Martin Smith**
Christine Daaé **Jill Washington (Iren Bartok)**
Raoul **Robert Meadmore**
M Firmin **Paul Leonard**
M André **James Paterson**
Carlotta Giudicelli **Morag McLaren**
Madame Giry **Mary Millar**
Ubaldo Piangi **Joan Aron**
M Reyer **Adrian Scott**
Porter/Marksman **Jay Jackson**
Meg Giry **Karen Lowe**
M Lefèvre/Auctioneer **John Griffiths**
Joseph Buquet **Janos Kurucz**
Don Attilio/Passarino **Duncan Smith**
Slave Master **Wayne Aspinall**
Policeman in the Pit **Justin Church**
Page **Lesley Windsor**
Porter/Fireman **Simon Tunkin**
Fireman **Kevin A J Ranson**
Page **Deborah Goody**
Wardrobe Mistress/Confidante **Jane Stoggles**
Princess **Penelope Brister**
Madame Firmin **Julia Goss**
Innkeeper **John Ayldon**
Innkeeper's Wife **Sharon Halliday**
The Ballet Chorus of the Opera Populaire **Sally Ashfield, Manda Gilliland, Caroline Heming, Tania Fairbairn, Rachel Smith, Emma Hardwicke, Lynne Jezzard and Phyllida Crowley-Smith**
Ballet Swing **Patricia Merrin**

Music **Andrew Lloyd Webber**
Lyrics **Charles Hart**
Additional Lyrics **Richard Stilgoe**
Book **Richard Stilgoe and Andrew Lloyd Webber from the novel, *Le Fantôme de l'Opéra*, by Gaston Le Roux**
Design **Maria Björnson**
Lighting **Andrew Bridge**
Sound **Martin Levan**
Orchestration **David Cullen and Andrew Lloyd Webber**
Musical Director **Jonathan Butcher**
Choreographer **Gillian Lynne**
Director **Harold Prince**

Le Roux's novel, which inspired films both silent and sound, provided the basis of the continuing musical success of Andrew Lloyd Webber's *The Phantom of the Opera*, which is produced by Cameron Mackintosh and the Really Useful Theatre Company. Revolving around events at the Paris Opera in 1881 and a disfigured and embittered musician, *The Phantom of the Opera* has so captured the imagination that one is surprised that it is only just entering its fourth year. It seems to have been a permanent part of the London theatre scene for as long as one can remember.

12. ... and Jan Hartley-Morris as Christine in Andrew Lloyd Webber's The Phantom of the Opera, *which continues to fill Her Majesty's Theatre. Martin Smith and Jill Washington have since taken over the roles of The Phantom and Christine.*

Lyric Theatre

SHAFTESBURY AVENUE, LONDON W1
01-437-3686

Steel Magnolias (1987)
ROBERT HARLING

7 March–5 August 1989

Truvy **Maggie Steed**
Annelle **Janine Duvitski**
Clairee **Stephanie Cole**
Shelby **Joely Richardson**
M'lynn **Rosemary Harris**
Ouiser **Jean Boht**

Design **Eileen Diss**
Costume **Lindy Hemming**
Lighting **Mick Hughes**
Sound **Kevin Malpass**
Music **Carl Davis**
Director **Julia McKenzie**

Robert Harling's first play was an immense success Off-Broadway. It is set in a Louisiana beauty parlour and covers a two and a half year span in the lives of six women who tell of their joys and griefs, births and deaths. Somewhat sentimental, it was firmly directed by Julia McKenzie and very well played by the six ladies, one of whom was Rosemary Harris, described by Clive Hirshhorn as 'one of the world's great actresses'. Her moving performance as a kidney-donating mother was warmly received.

Steel Magnolias replaced the revival of *Dry Rot*, which closed on 7 January.

Look Back in Anger (1956)
JOHN OSBORNE

7 August–7 September 1989

Jimmy Porter **Kenneth Branagh**
Cliff Lewis **Gerard Horan**
Alison Porter **Emma Thompson**
Helena Charles **Siobhán Redmond**
Colonel Redfern **Edward Jewesbury**

Design **Jenny Tiramani**
Lighting **Jon Linstrum**
Music **Patrick Doyle**
Director **Judi Dench**

There was a time some 15 years ago when *Look Back in Anger* seemed destined to become a period piece. Suddenly, within the last three years, it has been reclaimed, and its voice is as strident as ever, a fact emphasised in Judi Dench's excellent production for the Renaissance Theatre Company. Perhaps the tyrannies of the class-divided society and the erosions of the ideals of the welfare state are even stronger now than they were in 1956.

There were some critics who felt that Kenneth Branagh's Jimmy Porter was so unsympathetic that no woman could have loved him, let alone two – but this, surely, is to seek a logic in our human relationships which does not exist. Mr Branagh is an exciting actor. He has a facility for language which few possess. Words trip so easily and meaningfully from his tongue that, as in music, we can almost anticipate the next bar or phrase. He has no need of the extravagant gesture because he takes us into his confidence, and when he told of a father dying from wounds received in the Spanish Civil War, we shared the pain and bewilderment of the memory.

There were times, perhaps, when Miss Dench's production aimed too much for the humour of the play. There is humour, which has been neglected, but it is not levity. To allow Alison to throw away hurriedly lines like 'just one of those sturdy old plants left over from the Edwardian wilderness that can't understand why the sun isn't shining any more' was surely a mistake. This was a minor blemish on Emma Thompson's fine performance. She captured the exhaustion of the character, the battle fatigue, and the class difference was never laboured to the point of caricature.

Gerard Horan was a warm and companionable Cliff, but Siobhán Redmond was not the first to struggle with the unrewarding character of Helena, whose contradictions have defeated many actresses.

The production began with charity performances in Belfast and London, and its run at the Lyric was limited and played to full houses.

Anthony Newley's *Stop the World I Want To Get Off* opened on 19 October with the delightfully talented Rhonda Burchmore among the cast.

Lyric Theatre Hammersmith

KING STREET, HAMMERSMITH, LONDON W6 0QL
01-741-2311

Pentecost (1987)
STEWART PARKER

Studio 9–28 January 1989

Stewart Parker's last play is a work of outstanding quality. Set in Belfast, it is a tale of caring people in an uncaring world, steadfast in their belief that only common humanity can rid a society of hate.

Lenny **Adrian Dunbar**
Marian **Dearbhla Molloy**
Lily **Barbara Adair**
Ruth **Michelle Fairley**
Peter **Sam Dale**

Design **Poppy Mitchell**
Lighting **David Colmer**

The Woman in Black played in the main house from 17 January until 11 February. It transferred to the Strand Theatre and later to the Fortune, under which details of the production are to be found.

Sound **Alastair Goulden and John A Leonard**

Director **Nicolas Kent**

Siblings (1930)
KLAUS MANN

Studio 8–25 February 1989

Marietta **Rose Hill**
Elisabeth **Suzanna Hamilton**
Paul **Simon Cutter**
Gerard **Mark Tandy**
Agathe **Kitty Aldridge**
Michael **Steve Elm**

Design **Philippe Brandt**
Costume **Philippe Brandt and**
John Bright
Lighting **Ben Ormerod**

This was the British première of Mann's play, which was loosely based on Cocteau's *Les Enfants Terribles*. Set in the fashionable Paris of the 1920s, the play depicts the bizarre and ultimately destructive relationship of eccentric orphans Elisabeth and Paul. It was stylishly acted and directed.

Music **Chris Littlewood**
Director **Peter Eyre**

16 February–4 March 1989, the Vakhtangov Theatre of Moscow presented *The Peace of Brest* by Mikhail Shatrov; and The Moscow-Jewish Theatre 'Shalom' performed *The Train To Happiness*, scenes from Jewish life.

Chekhov's Women (1985)
VANESSA REDGRAVE and FRANCES DE LA TOUR

7–11 March 1989

with **Vanessa Redgrave, Frances de la Tour, David Hargreaves, Angela Richards, Julia Swift, Richard Vanstone and Rachel Kempson**

Director **Vanessa Redgrave and David Hargreaves**

It was Vanessa Redgrave's company which brought the two Russian groups to the Lyric Hammersmith, and the season was completed when Miss Redgrave presented the piece that she and Frances de la Tour had devised in 1985. Lilina (Vanessa Redgrave), the wife of Stanislavski, conducts a master-class in excerpts from Chekhov's plays, stories and letters, and in extracts from Stanislavski's *An Actor Prepares*.

Long Time Gone (1989)
CATHERINE HAYES

Studio 15 March–1 April 1989

Don **Jack Galloway**
Joe **William Roberts**
Phil **Colin Bruce**
Dennis **Christopher Quinn**
Mom **Diana Payan**
Sue/Venetia **Michele Costa**
Netia/Jackie **Lorraine Brunning**

Presented in association with Salisbury Playhouse, *Long Time Gone* moves backwards and forwards in time as it traces the eventual break-up of the singing partnership of the Everly Brothers. It is a play of family tensions, estrangements and eventual reconciliations.

Design **Anabel Temple**
Lighting **Mak Elliott**

Sound **Liz Cecil**
Director **Debbie Shewell**

A Farewell to Sequins (1989)
Devised and performed by
FASCINATING AIDA

30 March–15 April 1989

with **Dillie Keane, Adele Anderson and Denise Wharmby**

Costume **Chris Clyne and Murray Arbeid**

The farewell performance of 'one of the best cabaret acts in the entire history of the universe'.

Lighting **Kevin Sleep**
Sound **Teg Davies**

Choreographer **Nica Burns**
Director **Nica Burns**

Low Level Panic (1988)
CLARE McINTYRE

Studio 14–22 April 1989

Jo **Caroline Quentin**
Mary **Lorraine Brunning**
Celia **Alaine Hickmott**

Design **Lucy Weller**
Lighting **Stephen Watson**

First presented at the Royal Court Theatre Upstairs, *Low Level Panic* revealed a world of female worries and ambitions. Nicholas de Jongh described it as 'an unsettling, compulsive night out for men, and a sobering one for women'.

Sound **Christopher Shull**

Director **Nancy Meckler**

28 April–10 June 1989, *A Madhouse in Goa*. Transferred to the Apollo Theatre, under which details will be found.

Cleopatra and Antony (1989)

ACTORS TOURING COMPANY adapted from William Shakespeare and others

Studio 16 May–3 June 1989

Cleopatra **Pauline Black**
Charmian **Juliet Prague**
Iras/Octavia **Susan Henry**
Mark Antony **Patrick Wilde**

Design **Paul Brown**

This was not a satire, but a pared-down version of Shakespeare's play performed by a cast of four. It won few friends.

Costume **Cyndy Vogelsang**
Lighting **Kate Malik and Glen Weston**
Sound **Carl Sutton and Alan Woodhouse**
Director **Malcolm Edwards**

Blithe Spirit (1941)
NOEL COWARD

15 June–3 July 1989

Edith **Lynette McMorrough**
Ruth **Deborah Grant**
Charles **Neil Stacey**
Doctor Bradman **Michael Knowles**
Mrs Bradman **Eira Griffiths**
Madame Arcati **Peggy Mount**
Elvira **Rula Lenska**

Design **Terry Parsons**
Costume **Philippe Brandt**

A revival of the Coward favourite which was warmly received by most. Nicholas de Jongh particularly liked Peggy Mount's Madame Arcati: 'dressed in what looks like a personalised tent, socks and the odd feather, boots and black beret she looks a suitable full-scale eccentric'. There was praise from Charles Osborne for Rula Lenska's witty ghost and for Deborah Grant's 'nicely acerbic second wife'.

Lighting **Richard Caswell**
Director **John David**

Farrowland (1989)
ELIZABETH BOND

Studio 13 June–1 July 1989

Lesley/Isaac Stirner **Jane Belshaw**
Bea/Batey **Isabella MacKenzie**
Graham/Mr Day/Vicar/Stick **John Ioannou**
Mervin **Dale Savage**
Dad/Trendle **Stuart Rayner**

Design and Costume **Pip Nash**

First-rate performances marked this new play about the 'dispossession and despair' of those who work the land. It was very well received and should not be regarded as a play without hope of a longer run.

Lighting **Adrian Lochead**
Director **Peter Wardle**

A Song in the Night (1989)
ROGER FRITH

3–15 July 1989

A strong team combined to give a powerful and moving picture of the gentle poet who spent much of his life in a lunatic asylum.

John Clare **Freddie Jones**

Costume **Joyce Hawkins**
Director **Patrick Garland**

The Old Bachelor (1693)
WILLIAM CONGREVE

Studio 5–22 July 1989

A rarely performed comedy which Congreve wrote when he was 23 was presented with gusto by Great Eastern Stage. The play revolves around characteristic Restoration themes of misallied marriages and the battle of the sexes, and includes the related subterfuges. Most critics felt that it was all a little too blatant and strident.

Mr Bellmour/Capt. Bluffe **Gary Sharkey**
Mr Vainlove/Mr Heartwell/Sir Joseph Wittol **Michael Lumsden**
Mr Sharper/Ald. Fondlewife **Richard Pocock**
Belinda/Lucy **Carol Carey**
Araminta/Sylvia/Laetitia **Joanne Sergent**
Setter **Paul Marshall**

Design **Neil Richardson**
Lighting **Mel Sinnott**
Choreographer **Sara van Beers**

Music **Michael Fry, from Purcell**
Musical Director **Stuart Barham**
Director **Michael Fry**

Miss Julie (1889)
AUGUST STRINDBERG in a French version by Mathilde Eidemoc

25–30 July 1989

The Comédie de Genève provided Switzerland's contribution to the London International Festival of Theatre. It was their version of Strindberg's one-act play about sex and class.

Miss Julie **Laurence Calame and Anne-Cécile Moser**
Jean **François Chattot**
Christine **Martine Schambacher**

Costume **Conchita Salvador**

Lighting **Christian Michaud**
Sound **Louis Yerly and Jean-Jacques Burger**
Director **Matthias Langhoff**

Huis Clos (1944)
JEAN-PAUL SARTRE translated by Frank Hauser

Studio 26 July–12 August 1989

Garcin **Bruce Purchase**
Ines **Susan Drury**
Estelle **Kate Nicholls**
Valet **Reuben Purchase**

Design **Paul Farnsworth**
Lighting **Leonard Tucker**

The newly formed Cotswold Theatre Group offered what Katharine Way in *City Limits* described as a 'sumptuous production' of Sartre's play. It is about three characters in hell who survey, for the last time, the land of the living.

Director **Alison Sutcliffe**

Prin (1989)
ANDREW DAVIES

23 August–14 October 1989

Prin **Sheila Hancock**
Dibs **Susie Blake**
Boyle **Paul Copley**
Walker **John Michie**
Kite **David Howie**
Melanie **Victoria Worsley**

Design **Julian McGowan**
Lighting **Kevin Sleep**
Choreographer **Geraldine Stephenson**
Director **Richard Wilson**

The excellent Sheila Hancock gave what many considered to be the performance of her career as the lesbian principal of a teachers' training college who is made redundant when her college merges with a polytechnic. She is a mass of contradictions, arrogant and self-destructive, a socialist who has little time for the common herd. She can be sensitive but is often dismissive of others, and she believes that she is producing teachers who will work in 'the most ignorant, philistine country in Europe, East or West'. Charles Osborne, in *The Daily Telegraph*, described this as a 'delightful and thought-provoking play' and it was most capably acted and directed.

Back Street Mammy (1989)
TRISH COOKE

Studio 7–23 September 1989

with **Cecilia Noble, Pamela Nomvete, Stephen Persaud and Michael Stewart**

Design **Zara Conway**

Temba Theatre Company produced Trish Cooke's first play. It deals with the problems of a bright 16-year-old girl who becomes pregnant.

Lighting **Paul Armstrong**   Director **Paulette Randall**

Mermaid Theatre

PUDDLE DOCK, BLACKFRIARS, LONDON EC4
01-236-5568

The Tart and the Vicar's Wife (1986)
JOAN SHIRLEY

9 March–8 April 1989

Rev. Robert Parry **Allan Stirland**
Glenda Parry **Sylvia Keeler**
Rev. Henry Benson **Ian Dickens**
Joe Carpenter **Neale Birch**
Sindy O'Connor **Meg Duval**
Kate Spencer **Shaaron Jackson**
Pru **Gerrie Raymond**
Selina **Isabel Dinning**

Joan Shirley's touring farce opened in Preston in 1986. Since then it has had more than 500 performances. When it reached London and the Mermaid, it was very badly received by the critics and soon continued on its way. The play concerns a vicar's wife who turns her house into a brothel while her husband is away on a course. All is done for altruistic reasons.

Design **Ian Shirley**
Lighting **Bob Bustance**
Director **Danny Davies**

To Kill a Mockingbird (1988)
CHRISTOPHER SERGEL from the novel by Harper Lee

3 May–28 October 1989

Jean Louise Finch **Hildegard Neil**
Scout **Penny Gonshaw**
Jem **Nick Raggett**
Atticus **Alan Dobie**
Calpurnia **Jacqui Gordon-Lawrence**
Maudie Atkinson **Lisa Bermond**
Stephanie Crawford **Eileen Gourlay**
Mrs Dubose **Sarah Eyton**
Nathan Radley **Andrew Jolly**
Boo Radley/Mr Gilmer/ Walter Cunningham **Peter Banks**
Dill **Tom Davidson**
Heck Tate **Mel Cobb**
Judge Taylor **Mike Burnside**
Rev. Sykes **Mark Heath**

The Royal Theatre, Northampton, first staged this touring production in September 1988. It came to rest at the Mermaid for six months in 1989. Harper Lee's immensely popular, amusing and moving account of childhood and racial prejudice in the deep South in the 1930s has had an uncertain transformation to the stage. However, the court scene in which Atticus, a lawyer of the utmost integrity, defends a black man wrongfully accused of raping a white girl makes good theatre.

Tom Robinson/Zeebo **Lenny Aljernon-Edwards**
Helen Robinson/Lula **Sharon-Rose Alexander**
Mayella Ewell **Helene Kvale**
Bob Ewell **Adrian McLoughlin**
Link Deas **Mark Brailsford**

with **Arlene Banton, Louise Green** and **Tony Howard**

Design **Ray Lett**
Lighting **Dee Ashworth**
Music **Martin Waddington**
Director **Chris Hayes**

THE LONDON THEATRE: WEST END

New London Theatre

DRURY LANE, LONDON WC2
01-405-0072

General Manager **George Biggs**

Cats (1981)

Based on T S Eliot's *Old Possum's Book of Practical Cats*

Opened 11 May 1981

Cameron Mackintosh and the Really Useful Theatre Company's production of *Cats* is completing its eighth year at the New London Theatre. The quality of the lyrics, the fresh and invigorating staging, the intelligent direction and music which is both haunting and witty all enable it to remain exciting and compelling.

Admetus/Macavity **Adrian Goodfellow**
Alonzo **Cavin Cornwall**
Asparagus/Bustopher **Tom Jobe**
Bill Bailey **Darren McGarry**
Bombalurina **Heather Robbins**
Carbucketty **Douglas Howes**
Cassandra **Michelle Hodgson**
Coricocat **Derek Cullen**
Demeter **Linda Mae Brewer**
Deuteronomy **Donald Francke**
Electra **Robin Cleaver**
Etcetera **Marsha Bland**
George **Steven Wayne**
Grizabella **Ria Jones**
Jellylorum **Grace Kinirons**
Jemima **Siobhan Coebly**
Jennyandots **Sonia Swaby**
Mungojerrie **Scott Sherrin**
Munkustrap **Gary Martin**
Quaxo **Graham Fletcher**
Rumpleteazer **Anna-Jane Casey**
Rum Tum Tugger **Richard Lloyd King**
Skimbleshanks **Japheth Myers**
Tantomile **Diane Manou**
Victor **Christopher Molloy**
Victoria **Amanda Courtney-Davies**
The Cats Chorus **Cathy Cordez, Duncan MacVicar, Jacqui Harman, Hilton Jones, Nicola Keen and David Olton**

Music **Andrew Lloyd Webber**
Design **John Napier**
Lighting **David Hersey**
Sound **Abe Jacob and Martin Levan**
Choreographer **Gillian Lynne**
Orchestration **David Cullen and Andrew Lloyd Webber**
Production Musical Director **David Caddick**
Musical Director **Jae Alexander**
Director **Trevor Nunn**

Old Vic Theatre

WATERLOO ROAD, LONDON SE1 8NB
01-928-7616

Executive Director **Ed Mirvish**
Executive Producer **David Mirvish**
Administrator **Andrew Leigh**
Artistic Director **Jonathan Miller**

Candide (1972)

1 December 1988–7 January 1989

Voltaire/Pangloss/Cacambo/Martin **Nickolas Grace**
Captain/Governor/Gambler **Alexander Oliver**
Candide **Mark Beudert**
Cunegonde **Rosemary Ash/ Marilyn Hill Smith**
Old Lady **Patricia Routledge**
Paquette **Gaynor Miles**
Maximillian **Mark Tinkler**
The Baron/First Officer/Grand Inquisitor/First Jesuit/Slave Driver/Ragotski/Sailor **Leon Greene**
Don Issacher/Father Bernard/The Anabaptist/Second Officer/Sailor **Howard Goorney**
Baroness **Betsy Marrion**
Lisbon Women **Harriet Neave and Helen Garton**
Informer/Announcer/Aide **John Brackenridge**
Huntsman/Croupier **Jonathan Coad**
Archbishop **Bill Snape**
with **Juliet Arthur, Susan Ashley, Ian Baar, Christine Beaumont, Tony Crean, Christopher Dee, Timothy Evans Jones, Andrew Fearn, Helen Greenaway, Stephanie Kulesza, Robin Martin Oliver, Michael Neill, Jane Oakland, Elisabeth Stirling and Robert Traynor**

Music **Leonard Bernstein**
Book **Hugh Wheeler, from the novel by Voltaire**
Lyrics **Richard Wilbur**
Additional Lyrics **Stephen Sondheim, John Latouche, Lillian Hellman and Dorothy Parker**
Musical Director **Peter Stanger**
Assistant Musical Director **Stephen Clarke**
Choreography and Staging **Anthony Van Laast**
Design **Richard Hudson**
Lighting **Davy Cunningham**
Sound **Julian Beech**
Director **Jonathan Miller and John Wells**

The musical version of *Candide* has had a chequered history since it was first produced on Broadway in 1956. It was not a success there and was revised before being produced in Los Angeles. It again met with limited success. In 1972 it was produced by Hugh Wheeler with a completely new version of the book. This time it enjoyed a 12-month run on Broadway. A new two-act version opened at the New York City Opera in 1983.

The production at The Old Vic was first seen at the Theatre Royal, Glasgow, in conjunction with The Scottish Opera, in May 1988. John Mauceri rearranged the score for it and Hugh Wheeler agreed to adapt his script. He died before the task was completed, and the work was finished by John Wells.

Candide is the most unlikely subject for a musical. The novel scorns the philosophy of optimism in an amusing way, but it takes us through rape, earthquake, murder, cruelty, deformity and warfare. The ultimate feeling with which one is left is far removed from joy. Having said this, the musical version which arrived at The Old Vic in December 1988 was vital and inventive. Richard Hudson provided an excitingly fresh design. A grey box set with grotesque colourful giant masks hovering in the background and cities and castles appearing and disappearing in the front was dominated on occasions by chairs of graduating size. The conception proved an ideal blend against which to set the performers. A cast of actors who could sing and singers who could act sustained a lively and vigorous entertainment. At the centre, Nickolas Grace was witty and energetic in his four roles, while Patricia Routledge produced a delightfully funny and rich performance as the one-buttocked daughter of the Pope. Miller's direction was faithful to mood, music and text, and Bernstein's score was versatile and engaging without ever being memorable.

Candide was The Old Vic's happiest and seemingly most popular venture of 1988 and gave a good start to 1989.

The Wars of the Roses

26 January–11 March 1989

The English Shakespeare Company's production of Shakespeare's History Cycle. Including adaptations of *Henry VI, Parts One, Two* and *Three*, by Michael Pennington and Michael Bogdanov, titled *House of Lancaster* and *House of York*.

Richard II (1595)
WILLIAM SHAKESPEARE

Richard II **Michael Pennington**
Isabel **Francesca Ryan**
John of Gaunt/Groom **Clyde Pollitt**
Henry Bolingbroke **Michael Cronin**
Duke of York **Colin Farrell**
Duchess of York **Ann Penfold**
Duke of Aumerle **Phillip Bowen**
Thomas Mowbray/Sir Piers of Exton **Jack Carr**
Duchess of Gloucester **June Watson**
Duke of Exeter/Earl of Salisbury **Ian Burford**
Earl of Northumberland **Roger Booth**
Hotspur/Herald **Andrew Jarvis**
Lord Ross **John Dougall**
Lord Willoughby **Charles Dale**
Lord Berkeley/Servant/Gardener **Stephen Jameson**
Earl of Westmoreland **Ben Bazell**
Bishop of Carlisle **Hugh Sullivan**
Sir John Bushy **Siôn Probert**
Sir John Bagot **Paul Brennen**
Sir Henry Greene **Michael Fenner**
Sir Stephen Scroop/Herald **John Darrell**
Servant to Exton **Simon Elliott**
Welsh Captain **Barry Stanton**
Gardener/Keeper **John Tramper**
Gardener/Servingman **Phillip Rees**
Lady **Jenifer Konko**
Musicians **John Darrell, Ben Bazell, Ian Burford and Andrew Jarvis**

Ever anxious to crystallise what he sees as the essence of the play in a period which captures the required mood, Michael Bogdanov placed his *Richard II* among the sycophants of the Regency age. The play seemed to fit remarkably well there, not least because of Michael Pennington's deeply sensitive performance in the title role. Pennington had a mastery of Shakespeare's verse which gave the King an eloquent dignity. Richard is a flawed king, and Pennington's understanding of Richard's vanity, his artistic self-satisfaction, gave his interpretation a dimension few others have been able to attain. Richard is initially complacent, secure in the belief that his divine right as a king is sufficient for his authority and his survival. In the politics of the court and the intricacies of the affairs of state, he is naïve. It is his combination of innocence and vanity that bring about his downfall. Pennington's study showed a fine awareness of the subtle and gradual sense of awareness that comes to Richard all too late. He was most ably supported by some fine ensemble playing.

Henry IV – Part One (1597)
WILLIAM SHAKESPEARE

King Henry IV **Michael Cronin**
Henry, Prince of Wales **Michael Pennington/John Dougall**
Thomas, Duke of Clarence/Edmund Mortimer **Stephen Jameson**
Prince John of Lancaster **John Dougall/Robert Hands**
Humphrey, Duke of Gloucester/Earl of Douglas/Poins **Charles Dale**

Duke of Exeter/Vintner **Ian Burford**
Earl of Westmoreland/First Carrier
Ben Bazell
Sir Walter Blunt **Michael Fenner**
Lord Chief Justice **Hugh Sullivan**
Henry Percy, Earl of
Northumberland/Traveller **Roger Booth**
Earl of Worcester **Phillip Bowen**
Hotspur/Gadshill **Andrew Jarvis**

Lady Percy **Ann Penfold**
Lady Mortimer/Traveller **Jenifer Konko**
Owen Glendower **Siôn Probert**
Sir Richard Vernon/Peto **Paul Brennen**
Tarvers/Carrier **Simon Elliott**
Richard Scroop/First Traveller **John Darrell**
Sir Michael/Chamberlain **Clyde Pollitt**

Sir John Falstaff **Barry Stanton**
Mistress Quickly **June Watson**
Doll Tearsheet **Francesca Ryan**
Bardolph **Colin Farrell**
Francis/Traveller **John Tramper**
Musicians **Ben Bazell, Ian Burford, Charles Dale, Simon Elliott, Colin Farrell, Andrew Jarvis and Francesca Ryan**

Henry IV – Part Two (1598)
WILLIAM SHAKESPEARE

King Henry IV **Michael Cronin**
Henry, Prince of Wales **Michael Pennington/John Dougall**
Thomas, Duke of Clarence/Drawer/Snare **Stephen Jameson**
Prince John of Lancaster **John Dougall/Robert Hands**
Humphrey, Duke of Gloucester/Poins **Charles Dale**
Duke of Exeter **Ian Burford**
Earl of Westmoreland/Drawer/Fang **Ben Bazell**
Lord Chief Justice **Hugh Sullivan**
Harcourt **Andrew Jarvis**

Earl of Northumberland/Davy **Roger Booth**
Lady Northumberland **Susanna Best**
Lady Percy **Ann Penfold**
Lord Morton **Siôn Probert**
Sir Richard Vernon/Pistol **Paul Brennen**
Travers/Drawer/Simon Shallow **Simon Elliott**
Richard Scroop/Francis Feeble **John Darrell**
Lord Mowbray/Peter Bullcalf **Michael Fenner**

Lord Hastings/Mouldy **Jack Carr**
Sir John Coleville **Phillip Rees**
Sir John Falstaff **Barry Stanton**
His Page **John Tramper**
Mistress Quickly **June Watson**
Doll Tearsheet **Francesca Ryan**
Bardolph **Colin Farrell**
Robert Shallow **Clyde Pollitt**
Silence **Phillip Bowen**
Thomas Wart **John Dougall**
Musicians **Robert Hands, Ben Bazell, John Darrell, Simon Elliott, Colin Farrell and Andrew Jarvis**

Henry V (1599)
WILLIAM SHAKESPEARE

Chorus **Barry Stanton**
Archbishop of Canterbury/ Constable of France **Hugh Sullivan**
Bishop of Ely/Michael Williams/Governor of Harfleur **Roger Booth**
King Henry V **Michael Pennington/John Dougall**
Thomas, Duke of Clarence/John Bates/Nym **Stephen Jameson**
Prince John of Lancaster **Robert Hands**
Humphrey, Duke of Gloucester/Monsieur le Fer **Charles Dale**

Duke of Exeter **Ian Burford**
Earl of Westmoreland/Jamy **Ben Bazell**
Lord Scroop of Masham/Duke of Burgundy **Jack Carr**
Earl of Cambridge/Duke of Orleans **John Darrell**
Sir Thomas Grey **Phillip Rees**
Fluellen **Siôn Probert**
Macmorris **Michael Cronin**
Gower **Michael Fenner**
Sir Thomas Erpingham/Bardolph **Colin Farrell**
Alexander Court **Simon Elliott**

Mistress Quickly/Isabel **June Watson**
Pistol **Paul Brennen**
Nym **John Dougall/Stephen Jameson**
Boy **John Tramper**
Charles VI **Clyde Pollitt**
Lewis, the Dauphin **Andrew Jarvis**
Princess Katherine **Francesca Ryan**
Alice **Ann Penfold**
Montjoy, a Herald **Phillip Bowen**
Maid **Jenifer Konko**
Musicians **Ben Bazell and Colin Farrell**

The two parts of *Henry IV* and *Henry V* were the three plays first performed by the English Shakespeare Company and they formed the basis of their two and a half year world tour. Bogdanov's setting and costume for the plays aimed at a timeless effect, with punks and courtiers rubbing shoulders in the Boar's Head Tavern. The political aspects of the plays were clearly defined. Michael Cronin was a conscience-ridden Henry IV, his crown uneasily worn. In an intelligent interpretation, Cronin had the air of a man for whom the attainment of the crown had been all and who was wearied and close to being destroyed by the effort expended to reach the summit. Michael Pennington, who shared the role with John Dougall towards the end of the run, produced another highly commendable performance as Prince Hal, preparing himself for kingship by gaining knowledge of his subjects. His Hal was a prince burning with inward passion and controlled by an intelligence which was always acutely aware of others. His Henry V was a natural maturation of the younger Hal, not a different character. In the comic parts, Barry Stanton was a worthy successor to John Woodvine, and June Watson's Mistress Quickly was beautifully observed. One has not seen a better performance in this role. She was wonderfully at home in Eastcheap, considerate of her customers whose antics often bewildered her. Her narration of the death of Falstaff created one of those rare magical moments in the theatre, succeeded as it was by the departure for France, and searing contrast that Bogdanov achieved between the coarse, foul-mouthed English rabble of an army and the champagne-sipping, immaculately dressed French. As the Dauphin, Andrew Jarvis was waspishly petulant, a vital performance. The three productions breathed passionately and spoke intelligently from first to last.

Henry VI – Parts One, Two and Three (1589–91)
WILLIAM SHAKESPEARE

Adapted into two plays

House of Lancaster (Henry VI – Parts One and Two)

King Henry VI **Paul Brennen**
Humphrey, Duke of Gloucester **Colin Farrell**
Duchess of Gloucester **Ann**

Penfold
Duke of Bedford/Sir John Hume **John Dougall**
Bishop of Winchester **Clyde Pollitt**

Thomas, Duke of Exeter **Ian Burford**
Duke of Somerset **Siôn Probert**
Earl of Suffolk **Michael Pennington**

Sir Humphrey Stafford/Sir William
Lucy **John Darrell**
Earl of Hereford/Reignier **Hugh Sullivan**
Lord Talbot **Michael Fenner**
John Talbot/Keeper **John Tramper**
Bassett **Robert Hands**
Sir John Stanley **Phillip Rees**
Richard Plantagenet **Barry Stanton**

Edmund Mortimer **Stephen Jameson**
Richard Neville **Michael Cronin**
Vernon **Charles Dale**
Charles the Dauphin **Andrew Jarvis**
Margaret **June Watson**
Duke of Burgundy/Roger Bolingbroke **Jack Carr**
Duke of Alençon/John Southwell

Ben Bazell
Montjoy **Phillip Bowen**
Joan la Pucelle/Margery Jourdain **Francesca Ryan**
Lawyer/Saunder Simpcox **Roger Booth**
Mrs Simpcox **Jenifer Konko**

House of York (Henry VI – Parts Two and Three)

Richard Plantagenet **Barry Stanton**
Edward, Earl of March **Phillip Bowen**
George **John Dougall**
Richard **Andrew Jarvis**
Edmund/Smith the Weaver/A Son/Watchman **Stephen Jameson**
Duke of Norfolk/William Stafford **Ben Bazell**
Earl of Warwick **Michael Cronin**
Lady Grey **Ann Penfold**
Lord Rivers/Tutor/Sir Humphrey

Stafford/Keeper **John Darrell**
King Henry VI **Paul Brennen**
Queen Margaret **June Watson**
Edward **John Tramper**
John Beaufort/Keeper **Siôn Probert**
Lord Clifford/Lewis XI **Ian Burford**
Young Clifford **Charles Dale**
Earl of Hereford **Hugh Sullivan**
John de Vere **Michael Fenner**
Lord Say/Watchman **Clyde Pollitt**
Richmond **Dean Magri**
William Lord Hastings/Alexander

Iden/Father **Roger Booth**
Sir Robert Brackenbury/Clerk of Chatham **Colin Farrell**
Jack Cade **Michael Pennington**
Dick the Butcher **Jack Carr**
Michael **Robert Hands**
Lady Bona **Jenifer Konko**
Musicians **Ben Bazell, Ian Burford, Michael Cronin, Charles Dale, Simon Elliott, Colin Farrell and Francesca Ryan**

Even if one found some of the cutting too severe, one still could not fail to be impressed by the ESC's version of *Henry VI*. Once again Bogdanov concentrated on the strength of narrative. It was not possible to leave the theatre with the feeling of failing to understand the plays in spite of the intricacy of the politics and the vacillations of Warwick, who was played with surety by Michael Cronin. At the heart of the drama sits Henry VI, king before his time, son of a famous father whom he does not resemble in deed or thought, a man of gentility and piety in the midst of debris. Paul Brennen's Henry was a masterly achievement. Henry is a king utterly unsuited to kingship. There is a terrible poignancy at the end of *House of Lancaster* (Act IV, Scene Four of Part Two) where the bespectacled Henry turns to his prayer book with the words, 'Come, Margaret, God our hope will succour us' as rebellion rages in the streets of his capital and his wife clutches the head of her murdered lover, Suffolk. Henry is neither willing nor able to face the truth of the evil that surrounds his good. He would rather 'send some holy bishops to entreat' against the barbaric Cade than have 'so many simple souls' perish by the sword. Brennen made him a lonely figure and captured precisely the tragedy of a man thrust into the role of king when his gifts suit him better to be a country parson.

Alongside Brennen's Henry, June Watson's Margaret was the perfect foil. Margaret has the strength where Henry has the weakness, and that it is she who leads the forces into battle surprises us not a jot. June Watson's performance was such that it showed the seeds of this strength from her first appearance. At that point Suffolk courts her on his King's behalf. Here is no giddy girl, but a young woman destined to rule and to be obeyed. It is apparent from the start that only a man like Suffolk could be worthy of her bed. Michael Pennington grasped the sexuality and political scheming of Suffolk with a lyrical passion.

In *House of York*, Pennington took on the contrasting role of Jack Cade (scenes having been transposed) and his vocal qualities reminded us that the brashness that comes from Cade's mouth is still poetry. Bogdanov cast Cade and his men as National Front football hooligans, and if the conception was less successful than in *Henry V*, it still provided some chilling moments.

The ultimate defeat of Margaret had about it a tragic grandeur. It was to some extent deflated by some misplaced levity from Richard (Andrew Jarvis), but little could spoil the total effect. We were shown men and women lusting for power and the misery inflicted upon the innocent because of that lust. Shakespeare's warnings against civil strife and the violation of the natural order are loud and clear. In spite of the cuts and the reordering of scenes, a reverence for the verse and for the spirit of the plays themselves was maintained.

Richard III (1593)
WILLIAM SHAKESPEARE

Duchess of York **Susanna Best**
King Edward IV **Phillip Bowen**
Duke of Clarence **John Dougall**
Richard III **Andrew Jarvis**
Prince Edward **Simon Doe**
Richard, Duke of York **Rikki Belsham**
Queen Margaret **June Watson**
Lady Anne **Francesca Ryan**
Ghost of Henry VI/First Citizen **Paul Brennen**
Ghost of Edward/Marquess of

Michael Bogdanov is an idiosyncratic director, and the problem with idiosyncracy is that it borders on self-indulgence. He avoided self-indulgence in the first six plays in the cycle, but he lapsed in the seventh and last. Like the Birmingham Repertory Theatre's production of *Henry VI, Part Three*, at The Old Vic in the 1950s, Bogdanov's *House of York* ended with the opening soliloquy from *Richard III*. His *Richard III* opened with a prologue of his own invention. A fashionable cocktail party was the scene in which characters were introduced and the story was related in cynical, and often tasteless, fashion. The prologue set the tone. The play was set in modern dress with table-top computers and heavy artillery.

Dorset **John Tramper**
Queen Elizabeth **Ann Penfold**
Lord Rivers **John Darrell**
Lord Grey/Duke of Norfolk **Ben Bazell**
Lord Cardinal Bourchier/Third Citizen **Clyde Pollitt**
John Morton, Bishop of Ely **Ian Burford**
Lord Hastings **Roger Booth**
Duke of Buckingham **Michael Pennington**
Lord Stanley **Michael Cronin**
Lord Mayor of London/Tressel **Hugh Sullivan**
Sir Robert Brackenbury/Sir James Blunt **Colin Farrell**
Sir William Catesby **Siôn Probert**
Sir Richard Ratcliffe/Second Citizen **Stephen Jameson**
First Murderer/Earl of Oxford **Michael Fenner**
Sir James Tyrrel **Jack Carr**
Prologue/Second Murderer **Barry Stanton**
Berkeley **Phillip Rees**
Henry, Earl of Richmond **Charles Dale**
Musicians **Ben Bazell, Ian Burford, Michael Cronin, John Darrell, Colin Farrell and Andrew Jarvis**

Design **Chris Dyer**
Costume **Stephanie Howard**
Lighting **Mark Henderson**
Musical Director **Terry Mortimer**

Assistant Directors **Susanna Best and Stella Bond**

Director **Michael Bogdanov**

No Shakespeare play lends itself less readily to modern dress than *Richard III*. The keynote of this production was levity. Andrew Jarvis's Richard was all comic capers and had no sinister evil. Siôn Probert's Catesby was an unfortunate interpretation in which juvenile laughs were courted with theatrical mincing and executions were immediate, made with the pistol rather than the axe. From Olivier on film to John Wood at the National Theatre a few years ago, few actors appear willing to take the play seriously, and few take the opportunity of linking Richard with Vice of the morality plays. Yet Bogdanov's production was not without its moments. Ann Penfold and her confederates were able schemers, Pennington completed a triumphant cycle with a wonderfully astute and bristling Buckingham and June Watson's final exit as Margaret dragged the last vestige of nobility and dignity from a broken queen.

If one is disappointed with *Richard III*, that disappointment cannot detract from the overall delight at the ESC's monumental achievement in staging the cycle. The productions were greeted with acclaim at The Old Vic, as they had been at many other places all over the world. The seven plays told their stories with clarity and vitality. There was never a moment's boredom; never a moment when the intellect was not challenged or the emotions not stirred. From The Old Vic, the ESC took the cycle to Eastbourne, Norwich and Southampton. After that, two and a half years of bringing Shakespeare to the world, excitingly, came to an end, at least temporarily. Pennington and his team leave behind them cherished memories. Few have done as much for the prestige of the British theatre and won so many friends in so many places. Next time honours are awarded for services to the theatre, one hopes that those responsible will look further than the latest television sit-com.

King Lear (1605)

WILLIAM SHAKESPEARE

23 March–13 May 1989

With the memory of Dr Miller's *Tempest* still fresh in one's mind, one attended this production with some trepidation, but by the end of the evening one was captivated, even purged.

13. Paul Rogers as Gloucester is led off-stage to be blinded in Jonathan Miller's intelligent and extremely well-acted production of King Lear at The Old Vic in May.

Lear **Eric Porter**
King of France **Jasper Britton**
Duke of Burgundy/Gentleman **Stephen Caro**
Duke of Cornwall **David Sumner**
Duke of Albany **David Firth**
Earl of Kent **Ian Hogg**
Earl of Gloucester **Paul Rogers**
Edgar **Peter Eyre**
Edmund **Clive Russell**
Curan **Andrew Kitchen**
Oswald **Bill Snape**
Old Man **Robert Wentworth**
Doctor **John Scarborough**
Fool **Peter Bayliss**
Goneril **Gemma Jones**
Regan **Frances de la Tour**
Cordelia **Kim Thomson**
Knight/First Servant **Colin Tarrant**
Gentleman **Peter Needham**
Second Servant **Michael Cotterill**
Third Servant **Terence Dauncey**
Officer to Edmund **Robert Neil Kingham**
Herald **Greg Banks**
Gentlewoman **Annie Tyson**
Gentlewoman **Alison Fielding**
Attendants **James Allen, Conway Burns, Jim Douglas, Craig Duran, Stefan Meigh and Adrian Relph**

Design **Richard Hudson**
Lighting **Paul Pyant**
Music **Stuart Hutchinson**
Director **Jonathan Miller**

Miller's production, his third of *King Lear* in 20 years, was a traditional one. There were no gimmicks, and the result, ultimately, was a rendering of this great play which was sharp in clarity and intensely moving. Porter's magnificent Lear was without self-pity and his tragedy was unquestionably self-inflicted, the reward for emotional blackmail and for unthinking self-satisfaction. Gemma Jones and Frances de la Tour made Goneril and Regan credible human beings, tired of this old man who loved their sister most and whose heart ever ruled his head. Kim Thomson's Cordelia can rarely have been equalled; she was exquisite in beauty, tender in care, full of youthful integrity. When Lear entered with her dead in his arms the moment was almost unbearably poignant, and when he cried 'And my poor fool is hang'd' there was no ambiguity – it was clearly of Cordelia that he spoke.

The action was played before Richard Hudson's intelligently imaginative set: layer upon layer of unresponsive brick which gradually peeled away to reveal space and light. The design, in fact, became a metaphor of the play itself.

Miller chose to break with convention and with Shakespeare's instructions. He had Gloucester blinded off-stage, and we witnessed the horrendous act through the eyes of Regan. That denied us the physical equivalent of Lear's mental suffering, but it had a terrifying force, and Regan was revealed as a voyeur in evil, a cancer at the heart of the play.

Yet there were weaknesses. The Fool was too large a figure and missed pathos, for he was no other-Lear. Edmund was all surliness and missed the evil delight that the Machiavellian has in his actions – for the power that they bring him and for their own sake. Worst of all, the storm scene was so dominated by noise and billowing cloud that we heard little of what the mad King was saying. In those moments of madness there is a lucidity which brings us close to the inner Lear. The rages of the storm denied us this intimacy in Miller's production, which was a grievous loss. There were compensations, and one will remain ever grateful for Porter's Lear and Kim Thomson's Cordelia, for the plausibility of the evil of Regan and Goneril, for Peter Eyre's Edgar and Ian Hogg's rugged Kent and for the way in which Paul Rogers's Gloucester captured the reality of self-inflicted wounds. This was, indeed, a very fine *King Lear*.

As You Like It (1599)
WILLIAM SHAKESPEARE

23 May–8 July 1989

Orlando **Adam Kotz**
Adam **Daniel Thorndike**
Oliver **James Fleet**
Charles **Sean Blowers**
Rosalind **Fiona Shaw**
Celia **Helen Cooper**
Touchstone **David Cardy**
Le Beau **Brian Lipson**
Duke Frederick **John McEnery**
First Lord **Simon Harrison**
Second Lord **Gary Owston**
Duke Senior **Ronald Hines**
Lord **Mark Lewis**
Amiens **Aneirin Huws**
Jaques **Karl Johnson**
Corin **Sylvester Morand**
Silvius **Simon Roberts**
Phoebe **Polly Walker**
Audrey **Sarah Flind**

According to Shakespeare, the opening scene of *As You Like It* is played between Orlando and Adam. In Tim Albery's version, Rosalind, uncomfortably dressed, entered on a narrow parapet above the orchard, which resembled a racing stable. She opened a flap in the wall which revealed a single miniature tree at which she gazed wistfully while trying to keep her balance and spy what was going on below. A blood-red wall with a single opening, the door to the court, sloped menacingly towards the auditorium. The changes of scene or emphasis were marked by violent changes of light, although nothing could ever quite hide the threatening red wall. That put us into a world of heavy Jacobean tragedy, and the lightness of Shakespearean comedy seemed a million miles away. We entered the Forest of Arden through what looked like Harrods' window at Christmas, and the front of the stage accommodated what initially sounded like a gravel pit and was later revealed as a pool. The gravel pit was in keeping with a production which was ponderous and slow moving, weighed down with darkness. Fiona Shaw's Rosalind was so

Sir Oliver Martext **Alan Thompson**
William **Nigel Betts**
First Page **Samuel Holden/Ben Divers/Adam Osborne**
Second Page **Joseph Holden/Timothy Wright/Barnaby Powell**
Hymen **Rose English**
Jaques de Boys **Andrew Luce**

Design **Anthony McDonald**
Lighting **Peter Mumford**
Music **Orlando Gough**
Director **Tim Albery**

14. Fiona Shaw as Rosalind and Adam Kotz as Orlando in The Old Vic's heavyweight As You Like It.

heavily masculine, with cropped hair and casual clothes, that her moments of femininity – the swoon and the gasp of love – came almost as an embarrassing intrusion on the action. The humour had evaporated from the play. There was no fun in Touchstone, and the sun was perpetually behind the clouds. Only Karl Johnson's thoughtful Jaques emerged with any lightness from the gloom.

A Flea in Her Ear (1907)

GEORGES FEYDEAU translated from the French, *La Puce à l'Oreille*, by John Mortimer

8 August–18 November 1989

Camille Chandebise **Phelim McDermott**
Antoinette Plucheux **Julia Bardsley**

Farce is founded on truth. The fun, and its attendant element of cruelty, springs from the fact that credible human beings suddenly find themselves lost in a nightmare of mistakes and

15. Timothy Walker as Romain Tournel begs love from Linda Marlowe as Raymonde Chandebise in Richard Jones's version of Feydeau's A Flea in Her Ear *at The Old Vic. No remembrance of joys past on the same stage.*

Etienne Plucheux **Roger Lloyd Pack**
Dr Finache **David Ross**
Lucienne Homenides De Histangua **Rose English**
Raymonde Chandebise **Linda Marlowe**
Victor Emmanuel Chandebise **Jim Broadbent**
Romain Tournel **Timothy Walker**
Carlos Homenides De Histangua **Kevin Williams**
Eugenie **Angela Clerkin**
Augustin Feraillon **Matthew Scurfield**
Olympia **Rosalind Knight**
Baptistin **Johnny Hutch**
Herr Schwarz **Steven Beard**
Poche **Jim Broadbent**
Clerks and Servants **Paul Besterman, Suzy King, Penelope Dimond, Timothy Page, Brian Lipson and Vernon Gudgeon**
Dog **Schaefer**

Design **The Brothers Quay**
Costume **Sue Blane**
Lighting **Jonathan Collinson**
Sound **Larry Sider**
Director **Richard Jones**

mistimings. Unfortunately, Richard Jones, to whom Ostrovsky and Feydeau are apparently indistinguishable, created a world of caricature and the grotesque in his production of *A Flea in Her Ear*. The result was that the second act, one of the most amusing of theatrical creations, was totally unfunny. Indeed, at times, it was almost obscene and offensive. The first act had laboured as the women struggled, unsuccessfully, to come to terms with their characters and, seemingly, with the wishes of the director. The second act left no hope of recovery. Jim Broadbent, in the dual role of Victor Emmanuel Chandebise and Poche, strode bravely through the debris, but nothing could save or justify this ill-conceived production.

Open Air Theatre, Regent's Park

LONDON NW1 4NP
01-486-2431
New Shakespeare Company 01-935-5756

A Midsummer Night's Dream (1596)
WILLIAM SHAKESPEARE

30 May–9 September 1989

Theseus **David Henry**
Hippolyta **Brigitte Kahn**
Philostrate **Stefan Bednarczyk**
Egeus **William Haden**
Hermia **Vicky Licorish**
Demetrius **Teddy Kempner**
Lysander **Sam Miller**
Helena **Tricia Morrish**
Quince **Christopher Ettridge**
Bottom **Christopher Benjamin**
Flute **Robert Styles**
Starveling **David Mallinson**
Snout **Jo Jones**
Snug **Jason Hart**
Puck **Trevor Laird**

Blessed with a good summer, the Regent's Park season opened with the traditional *Dream*. Guy Slater's production set the play in the 1960s love era of flower power and caftans, 'fancy-dress costumes that suit the play's spirit of midsummer madness'. Saeed Jaffrey caressed the verse as Oberon; and Tricia Morrish, Christopher Benjamin, Robert Styles and Jason Hart received special praise in a production which was generally greeted with delight.

First Fairy **Kim Barry**
Titania **Sally Dexter**
Oberon **Saeed Jaffrey**
Moth **Annette Fraser**
Cobweb **David Jarvis**
Peaseblossom **Kathryn Salt**

Design **Simon Higlett**
Lighting **Ian Callander**
Choreographer **Kenn Oldfield**
Director **Guy Slater**

Twelfth Night (1602)
WILLIAM SHAKESPEARE

14 June–7 September 1989

Orsino **Christopher Ettridge**
Viola **Juliette Grassby**
Sebastian **Sam Miller**
Antonio **Trevor Laird**
Valentine **Robert Styles**
Olivia **Sally Dexter**
Curio **Jason Hart**

The New Shakespeare Company notched up a second success in their Regent's Park repertoire with Ian Talbot's 'fluently orchestrated' production of *Twelfth Night*. Ann McFerran, in *Time Out*, was not alone in singling out Bernard Bresslaw's Malvolio for special mention. She described his performance as 'upwardly mobile, socially naff, desperately nouveau, pitifully vulnerable' and a 'joy to behold'.

Sir Toby Belch **David Henry**
Sir Andrew Aguecheek **David Mallinson**
Maria **Vicky Licorish**
Malvolio **Bernard Bresslaw**
Fabian **Stefan Bednarczyk**
Feste **Teddy Kempner**
Sea Captain **William Haden**
Ladies in Waiting **Tricia Morrish, Kim Barry, Annette Fraser and Kathryn Salt**
Officers **David Jarvis and Jo Jones**
Design **Simon Higlett**
Lighting **Ian Callander**
Musical Director **John du Prez**
Director **Ian Talbot**

The Swaggerer (c. 200 BC)

PLAUTUS adapted by Brian Trueman from *Miles Gloriosus*

2 August–2 September 1989

The season in Regent's Park was completed by a musical version of a romp by Plautus. Bernard Bresslaw was the cowardly swaggerer and Sally Dexter the sex siren.

Trogo **Ian Talbot**
Wrestlers/Tumblers **David Jarvis and Robert Styles**
Leader of Troupe **Stefan Bednarczyk**
Cantors **Kim Barry, Paul Hegarty, Teddy Kempner and Tricia Morrish**
The Captain **Bernard Bresslaw**
Little Soldier **Jason Hart**
Lucius **Sam Miller**
Philippa **Juliette Grassby**
Senator **David Henry**
Gluteus Maximus **David Mallinson**
Lurcio **Teddy Kempner**
Acerbita **Sally Dexter**
Ancila **Liz Gebhart**
Tumbler **Annette Fraser**
Bear's Keeper **Kathryn Salt**
Bear **Jo Jones**
Design **Simon Higlett**
Lighting **Ian Callander**
Choreographer **Kenn Oldfield**
Music **Carl Davis**
Musical Director **Stefan Bednarczyk**
Director **Caroline Smith**

Palace Theatre

CAMBRIDGE CIRCUS, SHAFTESBURY AVENUE, LONDON W1
01-434-0909

Administrator **Harry Dagnall**

Les Misérables (1980)

ALAIN BOUBLIL and **CLAUDE-MICHEL SCHÖNBERG**, based on the novel by Victor Hugo

Opened 4 December 1985

Jean Valjean **Peter Karrie**
Courfeyrac **Michael McLean**
Whore/Factory Worker **Janet Mooney**

The Cameron Mackintosh/RSC production has become so much a permanent fixture in Cambridge Circus that it seems hard to remember that it started in England at the Barbican in October 1985. Its success is hard to define. In an interesting

Javert **Philip Quast**
Fantine **Grania Renihan**
Pimp/Claquesous **Matthew Ryan**
Whore **Paula Simpson**
Madame Thénardier **Gay Soper**
Babet **Bernard Tagliavini**
Bishop of Digne/Lesgles **Rex Taylor-Craig**
Whore/Factory Worker **Elizabeth Watts**
Feuilly **Matthew White**
Factory Girl **Jacinta Whyte**
Old Woman/Factory Worker **Norma Atallah**
Crone **Sally Bentley**
Factory Worker **Clare Burt**
Bramatabois/Grantaire **Michael Cantwell**
Montparnasse **Glenn Carter**
Joly **Danny Coll**
Jean Prouvaire **Julian Forsyth**
Marius **Mario Frangoulis**
Eponine **Linzi Hateley**
Factory Foreman/Combeferre **Mark Heenehan**
Enjolras **Christopher Howard**
Cosette **Lisa Hull**
Old Beggar Woman **Ellen Jackson**
Thénardier **Barry James**
Brujon **Halcro Johnston**
with **John Dulieu, Julie Michaels, Caroline Tatlow and Tony Whittle**

Lyrics **Herbert Kretzmer**
Music **Claude-Michel Schönberg**

article, 'What Makes a Subject for a Good Musical?', Trevor Nunn admitted that the idea of 'proposing a different sort of music drama based on the difficult and inescapably serious 19th Century French novel' was greeted with 'snickers and guffaws'. Although not to the liking of all critics and unquestionably weak in libretto on occasions, Les Misérables continues to prosper and entertain.

Design **John Napier**
Costume **Andreane Neofitou**
Lighting **David Hersey**
Sound **Andrew Bruce (Autograph)**
Orchestration **John Cameron**
Musical Director **Martin Koch**
Director and Adaptor **Trevor Nunn and John Caird**

16. *To the barricades!* Les Misérables – and no sign of the end of hostilities at the Palace Theatre, where the RSC's production continues to play to full houses.

Palladium

8 ARGYLL STREET, LONDON W1
01-437-7373

The revival of *'Allo 'Allo* ran 21 December 1988–27 May 1989. There are plans to revive it for the Christmas season 1989–90.

Singin' in the Rain (1983)
BETTY COMDEN and ADOLPH GREEN based on the MGM film

29 June–11 November 1989

When it first came on to the Palladium stage, *Singin' in the Rain* ran for a record two and a half years. It was resurrected in 1989. Colourful and slick, and based on a deservedly popular musical film, it again made people happy with its tale of Hollywood at the time when the film world was coping with the advent of sound.

Dora Bailey **Rachel Izen**
Zelda Saddler **Debbie Kenwood**
Olga Nerg **Stephanie Vivaudou**
Baron de la Rattele de la Tolerone/Ziegfeld Dancer **Roger Sutton**
Cosmo Brown **Bunny May**
Chauffeur/Man in Rain **Mark Canton**
Lina Lamont **Sarah Payne**
Don Lockwood **Tommy Steele**
Miss Detroit **Angela Kemp**
Roscoe Dexter **Graham Hoadly**
Bertram B Bertram **Mason Taylor**
R F Simpson **Kalman Glass**
Gozark **Joe Montana**
Kathy Selden **Danielle Carson**
Man on the Screen **Frank Williams**
Valentine Girl/Girl in Rain **Alexandra Moore**
Valentine Girls **Joanne Farrell, Stephanie Hicks, Debbie Kenwood and Teri James**
Indian Brave **Johnny Havelock**
Indian Chief **Mark Waghorn**
Train Driver **Gerald Armin**
Steve **Russell Richardson**
Tea Lady **Gynna Oladjins**
Miss Ginsmore **Joyce Carpenter**
Hairdresser **Sandra Carrier**
Sound Man **Roy Sone**
Clapper Boy **William Folan-Conroy**
Ladies in Waiting **Denise Kelly and Alison Temple Savage**

Villain **Edward Brayshaw**
Policeman **Gary Hoof**
Contract Players **Alison Edge, Julie Michelle, Cherith Towler, Paul Nield, Sarah Jane Raynsford, Gary Forecast and Stephen Richards**

Music **Nacio Herb Brown**
Lyrics **Arthur Freed**
Design and Costume **Terry Parsons**
Director **Tommy Steele**

Phoenix Theatre

CHARING CROSS ROAD, LONDON WC2
01-836-2294

General Manager **David Lyness**

Richard II (1595)
WILLIAM SHAKESPEARE

28 November 1988–13 May 1989

Richard II **Derek Jacobi**
John of Gaunt **Robert Eddison**
Henry Bolingbroke **David Rintoul**
Thomas Mowbray/Gardener/Sir Piers of Exton **Peter Postlethwaite**
Duchess of Gloucester **Rachel Gurney**
Earl of Salisbury **Patrick Marley**
Duke of Aumerle **Clive Arrindell**
Sir Stephen Scroop/Groom **Tom Durham**
Lord Fitzwater **Adam Norton**
Sir Henry Green/Keeper of Pomfret Prison **Scott Cherry**
Sir John Bushey **Gwynn Beech**

Sir John Bagot **Malcolm Mudie**
Edmund, Duke of York **Malcolm Tierney**
Earl of Northumberland **Jeffery Dench**
Lord Ross **Leon Eagles**
Lord Willoughby **Richard Wilkes**
Queen Isabel **Kathryn Pogson**

Henry Percy **Sam Miller**
Welsh Captain/Abbot of Westminster **Ray Llewellyn**
Bishop of Carlisle **Robert Swann**
Ladies attending the Queen **Jan Dunn and Jennifer Thorne**
Man **Jason Salkey**
Duchess of York **Barbara Jefford**

Attendant **Graham Rowe**

Design **Carl Toms**
Lighting **Mick Hughes**
Music **Marc Wilkinson**
Musical Director **Ian MacPherson**
Director **Clifford Williams**

Richard III (1593)
WILLIAM SHAKESPEARE

8 February–13 May 1989

Richard of Gloucester **Derek Jacobi**
George, Duke of Clarence **Malcolm Tierney**
Sir Robert Brackenbury **Patrick Marley**
Lord Hastings **Robert Swann**
Lady Anne **Kathryn Pogson**
Halberdier/Messenger **Jason Salkey**
Queen Elizabeth **Heather Canning**
Earl Rivers **Malcolm Mudie**
Lord Grey **Scott Cherry**
Marquis of Dorset **Gwynn Beech**
Duke of Buckingham/Sir James Blunt **Leon Eagles**
Lord Stanley **Jeffery Dench**
Queen Margaret **Barbara Jefford**
Sir William Catesby **Clive Arrindell**
First Murderer **Ray Llewellyn**
Second Murderer/Earl of Oxford **Sam Miller**
King Edward IV/Henry, Earl of Richmond **David Rintoul**
Sir Richard Ratcliffe **Richard Wilkes**
Duchess of York **Rachel Gurney**
Archbishop of York/Sir James Tyrrel **Tom Durham**
Richard, Duke of York **Robbie Engels/Ian Harris**
Edward, Prince of Wales **Corrin Helliwell/Sam Hails**
Archbishop of Canterbury/Duke of Norfolk **Adam Norton**
Bishop of Ely **Robert Eddison**
Lord Mayor of London/Sir Walter Herbert **Graham Rowe**
Jane Shore **Jan Dunn**

At the close of 1988 and for the first four and a half months of 1989, the Phoenix Theatre was home to Derek Jacobi's two Richards. The plays were later taken to Washington, where they were performed at the Kennedy Center.

Richard II proved to be a rather stolid production. Jacobi's ill-starred King who never became a man was seen by Christopher Edwards in *The Spectator* as 'unusual in its sardonic, mood-switching variety'. In addition to Jacobi's generally praised performance there was a good supporting cast, of which the eloquent Robert Eddison inevitably earned special commendation. Surely, his is one of the loveliest voices to be heard on the London stage. The production as a whole, however, was considered clear rather than inspired or inspiring.

Richard III gave Derek Jacobi a further opportunity to display his variety of talents, but the production was seen as presenting the action in something of a vacuum. There were capable performances from supporting players, notably David Rintoul and Barbara Jefford. Martin Hoyle in *The Financial Times* summarised most people's objections to the production when he said that by the time it realised Richard was 'a homicidal maniac as well as a lovable clown', it was too late.

Princess Elizabeth **Tara Williams**

Design **Carl Toms**
Lighting **Mick Hughes**
Music **Marc Wilkinson**
Director **Clifford Williams**

The Merchant of Venice (1597)
WILLIAM SHAKESPEARE

1 June–23 September 1989

Antonio **Leigh Lawson**
Bassanio **Alex Hardy**
Lorenzo **Richard Garnett**
Gratiano **Michael Siberry**
Salerio **Robert Arnold**
Solanio **Ian Lavender**
Leonardo **Ian Bolt**
Shylock **Dustin Hoffman**
Jessica **Francesca Buller**
Tubal **Leon Lissek**
Lancelot Gobbo **Peter-Hugo Daly**
Old Gobbo **John Cater**
Portia **Geraldine James**
Nerissa **Abigail McKern**
Balthasar **Brian Poyser**
Stephano **Simon Beresford**
Prince of Morocco **Jeffery Kissoon**
Prince of Aragon **Michael Carter**
Duke of Venice **Basil Henson**
with **Kammy Darweish, Leigh Funnelle, Heather Ramsay, David Summer, Michael John Wade and Lawrence Werber**
Musicians **Nicola Lewis, Jo Maggs, Karl Morgan and Alison Smart**

Design **Chris Dyer**
Lighting **Mark Henderson**
Sound **Paul Arditti**
Music **Robert Lockhart**
Director **Peter Hall**

Peter Hall said farewell to the National Theatre in 1988 with productions of Shakespeare's three late plays which, whatever faults they may have had, were distinguished by their clarity of exposition. The same comment can be applied to his *Merchant of Venice* at the Phoenix, which played to capacity audiences throughout its four-month run. Indeed, it was so popular that the run was extended for a fortnight more than was originally scheduled. The presence of Dustin Hoffman was obviously a great attraction, and he did not disappoint his followers. His Shylock, outwardly more genial than is customary but essentially a private man, was an honest and thoughtful piece of characterisation. His control and essays at humour in the early part of the play brought his demand for the bond into sharper relief, and he came close to gaining our sympathy.

The outstanding performance, however, was that of Geraldine James as Portia. She achieved what might have been thought to be impossible in that she made this generally priggish woman appear both credible and likeable. There seemed to be nothing strange in Miss James's Portia going off to

17. *An accusing finger from Dustin Hoffman's genial Shylock in Peter Hall's production of* The Merchant of Venice *at the Phoenix Theatre.*

Venice and winning her case while disguised as a man, for, from the start, she was both stronger and more intelligent than the men around her. It was no surprise that she had been guarded from mercenary suitors by her father's stratagem, for she made it clear that she had inherited his wisdom and perspicacity as well as his wealth. In Venice, she was totally convincing. When she offered the 'quality of mercy' speech, it was with a gesture of compromise and compassion – she was not merely delivering a passage learned for an elocution examination. She was most ably supported by Abigail McKern as Nerissa, and it was quite apparent in their handling of their husbands who would be dominant in their marriages. This, surely, is as it should be. Bassanio does little to show that he is worthy of such a splendid woman. This is a play in which the wishes and wiles of women rule.

Inevitably, Peter Hall's production was straightforward and intelligent. The text ruled. The days of gimmick were long in the past. Paradoxically, what we were left with was the realisation that this is neither a very good nor, to modern audiences, a very pleasant play; but Hall's production made it a thoughtful and interesting experience.

Napoleon – the Untold American Story (1987)
JOHN SESSIONS

27 September–28 October 1989

Napoleon *et al.* **John Sessions**

Design **Jenny Tiramani**
Director **Kenneth Branagh**

First performed at the Riverside Studios in 1987, John Sessions's one-man show was presented in its rewritten version for a limited season at the Phoenix. Sessions told the story of Napoleon from womb to tomb in a way that was both erudite and highly entertaining. This stunning performer ranged widely over art, history, literature and much else. 'The real joy of the production', wrote Charles Spencer in *The Daily Telegraph*, 'is Sessions's magpie mind and his gift for instant impersonation.' The collapse of Napoleon's marriage, for example, was played as if by Richard Burton and Elizabeth Taylor in *Who's Afraid of Virginia Woolf?* And Bilko, Woody Allen, Diane Keaton, Sylvester Stallone and many others tumbled through the evening. It is, indeed, 'an exhilarating *tour de force*'. To quote again from Charles Spencer, 'Something of the tragic grandeur of Napoleon's story, and a sense of the waste and pity of war, survives the barrage of gags and word-play.'

The Baker's Wife opened on 17 November 1989. Full details of this musical will be found under Ipswich, Wolsey Theatre.

Piccadilly Theatre

DENMAN STREET, LONDON W1
01-867-1118

Metropolis (1989)

8 March–28 August 1989

A spectacular and expensive adaption of Fritz Lang's silent film about the future. The black and metal set tended to dominate a venture which most judged to be ill-conceived and which was short lived.

John Freeman **Brian Blessed**
Maria/Futura **Judy Kuhn**
Steven **Graham Bickley**
Warner **Jonathan Adams**
Jeremiah **Paul Keown**
George **Stifyn Parri**
Jade **Linsey Danvers**
Groat **Colin Fay**
Lake **Megan Kelly**
Marco **Robert Fardell**
Lulu **Lucy Dixon**
Workers and Elitists **Buz Butler, Stephen J Colley, Geoffrey Dallamore, Mark Fredrick, Liz Izen, Gael Johnson, Martyn Knight, Bo Light, Joseph Lloyd Collatin, Mhairi Nelson, Kevin Power, Teresa Revill, Scott St Martyn, Charles Shirvell, Julie Ann Ward and Simon Warwick**
Swings **Jason Barker, Caroline Jameson and Christian Solari**
Children of Metropolis **Oswald Bailey, Amanda Cannon, David Cooper, Clare Humphrey, Lucy Indrisie, Ian McGregor, Jean Paul Pfluger, Elizabeth Pearce, James Tovell and Emmaline Wood**

Music **Joe Brooks**
Book and Lyrics **Joe Brooks and Dusty Hughes**
Additional Material **David Firman**
Design **Ralph Koltai**
Lighting **David Hersey**
Sound **Bobby Aitken**
Choreographer **Tom Jobe**
Musical Director **Mark Warman**
Director **Jerome Savary**

The Chichester Festival Theatre production of *A Little Night Music* opened on 10 October 1989. Details of the production will be found under Chichester. It is likely that this mainly good production will find a more comfortable home at the Piccadilly. There the stage is more suited to a musical than it is at Chichester.

Playhouse Theatre

NORTHUMBERLAND AVENUE, LONDON WC2N 5DE
01-839-4401

The World According to Me (1989)

15 February–15 April 1989

The comedian and ex-rabbi Jack Mason won great acclaim for his slick, fast-talking Jewish-American humour. It has no equivalent in Great Britain.

---

18 April–3 June 1989, *The Woman in Black* (see under Fortune Theatre).

A Room of One's Own (1989)

PATRICK GARLAND adapted from the writings of Virginia Woolf

5–24 June 1989

Virginia Woolf **Eileen Atkins**

Music **Nigel Hess**
Sound **John Leonard**
Director **Patrick Garland**

Originally presented at the Purcell Room and later at Hampstead, *A Room of One's Own* was a delicately produced and performed piece based on the writings of Virginia Woolf.

Boswell for the Defence (1989)

PATRICK EDGEWORTH

6 September–25 November 1989

James Boswell **Leo McKern**
Voice of Abigail **Sarah Monroe**

Design **Kristian Fredrikson**
Lighting **Keith Edmundson**
Director **Frank Hauser**

The National Youth Theatre performed the *Marat/Sade* play in August, after which Leo McKern opened in *Boswell for the Defence*. Dr Johnson's biographer is seen as the lawyer he was, engaging himself with the case of Mary Broad. She was transported and rowed a mammoth distance to save her starving children, only to be sentenced to death. It was welcomed as good talk and good acting, funny and moving.

Prince Edward Theatre

OLD COMPTON STREET, LONDON W1
01-734-8951

Anything Goes (1934)

Opened 4 July 1989

Louie **Philip Griffiths**
Elisha Whitney **Harry Towb**
Fred **Nigel Waugh**
Billy Crocker **Howard McGillin**
Reno Sweeney **Elaine Paige**
Young Girl **Anita Pashley**
Sailor **Anthony Lyn**
Captain **David Bacon**
Purser **David Bexon**
Purity **Jacqui Boatswain**
Chastity **Sarah Drummond**
Charity **Nicola Meerloo**
Virtue **Suzanne Maria Thomas**
Minister **Brian Ellis**
Luke **Hi Ching**
John **John Shin**
Hope Harcourt **Ashleigh Sendin**
Mrs Evangeline Harcourt **Ursula Smith**
Lord Evelyn Oakleigh **Martin Turner**
Erma **Kathryn Evans**
Moonface Martin **Bernard Cribbins**
Mrs Wentworth Frick **June Bland**
with **Chris Baldock, Stephen Graf, Darryl Knock, Lorraine Lacey, Patrick Long, Jason Di Mascio, Stephen Mear, Peter Alex Newton, Denise Ranger, David Samuel, Nils Seibaek, Janice Torrens and Stephen Tye**

To succeed *Chess* at the Prince Edward Theatre, Robert Fox Ltd, Anchorage Productions and Joan and Joe Cullman brought Jerry Zaks's Lincoln Center Theater production of Cole Porter's 55-year-old *Anything Goes* to London. The original book about

18. Elaine Paige and Bernard Cribbins showing their paces in Anything Goes *at the Prince Edward Theatre.*

Music and Lyrics **Cole Porter**
Original Book **P G Wodehouse, Guy Bolton, Howard Lindsay and Russell Crouse**
New Book **Timothy Crouse and John Weidman**
Musical Director **John Owen Edwards**
Choreographer **Michael Smiun**
Design and Costume **Tony Walton**
Lighting **Paul Gallo**

a shipwreck aboard a luxury liner had to be drastically revised, and the show survived entirely on the strength of its familiar and friendly songs, such as 'I Get a Kick Out of You' and 'The Gypsy in Me'. Although some critics, specifically Michael Billington, found the production full of 'energy and zest', they found the story of criss-cross romances aboard an ocean liner very thin and the show 'a piece of vacuous escapism'.

Sound **Tony Meola (for Autograph)**
Dance Arrangements **Tom Fay**
Director **Jerry Zaks**

Prince of Wales

COVENTRY STREET, LONDON W1
01-839-5987

Aspects of Love (1989)

Opened 17 April 1989

Rose Vibert **Ann Crumb**
Alex Dillingham **Michael Ball**
George Dillingham **Kevin Colson**
Giulietta Trapani **Kathleen Rowe McAllen**
Marcel Richard **Paul Bentley**
Jenny Dillingham, 12 **Zoe Hart/Natalie Wright**
Jenny, 14 **Diana Morrison**
Elizabeth **Laurel Ford**
Hugo Le Meunier/Friend **David Greer**
Chanteuse/Pharmacist **Sally Smith**
Barker/Hotelier **David Oakley**
Barker/Gondolier/Knife Thrower **John Barr**
Friend **Michael Sadler**
Girl/Hotel Cashier **Carol Duffy**
Girl/Nun **Susie Fenwick**
Alex's Date/Assistant **Trilby Harris**
Doctor/Friend of Marcel/Clown **Tim Nilsson-Page**
Clown **Geoffrey Abbott**
Clown/Young Peasant **Sandy Strallen**

Music **Andrew Lloyd Webber**
Lyrics **Don Black and Charles Hart**, based on the novel by David Garnett
Design **Maria Bjornson**
Lighting **Andrew Bridge**
Sound **Martin Levan**
Choreographer **Gillian Lynne**
Musical Director **Michael Reed**
Director **Trevor Nunn**

The withdrawal of Roger Moore from the leading role gave rise to the suspicion that Andrew Lloyd Webber could be heading for a failure. Those who anticipated this were to be disappointed, for *Aspects of Love*, like *Phantom of the Opera* and *Cats*, was rapturously received and would seem to be with us for ever. It is totally different in style from Lloyd Webber's other works, closer to opera than to operetta, and many see it as a most courageous venture. 'Love Changes Everything' is a key song and an underlying theme of the musical, which revolves around the love of a young girl for an older man. Some critics had their reservations, but many found tenderness, lyricism and innovation.

Queen's Theatre

SHAFTESBURY AVENUE, LONDON W1
01-734-1166

Single Spies (1988)
ALAN BENNETT

28 February–26 August 1989

Jeffrey Archer's *Beyond Reasonable Doubt* closed in February prior to a national tour. It was replaced by the National Theatre production of Alan Bennett's two one-act plays, *Single Spies*. The first, an adaptation of his earlier television play, deals with a meeting between the actress Coral Browne and the defector Guy Burgess in Moscow. The second is a study of Blunt and is a delicately structured piece involving the examination of a painting and a conversation with Her Majesty the Queen. Both plays, commented upon in last year's edition, were impeccably acted and were a delight to the intellect and to the imagination.

An Englishman Abroad

Coral **Prunella Scales**
Burgess **Simon Callow**
Tolya **Renny Krupinski**
Shop Assistant **Edward Halstead**

Tailor **Alan Bennett**

Director **Alan Bennett**

A Question of Attribution

Blunt **Alan Bennett**
Restorer **David Terence**
Chubb **Simon Callow**
Phillips **Patrick Bailey**
Colin **Sean Chapman**

HMQ **Prunella Scales**

Design **Bruno Santini**
Lighting **Paul Pyant**
Music **Dominic Muldowney**
Director **Simon Callow**

Shadowlands opened on 17 October 1989, having premièred at the Theatre Royal, Plymouth, under which details of the production are to be found.

Royal Court Theatre

SLOANE SQUARE, LONDON SW1
01-730-1745

Artistic Director **Max Stafford-Clark**

A Man with Connections (1988)
ALEXANDER GELMAN translated by Stephen Mulrine

10 January–4 February 1989

Natasha Gladkov **Marty Cruickshank**
Andrei Gladkov **Bill Paterson**
Voice of Alyosha **Simon Donald**

Design **Dermot Hayes**
Lighting and Sound **George Tarbuck**
Director **Jenny Killick**

First presented by the Traverse Theatre as part of their programme at the Edinburgh Fringe Festival in 1988, *A Man with Connections* is a powerful Russian domestic drama which has been immensely popular in the Soviet Union since Gorbachev's liberal reforms. It is severely critical of the Soviet economic planning and its effect on the lives of ordinary people.

My Mother Said I Never Should (1987)
CHARLOTTE KEATLEY

2 March–1 April 1989

Doris **Elizabeth Bradley**
Margaret **Sheila Reid**
Jackie **Jane Gurnett**
Rosie **Shirley Henderson**

Design **Tanya McCallin**
Costume **Jennifer Cook**
Lighting **Mark Henderson**
Sound **Bryan Bowen**

A revision of a play first presented in Manchester in 1987, *My Mother Said I Never Should* concerns four generations. It moves in and out of time over a period of 50 years, weaving the lives of the four women together and tracing parallels and paradoxes in mothers, daughters and granddaughters. The splendid cast rose to all that was asked of them under Michael Attenborough's excellent direction.

Director **Michael Attenborough**

Icecream (1989)
CARYL CHURCHILL

6 April–13 May 1989

Two middle-aged Americans tour England in search of their

Lance **Philip Jackson**
Vera **Carole Hayman**
Phil **David Thewlis**
Jaq **Saskia Reeves**
Man in Devon/Shrink/Colleague/
Guest/Hitcher/Professor **Allan Corduner**
Waitress/Drunk/Mother/Venezuelan Passenger **Gillian Hanna**

ancestors. They find their way through idyllic countryside to the East End of London. Accident and murder jostle with the comedy in a play about conflicting cultures which some described as fun, others as formless.

Design **Peter Hartwell**
Costume **Jennifer Cook**
Lighting **Christopher Toulmin**

Sound **Bryan Bowen**
Director **Max Stafford-Clark**

Iranian Nights (1989)
TARIQ ALI and HOWARD BRENTON

20–29 April 1989

A short early evening play which was a response to the Salman Rushdie affair. It pointed out the difference between the prophet and his mouthpieces and depicted a divided Moslem community within Britain.

Omar Khayyam **Paul Bhattacharjee**
The Caliph **Nabil Shaban**
Scheherezade **Fiona Victory**

Design **Debra Overton and Colin Pigott**
Costume **Chrissy Robinson**

Lighting **Christopher Toulmin**
Director **Penny Cherns**

American Bagpipes (1988)
IAIN HEGGIE

4 June–1 July 1989

Sandra Michigan **Lesley Manville**
Rena Nauldie **Eileen Nicholas**
Willie Nauldie **Ken Scott**
Patrick Nauldie **Paul Higgins**

Design **Julian McGowan**
Lighting **Rick Fisher**
Sound **Bryan Bowen**
Choreographer **Geraldine Stephenson**
Director **Lindsay Posner**

Performed previously in both Glasgow and Manchester, *American Bagpipes* is a black comedy about a tyrannical Glasgow policeman and his family. Daughter Sandra comes back from America in an effort to liberate her mother. It was very well received as a play and its performance and direction were commended.

A Whistle in the Dark (1961)
TOM MURPHY

7–29 July 1989

Des Carney **Lorcan Cranitch**
Michael Carney **Dermot Crowley**
Iggy Carney **Gerard Horan**
Much **Ray McBride**
Harry Carney **Sean McGinley**
Dada **Godfrey Quigley**
Betty **Corrine Ransom**
Hugo Carney **Maeliosa Stafford**

The Dublin Abbey Theatre's production of Tom Murphy's powerful play about a clan of Irish immigrants in Coventry. This was part of the London International Festival of Theatre.

Design **Brien Vahey**
Costume **Claudia Mayer**
Lighting **Andy Phillips**

Sound **Bryan Bowen**
Director **Garry Hines**

The Recruiting Officer (1706)
GEORGE FARQUHAR

10 August–30 September 1989

Mr Scruple/Pluck **Mark Lambert**
Mr Balance/Costar Pearmain/Servant **Jude Akuwudike**
Mr Worthy/Bridewell **Nigel Cooke**
Capt. Plume **Julian Wadham**
Capt. Brazen/Bullock **Ron Cook**

Kite **Clive Russell**
Thomas Appletree/Melinda **Kathryn Hunter**
Silvia **Amanda Redman**
Lucy **Suzanne Packer**
Rose **Mossie Smith**

Design **Peter Hartwell**
Lighting **Christopher Toulmin**
Sound **Andy Pink**
Director **Max Stafford-Clark**

Our Country's Good (1988)
TIMBERLAKE WERTENBAKER based on the novel by Thomas Keneally

10 August–30 September 1989

Capt. Arthur Phillip, RN/John Wisehammer **Ron Cook**
Maj. Robbie Ross, RM/Ketch Freeman **Mark Hunter**
Capt. David Collins, RM/Robert Sideway **Nigel Cooke**
Capt. Watkin Tench, RM/Aboriginal/Black Caesar **Jude Akuwudike**
Capt. Jemmy Campbell, RM/Mid.

Harry Brewer, RN/John Arscott **Clive Russell**
Rev. Johnson/Mary Brenham/Meg Long **Amanda Redman**
Lt George Johnston, RM/Duckling Smith **Suzanne Packer**
Lt Will Dawes, RM/Liz Morden **Kathryn Hunter**
2nd Lt Ralph Clark, RM **Julian Wadham**
2nd Lt William Faddy, RM/Dabby Bryant **Mossie Smith**

Design **Peter Hartwell**
Lighting **Jenny Cane**
Sound **Bryan Bowen**
Director **Max Stafford-Clark**

The Royal Court re-presented their successful productions of 1988 when *The Recruiting Officer* and *Our Country's Good* were offered in repertoire. The plays have a link in that Timberlake Wertenbaker's prize-winning drama concerns a group who are deported to Australia and rehearse a production of *The Recruiting Officer*. The plays had toured extensively and there were many differences in the casts from the original 1988 productions.

Royal Court Theatre Upstairs

A Rock in Water (1989)
WINSOME PINNOCK

Upstairs 16–28 January 1989

The Royal Court Young People's Theatre presented this play with music, inspired by the life of Claudia Jones, the American Black Rights campaigner. It was directed by Elyse Dodgson.

A Hero's Welcome (1989)
WINSOME PINNOCK

Upstairs 20 February–11 March 1989

Set in Jamaica in 1947, the play tells of a gentle young man who returns to the island and invents a war record to explain an injury sustained in a factory. His tale is overwhelmed as three adolescent girls scramble to leave for England in their aspirations for a better life. *The Independent* thought it 'a hugely talented cast in a highly recommended production'.

Len **Brian Bovell**
Nana **Mona Hammond**
Charlie **Andrew Fraser**
Minda **Suzanne Packer**
Sis **Pamela Nomvete**
Ishbel **Joanne Campbell**
Stanley **Gary McDonald**

Design **Lucy Weller**

Lighting **Tina MacHugh**
Sound **Bryan Bowen**

Director **Jules Wright**

Blood (1989)
HARWANT S BAINS

Upstairs 30 August–16 September 1989

Third Man/Indian Worker/Official/Henchman **Bhasker**
Balbir/Balbir's Father **Paul Bhattacharjee**
Second Man/Indian Prime Minister/Henchman **Kulvinder Ghir**
Jane **Debra Gillett**
Young Balbir **Ronak Manek**
Young Manmohan **Sean Ramnath-O'Neil**
Manmohan **Dev Sagoo**
Surinder **Meera Syal**

First Man/Harjeet **Gordon Warnecke**
Landlord/White Worker/Bodyguard **Jimmy Yuill**

After months of closure through lack of funds, the Theatre Upstairs reopened with a play which begins in India at the time of partition and moves to England. The brutality which Balbir witnesses as a child fashions his life as he becomes a murderer. Indeed, blood and corruption run through all he touches.

Design **Julian McGowan**
Lighting **Tina MacHugh**
Music **Stephen Warbeck**
Sound **Bryan Bowen**
Director **Lindsay Posner**

The Astronomer's Garden, which was covered in last year's edition, returned for a season, 28 September–21 October 1989.

Royalty Theatre

PORTUGAL STREET, LONDON WC2
01-831-0660

Cross Country (1988)

31 January–18 February 1989

with **Mark Sexton, Brandi Chapman, Barbara Ramos** and **Leo Case**
Dancers **Debi Thompson, Kelly George, Debbie Scamp** and **Simon Embleton**

A 'fabulous country music spectacular' which aimed to be a musical history of country and western music. It was said to have come straight from Las Vegas. *Cross Country* was not well received by the few critics who gave it space.

Sound **Liam Walsh**   Director **Gui Andisano**

St Martin's

WEST STREET, LONDON WC2
01-836-1443

Manager **Wallace G Stewart**

The Mousetrap (1952)
AGATHA CHRISTIE

Opened 25 November 1952 (Ambassadors Theatre)
Opened 25 March 1974 (St Martin's Theatre)

Mollie Ralston **Sandra Miller (Sophie Doherty)**
Giles Ralston **Christopher Bramwell (Jonathan Drysdale)**
Christopher Wren **John Elnaugh (Richard Croxford)**
Mrs Boyle **Kay Woodman (Kathleen Byron)**
Major Metcalf **Anthony Bailey (Brian Spink)**
Miss Casewell **Susan Tordoff (Penelope Freeman)**
Mr Paravicini **Richard Klee (Charles Stapley)**
Det. Sgt Trotter **William Hart (Liam Kennedy)**

Design **Anthony Holland**
Lighting **Michael Northen**
Director **Kim Grant (Ian Watt-Smith)**

On 25 November 1989, *The Mousetrap* celebrated its 37th birthday. Two days later a new cast, those in brackets in the list, took over. Sophie Doherty became the 36th actress to play the part of Mollie Ralston, and Ian Watt-Smith is the 19th director that the production has had. It all began with Richard Attenborough and Sheila Sim, and all together 238 actors and actresses have now appeared in a production which has been seen by more than eight million people. The play has been presented in 44 different countries and in 24 languages. There is no sign of interest waning.

19. John Elnaugh, Anthony Bailey and Susan Tordoff in the cast of The Mousetrap in 1989 at the St Martin's Theatre when the play celebrated its 37th birthday.

Savoy Theatre

STRAND, LONDON WC2R 0ET
01-836-8888

Over My Dead Body (1989)
MICHAEL SUTTON and ANTHONY FINGLETON

20 February–12 August 1989

Trevor Foyle **Donald Sinden**
Dora Winslow **June Whitfield**
Bartie Cruickshank **Frank Middlemass**
Charters **Ken Wynne**
Simon Vale **Marc Sinden**
Chief Insp. Smith **Paul Ridley**
Leo Sharp **Chris Tranchell**
Det. Sgt Trask **William Sleigh**

Over My Dead Body presents the three surviving founder members of the Murder League, a Pall Mall club for writers of detective fiction. They see that their style of writing is out of fashion and set out to bring down justice upon a murderer. Unfortunately, they sight the wrong man. A comedy thriller which won few friends.

Design **Saul Radomsky**
Lighting **Leonard Tucker**
Sound **Peter Still**
Director **Brian Murray**

Productions of *The Mikado* and *The Pirates of Penzance*, the Gilbert and Sullivan operas, by the reconstituted D'Oyly Carte company occupied the Savoy Theatre from September onwards. The vaudeville show *Sugar Babies* with Mickey Rooney and Ann Miller closed some time before, in January.

Shaftesbury Theatre

SHAFTESBURY AVENUE, LONDON WC2
01-379-5399

Managing Director **Ian B Albery**

Eartha Kitt in Concert (1989)

13 March–8 April 1989

Eartha Kitt with **Steve Agyei, Heavon Grant, Julian Redmond and Stephen Shane**

Follies, an over-praised Sondheim musical, closed in January. Eartha Kitt, one of the redeeming features in the last cast of that show, took the stage at the Shaftesbury after the theatre had

Design **David Bight**
Lighting **Kevin Sleep**
Sound **Julian Beech**
Choreographer **David Toguri**
Musical Director **Roger Webb**
Director **Nica Burns**

undergone refurbishment. 'Enduring, enigmatic', 'an electrifying stage presence' and 'the last great diva' were some of the words and phrases used to describe her magnetic performance. Lydia Conway spoke of her as 'the world's greatest manipulator'.

M. Butterfly (1988)
DAVID HENRY HWANG

Opened 20 April 1989

Kurogo **Darren Chan, David K S Tse and Tom Wu**
Rene Gallimard **Anthony Hopkins (Peter Egan)**
Song Liling **G G Goei**
Marc/Man 2/Consul Sharpless **Ian Redford**
Renee/Woman at Party/Girl in Magazine **Catherine McQueen**
M Toulon/Man 1/Judge **Don Fellows**
Comrade Chin/Suzuki/Shu Fang **Tsai Chin**
Helga **Lynn Farleigh**

Design and Costume **Eiko Ishioka**
Lighting **Andy Phillips**
Music **Giacomo Puccini and Lucia Hwong**
Sound **Julian Beech**
Director **John Dexter**

M. Butterfly had its first performance in Great Britain at the Leicester Haymarket Theatre before moving to the Shaftesbury. The play was inspired by newspaper accounts of a remarkable case of a French diplomat charged with espionage who had a love affair lasting 20 years with a Chinese actor whom he had taken to be a woman. The story is told in flashbacks as Rene Gallimard reflects on his past from his prison cell. Scraps of conversation by guests at a party tell us in the opening minutes of the play that Gallimard's lover was a man and, indeed, G G Goei's first appearance as an opera singer at a reception in Beijing shows him in a guise that is

20. Anthony Hopkins – a mighty performance in M. Butterfly at the Shaftesbury Theatre. Hopkins left the cast in October 1989 and was succeeded by Peter Egan.

penetrable. Yet, as the evening wears on, he sows seeds of doubt in our minds as to his gender, and this is of great credit to G G Goei, who is appearing in his first major role. There is, too, a mighty performance by Anthony Hopkins in what is essentially a 'theatrical' part littered with confidential asides to the stalls. Mr Hopkins revels in the role and is faithful to the play's main theme that we love and are true to an imaginative ideal and that we are reluctant to accept the intrusion of any 'truth' that would tell us that things are not as we want them to be. Puccini's *Madame Butterfly* is cited throughout as the parallel – Pinkerton is the cad whom it is customary to despise and whom most men, in their hearts, envy.

The production is excitingly designed, and it has two central characters who are played with intelligence, strength and conviction; but this is not enough. There is no hint of Frenchness about the play whatsoever, even though the story, with its emphasis on the mistress and the congratulations of the consul are essentially French. Indeed, one wonders for much of the time if one is in the American Embassy, so distorted is the picture. It is not helped by the acting in the supporting roles. Lynn Farleigh as Gallimard's wife and the two principals apart, the cast is dreadful. Scenes such as that in which Gallimard is seduced by a young girl at a party and that in which Song Liling undergoes rehabilitation after the cultural revolution are so bad as to be embarrassing. In defence of the actors, one must say that the writing outside the two central roles is pretty poor stuff.

In spite of these deficiencies, *M. Butterfly* remains a mostly engaging theatrical experience. Peter Egan took over the part of Rene Gallimard in October.

Strand Theatre

ALDWYCH, LONDON WC2
01-836-2660

General Manager **Nigel P Everett**

Can-Can closed in January and was followed by *The Woman in Black*, 15 February–18 March 1989. This transferred to the Playhouse and later to the Fortune Theatre, under which details will be found.

Ivanov (1887)
ANTON CHEKHOV

10 April–29 July 1989

Nikolai Ivanov **Alan Bates**
Borkin **Nicky Henson**
Count Shabyelsky **Frank Thornton**
Anna Petrovna **Felicity Kendal**
Doctor Lvov **Philip Franks**
Lyebedev **Peter Sallis**
Ziusiushka **Sheila Steafel**
Kosyh **Robert Gwilym**

Sasha **Karen Ascoe**
Avdotya **Anthea Holloway**
Babakina **Cherith Mellor**
Gabrila **Judith Porter**
Piotr **Christopher Banks**
Party Guests **Liz Digby-Smith, Richard Harradine, Christopher Hollis, Tom Kelly and Colin Marsh**

Design **Mark Thompson**
Lighting **Davy Cunningham**
Music **Stephen Oliver**
Sound **Paul Farrah**
Director **Elijah Moshinsky**

Much Ado About Nothing (1599)
WILLIAM SHAKESPEARE

10 April–29 July 1989

Leonato **Frank Thornton**
Messenger/Watchman **Colin Marsh**
Beatrice **Felicity Kendal**
Hero **Karen Ascoe**
Don Pedro **Nicky Henson**
Benedick **Alan Bates**
Don John **Robert Gwilym**
Claudio **Philip Franks**
Antonio/Verges **Geoffrey Wright**
Conrade **Tom Kelly**

Borachio **Christopher Hollis**
Margaret **Sheila Steafel**
Ursula **Cherith Mellor**
Boy/Friar Francis/Sexton **Christopher Banks**
Dogberry **Peter Sallis**
George Seacoal **Richard Harradine**
Watchman **Patrick Gordon**
Members of Household **Anthea Holloway, Judith Porter and Liz Digby-Smith**

Gamba Player **Frank Schaefer**

Design **Mark Thompson**
Lighting **Davy Cunningham**
Choreographer **Anthony van Laast**
Music **Stephen Oliver**
Sound **Paul Farrah**
Musical Director **Philip Hawkes**
Director **Elijah Moshinsky**

Ivanov opened on 10 April and was joined in repertory by *Much Ado About Nothing* a month later. Although the Chekhov was received with less than enthusiasm for 'its ugly and ridiculous set' and its 'chilly, wintry' production, the Shakespeare was more warmly received. Sheridan Morley welcomed the 'joyously intelligent staging', and Rhoda Koenig, in *Punch*, felt that the company was 'more comfortable with Shakespeare's demonstration of how intelligent people can create a harmonious relationship than with Chekhov's portrayal of how they find it impossible'. The set came in for much criticism.

Last of the Red Hot Lovers (1969)
NEIL SIMON

1 August–2 September 1989

Barney Cashman **Bruce Montague**
Elaine Navazio **Judy Buxton**
Bobbie Michele **Debbie Arnold**
Jeanette Fisher **Josephine Tewson**

Design **Terry Parsons**
Lighting **Matthew Evered**
Director **Christopher G Sandford**

The Theatre Royal, Windsor, production tended to emphasise the fact that Neil Simon's play has neither lasted nor travelled well. Barney, a fish restaurateur, decides after 23 years of happy marriage to bring some adventure into his life. He proceeds unsuccessfully to try to seduce three women. It is a mid-life crisis comedy.

Exclusive (1989)
JEFFREY ARCHER

Opened 19 September 1989

21. Paul Scofield in Jeffrey Archer's Exclusive *at The Strand Theatre.*

Sally Kershaw **Eileen Atkins**
Peter Webb **Michael Beint**
Sean Bryant **Michael Gyngell**
Nicholas Berkeley **Paul Scofield**
Charlie Matthews **Jeffry Wickham**
Ian Miller **Peter Bourke**
Anne Crowe **Pamela Buchner**
Jack Taylor **Peter Halliday**
Andrew Pierson **Ronnie Letham**
Simon Rodway **Ewart James Walters**
Dr Wilkie **James Taylor**
Stone Hand/Terry Bailey **David Bauckham**
Stone Hand/Secretary **Juliet**

Douglas
Cartoonist/Photographer in Kent **Alan Towner**
Vincent Dexter **Steven Pacey**
Copy Girl/Maureen **Ruth Hudson**
Harry Rivers **Alec McCowen**
Arnold Carter **Alan Leith**
Sub 1 **Michael Shallard**
Sub 2 **Simon Fisher-Becker**

Design **Timothy O'Brien**
Costume **Lindy Hemming**
Lighting **Robert Bryan**
Sound **Paul Arditti**
Director **Michael Rudman**

Jeffrey Archer's latest play, set in the offices of a national newspaper and having political overtones, opened at the Strand with a star-filled cast. The presence of Paul Scofield, Eileen Atkins, Alec McCowen and the rest failed to save the play from the scorn of the critics, but the public, no doubt, will ensure it has a fruitful run.

Vaudeville Theatre

STRAND, LONDON WC2R 0NH
01-836-9988

Henceforward... (1987)
ALAN AYCKBOURN

14 November 1988–16 September 1989

Jerome **Martin Jarvis**
Lupus **Robin Herford**
Zoe **Sara Crowe**
Rita **Emma Gibbins**
Geain, aged 9 **Victoria Horsfield**
Corinna **Joanna Van Gyseghem**
Mervyn **Peter Forbes**
Geain, aged 13 **Susanna Newman**

Design **Roger Clossop**
Lighting **Mick Hughes**

Synclavier Programmer **Yasmin Hashmi, with Paul Todd**

Music **Paul Todd**
Director **Alan Ayckbourn**

Ayckbourn's immensely funny and equally disturbing play set in a Britain of the not-too-distant future, which was originally produced at Scarborough in 1987, ran until September. Martin Jarvis, Joanna Van Gyseghem, Sara Crowe and Peter Forbes took over the leading parts. Those were first played at the Vaudeville by Ian McKellen, Jane Asher, Serena Evans and Michael Simkins.

Re: Joyce! (1988)
JAMES ROOSE-EVANS and MAUREEN LIPMAN

Opened 19 September 1989

Joyce Grenfell **Maureen Lipman**
Accompanist **Denis King**

Design **Peter Rice**
Costume **Ben Frow**
Lighting **Adam Grater**
Choreographer **Geraldine Stephenson**
Music **Joyce Grenfell and Richard Addinsell**
Director **Alan Strachan**

Originally produced at the Redgrave Theatre, Farnham, and, late in 1988, at the Fortune Theatre, *Re: Joyce!*, an affectionate glance at an artist who gave much pleasure, was revived at the Vaudeville Theatre in autumn 1989.

Victoria Palace

VICTORIA STREET, LONDON SW1
01-834-1317

Brigadoon, which many prophesied would not survive, ran in good health until 9 September 1989. The production, originally seen in Plymouth, had opened on 25 October 1988, and full details can be found in last year's edition.

Buddy, a musical centred on rock star Buddy Holly, opened on 19 October 1989. The cast list and comments on it will be found in next year's edition.

Westminster Theatre

PALACE STREET, LONDON SW1
01-834-0283

An Ideal Husband (1895)
OSCAR WILDE

Opened 24 April 1989

Lady Basildon **Rachel Preece**
Mrs Marchmont **Shauna Baird**
Earl of Caversham **Richard Murdoch**
Lady Chiltern **Liz Bagley**
Mabel Chiltern **Emma Watson**
Lady Markby **Moira Redmond**
Mrs Chevely **Delia Lindsay**
Vicomte de Nanjac **Sean Aita**
Sir Robert Chiltern **Jeremy Child**
Lord Goring **Jeremy Sinden**
Mason **Deborah Blake**
Phipps **Roy Boutcher**

Design **Juliet Shillingford**
Lighting **Vincent Herbert**
Director **Patrick Sandford**

Three members of the cast remain from the Redgrave Theatre, Farnham, production, and they have changed roles. After an extensive national tour, *An Ideal Husband* came to rest at the Westminster Theatre with the delightful Liz Bagley moving from Mabel to Lady Chiltern, and Jeremy Sinden forsaking the role of Sir Robert to become Lord Goring.

Wilde's melodrama tells of a scheming woman, Mrs Chevely, who threatens to destroy an idealistic politician, Sir Robert Chiltern, by revealing the 'insider dealings' of his youth unless he helps her with political support for her monetary ambitions. The situation is saved by the intervention of Lord Goring, a witty fop in the Wilde fashion, played by Jeremy Sinden. Liz Bagley, 'sweetly naïve, shamed by her husband's sin but eventually ready to help him get away with it', is the wife who must come to terms with the fact that 'a man's life is more important than a woman's'. Richard Murdoch was plausible as Lord Goring's father. D A N Jones in the *Sunday Telegraph* found it 'an elegant and sinister show, as relevant to modern politics as it is to Wilde's downfall'. Not all agreed, but the majority found it an enjoyable production.

Whitehall Theatre

WHITEHALL, LONDON SW1
01-930-7765

Run For Your Wife (1982)
RAY COONEY

Opened 6 March 1989

Mary Smith **Carol Hawkins (Linda Hayden)**
Barbara Smith **Heather Alexander (Anita Graham)**
John Smith **Jeffrey Holland (Geoffrey Davies)**
Det. Sgt Troughton **Ken Farrington (David Griffin)**
Stanley Gardner **Paul Shane (Roy Hudd/Henry McGee)**
Reporter **Michael Boothe (Stirling Rodger)**

When the Criterion Theatre in Piccadilly Circus closed for refurbishment as part of the redevelopment plan for the area, *Run For Your Wife* moved to the Whitehall Theatre. It succeeded Francis Durbridge's *A Touch of Danger*.

Paul Elliott and Ian B Albery's production of *Run For Your Wife* for the Theatre of Comedy has had a remarkable career and is rapidly passing into theatre history. It was first produced at the Yvonne Arnaud Theatre, Guildford, on 26 October 1982. On 18 March of the following year, it opened at the Shaftesbury Theatre and it transferred to the Criterion Theatre nine months later. The cast is changed every three months in order to keep the farce fresh, and the change on 4

22. *Run For Your Wife* moved from the Criterion Theatre to the Whitehall Theatre in 1989. It looks as if it will continue for several years to come. The play is recast every three months. The squad that took over in October 1989: back *David Griffin and Stirling Rodger;* middle *Alfred Marks, Anita Graham, Geoffrey Davies, Linda Hayden and Roy Hudd;* on floor *Brian Godfrey*.

Det. Sgt Porterhouse **Windsor Davies (Alfred Marks)**
Bobby Franklin **Brian Godfrey**

Design **Douglas Heap**
Lighting **James Baird**
Director **Ray Cooney**

September 1989 brought the 26th consecutive company into action. The company which took over then is shown in brackets in the cast list.

Linda Hayden was returning to the company for her seventh season, Anita Graham for her fifth, Alfred Marks for his third and Roy Hudd for his second. Roy Hudd left the cast temporarily for an eye operation and was replaced by Henry McGee, who had also appeared at the Criterion.

By September 1989, *Run For Your Wife* had notched up 2,700 performances, had been translated into 18 languages and had played in 35 countries outside Great Britain. A front page of the *Evening Standard* is eaten at every performance, and 208 actors have so far appeared in the play. Geoffrey Davies and David Griffin were the latest to make their first appearances in the seven-year run. It has so far netted more than £7,200,000, and there seems to be no sign of interest diminishing. Indeed, there is even speculation about a permanent home for the farce.

It has established a formidable record.

Wyndham's Theatre

CHARING CROSS ROAD, LONDON WC2
01-867-1116

The Secret of Sherlock Holmes (1988)
JEREMY PAUL

22 September 1988–16 September 1989

Sherlock Holmes **Jeremy Brett**
Doctor Watson **Edward Hardwicke**

Design **Poppy Mitchell**
Costume **Esther Dean**
Lighting **Mark Pritchard**
Music **Nigel Hess**
Musical Director **David Firman**
Sound **John Leonard**
Director **Patrick Garland**

Having run for a year in Charing Cross Road, *The Secret of Sherlock Holmes* closed in September 1989 and began a national tour. Jeremy Paul's play sees the famous sleuth and his faithful companion setting up house in Baker Street. The secret that is revealed is that Holmes's arch-enemy is the darker, repressed side of his own personality. A hundred years since his adventures were documented, the mere name of Sherlock Holmes draws devotees in their thousands.

Ronald Harwood's new play, *Another Time*, with Albert Finney, Janet Suzman, Sara Kestleman, David de Keyser and Christien Anholt, and directed by Elijah Moshinsky, opened on 25 September 1989. It will be fully covered in the next edition.

The Young Vic

66 THE CUT, LONDON SE1 8LZ
01-928-6363

Artistic Director **David Thacker**

Two-Way Mirror (1982)
ARTHUR MILLER

19 January–4 March 1989

23. Helen Mirren and Bob Peck in pensive mood in David Thacker's production of Some Kind of Love Story at The Young Vic.

Some Kind of Love Story

Angela **Helen Mirren**
Tom O'Toole **Bob Peck**

Elegy for a Lady

Man **Bob Peck**
Proprietress **Helen Mirren**

Design **Bob Crowley**
Lighting **Paul Denby**

Sound **Dick Crabbe**
Director **David Thacker**

The year began with a characteristic scoop by The Young Vic in presenting Arthur Miller, one of the world's greatest – arguably the greatest – living playwrights before an invited audience who bombarded him with questions. The present writer asked him whether he found difficulties in accepting British actors acting in his plays. Miller's reply was both interesting and encouraging; he felt that the British open expression of large emotions and the more lyrical, heroic approach suited his work better than the 'crocheting and knitting of a naturalistic portrayal' prevalent in the United States.

Inevitably, he was asked whether or not the first of the two one-act plays which comprise *Two-Way Mirror* was autobiographical. He thought not, but critics have continued to worry him on the subject.

In *Some Kind of Love Story*, Helen Mirren played a schizophrenic prostitute who was being quizzed by a New York detective; in *Elegy for a Lady*, she played a woman in an expensive shop who helped a man to choose a gift for his dying

24. In the second of Arthur Miller's two one-act plays, Helen Mirren is the assistant in an expensive store trying to aid Bob Peck who is in search of a present for his dying lover. Elegy for a Lady, *polished production at The Young Vic.*

lover. The suggested autobiographical link in the first play is that the woman has been raped by her father and has her 'heart hanging by a thread'. A mournful saxophone heralded the first play; a deep cello welcomed the second. The mirror, in Bob Crowley's imaginative set, changed sides from the first play to the second, and the scene became both more expensive and more expansive. This was a reflection of the two plays. In the first play, information is withheld; in the second, confidences are offered. The bond between them is the barrier that prevents ultimate communication.

The quality of the acting was of the highest level. As Angela, Helen Mirren was agitated, nervous, fluctuating in mood, now giving, now withdrawing from this man whose constant enquiries have brought a unity between them. Peck exuded an air of eager anticipation qualified by a sense of life lived, a time outside the play.

In *Elegy for a Lady*, Peck's character is a man clarified by grief, the concern for a dying woman with whom his meetings have been purely for pleasure. His affair with her has happened because he needs the 'dangerous mountains' not met in the valley of marriage. He is a man with a desperate ambition to overcome the facts that each morning when he looks in the mirror he sees himself shaving his father and that each evening he is sleepy by 9.30p.m.

These are subtle and challenging plays in that they confront us with the solitariness of ourselves and with the way in which that loneliness becomes deeper as we grow older and despair of ever being able to escape from the prison of ourselves.

Waiting for Godot (1953)
SAMUEL BECKETT

Studio 21 February–25 March 1989

Estragon **Reg Stewart**
Vladimir **Peter Theedom**
Pozzo **Howard Crossley**
Lucky **James Walker**
The Boy **Simon Bright**

Design **Anny Evanson**
Lighting **Jim Simmons**
Director **David Thacker**

Following a tour which has taken the play throughout Great Britain and to the Low Countries, *Waiting for Godot* ended its run with a month in the Young Vic studio. There has suddenly been an abundance of Godots, and David Thacker's production compared favourably with the National Theatre's offering. He brought back the menace. Peter Theedom's Vladimir was an altogether more disturbed and more disturbing portrayal than Alec McCowen's. This is not to say that the humour of the piece was lost; indeed a weakness was that Howard Crossley's Pozzo was all too jolly – a north country travelling salesman who threatened no one. Yet the production overall showed the bleakness and despair which never degenerated into self-pity. It is not a play without hope, but it is a play of dread which James Walker's white-haired Lucky, gasping for breath, epitomised chillingly. Reg Stewart's Estragon, seeking perpetually to recall, was at one with the lethargy and decline.

Special mention must be made of Simon Bright's brief appearance as the boy who brings news only of false hope. David Thacker seems to bring more out of child actors than any other director operating at present.

Solomon and the Big Cat, by David Holman, which is covered in last year's edition, played for one week, 10–18 March 1989, in the main house. After that it began a national tour.

Measure for Measure (1604)
WILLIAM SHAKESPEARE

13–22 April 1989

The outstanding quality of a David Thacker production is that he can take a complex, 'difficult' or dusty play and send you from the theatre at the end of an evening full of understanding. His *Measure for Measure*, a reworking of his 1987 production, was no exception. It blazed with clarity.

The play moved easily into modern dress, for Thacker's production emphasised a society's obsession for sex and money that was not too different from our own. The Duke

25. Rob Edwards as the Duke and Sarah-Jane Fenton as Isabella in Measure for Measure at The Young Vic, a production of utmost clarity.

26. A chillingly fine performance by Stephen Jenn as Angelo in Measure for Measure at The Young Vic. He towers over Jane Maud as Mariana and Sarah-Jane Fenton as Isabella. Rob Edwards as the Duke gazes down from behind his chair of authority on the women.

Duke **Rob Edwards**
Escalus **Randal Herley**
Angelo **Stephen Jenn**
Lucio **Dominic Letts**
Gentleman/Friar/Froth/Abhorson **Gary Lucas**
Mistress Overdone/PA **Janet Crawford**
Pompey **Reg Stewart**
Claudio **Clive Owen**
Provost **James Walker**
Isabella **Sarah-Jane Fenton**
Francisca/Mariana **Jane Maud**
Elbow/Barnadine **Howard Crossley**
Juliet **Catriona Elliott**

Design **Fran Thompson**
Lighting **Jim Simmons**
Director **David Thacker**

abnegates his responsibility and leaves his province in the power of Angelo, a chilly puritan who revives the law that insists on the death penalty for fornication. It is a measure of Stephen Jenn's brilliant portrayal of Angelo that he conveyed the duplicity of the character, the burning lust that lies beneath the icy exterior. As he misuses the power entrusted in him, the desk from which he administers his justice turns from the straight, symbolising the distortion that is now rampant in the law.

The confrontation between Angelo and Isabella is the crux of the play as he, unable to repress his own desires, bargains Claudio's life for her virginity. It is a scene of oppressive evil, not only for the intended seduction but because of the truths that Angelo learns about himself.

Sarah-Jane Fenton's Isabella was sufficiently pure and noble, but, as a young actress of much talent, she lacked something of the strength that the part demanded. Perhaps Isabella is one of those Shakespearean roles which you are really too old to play by the time you have gained the wisdom and maturity needed.

There was some splendid, meaningful comic interchange between Janet Crawford's Mistress Overdone and Reg Stewart's Pompey which grasped the sexual energy and corruption of the play. Only Rob Edwards's Duke failed to find the right level of understanding in this highly intelligent and vital production.

Measure for Measure later toured Britain and the Continent.

Coriolanus (1608)
WILLIAM SHAKESPEARE

3–27 May 1989

Coriolanus **Corin Redgrave**
Titus Lartius **Simon Green**
Cominus **Terence Bayler**
Menenius Agrippa **John Franklyn-Robbins**
Sicinius Velutus **Michael O'Hagan**
Junius Brutus **Peter Sproule**
Young Martius **Elliott Bromley/Harvey Redgrave**
Aufidius **Colin McFarlane**
Citizens/Servants **Richard Albrecht, Harry Miller, Doyle**

Three generations of Redgraves took part in The Young Vic production of *Coriolanus*, but for once this exciting theatre failed to live up to its usual high standards. The initial problem was the set. The stage was a cross between a bandstand and a cage. It was constantly swept clear of leaves by four mournful, faceless characters who might have been better employed in bolstering understrength armies. There must be something wrong with a set which prevents parts of the audience from seeing what is happening at various times in the play.

The second problem raised by this production was that the text had been so pared down to the bone as to leave us with little meat. There were falls of poppies when men were

Richmond and Andrew Secombe
Volumnia **Rachel Kempson**
Virgilia **Geraldine Griffiths**
Valeria **Alphonsia Emmanuel**
Slaves **Anita Cahill, Davina McGee, Gary Moynihan and Jess Walters**

Design **Hayden Griffin, Claudia Mayer and David Neat**

Lighting **Paul Denby**
Music **Mark Vibrans**

Director **Jane Howell**

slaughtered, reminiscent of *Oh What a Lovely War!*, and there were moments of wonderful arrogance from Corin Redgrave and the occasional flash of nobility and cynicism. There was discord in the music which echoed the discord in a world for whom Coriolanus's spirit was too noble, but there was too little trust in the nobility of the play itself.

From the Mississippi Delta (1984)
ENDESHA IDA MAE HOLLAND

Studio 28 September–28 October 1989

Woman One **Josette Bushell-Mingo**
Woman Two **Joy Richardson**
Woman Three **Angela Bruce**

Design **Iona McLeish**
Lighting **Nick Beadle**
Music **Helen Glavin**
Director **Annie Castledine and Sue MacLennan**

'Set your aims up high yonder with the birds' is the clarion call towards the end of this powerful, amusing and moving autobiographical play which, to their great credit, The Young Vic at last brought before an English audience. It tells the story of a black girl from the Mississippi Delta whose mother was a midwife and who also ran a boarding house. The girl is raped by a white man on her eleventh birthday, his wife acting as procurer. She works briefly as a prostitute and becomes a sexy dancer at a fair – again briefly. After her mother is burned to death in the white South's reaction to the Civil Rights' movement she goes north to the University of Minnesota where she gains a doctorate. It is an amazing story and a dynamic piece of theatre.

Three actresses of immense talent play all the characters. Aint Baby, the mother, is played primarily by Angela Bruce, but, at times, by one of the other two instead.

A hollow in centre stage, a ledge, a corrugated, rusty wall and two ladders were all the scenery and properties that were needed in this most imaginative of productions. It was irrepressibly happy, fluent and exciting in movement and full of a sense of wonder as the actresses made quick transitions from one character to another. The ladders were used to portray the birth of a child in a scene which was gripping and tense. Then they served as the steps which the eleven-year old climbed to her birthday deflowering. The hollow was the scene of the dance ring in the fair in which Miss Candy was followed by the Delta Queen in a wonderfully funny sequence, and later was the setting for Miss Rosebud's defence of her water meter and for the funeral of Aint Baby. Laughter was not far away, even at this solemn moment, for as the preacher implored the Lord to accept one who had taken up the Cross one of the mourners tottered away drunk.

The overwhelming strength of the play is that the heroine, or heroines, no matter what they endure, are 'dismayed but not hopeless'. It is a play that reaches outside the confines of the titanic struggle of a black girl in the southern part of the United States between the 1940s and the 1980s to emphasise the unquenchable human spirit that is mankind's finest quality.

As a play, *From the Mississippi Delta* is some ten minutes too long. There is no need to go beyond the triumph of the graduation scene to the roll of honour for black women writers and activists; the point has already been made. However, it is a fine and powerful piece of work, hugely entertaining. In the hands of Angela Bruce, Josette Bushell-Mingo and Joy Richardson and under the direction of Annie Castledine and Sue MacLennan, it was a thrilling theatrical experience.

27. Josette Bushell, Joy Richardson and Angela Bruce in the British première of From the Mississippi Delta *by Endesha Ida Mae Holland, directed at The Young Vic by Annie Castledine and Sue MacLennan. Thrilling and challenging theatre.*

The Glass Menagerie (1944)
TENNESSEE WILLIAMS

Touring Production

Tom Wingfield **Richard Garnett**
Amanda Wingfield **Susannah York**
Laura Wingfield **Suzan Sylvester**
The Gentleman Caller **Daniel Flynn**

Design **Shelagh Keegan**
Lighting **Jim Simmons**
Music **Paul Bowles**
Sound **Dick Crabbe**
Director **David Thacker**

A highly acclaimed revival of Williams's play about personal deprivation and the conflict between the sensitive being and the harsh world of materialism. Susannah York, as the mother hopeful of arranging a romance that will free her lame daughter from her shyness and her world of glass animals, gave 'a beautiful study of a woman cocooned in a romantic dream'. Suzan Sylvester brought to Laura 'the right introverted prettiness and a wonderful look of doomed resignation'.

Richard Garnett and Daniel Flynn were equally impressive in a production which was typical of David Thacker in its clarity and sensitivity.

The Young Vic's future plans include a revival of David Holman's splendid *A Christmas Carol*, performances of *Can't Pay? Won't Pay!* at the end of its tour, and New Year productions of *The Cherry Orchard* and *The Price* by Arthur Miller.

The theatre remains among the most exciting in the country, jealous of its high standards and never compromising its artistic integrity. It boasts a press and publicity director, Anne Mayer, whose administration and public relations flair keep the theatre ever alive and harmonious, and an artistic director who constantly seeks truth and quality in all facets of his art.

SECTION TWO
The National Theatre

1. The pile of clothes in the opening scene in Ghetto. The production of the year, and one of the outstanding productions of a lifetime.

The Royal National Theatre of Great Britain

SOUTH BANK, LONDON SE1 9PX
01-928-2252

Artistic Director **Richard Eyre**
Executive Director **David Aukin**

The Shaughraun, Bartholomew Fair, Roots, The Secret Rapture, The Magic Olympical Games, The Father and *Single Spies* were the 1988 National Theatre productions which continued in the repertory into the New Year. *The Shaughraun* and *The Secret Rapture* were to be recast and reintroduced into the repertory, while *Single Spies*, like *Mrs Klein*, transferred to the West End.

Making History (1988)
BRIAN FRIEL

Cottesloe Theatre 5 December 1988–18 January 1989

Hugh O'Neill **Stephen Rea**
Harry Hovenden **Niall O'Brien**
Archbishop Lombard **Niall Toibin**
Hugh O'Donnell **Peter Gowen**
Mabel Bagenal **Clare Holman**
Mary Bagenal **Emma Dewhurst**

Design **Julian McGowan**
Costume **Martin Chitty**
Music **Arty McGlynn/Nollaig O'Casey**
Lighting **Christopher Toulmin**
Director **Simon Curtis**

Originally presented at the Guildhall, Derry, in September 1988, Brian Friel's new play is set in County Tyrone at the end of the 16th century and at the beginning of the 17th. It concerns Hugh O'Neill, the Earl of Tyrone, who fled to Europe in 1607, six years after he had been defeated by the English army at the Battle of Kinsale. The play is an exploration of Irish identity and of the way in which history comes to be written to serve the ambitions of its authors, rather than the truth. The play enjoyed a brief run. Many found that the intellectual discourse weighed rather heavily and that the dramatic action was ponderous.

Fuente Ovejuna (1612)
LOPE DE VEGA in a version by Adrian Mitchell

Cottesloe Theatre 10 January–28 August 1989

The National Theatre chose to open their 1989 season with a

2. Declan Donnellan's production of Fuente Ovejuna. James Laurenson as Commander Fernando Gomez de Guzman and Wilbert Johnson as Frondoso. An exciting production with ensemble playing of the highest order.

Commander Fernando Gomez de Guzman **James Laurenson**
Captain Flores **David Beames**
Sergeant Ortuno **Jim Barclay**
The Grand Master of Caltrava, Rodrigo **Mark Lockyer**
Queen Isabella of Castille **Ellen Thomas**
King Ferdinand of Aragon **Jon Rumney**
Don Manrique **Ivan Kaye**
Cimbranos **Nicholas Blane**
Soldiers **Trevor Sellers, Oliver Beamish and Jo Stone-Fewings**
Laurencia **Rachel Joyce**
Pascuala **Joy Richardson**
Frondoso **Wilbert Johnson**
Barrildo **Jonathan Cullen**
Mengo **Clive Rowe**
Juan Rojo **Tam Dean Burn**
Esteban **George Harris**
Alonso **Gilbert Wynne**
Jacinta **Sandy McDade**
A boy **Timothy Matthews**
Ines **Sandra Butterworth**
Olalla **Laura Shavin**
Leonelo **Glyn Pritchard**
Farmers **David Schneider, Trevor Sellers and Merlin Shepherd**
Aldermen **Trevor Sellers and John Fitzgerald-Jay**

Design **Nick Ormerod**
Lighting **Mick Hughes**
Music **Paddy Cunneen**
Director **Declan Donnellan**

classical Spanish play of the 17th century, directed by the founder of Cheek By Jowl and designed by his collaborator in that wonderful touring company. The result was that a standard was set by which all else during the year had to be measured. Fuente Ovejuna is a small village in southern Spain. At the time of the action, 1476, it is under the rule of a military commander, Fernando, a local tyrant who cannot understand why those whom he abuses do not love him. Fernando persuades the new, young Grand Master of the military order of Calatrava to side with the King of Portugal against Ferdinand of Aragon. Initially he is victorious; ultimately he learns to ally himself to Ferdinand. Against this political background is set the local and major action.

Fernando returns from his initial victory to receive the acclaim and the gifts of the peasants and farmers of Fuente Ovejuna, where his fortress is situated. We learn that he believes it is his right to take any of the women of the village for whom he has a fancy. His fancy turns towards Laurencia, the daughter of the mayor, but she both resists and evades him. He revenges himself by interrupting her wedding, imprisoning her groom, having her father beaten and abducting her. The raped heroine returns to taunt the men of the village into action. The villagers rise as one, and they overthrow and kill the commander.

Ferdinand and Isabella send an inquisitor to discover the identity of the murderer. He uses all the prescribed tortures, but the only reply that he can elicit from anyone – boys, men or women – is 'Fuente Ovejuna did it.'

The inquisitor is unable to place any written evidence before the King and Queen. The villagers are loyal to Ferdinand and Isabella. They return to a life of happier normality, tending their sheep and working in the fields. The only monuments to the uprising are Lope de Vega's play and the fact that the name of the village has become part of a Spanish proverb to explain a crime for which no culprit can be found.

In Nick Ormerod's design, seats are arranged in traverse style across the length of the auditorium so that actors must run the gauntlet of the audience for much of the time. The drama begins with a trapdoor at the centre of the acting oblong opening and gushing forth the people of Fuente Ovejuna, who immediately go about their daily work. Foot-stamping and staccato clapping announce the ceremonial entry of the Knights of Calatrava. The arrogant Fernando, a complex mixture of vicious arrogance and uncertainty played with great understanding and physical presence by James Laurenson, awaits audience with the new Grand Master, whose mentor he has been. As the action proceeds, Ferdinand and Isabella remain seated on their thrones at one end of the oblong; the people of Fuente Ovejuna are, for the most part, assembled at the other. There is not a sound, a gesture, a prop or a movement which does not, in some way, advance the dramatic action and the emotional intensity of the play.

When Laurencia, in a beautifully judged strong performance by Rachel Joyce devoid of all self-pity, first escapes Fernando, she is swallowed by the crowd of villagers. Here there is ensemble playing of the very highest quality; we see it again in the torture scene, where the inquisitor stands in the middle of the acting space simply naming and questioning as the people stand in file at their end of the oblong. The screams that we hear come from those ranks of people. They are piercing and agonising, all the more so because they come from individuals within ranks which are never broken.

From such strong ensemble playing, it is wrong, perhaps, to single out any individual, for all deserve our warmest thanks. However, George Harris as mayor, the father of Laurencia, is a diplomatic and tender figure whose strength is drawn from his integrity; and Clive Rowe as the cowardly Mengo who ultimately draws courage from the townsfolk is a deeply sensitive creation of both humour and durability.

It was a production played without gimmick and in the costume of the period. It was totally comprehensible and unsentimental – the people were victorious in their uprising against tyranny, but they still had to bow the knee to the King and Queen in whose hands lay their fate. It was directed by a man whose theatrical vision was shot by clarity and excitement. Declan Donnellan's first venture at the National Theatre was a total triumph. The memory of the revitalisation of this classical Spanish play will warm those who were lucky enough to see it for many years to come.

Speed-the-Plow (1988)
DAVID MAMET

Lyttleton Theatre 25 January–23 August 1989

Bobby Gould **Colin Stinton**
Charlie Fox **Alfred Molina**
Karen **Rebecca Pidgeon**

Design **Michael Merritt**
Lighting **Kevin Rigdon**
Director **Gregory Mosher**

Bobby Gould is the head of production at a Hollywood studio. His old friend, Charlie Fox, approaches him with a package for a film. It is a prison drama with a popular and established star, and is a safe commercial package. Attention is distracted by Gould's temporary secretary. As a way of persuading her into bed Gould invites her to his home to read a pretentious apocalyptic novel on which she is to pronounce judgement as to whether he should film it or not – although he is already rightly convinced that it would be a financial disaster. She persuades him otherwise, not least because of her sexual charms. Back in the office, she reveals enough of herself to show that she, too, is young and upwardly mobile and therefore a threat. She is ousted, and Charlie and his prison drama win the day.

It is a very amusing play, full of scathingly witty dialogue. Many critics have denied that it is a satire on Hollywood, presumably because none of the three characters deserves our sympathy and pleasant people are not victorious in the end. Yet the play clearly is an anti-Hollywood satire, and more. It shows those in power in the movie industry, and elsewhere, as threadbare and insecure people, and it shows, moreover, their use and abuse of language. Bobby and Charlie are convinced that they are in 'the people business', but, realistically, they see their success as somebody else's failure and gloat about the fact. The chilling line of sobriety that Charlie utters among the bantering, the sexual muscle flexing and the business jargon is, 'It's only words, unless they're true.'

Under Gregory Mosher's direction – and it is his twelfth collaboration with David Mamet – the play moves at a brisk, invigorating pace, and the text is well served by three fine actors. Alfred Molina is a gloriously large, eager and devious Charlie. Colin Stinton follows his assured performance in *The Father* with a Bobby which is flashy and confident on the outside, but vulnerable not too far below the surface. As Karen, the part played by Madonna in the New York production,

3. Colin Stinton as Bobby Gould, head of production in Speed-the-Plow, *a sharp stab at Hollywood and at the use and abuse of language.*

Rebecca Pidgeon exudes sexual surety and intellectual transparency in the right proportions.

It is a bustling play about superficial people, but it is far from being a superficial play.

Hedda Gabler (1890)

HENRIK IBSEN in a version by Christopher Hampton

Olivier Theatre 2 February–7 October 1989

Aunt Julia **Bridget Turner**
Berta **Janet Whiteside**
George Tesman **Paul Shelley**
Hedda Tesman **Juliet Stevenson**
Mrs Elvsted **Suzanne Burden**
Judge Brack **Norman Rodway**
Eilert Lovborg **Paul Jesson**

Howard Davies enjoyed a year of spectacular success in 1988. He began 1989 with another triumphant production, yet one welcomes his *Hedda Gabler* with reservations. Those reservations have nothing to do with acting, understanding, clarity or tone; but with set and size. From the start, Bob Crowley's splendid sweeping staircase, giant portrait and massive drawing-room make one feel that the play has been scheduled for the wrong theatre. We are denied the

4. Juliet Stevenson as Hedda Gabler, a sensitive blend of power and subtlety.

Design **Bob Crowley**
Lighting **Mark Henderson**
Music **Dominic Muldowney**
Director **Howard Davies**

claustrophobia that Ibsen's chilling study of a woman torn by social convention and artistic envy demands. She has neither occupation nor interest. She is without the wealth to entertain as the vast house, her social upbringing and her own inclination would demand. She is a woman trapped, able only to assert a spiritual power, and when that fails her she is torn by an envy which brings about her own destruction.

In the title role, Juliet Stevenson gives a performance which is a sensitive blend of power and subtlety. You feel her abhorrence of sexual relationships through her every shudder, and the frigidity and cruelty of her contempt for others is shown in her opening scene with Aunt Julia, played with a delightful sense of comic bewilderment by Bridget Turner.

From the outset, one is convinced by Juliet Stevenson's Hedda. Here is no woman with whom to meddle. Only Judge Brack can match her, for only he can see into her. They are almost two of a kind. He is a man of power, but also a man of lonely intelligence. One cannot believe that there has been a better Judge Brack than Norman Rodway.

Paul Shelley is, perhaps, a little too insubstantial, but Paul Jesson's Lovborg is an intelligent, waspish study.

Howard Davies's direction, as ever, takes us to the very heart of the play, but, eventually, we are crushed by the gigantic setting.

Juno and the Paycock (1924)
SEAN O'CASEY

Lyttleton Theatre 22 February–10 June 1989

Mary Boyle **Rosalind Bennett**
Juno Boyle **Linda Bassett**
Johnny Boyle **Linus Roache**
Jerry Devine **Fabian Cartwright**
Captain Jack Boyle **Tony Haygarth**
Joxer Daly **Tom Hickey**
Sewing Machine Man **Harry Webster**
Coal Block Vendor **Paul Conway**
Charles Bentham **Richard Bonneville**
Mrs Maisie Madigan **Aine Ni Mhuiri**
Mrs Tancred **Pauline Delaney**
Neighbours **Deidre Halligan, Melee Hutton and Tricia Kelly**
Needle Nugent **Derry Power**
An Irregular Mobiliser **Paul McCleary**
Removal Men **Neil Clark and Peter Dineen**
Irregular Soldiers **Paul Conway and Aidan Gillen**

Design **Deidre Clancy**

If a customer pays £14 for a seat, he at least has the right to expect to be able to see all the play. He would be disappointed with *Juno and the Paycock* at the Lyttleton where, from the fourth and fifth row of the stalls, part of the stage was invisible. Sadly, not only was the design insensitive to the needs of the paying customer, it was also insensitive to the needs of the play. Unfortunately, the design was not the only problem in this production of O'Casey's masterly play. It is a mixture of the comic and the tragic, which involves the abduction and execution of the informer Johnny, the pregnancy of his sister Mary, the posturings of Captain Jack (Juno) and an inheritance which turns out to be a false dream.

The might of the play is in its relationships and the reactions of the characters to personal and political issues. Little of this was apparent in a laboured production in which only the performances of Tony Haygarth and Rosalind Bennett came close to an understanding of the nature of the play itself.

This was advertised as being the first in a series of productions which would cover O'Casey's famous trilogy, but nothing more has been heard of the plan since the demise of this unhappy offering of *Juno and the Paycock*.

Lighting **Mark Seaman**
Director **Peter Gill**

Bed (1989)
JIM CARTWRIGHT

Cottesloe Theatre 8 March–2 May 1989

Bosom Lady **Ruth Kettlewell**
Captain **John Boswall**
Charles **Charles Simon**
Spinster **Vivienne Burgess**
Marjorie **Margery Withers**
The Couple **Joan White and Donald Bisset**
Sermon Head **Graham Crowden**

Design **Peter J Davison**
Lighting **Christopher Toulmin**

Bed is an interesting play about old age, sleep and dreaming. Seven elderly people are tucked up in a massive bed. We learn a little about each of them – a couple, an old sea captain, a religious spinster, a neglected wife and an ex-showgirl. The wild head of an insomniac disturbs all the others as he rages piercingly from a book-shelf – only his head is ever visible.

Graham Crowden was splendidly demonic as the head, and indeed all the acting was fine, but eventually one felt it had been something of a slight evening. After the success of Jim Cartwright's last play, *Road*, perhaps that was inevitable.

Music **John Winfield**   Director **Julia Bardsley**

Hamlet (1602)
WILLIAM SHAKESPEARE

Olivier Theatre 16 March–13 December 1989

Barnardo **Douglas McFerran**
Francisco **Toby E Byrne**
Horatio **David Bamber (Paul Jesson)**
Marcellus **Ian Flintoff**
Ghost of Hamlet's Father **David Burke**
Claudius **John Castle**
Voltimand **Alan Brown**
Cornelius **Alan White**
Laertes **Peter Lindford (Jeremy Northam)**
Polonius **Michael Bryant**
Hamlet **Daniel Day-Lewis (Ian Charleson)**
Gertrude **Judi Dench (Sylvia Syms)**
Ophelia **Stella Gonet**
Reynaldo **Stephen Rashbrook**
Rosencrantz **Crispin Redman**
Guildenstern **Guy Henry**
Player King **Oliver Ford Davies**

In the vaults of the castle at Elsinor in Denmark, there is a massive statue, Holge Danske, the Viking who will wake from his slumbers when Denmark is threatened. The stage for Richard Eyre's *Hamlet* was dominated by a similar statue, only this was of the dead Hamlet senior, the product of the director's fertile imagination and not inspired by a visit to Elsinor. It fitted well with John Gunter's set, which divided the stage with a wall which varied in length and purpose as the occasion demanded. There was a moment when it rolled back to reveal Fortinbras's weary, marching army in shades of blue, reminiscent of a painting by Albrecht Altdorfer of the Battle of Issus. It was a moment of magical theatre, but it is significant that memories of the production are of visual images rather than of any of its verbal or interpretative qualities.

Inevitably, if a production of *Hamlet* fails, as this did, the weakness is at the centre. It is a play of inaction until the final massacre, for the movement is in the mind, a point which Daniel Day-Lewis quite failed to recognise. The result was that he presented us with soliloquies which he failed to distinguish with the slightest change of emphasis or nuance. For this he sought compensation in an 'antic disposition', and his grotesque cavortings about the stage reached a point where

Player Queen **Grant Olding/Brian Swanton**
Prologue **Peter Searles**
Lucianus **Richard Lawry**
Player Musicians **Mary Chater and Charles Spicer**
Fortinbras **Fintan McKeown**
Captain to Fortinbras **Harry Waters**
Gentlewoman **Judith Coke**
Osric **Jeremy Northam**
Grave-digger **David Burke**
His Companion **Dean Hollingsworth**
Priest **Morris Perry**
Courtiers, Soldiers etc. **Christopher Armstrong, Melvyn Bedford, Ciaran McIntyre and Peter Nicholas**

Design **John Gunter**
Costume **Liz da Costa**
Lighting **Mark Henderson**
Music **Dominic Muldowney**
Director **Richard Eyre**

5. Daniel Day-Lewis as Hamlet attacks Claudius, played by John Castle, from the rear. Jeremy Northam (Osric) looks on.

they were not only irrelevant but distracting.

The relationships, too, collapsed. There was neither warmth nor intellectual companionship between this Hamlet and this Horatio, and, after an entrance of great splendour and regality, Claudius and Gertrude failed to suggest a passion that has moved them to murder. Judi Dench was left lost, like a Cleopatra without an Antony.

Michael Bryant was an excellent Polonius, but this was scant consolation for a very disappointing production.

In the autumn, the principal roles were recast. From 9 October until the end of the run, they were played by those named in brackets in the cast list.

The production, sponsored by Ladbroke Group plc, played at the Dubrovnik Festival and toured Hong Kong and Japan.

The March on Russia (1989)
DAVID STOREY

Lyttleton Theatre 6 April–10 August 1989

Colin **Frank Grimes**
Pasmore **Bill Owen**
Mrs Pasmore **Constance Chapman**
Wendy **Rosemary Martin**
Eileen **Patsy Rowlands**
Postman **Michael Goldie**

David Storey returns to the theme of his earlier play, *In Celebration*, with *The March on Russia*, in which the Pasmores 'celebrate' their diamond wedding. They are visited by their three children. The two daughters are in differing states of matrimonial disharmony, and the son, Colin, has had so much success as an author of a popular history that he has been able to buy his parents the house in which they live. He arrives

Design **Jocelyn Herbert**
Lighting **Mick Hughes**
Music **Alan Price**
Director **Lindsay Anderson**

desperate to tell them something, but leaves with his secret intact as the elderly couple renew their battle.

This is a powerful play, not least because of the strength of Bill Owen and Constance Chapman as the Pasmores, so credible in their every phrase and gesture. He is a retired miner who harks back to his march on Russia, which was ordered by Churchill in an attempt to save the Tsar in 1918. It is an escapade which is remembered with humour, pride and a little embarrassment; for he is a socialist whose wife has betrayed him as she has moved further and further to the right with increasing affluence. Their bickering provides both humour and a dark portrayal of human relationships as people pass the last years of their lives together. He, defenceless in his need of her, finds refuge only in crossword puzzles and a way of recognition only in shop-lifting.

Directed with sensitivity and control and acted with compassion, *The March on Russia* was a human, and therefore at times harrowing, experience.

Ghetto (1984)

JOSHUA SOBOL in a version by David Len

Olivier Theatre 27 April–9 November 1989

Srulik **Jonathan Cullen**
Kittel **Alex Jennings**
Hayyah **Maria Friedman**
Djigan **Linda Kerr Scott**
Gens **John Woodvine**
Weiskopf **Anthony O'Donnell**
Kruk **Paul Jesson**
Dessler **Ivan Kaye**
Yosef Gerstein **David Schneider**
Judith Azra **Nicola Scott**
Oomah Orshevskaya **Angela Pleasence**
Yitshok Elmis **Jon Rumney**
Avrom Bliakher **Nicholas Blane**
Luba Grodzenski **Laura Shavin**
Elia Geivish **Mark Lockyer**
Yitzhok Geivish **Glyn Pritchard**
Yankel Polikanski **Mark Addy**
Alexander Gertner (trumpeter) **Jo Stone-Fewings**
Shabse Gottlib (bass player) **Sandy Burnett**

In a middle-class apartment in Tel Aviv in 1983, a man is being interviewed although the interviewer is unseen: 'Our last performance... It was the night before Kittel murdered Gens. Ten days later the Ghetto was destroyed. That was the last performance. A good house? Listen to what I'm going to tell you. The theatre was full.'

The speaker is revealed as Srulik, the director of the theatre company in the Jewish Ghetto in Vilna, Lithuania. The story he reveals is of the activities of that company between January 1942 and September 1943, when all but he were killed. A pile of clothes is unloaded on to the stage, and weary people sort them. They are, of course, clothes that belonged to those liquidated in the camp a few miles away. Hayyah, a singer, clothes herself from the pile, but as she is doing so Kittel, the SS officer in charge, discovers that she is carrying a kilo of beans. They have either been stolen or obtained on the black market. Either way she could be instantly shot, but the bargaining begins. She sings for her life, and each time she offers a performance a few grams of beans are deducted from her debt.

That she survived after the initial discovery of the illicit beans is due to the intervention of Srulik and his dummy,

6. Maria Friedman. In Ghetto, she gave a vigorous, heroic performance as Hayyah, the singer who sings as if her life is at stake.

Sonia Grudberg **Sandra Butterworth**
Haikin (violinist) **Vladimir Asriev**
Yakob Iris **Ged McKenna**
Helena Lares **Jill Stanford**
Yitzhok Lipovsk **John Fitzgerald Jay**
Shmuel Mandelblit (trumpeter) **Oliver Beamish**
Sasha Molevsky **Ivan Kaye**
Nemi Madir (violinist) **Judith Sim**
Brauch Natan **Trevor Sellers**
Yakob Nemi (guitarist) **Michael O'Connor**
Moishe Norvid (saxophonist) **Merlin Shepherd**
Leah Rudkov **Jennifer Hill**
Zigmund Samberg (clarinettist) **David Roach**
Henry Taytlboym (trombonist) **Keith Woodhams**
Avrom Walter (accordionist) **Brian Greene**
Avrom Wittenberg **Tam Dean Burn**
Polia Wittenberg **Sandy McDade**
Gestapo Guards **Christopher Armstrong, Melvyn Bedford, Toby E Byrne and Ciaran McIntyre**
Jewish Police Officers **Mark Addy, Mark Lockyer, Christopher Armstrong, Melvyn Bedford, Glyn Pritchard, John Fitzgerald Jay and Trevor Sellers**

Djigan, for Srulik is both director of the theatre company and a ventriloquist. There are times when Djigan, in a remarkable performance by Linda Kerr Scott – who has the flexible humour and pathos of the clown, took on a life of its own. The dummy is the licensed fool, and within the terrible confines of the ghetto can offer in word and gesture criticism forbidden to others.

Kittel is a young music-loving SS officer who rules over the ghetto with a saxophone in one hand and an automatic pistol in the other. Alex Jennings avoided all the clichés in his performance. He is a handsome young man, ruthless in his application of the Führer's policies, but needing the Ghetto Theatre, which he orders to be resurrected, for his own artistic and spiritual sustenance. That Jennings played the part with a

Design **Bob Crowley**
Lighting **David Hersey**
Sound **Richard Borkum**
Movement **Jane Gibson**
Lyrics and Music **Jeremy Sams, translated and arranged from the music and lyrics by inhabitants of the Vilna Ghetto**
Musical Director **Sandy Burnett**
Director **Nicholas Hytner**

7. John Woodvine as Gens and Angela Pleasence as the demented once-star actress take centre stage in a scene from Ghetto. Srulik (Jonathan Cullen) has his dummy Djigan (Linda Kerr Scott) on his shoulders. Outstanding ensemble playing in a memorable production.

certain chilling charm and without the stereotype Nazi clicks and growls made him all the more terrifying.

His sudden whims jeopardise the lives of thousands. 'Suddenly, out of the blue, I just had to hear Gershwin. Isn't that strange?' 'Where's the singer who owes me fifty grams of beans?' Hayyah and the band give a stunning performance of *Swanee* with Kittel joining in on his saxophone. Her performance is sensuous and sparkling, 'her life depends upon it'. There was never a hint of self-pity in Maria Friedman's performance. She is a singer, an actress, on the edge of death, and as both singer and actress, she gives a vigorous and moving reminder of the heroic indestructibility of the human spirit. The *Swanee* sequence was stunning, for we were invigorated by the performance, and only gradually did we comprehend the context in which we were seeing it.

It is a microcosm of the play, which is about survival and the tactics of survival. Jacob Gens, the leader of the Jewish council, for whom 'jobs mean lives', was played with impassioned strength and belief by John Woodvine. He will co-operate and negotiate, for he sees it as his duty to bring as many Jews as possible through this horror which he believes will end. Hermann Kruk, the librarian with his stack of books affirming that these crimes will not be forgotten, asserts 'No theatre in a graveyard' as he cries for links with the socialist resistance. The two opposing views are the debate at the centre of the play. If our passions lead us towards Kruk, our intellect can share Gens's motives when, at an orgiastic party, he is ordered by Kittel to murder 2,000 Jews in a neighbouring ghetto, but negotiates the number down to 410.

There is the third view, that of the apolitical tailor Weiskopf. 'When did Jews ever have it easy?' he asks. He simply wants to get on with the job he knows and looks for efficiency and profit. He is, of course, deceived. You cannot negotiate with tyranny and insane cruelty, for there is no point of rationalisation. Gens discovers this too, for when Hayyah escapes to join the resistance the theatre company and the ghetto are liquidated. Only Srulik lives to tell the tale. Djigan has been the last to die as he wriggles free from his master and waves the defiant hand of the clown.

But this is no morbid play. There is a life of the spirit, and of art, that cannot be crushed. The dead rise and sing with heroic defiance: 'Never say the final journey is at hand/Never say we will not reach the promised land.'

Sobol has used theatre and music as the metaphor of the indestructibility of the human spirit: 'We will live for ever – beyond the flames/And you will never forget our names.'

This is not another *Holocaust*, another contribution to a topic which Sobol says has been 'overexposed', but a piece of theatre which one has rarely seen equalled. In design, direction and in ensemble and individual performance, it reached heights not often reached on the stage. If one has given more space to it than to any other of more than 150 productions seen in 1989, it is because one will remain eternally grateful for having seen it.

The Secret Rapture (1988)
DAVID HARE

Lyttleton Theatre 17 May–26 September 1989

Katherine **Anna Calder-Marshall**
Rhonda **Valerie Gogan**
Isobel **Diana Hardcastle**
Tom **Richard O'Callaghan**
Irwin **Simon Templeman**
Marion **Susan Tracy**

Completely recast, *The Secret Rapture* returned to the repertoire for the summer months. On reflection, one feels that this play says what one wants to hear said and that it contains some fine and eloquent writing, but that it has limitations as a piece of theatre.

The Misanthrope played in the Lyttleton Theatre from 31

Design **John Gunter**
Costume **Fotini Dimou**
Lighting **Laurence Clayton and Brian Ridley**

May to 4 November 1989. It was a co-production with the Bristol Old Vic, under which details will be found.

Music **Ilona Sekacz**   Director **Howard Davies**

The Voysey Inheritance (1906)
HARLEY GRANVILLE BARKER

Cottesloe Theatre 27 June 1989–18 January 1990

Mr Voysey **David Burke**
Peacey **Michael Bryant**
Edward Voysey **Jeremy Northam**
Major Booth Voysey **Robert Swann**
Denis Tregoning **Guy Henry**
George Booth **Graham Crowden**
Rev. Evan Colpus **Morris Perry**
Ethel Voysey **Sarah Winman**
Alice Maitland **Stella Gonet**
Honor Voysey **Selina Cadell**
Beatrice Voysey **Suzanne Burden**
Phoebe **Janet Whiteside**
Mrs Voysey **Barbara Leigh-Hunt**
Mary **Wendy Nottingham**
Emily Booth Voysey **Judith Coke**
Trenchard Voysey **Ian Flintoff**
Hugh Voysey **Crispin Redman**
Christopher Voysey **Daniel Macklin**

Design **William Dudley**
Lighting **Mark Henderson**
Music **John Woolrich**
Musical Director **Gabriel Amherst**
Sound **Scott Myers**
Director **Richard Eyre**

The first thing to applaud was that Richard Eyre gave us the opportunity to see a very fine and unjustly neglected play by an exceptionally fine and much underrated and under-

8. *Jeremy Northam as Edward intent on honesty and correct dealing in Richard Eyre's excellent revival of Harley Granville Barker's mighty play* The Voysey Inheritance.

performed dramatist. The only thing of which to complain is that the production was confined to the Cottesloe Theatre in a well between two banks of audience rather than being given the freedom of a larger auditorium and stage that it needed and deserved.

The strength of the play is that more than 80 years on, its concern for financiers speculating with their clients' money for their own ends is totally relevant. Early in the play, Edward Voysey, an idealist, discovers that his father has been using the clients' fund for personal profit. There is no shame in Mr Voysey who thrives on the corruption he has inherited and would pass it on as 'a great edifice' to his son.

Edward is at first willing to bankrupt the firm and stand trial himself, but he later compromises as he attempts to right matters by what are, in effect, illegal means. It is an Edwardian family drama which says more about the corruptions of capitalism and the City, and says it more sharply, than Caryl Churchill managed to do in *Serious Money* – which was lavishly praised.

What Granville Barker captured so surely was the smugness, the self-satisfied élitism of the middle class. In his excellent production, Richard Eyre missed none of the points which the playwright subtly explores, and he was wonderfully served by a consistently fine cast, from David Burke's assured Voysey senior to Michael Bryant's pressing senior clerk desirous of his crumbs from the rich man's table. The ladies were equally fine in this revival. There was no need to tamper with or modernise this play to make its message plain to an audience to whom the world of insider dealings and financial fraud has become everyday news.

The Grapes of Wrath (1988)
FRANK GALATI adapted from the novel by John Steinbeck

Lyttleton Theatre 22 June–1 July 1989

Jim Casy **Terry Kinney**
Tom Joad **Gary Sinise**
Muley Graves **Alan Wilder**
Pa Joad **Robert Breuler**
Ma Joad **Lois Smith**
Granma **Lucina Paquet**
Grampa **Nathan Davis**
Ruthie **Laura McMahon**
Winfield **Luke Goodrich**

The National Theatre's international season of 1989 saw the Moscow Art Theatre in *Uncle Vanya*, the Ninagawa Company from Tokyo in *Suicide for Love*, Teatro del Sur from Buenos Aires in *Tango Varsoviano* and the Steppenwolf Theatre Company of Chicago in *The Grapes of Wrath*.

Steinbeck's novel is not one that lends itself easily to the stage. It tells the story of a family from Oklahoma who are driven westward by the dustbowl depression in the 1930s and suffer hardship, degradation and exploitation in California. It

Noah **Jeff Perry**
Uncle John **James Noah**
Rose of Sharon **Sally Murphy**
Connie Rivers **Mark W Deakins**
Al Joad **Jim True**
Floyd Knowles **Rick Snyder**
Ensemble **Jessica Black, Cheryl Lynn Bruce, Keith Byron-Kirk, Kevin Connell, Ron Crawford, Leelai Demoz, Jessica Grossman, Tom Irwin, David Ledingham, Nancy Lollar, Terrance MacNamara, Molly Powell, Rondi Reed, Theodore Schulz, Eric Simonson and Skipp Sudduth**
Musicians **Willy Schwarz, L J Skavin, Michael Smith and Miriam Sturm**

Design and Lighting **Kevin Rigdon**
Costume **Erin Quigley and Kevin Rigdon**
Sound **Rob Milburn**
Musical Director **Michael Smith**
Director **Frank Galati**

is a moving novel, often harrowing, heavily laden with social philosophy and comment. The essential realism of the truck journey cannot be captured on stage. Frank Galati's adaption was faithful to the line of Steinbeck's story, but it remained nothing more than an adequate representation.

Some liberties were taken with characters. The Joads would not have been abused by a black woman in the 1930s, nor would Rose of Sharon have suckled a black man – for the American black was then most positively lower than any white – but the general tone and journey of the novel were preserved. The reality was broken by the obviousness of the mechanics, and although the performances and the ensemble playing were mostly good, they were never of a standard that explained why this company has an international reputation. At the end, one was left believing that they had chosen the wrong vehicle with which to display their talents.

9. *Lois Smith (Ma Joad) and Gary Sinise (Tom Joad) in the Steppenwolf Theatre Company's version of* The Grapes of Wrath.

The Long Way Round (1981)
PETER HANDKE translated by Ralph Manheim

Cottesloe Theatre 6–22 July 1989

Nova **Tilda Swinton**
Gregor **Andrew Rattenbury**
The Caretaker **Mary Macleod**
Hans **David Bamber**
Albin **Aidan Gillen**
Ignatz **Peter Dineen**
Anton **Douglas McFerran**
Sophie **Linda Henry**
The Old Woman **Deidre Halligan**
Hans's Child **Marc Bellamy**

This was the English language première of a work by the Austrian playwright and novelist Peter Handke. Milton Shulman described it as 'the allegorical pilgrimage that Gregor takes to his village to discover not only his own roots but the spiritual essence of the community he has left behind'. It is a play not to the general English taste.

Design **Bunny Christie**
Lighting **Paul Jozefowski**
Music **John Leach**

Sound **Christopher Shutt**
Director **Stephen Unwin**

The Shaughraun (1874)
DION BOUCICAULT

Olivier Theatre 10 August 1989–27 January 1990

Claire Ffolliott **Suzanne Burden**
Mrs O'Kelly **Bridget Turner**
Capt. Molyneaux **Jeremy Northam**
Arte O'Neill **Stella Gonet**
Corry Kinchela **Geoffrey Hutchings**
Father Dolan **Oliver Ford Davies**
Harvey Duff **Anthony O'Donnell**
Robert Ffolliott **Fintan McKeown**
Moya **Wendy Nottingham**
Conn 'The Shaughraun' **Stephen Rea**
Tatters **Scamp**
Sgt Jones **Ged McKenna**
Nancy Malone **Mary Chater**
Bridget Madigan **Janet Whiteside**

Recast, *The Shaughraun* returned to the repertoire for the last five months of the year. An exuberant production, excitingly and spectacularly staged, it remained faithful to Boucicault's humour and melodrama and the more sombre undertones of the 'Irish problem'.

Donovan **Melvyn Bedford**
Keeners **Jennifer Hill, Judith Sim and Alan White**
Reilly **Mark Addy**
Sullivan **Michael O'Connor**
Mangan **Toby E Byrne**
Doyle **Douglas McFerran**

Design **William Dudley**

Costume **Liz da Costa**
Lighting **Mark Henderson**
Music **Dominic Muldowney**
Musical Director **Claire van Kampen**
Sound **Paul Groothius**
Director **Howard Davies**

Man, Beast and Virtue (1919)
LUIGI PIRANDELLO in a version by Charles Wood

Cottesloe Theatre 7 September–12 December 1989

Toto **William Hoyland**
Rosaria **Brid Brennan**
Paolina **Trevor Eve**
Giglio **Neil Clark**
Belli **Sean Gascoine**
Mrs Perella **Marion Bailey**
Nono **Mark Goodwin and Todd Welling**
Dr Pulejo **Tom Chadbon**
Grazia **Pauline Delany**

A revival of Pirandello's farce which Michael Billington greeted as 'explosively funny' and a 'minor gem', and Ian Herbert thought was 'Britain's entry for the Eurovision Mugging Contest'. Inevitably, the comedy revolves around a husband, a wife and a lover.

Filippo **Anthony Douse**
Capt. Perella **Terence Rigby**

Design **Annie Smart**

Lighting **Mick Hughes**
Sound **Mike Clayton**
Director **William Gaskill**

Schism in England had twelve preview performances at the Cottesloe before its première in Edinburgh.

The National Theatre's programme at the close of 1989 and into the New Year included *Ma Rainey's Black Bottom*; the touring production of *The Beaux Stratagem*, details of which can be found under the Belgrade Theatre, Coventry; the débuts at the National Theatre of Steven Berkoff and Deborah Warner as directors of *Salome* and *The Good Person of Sichuan* respectively; *Whale*, the Christmas play by David Holman; *Bent*; and, in March 1990, Sondheim's *Sunday in the Park with George*.

It has not been an easy year for the National with financial restrictions biting deep, but Richard Eyre has shown a bold and courageous leadership and has not allowed commercial considerations to compromise his artistic values. In *Fuente Ovejuna* and *The Voysey Inheritance*, the National Theatre gave us two of the outstanding productions of the year. In *Ghetto*, they gave us one of the outstanding productions of a lifetime.

SECTION THREE

Royal Shakespeare Company

This section includes an article by Michael Billington who describes his role as director of the RSC's production of *The Will*.

1. *A year of variety and great achievement for John Wood, seen here as Sheridan Whiteside in* The Man Who Came To Dinner. *In contrast to this comic role, he gave towering dramatic performances in* The Master Builder *and* The Tempest.

Royal Shakespeare Company

BARBICAN CENTRE, BARBICAN, LONDON EC2Y 8BF
01-628-8795
STRATFORD-UPON-AVON, WARWICKSHIRE
0789-295623

Artistic Director and Chief Executive **Terry Hands**
Artistic Director, London, 1989 **Adrian Noble**

Terry Hands announced a new work structure for the RSC at the beginning of 1989. The new system introduced a one-year cycle within which company members would play the first half in Stratford and the second half in London. The Spring Company played in Stratford from March to August, toured for two months and transferred to London in November. The Autumn Company played in Stratford from September 1989 to January 1990, transferred to Newcastle and are scheduled to move to London in March 1990.

Productions were mounted in the Royal Shakespeare Theatre, the Swan Theatre, the Barbican Theatre and the Pit. The Other Place underwent a period of rebuilding in 1989. Work should be completed in 1990. It will continue to house productions of plays by contemporary writers and the RSC's productions which are within their policy of rediscovering classic plays.

The RSC continued to gain considerable benefit from the sponsorship accorded by Royal Insurance. English Estates helped with the Newcastle season and British Telecom with the eight-week tour to community venues. IBM, Jaguar, Manulife and British Alcan Aluminium sponsored individual performances.

The RSC had ended 1988 on a note of triumph with Adrian Noble's production of *The Plantagenets*, and this moved to the Barbican in March 1989. Full details of the production were given in the first edition of the *British Theatre Yearbook*.

A most interesting, if brief, addition to the RSC's repertoire in the early part of 1989 was a production by Michael Billington, theatre critic of *The Guardian*, of *The Will* by Marivaux. **Michael Billington** himself describes below how this production came about.

The Will (1736)
PIERRE MARIVAUX translated by Michael Sadler from *Le Legs*

Barbican Conservatory 27 January–13 February 1989

Chevalier **Paul Spence**
Hortense **Emma Hitching**
Lisette **Helen Sheals**
Lepine **Gordon Warnecke**
The Marquis **Ian Barritt**

The Countess **Jane Leonard**

Design **Helen Weatherburn**
Lighting **Stanley Osborne White**
Sound **Monkey**

Music and Musical Director **Richard Brown**
Director **Michael Billington**

The Critic as Director

I shall remember 1989 for one thing: it was the year I directed a play. As an aisle-squatting critic, I spend two nights a week watching other people at work. But I recall Gore Vidal once saying that he stopped going to the theatre when he realised that the people on stage were having more fun than he was. And, inevitably, there are times when, as a critic, you sit there nursing your impotence complex speculating on what it would be like to be involved in the hurly-burly of putting on a show.

How did I come to direct? Like the lady in Webster's play, I was 'drawn arsie-varsie into the business'. It all goes back to the winter of 1987 when I was invited by Estelle Kohler to give an informal talk about criticism to the RSC actors in Stratford. I was inevitably asked if I thought it would be a good idea for critics to attend rehearsals to familiarise themselves with the theatrical process. I said I thought it was a dreadful idea: I tried it once and simply felt a redundant spectator sitting at the back of the Royal Court stalls looking furtively inconspicuous. Far better, I suggested, if a critic were asked occasionally to direct a play.

Over lunch afterwards Greg Doran (then a young actor in the company, now on the RSC's directorial staff) asked me if I were serious. I said 'Yes' and he promised to keep in touch. Nine months later he sent me a note suggesting that we take it further. We discovered that there would be a group of RSC actors free of commitments during the Christmas run of *The Wizard of Oz* and he asked me to come up with a list of plays. I quickly stubbed my toe against the reality of theatre: the piece in question would need to be about an hour long and ideally would have a cast of six and (since the budget was coming out of the actors' own kitty) minimal scenery.

In November 1988, I turned up at the Barbican one Saturday

morning to meet a group of actors interested in taking part in the project. We read through three possible plays. My own favourite, Strindberg's *The Pelican*, was quickly discounted both because of a risible translation ('I can't stand this smell of carbolic acid and fir twigs') and because it ended with an immolation scene more demanding than the climax of *Götterdämmerung*. Marivaux's *Slave Island*, a comedy about role-swapping between masters and servants, was liked but felt to be rather schematic. The play that made everybody fall about was another Marivaux piece, *The Will*, about a plot to get a nervous marquis to marry a domineering countess even though he has to sacrifice 200,000 francs in the process. In Michael Sadler's brilliant translation, it emerged as a very funny piece about emotional inhibition and the high cost of loving.

Thus it was that I found myself spending much of January 1989 in the RSC's Clapham rehearsal room with six highly gifted and willing actors, trying to crack the problem of staging a 1736 comedy. I soon discovered that the play posed real difficulties. The main one was that Marivaux's characters talked endlessly and manoeuvred for advantage – I kept comparing the play to emotional chess – but that they never *did* anything. Seizing on the fact that we were going to be mounting the play in the Barbican Conservatory – an urban jungle where few playgoers had ever trod – I decided to fill the stage with gardening implements and (with the actors' ready consent) to set the action in the 1930s. At least that would prevent us looking like an inferior version of *Les Liaisons Dangereuses*. It would also give the actors a chance to light cigarettes, flick through magazines, take off their wellies and relate the language to a world of realistic behaviour. I now understand, in fact, why so many directors transpose classic plays to a quasi-modern setting.

The rehearsal process itself was an almost unadulterated joy. I discovered that actors love analysing, talking about and chewing over a scene before getting up and doing it. I also learned that they have an amazing flexibility and willingness to try anything: new moves, new business, new accents even. I greatly enjoyed their company and admired their expertise while sympathising with their insecurity (they were all approaching the end of their RSC contracts and lived in uncertainty as to whether those would be renewed).

The only real problems were technical ones. I remember a fraught Saturday morning when we ran the play through in the Conservatory only to discover that an obtrusive, irremovable plant rendered many of the moves impractical. I also recall the final performance day panic when there was not time for a full-scale dress rehearsal. But I also remember, with gratitude, the lift given to the show when two RSC musicians (Richard Brown and Victor Slaymark) turned up on that last day to top and tail the show with a pungent, lively score.

In the event, it all seemed to go OK. We filled the space for six performances. Audiences seemed to have a good time. The reviews, mind you, were mixed. Two or three of my professional colleagues were pretty scathing. But the most interesting and detailed review came in *The Guardian* from Terry Hands. He made some rightly generous remarks about the actors. But he complained that I had made the whole thing too English and that I had failed to relate the servants to the main theme. There was some justice in both points which makes me think that Mr Hands, if ever he should want to relinquish directing, would make a very good critic.

What, everyone has asked me since, did I learn from the experience? To be honest, the most fundamental lesson was one that is of no immediate help to a critic. I discovered (something that people in the business already know) that directing is an essentially collaborative process and that no one out front can ever know where an idea came from. Someone congratulated me on a particularly good bit of business in which Ian Barritt as the Marquis retreated in high dudgeon behind the overhanging fronds of a Barbican plant; needless to say, the idea was his, not mine. But as a critic one constantly has to attribute praise or blame to an author, an actor, a director, a designer without ever being sure whether one has hit the mark.

On a more positive note, I came away convinced that it is a healthy thing for critics to immerse themselves in the practical process of play-making. Directing, in a sense, is criticism made manifest. A director, very like a critic, has to discover a writer's governing themes and interpret his or her intentions. The crucial difference is that a director has to find a way of creating a world on stage in which those ideas can clearly emerge. A critic also flits from play to play. A director worries away incessantly at a specific text, seeking to discover its elusive rhythms and hidden meanings.

'How's it going?' Richard Eyre asked me one night at the National. I said I was having a great time. 'Given the right circumstances,' he said, 'a rehearsal room is the nearest thing to paradise on earth.' Of course, he added, if the chemistry is not right, it can also be hell. I was fortunate in that I had a good play, a perfect cast, an atmosphere of unpaid, enthusiastic co-operation. Would I do it again? Like a shot, not because I entertain any delusions of directorial adequacy but because I believe that we erect false barriers between doing and commentating and because the process of taking a play apart to see how it works is bound at some stage to inform one's criticism. I resumed my seat on the aisle a happier and, I hope, a marginally wiser man.

MICHAEL BILLINGTON

Restoration (1981)
EDWARD BOND

The Pit from 29 March 1989

The production was first seen at The Swan in September 1988, and the play has been adapted from that which was originally produced at the Royal Court in 1981. It is a parody, a black comedy, of Restoration morality which begins with Lord Are accidentally murdering his wife.

Lord Are **Simon Russell Beale**
Frank **Mark Sproston**
Bob Hedges **Duncan Bell**
Mr Hardache **Colin McCormack**
Ann, Lady Are **Melanie Thaw**
Rose **Vivienne Rochester**
Mrs Hedges **Pip Hinton**
Parson **Joe Melia**
Gaoler **Paul Hargreaves**
Gabriel Hedges **Alfred Burke**
Mrs Wilson **Jane Cox**

Old Lady Are **Patricia Lawrence**
Messenger **Timothy Stark**

Design **David Fielding**
Lighting **Rick Fisher**

Sound **Steff Langley**
Music **Ilona Sekacz**
Musical Director **Peter Pontzen**
Director **Roger Michell**

Romeo and Juliet (1595)
WILLIAM SHAKESPEARE

The Swan from 5 April 1989

Described by Jack Tinker as a 'sensational start' to the Stratford season, Terry Hands's *Romeo and Juliet* was generally welcomed with great warmth for its excellent use of the space at The Swan, for the quality of its verse speaking and for the sense of unity which it achieved. There were very few dissenting voices.

Chorus **Rob Heyland**
Sampson **Francis Johnson**
Gregory **Jared Harris**
Abraham/Friar John **Ben Miles**
Balthasar **William Oxborrow**
Benvolio **Patrick Brennan**
Tybalt **Vincent Regan**
Capulet **Bernard Horsfall**
Lady Capulet **Linda Spurrier**
Montague **Michael Loughnan**
Lady Montague **Katherine Stark**
Escalus **Rob Heyland**
Romeo **Mark Rylance**
Paris **Michael Howell**
Peter **Evan Russell**

Nurse **Margaret Courtenay**
Juliet **Georgia Slowe**
Mercutio **David O'Hara**
Old Capulet/Apothecary **Griffith Jones**
Ladies **Hilary Jones and Jennie Heslewood**
Friar Lawrence **Patrick Godfrey**

Paris's Page **Richard Doubleday**
First Watch **Peter Carr**

Design **Farrah**
Lighting **Terry Hands**
Choreographer **Anthony van Laast**
Music **Claire van Kampen**
Director **Terry Hands**

A Midsummer Night's Dream (1596)
WILLIAM SHAKESPEARE

Royal Shakespeare Theatre from 11 April 1989

The wood near Athens is a junkyard of broken bicycles and pianos, and a small band is on stage throughout the production. The fairies wear Doc Martens and Puck is clad in boots and motoring goggles. Far from offending critics, John Caird's production was hailed as a triumph, a sensational reworking of the play which breathed new life into a tired vehicle and delivered Shakespeare with 'something like a first freshness'.

Theseus/Oberon **John Carlisle**
Hippolyta/Titania **Clare Higgins**
Egeus **Russell Enoch**
Hermia **Amanda Bellamy**
Demetrius **Paul Lacoux**
Lysander **Stephen Simms**
Helena **Sarah Crowden**
Quince **Paul Webster**
Bottom **David Troughton**
Flute **Graham Turner**
Starveling **Dhobi Oparei**
Snout **David Shaw-Parker**
Snug **Jimmy Gardner**
Puck **Richard McCabe**
Fairy **Liza Hayden**
Oberon's Fairies **Keith Goozee, Peter Hamilton Dyer, Andrew Havill and Neil Richardson**
Titania's Fairies **Sharon Hinds, Polly Kemp and Jacqueline Leonard**
Changeling Boy **Krishnan Chauhan/Mandip Jheeta**
Peaseblossom **Charlotte Bridgewater/Fiona Gibson**
Cobweb **Richard Handy/Zachary Gregory**
Moth **Curtis Mason/Mark Seavers**
Mustardseed **Chloe Trotman/Jodie Ball**

Design **Sue Blane**
Lighting **Alan Burrett**
Choreographer **Anthony van Laast**
Sound **Paul Slocombe**
Music **Ilona Sekacz**
Musical Director **Michael Tubbs**
Director **John Caird**

The Man of Mode (1676)
GEORGE ETHEREGE

The Pit from 13 April 1989

Transferred from The Swan, where it opened in July 1988, *The Man of Mode* revolves around Sir Fopling Flutter and his energetic pretensions to be fashionable, but it is also the love affairs of Dorimant that engage us. Some felt that the production had been more at home in Stratford.

Mr Dorimant **Miles Anderson**
Handy **John Bott**
Foggy Nan **Jane Cox**
Mr Medley **Pip Donaghy**
Shoemaker **David Acton**
Young Bellair **Mark Sproston**
Lady Townley **Joan Blackham**
Emilia **Jenni George**
Old Bellair **Joe Melia**
John Trott/Footman **Ian Embleton**
Page/Footman **Paul Sykes**
Mrs Loveit **Marie Mullen**
Pert **Maureen Beattie**
Bellinda **Katy Behean**
Harriet **Amanda Root**
Busy **Claudette Williams**
Lady Woodvill **Patricia Lawrence**
Chairman/Footman **Dominic Rickhards**
Sir Fopling Flutter **Simon Russell Beale**
Smirk/Chairman/Footman **Timothy Stark**
Page **Charles Miller/Anthony Watson**

Design **Di Seymour**

Lighting **Geraint Pughe**
Sound **Tony Brand**

Choreographer **Michael Popper**
Music **Ilona Sekacz**

Musical Director **John Francis**
Director **Gary Hynes**

Hamlet (1602)
WILLIAM SHAKESPEARE

Royal Shakespeare Theatre from 26 April 1989

This production was originally seen on tour in the autumn of 1988. It has been described as a 'lean' production in its staging, but one that created immense interest. Mark Rylance's portrayal of the prince is of a man 'tragically human to the core', and, under Ron Daniels's direction, he sees Hamlet as having been driven to madness. Generally recognised as a vital and fascinating interpretation.

Francisco/Violinist **William Oxborrow**
Bernando **Ben Mills**
Marcellus/Priest **Neil Richardson**
Horatio **Jack Ellis**
Ghost/First Player **Russell Enoch**
Claudius **Peter Wight**
Gertrude **Clare Higgins**
Hamlet **Mark Rylance**
Valtimand **Mark Brignal**
Cornelius **Peter Carr**
Polonius **Patrick Godfrey**
Laertes **John Ramm**
Ophelia **Rebecca Saire**
Reynaldo **Andrew Havill**
Rosencrantz **Andrew Bridgemont**
Guildenstern **Patrick Brennan**

Second Player **Katherine Stark**
Third Player **Roger Tebb**
Fortinbras **Jared Harris**
Lady **Hilary Tones**
Sailor **Michael Howell**
Gravedigger **Jimmy Gardner**
Second Gravedigger **William Oxborrow**
Osric **Paul Lacoux**

Design **Antony McDonald**
Lighting **Thomas Webster**
Music **Claire van Kampen**
Choreographer **Siobhan Davies**
Sound **John A Leonard**
Musical Director **Michael Tubbs**
Director **Ron Daniels**

King John (1597)
WILLIAM SHAKESPEARE

The Pit from 2 May 1989

Originally seen at The Other Place in the summer of 1988, Deborah Warner's production of *King John* reduces the play to its basic shape. She requires the minimum of scenery, but an abundance of ladders, and her stock is rising quickly after a succession of triumphs – of which *King John* is one.

King John **Nicholas Woodeson**
Queen Eleanor **Cherry Morris**
Prince Henry/Robert Faulconbridge/Messenger **Jack James**
Blanche of Spain/Messenger **Caroline Harding**
Earl of Pembroke **Richard Bremner**
Earl of Salisbury **Edward Harbour**
Lord Bigot/Limoges **Simon Dormandy**
Philip Faulconbridge **David Morrissey**

Lady Faulconbridge **Cissy Collins**
James Gurney/Melun **Patrick Robinson**
Arthur, Duke of Brittany **Nehme Fadlallah**
Constance **Susan Engel**

Philip of France **David Lyon**
Lewis the Dauphin **Ralph Fiennes**
Chatillon/Peter of Pomfret/Executioner **Roger Watkins**
Hubert **Robert Demeger**
Cardinal Pandulph **Julian Curry**

Design **Sue Blane**
Lighting **Robert Jones**
Music **Guy Woolfenden**
Director **Deborah Warner**

Macbeth (1606)
WILLIAM SHAKESPEARE

Barbican from 4 May 1989

First Witch **Pip Hinton**
Second Witch **Vivienne Rochester**
Third Witch **Candida Gubbins**
Duncan **Nicholas Selby**
Donalbain/Loon **James Purefoy**
Sergeant/Murderer **Ken Shorter**
Macduff **Colin McCormack**
Ross/Porter **Desmond Barrit**
Angus/Murderer **Mark Sproston**
Menteith **Peter Lennon**
Lennox **Ken Sabberton**
Macbeth **Miles Anderson**
Banquo **Tony Armatrading**
Lady Macbeth **Amanda Root**
Seyton **Patrick Miller**
Fleance **Curt Clement-Fletcher/ Harry Jameson**
Doctor **John Bott**
Lady Macduff **Maureen Beattie**
Young Macduff **Paul Fowling/ Nimer Rashed**
Macduff's Daughter **Allison Hamilton/Sarah Morrish**
Macduff's son **Jamie Bradley/ Jethro Ross-Wood**
Gentlewoman **Jill Spurrier**
Old Siward **Michael Gardiner**
Young Siward **Ian Embleton**

Design **Bob Crowley**
Lighting **Mark Henderson, Chris Parry and Clive Morris**
Choreographer **Jane Gibson**
Music **Geoffrey Burgon**
Director **Adrian Noble**

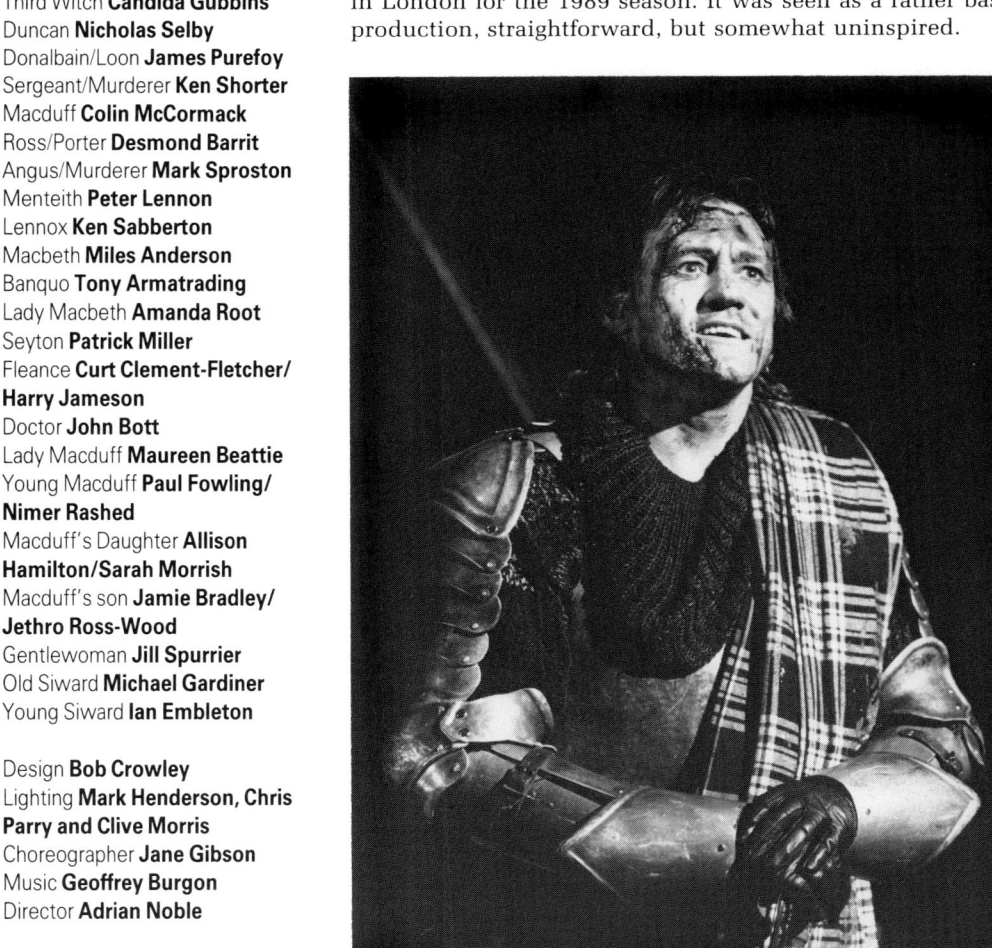

The production of *Macbeth* which started out in 1986 with Jonathan Pryce and was re-created at Stratford in 1988 arrived in London for the 1989 season. It was seen as a rather basic production, straightforward, but somewhat uninspired.

2. Miles Anderson as Macbeth.

3. *'My hands are of your colour: but I shame/To wear a heart so white.'* Amanda Root as Lady Macbeth and Miles Anderson as Macbeth in Adrian Noble's production of Shakespeare's tragedy at The Barbican.

Dr Faustus (1589)
CHRISTOPHER MARLOWE

Royal Shakespeare Theatre from 10 May 1989

The RSC's fourth revival of *Dr Faustus* in 21 years featured an all-male cast and a design which suggested that the action takes place in the dark depths of Faustus's mind.

Dr Faustus **Gerard Murphy**
Wagner **Richard McCabe**
Good Angel/Wrath/Emperor/Helen of Troy **Vincent Regan**
Evil Angel/Envy/The Pope/Horse-Courser **David Shaw-Parker**
Valdes/Pride/Cardinal of Lorraine/Duke of Vanholt **William Chubb**
Cornelius/Gluttony/Robin/Alexander the Great **Stephen Simms**
Scholar/Lucifer **Dhobi Oparei**
Beelzebub/Knight **Francis Johnson**
Covetousness/Vintner **Michael Loughnan**
Sloth/Ralph **Graham Turner**
Lechery/Paramour **Richard Doubleday**
Duchess of Vanholt **Keith Goozee**

Design **Ashley Martin-Davis**
Lighting **Wayne Dowdeswell**
Sound **Paul Slocombe**
Choreographer **Beyham**
Director **Barry Kyle**

The Plain Dealer (1676)
WILLIAM WYCHERLEY

The Pit from 22 May 1989

Another transfer from The Swan and with only a few changes in cast. Wycherley's play tells of Manly's return from the wars to find his beloved Olivia has betrayed him. He employs a sailor to avenge him, but the sailor turns out to be a woman in disguise who is desperately in love with him. Most felt that it was a masterly revival.

Manly **David Calder**
My Lord Plausible **Tom Fahy**
Sailor/Bailiff **Trevor Gordon**
Sailor/Petulant/Knight of the Post **Kevin Doyle**
Freeman **Pip Donaghy**
Fidelia **Geraldine Alexander**
The Widow Blackacre **Marjorie Yates**
Jerry Blackacre **Jason Watkins**
Olivia **Joanne Pearce**
Eliza **Jaye Griffiths**
Lettice/Splitcause/Knight of the Post **Cissy Collins**
Olivia's Boy/Waiter/Bookseller's Boy **Christian Dixon**
Maid/Waitress/Quaint **Kathleen Christof**
Novel **Mark Hadfield**
Major Oldfox **Nicholas Smith**
Alderman/Vernish **Edward Peel**

Design **David Fielding**
Lighting **Geraint Pughe**
Choreographer **Jane Gibson**
Musical Director **Richard Brown**
Director **Ron Daniels**

The Tempest (1611)
WILLIAM SHAKESPEARE

Barbican from 25 May 1989

Alonso **Nicholas Selby**
Sebastian **Colin McCormack**
Prospero **John Wood**
Antonio **Richard Haddon Haines**
Ferdinand **James Purefoy**
Gonzalo **Alfred Burke**
Adrian **Paul Hargreaves**
Francisco **Patrick Miller**
Ariel **Duncan Bell**
Caliban **John Kane**
Trinculo **Desmond Barrit**
Stephano **Campbell Morrison**
Master of a Ship **Peter Lennon**
Boatswain **Ken Shorter**
Miranda **Melanie Thaw**
Iris **Darlene Johnson**
Ceres **Cate Hamer**
Juno **Julia Lintott**
Spirits/Mariners **Michael Bott, Maggie Carr, Stephen Gordon,**

The initial impression created by Nicholas Hytner's *Tempest* is a sense of awe. A bleak, oval, tilted platform is diffused in grey and white. The storm rages with flickering light, illuminating the characters as in an old film. Then there is stillness and quiet, and the sailors are disturbed by the eerie feeling of the supernatural. Surprisingly, John Wood does not take the tone of his Prospero from this mood. His Prospero is essentially a vulnerable human being rather than an archmagician. He is bitter, angry and weeping. His cue seems to come from Miranda's words, 'Never till this day/Saw I him touch'd with anger, so distemper'd.' He is a man in a high state of excitement as his revenge and rehabilitation approaches after his years of exile. There is a constant sense of anticipation in him, of a great event about to take place. It is an exciting and human interpretation of the role, but a criticism must be that in these moments of high excitement and anger, there are times when we cannot hear what he is saying.

His relationship with his daughter is a delight. Melanie Thaw is heaped in wonder and wide-eyed innocence. Her love for Ferdinand, and his for her, is totally credible. Prospero's

Paul Hargreaves, Peter Lennon, Patrick Miller, Ken Shorter and Julia Tarnoky
Spirits **Leona Asamoah, Charlotte Hawkins, Nicole Merton, Jennifer Minott, Emma Preston and Leigh Saville**

Design **David Fielding**
Lighting **Mark Henderson and Clive Morris**
Sound **John A Leonard and Andrea J Cox**
Music **Jeremy Sams**
Musical Director **Peter Washtell**
Director **Nicholas Hytner**

4. A wonderfully funny and mournful Trinculo (Desmond Barrit) is looked down upon by a rollicking Stephano (Campbell Morrison).

joy in their love is that of a father for a daughter. It is an essential part of the harmony achieved in the production.

A ghost-like, restless and impatient Ariel adds urgency to this island full of noises, and the comic scenes are a clear parallel to the usurption by the nobles. Trinculo is a jester lost, a wonderful comic comment on the more serious events we witness. In Desmond Barrit's interpretation, he is gorgeously precious, uncomfortable and ill at ease outside the protection of the court. He is gloriously funny in his discomfort and also in the moments of radiant wisdom that he brings to the comic scenes: 'They say there's but five upon this isle; we are three of them, if th' other two be brain'd like us, the state totters.'

5. John Wood – a Prospero in a state of high excitement with Miranda (Melanie Thaw) in his arms.

Barrit's is a masterly performance.

Like Peter Hall's production at the National Theatre in 1988, the play flags in the masque scene, but for the rest of the time it is rich in humour and intelligence. It exudes the feeling of unity and harmony and is a most thought-provoking and challenging production.

Epicoene (1609)
BEN JONSON

The Swan from 5 July 1989

Ned Clerimont **Jared Harris**
A Boy **Liza Hayden**
Truewit **Richard McCabe**
Sir Dauphine Eugenie **Peter Hamilton Dyer**
Sir Amorous La Foole **Michael Mears**

The aptly named Morose plans to marry in order to disinherit his disagreeable nephew Dauphine. He has a detestation of noise and is found a silent bride, Epicoene. Dauphine is made conversant with the plans, and the resulting comedy in which Morose is thwarted is Jonson's rather malicious and anti-feminist play. It is no secret, although the RSC would have it so, that Epicoene is no woman. It is rather hard on the very

Morose **David Bradley**
Mute **Graham Turner**
Cutbeard **William Chubb**
Sir John Daw **John Ramm**
Epicoene **John Hannah**
Master Otter **David Shaw-Parker**
Mistress Otter **Jennie Heslewood**
Parson **Paul Lacoux**
Madame Haughty **Amanda Bellamy**
Madame Centaur **Rebecca Saire**
Mistress (Dol) Mavis **Sarah Crowden**
Mistress Trusty **Polly Kemp**
Pages/Servants **Richard Doubleday, Michael Howell, Jacqueline Leonard, William Oxborrow, Neil Richardson, Georgia Slowe and Hilary Tones**

talented John Hannah that for his début for the RSC he has to be recorded as Hannah John on the programme in order to try to keep the secret.

Design **Kandis Cook**
Lighting **Rory Dempster**
Sound **Andrea J Cox**
Choreographer **Lesley Hutchinson**
Music **Barrington Pheloung**
Musical Director **Roger Hellyer**
Director **Danny Boyle**

Cymbeline (1610)
WILLIAM SHAKESPEARE

Royal Shakespeare Theatre from 11 July 1989

Bill Alexander has developed and recast his studio production of 1987 into the final full-scale offering at the Royal Shakespeare Theatre for the summer season. It had a mixed reception, but most critics thought that it had much to commend it.

Members of the Court **Evan Russell, Dhobi Oparei, Andrew Havill, Roger Tebb and Keith Goozee**
Lords **Ben Miles and Andrew Bridgemont**
Cornelius **Jack Ellis**
Helen **Sharon Hinds**
Lady to the Queen **Katherine Stark**
The Queen **Linda Spurrier**
Imogen **Naomi Wirthner**
Posthumus Leonatus **David O'Hara**
Cymbeline **Bernard Horsfall**
Pisanio **Rob Heyland**
Cloten **David Troughton**
Iachimo **John Carlisle**
Philario **Mark Brignal**
A Frenchman **Francis Johnson**
Guest/British Captain **Andrew Havill**
Guest/Roman Captain **Roger Tebb**
Guest/British Captain **Keith Goozee**
Guest/Ghost of Sicilius **Peter Carr**
Guest/Philarmona **Sharon Hinds**
Caius Lucius **Michael Loughnan**
Belarius **Paul Webster**
Guiderius **Stephen Simms**
Arviragus **Vincent Regan**
Gaolers **Dhobi Oparei and Evan Russell**

Design **Timothy O'Brien**
Lighting **Mark Henderson**
Sound **Paul Slocombe**
Music **Ilona Sekacz**
Choreographer **Lesley Hutchinson**
Musical Director **John Woolf**
Director **Bill Alexander**

Some Americans Abroad (1989)
RICHARD NELSON

The Pit from 19 July 1989

Joe Taylor **Anton Lesser**
Philip Brown **Oliver Cotton**

One of the new productions for the season in London, *Some Americans Abroad* is about a group of American academics

Henry McNeil **Simon Russell Beale**
Betty McNeil **Amanda Root**
Frankie Lewis **Diane Fletcher**
Katie Taylor **Kate Byers**
Harriet Baldwin **Patricia Lawrence**
Orson Baldwin **John Bott**
Joanne Smith **Candida Gubbins**
An American **Joe Melia**

and students on an annual culture tour of theatres in England. It is a dark comedy of manners which views British culture through pretentious American eyes.

Donna Silliman **Caroline Harding**
Singer **Pip Hinton**

Design **Alexandra Byrne**

Lighting **Rick Fisher**
Sound **Paul Spedding**
Music **Jeremy Sams**
Director **Roger Michell**

The Man Who Came To Dinner (1939)
GEORGE S KAUFMAN and MOSS HART

Barbican from 20 July 1989

Mrs Stanley **Marjorie Yates**
Miss Preen **Marie Mullen**
Richard Stanley **James Purefoy**
John **Stephen Gordon**
June Stanley **Melanie Thaw**
Sarah **Marjie Lawrence**
Mrs McCutcheon **Penny Jones**
Mrs Dexter **Elizabeth Stewart**
Mr Stanley **Richard Haddon Haines**
Maggie Cutler **Maureen Beattie**
Dr Bradley **Jeffrey Segal**
Sheridan Whiteside **John Wood**
Harriet Stanley **Cherry Morris**
Bert Jefferson **Ralph Fiennes**
Professor Metz **Michael Gardiner**
Luncheon Guest/Deputy **Paul Sykes**
Luncheon Guest/Deputy **Ian Embleton**

The RSC's decision to revive *The Man Who Came To Dinner* may have surprised many, but very few could have been disappointed with the result. The famous American comedy revolves around Sheridan Whiteside (a thin disguise for

6. Barrie Ingham as Beverly Carlton, 'a delight and a gem', consoles Maureen Beattie as Maggie Cutler. Miss Beattie gave a splendid performance – cool, witty, sensitive and controlled in Whiteside's mad world – in The Man Who Came To Dinner.

Luncheon Guest/Plain Clothes Man
Simon Downes
Baker/Westcott **Ken Shorter**
Expressman **Dominic Rickhards**
Sandy **Mark Strong**
Lorraine Sheldon **Estelle Kohler**
Beverly Carlton **Barrie Ingham**
Radio Technicians **Paul Sykes and Ian Embleton**
Young Boys **Jonathan Ardill, Damian Aziz, Paul Gorney, William Harper, Charley Henderson, Daniel Ison, Paolo Macis, Emmanuel Papadakis, Matthew Rhys-Evans, Adam Seton, Benjamin Sandbrook, Ben Segal, Raphael Schneebeli, Tom Smith and Jonathan Taylor**
Banjo **Desmond Barrit**
Expressman **Ian Embleton**

Design **Carl Toms**
Costume **Alexander Reid**
Lighting **Mark Henderson**
Sound **Steff Langley**
Musical Directors **Richard Brown and Peter Washtell**
Vocals **Bronwyn Baud**
Director **Gene Saks**

Alexander Woollcott), critic, lecturer and massive radio personality, who wreaks havoc in a small town in Ohio when he is supposedly incapacitated and commandeers the home of the Stanleys. The comedy is centred on Whiteside's gigantic ego and on his attempt, which he later regrets and for which he makes restitution, to prevent his secretary from leaving him to marry the editor of the local newspaper. It is essentially a period piece littered with the gossip, show business news, historical figures and personalities of the 1930s. In his production, Gene Saks has shown reverence for this fact and demonstrated his belief in the worth of the play. Would that more directors did the same.

Carl Toms's set is a discreet and dignified embodiment of the Stanley family. It has a calm and coolness which allows Whiteside's intrusion to be a violation of place as well as of manners. If John Wood lacks the Falstaffian physical presence that some would want to see in Whiteside, he has a vocal command which is pitched at just the right level so that his insults are waspish and funny. His mannerisms are controlled, and the raising of his eyebrows can dominate an audience. He is ably supported by a fine cast in which there are several delightful cameos, such as Jeffrey Segal's Dr Bradley.

As the extravagant actress Lorraine Sheldon, Estelle Kohler descends to the appropriate level of coarseness when things are not going her way. Desmond Barrit's Banjo is a delightful blend of Groucho Marx, Jimmy Durante and his own comic invention. Above all, Barrie Ingham's Beverly Carlton, English playwright, composer and star of Broadway, is a delight and a gem.

Across Oka (1988)
ROBERT HOLMAN

The Pit from 31 July 1989

Jolyon **Alfred Burke**
Matty **Edward Rawle-Hicks**
Eileen **Patricia Lawrence**
Tessa **Jane Cox**
Pavel **Christopher Rozycki**
Margaret **Joan Blackham**
Nikolai **Timothy Stark**

Design **Ashley Martin-Davis**

The transfer from The Other Place of Holman's play about the involvement of a Middlesbrough family with a nature reserve in the Soviet Union where an ornithologist is working to return the Siberian crane to the wild. It is an allegory of East–West relations.

Lighting **Geraint Pughe**
Music **Ilona Sekacz**
Musical Director **Peter Washtell**
Director **Sarah Pia Anderson**

Othello (1604)
WILLIAM SHAKESPEARE

The Other Place 24 August–16 September 1989
The Young Vic 20 September–11 November 1989

Roderigo **Michael Grandage**
Iago **Ian McKellen**
Brabantio/Gratiano **Clive Swift**
Othello **Willard White**
Cassio **Sean Baker**
Senator/Soldier **Brian Lawson**
Servant/Soldier **David Hounslow**
Duke of Venice/Lodovico **John Burgess**
Desdemona **Imogen Stubbs**
Montano **Philip Sully**
Emilia **Zoe Wanamaker**
Bianca **Marsha Hunt**

Design **Bob Crowley**
Lighting **Chris Parry**
Sound **Paul Slocombe**
Music **Guy Woolfenden**
Musical Director **Jonathan Goldstein**
Director **Trevor Nunn**

Trevor Nunn returned to the RSC and to Shakespeare after his sojourn with musicals to give us a production of *Othello* that was highly intelligent in conception and radiantly illuminating in performance. He sets the action in the late 19th century although the costumes have a hint of the American cavalry, and the immediate emphasis on the military gives much clarity to what is to follow. When Cassio is duped into a drunken brawl it is the natural outcome of a barrack-room romp, and the distinction between the commissioned and the non-commissioned officer emphasises the class divisions within the play.

Ian McKellen's Iago emerges as one of the great Shakespearean performances of recent times. In character and cause he is instantly recognisable. He anticipates Othello's jealousy in his nervous musings upon Emilia's supposed infidelity, and you feel you can see the wheels of revenge rotating in his mind. He is a man who has no feeling but for his own ambition, and that ambition has been thwarted by the promotion of Cassio. Yet the great strength of McKellen's performance is that he plays Iago as one who is, in fact, not 'officer material', a truth of which he is unaware.

McKellen's performance gains strength from his relationship with his wife, for Zoe Wanamaker's Emilia is a woman of integrity in love with her husband and somewhat perplexed by his oddities and whims. It is a wonderfully human portrayal.

In her affection for Desdemona, too, this Emilia is essentially human. The bond between the two women gives an added poignancy to the play's closing moments, in which Miss Wanamaker is magnificent.

She is matched by Imogen Stubbs's delightful study of youthful love and innocence as Desdemona. She leaps into Othello's arms and is blissfully happy in the early stages of her married life. When the Moor strikes her it is a terrible moment, and when she sinks into isolation in the final scene the agony is intense.

Alongside these three outstanding performances, however, there are two which are less satisfying. Willard White has majesty, and is often melodious and mighty, but he misses the music. He relates the story of his past adventures in a way that would have captivated no woman, and, in effect, he never

7. A major theatrical event, Trevor Nunn's production of Othello at The Other Place and The Young Vic. Willard White as Othello and Imogen Stubbs as Desdemona.

recovers his poetic standing in our eyes.

Cassio is arrogant and class conscious. He barges his way into Cyprus with a swagger that makes him less than popular, but what he lacks is the charm that balances these traits – the charm that makes him recognisable as Othello's successor and persuades Desdemona to help him. Sean Baker misses this vital ingredient.

There are some excellent supporting performances from Clive Swift and Michael Grandage, and, even with its faults, this is a memorable production.

The Love of the Nightingale (1988)
TIMBERLAKE WERTENBAKER

The Pit 22 August–4 October 1989

Male Chorus **David Acton, Stephen Gordon, Patrick Miller and James Smith**
Soldier/Hippolytus **Patrick Miller**

Timberlake Wertenbaker's reworking of the legend of Philomele is a tale of love, violence and the cost of silence. It was first presented at The Other Place in 1988 and won the Central TV Eileen Anderson Drama Award for 1989.

Soldier/Theseus **David Acton**
Procne **Marie Mullen**
Philomele **Katy Behean**
King Pandion **James Smith**
Queen/Servant **Darlene Johnson**
Tereus **Peter Lennon**
Female Chorus **Cate Hamer,**

Darlene Johnson, Jill Spurrier and Claudette Williams
Captain **Tony Armatrading**
Niobe **Jenni George**
Itys **James Black/James Pratt**
Aphrodite **Claudette Williams**
Phaedra **Cate Hamer**

Nurse/Female Chorus **Jill Spurrier**
Male Chorus **Stephen Gordon**

Design **Iona McLeish**
Lighting **Geraint Pughe**
Music **Ilona Sekacz**
Director **Garry Hynes**

Pericles (1608)
WILLIAM SHAKESPEARE

The Swan from 12 September 1989

Gower **Rudolph Walker**
Pericles **Nigel Terry**
Marina **Suzan Sylvester**
Antiochus/Pandar **Michael Cadman**
Daughter of Antiochus **Sarah McVicar**
Thaliard **Niall Refoy**
Helicanus **Randall Herley**
Cleon **Peter Theedom**
Dyoniza **Jane Maud**
Messenger **Ade Sapara**
Leonine **Harry Miller**
Master Fisherman **Dennis Clinton**
King Simonides/Boult **Russell Dixon**
Thaisa **Sally Edwards**
Marshal/Philemon **Ian Driver**

David Thacker's début for the RSC came with this production of one of Shakespeare's least performed plays. It is a lively tale of lost and found, adventure, prostitution and murder. The text is uneven and uncertain, as is the play, but there are some powerful scenes ranging from fairy tale to brothel.

Lychorida **Jane Gwilliams**
Cerimon/Bawd **Helen Blatch**
Lysimachus **Rob Edwards**
Diana **Sally Edwards**
Princes, Pirates, Knights, Sailors, Fishermen etc. **Ian Driver, Daniel James, Harry Miller, Ade Sapara, Steven Waddington, Rob Edwards and Niall Refoy**
Citizens, Ladies, Whores **Helen Blatch, Sarah Booth, Jane Gwilliams and Sarah McVicar**

Design **Fran Thompson**
Lighting **Jimmy Simmons**
Choreographer **Lesley Hutchinson**
Sound **Tim Oliver**
Music **Mark Vibrans**
Musical Director **Roger Hellyer**
Director **David Thacker**

As You Like It (1599)
WILLIAM SHAKESPEARE

Royal Shakespeare Theatre from 13 September 1989

Oliver **Howard Ward**
Jaques de Boys **Jason Flemyng**
Orlando **Jerome Flynn**
Adam **Eric Francis**
Dennis **Adrian Hilton**
Duke Frederick/Duke Senior **Clifford Rose**

Harriet Walter was originally publicised to play the role of Rosalind, but the part was eventually played by Sophie Thompson, who had been touring with the Renaissance Theatre Company. This was the fourth Stratford production of *As You Like It* in 12 years, and John Caird emphasised the theme that the characters only discover their real selves in the forest away from the trappings of the court.

Celia **Gillian Bevan**
Rosalind **Sophie Thompson**
Touchstone **Mark Williams**
Monsieur Le Beau/Jaques **Hugh Ross**
Charles/William **Andrew Tansey**
Amiens **Craig Pinder**
Corin **George Malpas**
Silvius **Alan Cumming**
Audrey **Joanna Mays**
Sir Oliver Martext **Andrew Hesker**
Phebe **Cassie Stuart**

Goatgirls, Courtiers and Foresters **Judith Brydon, Joanna Mays, Clara Onyemere, Alison Ruffelle, Cassie Stuart, Alan Cumming, Simon D'Arcy, Jason Flemyng, Andrew Hesker, Adrian Hilton, Maxwell Hutcheon, David Joyce, George Malpas and Craig Pinder**
Children **Charlene O'Dowd, Louise Potter, Charlotte Potts, Minna Zouhou, Paul Brookes, Andrew Kwan, Robert Langley and Ray Lawley**

Design **Ultz**
Lighting **Alan Burrett**
Sound **Charles Horne**
Choreographer **Matthew Bourne**
Music **Ilona Sekacz**
Musical Directors **Michael Tubbs and John Woolf**
Director **John Caird**

The Master Builder (1892)

HENRIK IBSEN translated by Michael Meyer

Barbican from 26 September 1989

8. *Alfred Burke as Brovnik argues in vain with John Wood as Solness in Adrian Noble's mighty production of* The Master Builder.

Ibsen returned from his 28-year exile in Germany and Italy to his native Norway in 1892 and wrote *The Master Builder*. A few years later, he admitted that Solness 'is a man who is somewhat related to me', an admission that surprises none

Knut Brovik **Alfred Burke**
Ragnar Brovik **Duncan Bell**
Kaja Fosli **Geraldine Alexander**
Halvard Solness **John Wood**
Aline Solness **Marjorie Yates**
Dr Herdal **John Bott**
Hilde Wangel **Joanne Pearce**
Townspeople **Teresa Banham, Penny Jones, Lynn Kitch, Marjie Lawrence, Elizabeth Stewart, Richard Conway, Ian Embleton and Michael Gardner**
Musicians **Roderick Tearle, Peter Wright, Brian Newman, David Hissey, John Elliott and Richard Brown**

Design **Richard Hudson**
Lighting **Chris Parry**
Sound **Steff Langley**
Music **Howard Blake**
Musical Director **Richard Brown**
Director **Adrian Noble**

who have read or seen this soul-searching masterpiece.

The play revolves around Halvard Solness, a middle-aged architect who has swept all before him but now fears the threat of youth. He exploits and has exploited everyone to attain his eminent position, but his life is dry and cold, shadowed by a sense of guilt. He feels guilt that he was, in part, responsible for the loss, through fire, of the family house and of the subsequent death of his sons through infection. His wife mourns the loss of her house and her collection of dolls and accepts the loss of her children as an act of God.

Marjorie Yates plays Aline Solness with a dark understanding that has a chill about it. She convinces us that she has indeed 'just come up out of the tomb' – that she is, to all intents and purposes, dead and that Solness is chained to the corpse.

Richard Hudson's set is an inclined wall with the minimum of furniture, seemingly a denial of Ibsen's detailed realism, yet dramatically totally effective. John Wood's first entrance is through the gap, centre stage. He is dressed in black, a commanding figure, controller of the lives of those around him: Knut Brovik, the architect whose practice he has destroyed and whom he now employs; Ragnar, Brovik's son, whose talents and ambitions he frustrates out of fear for his own position; and Kaja, Ragnar's betrothed, whose affection he exploits so that he may tie her and Ragnar to his firm.

He talks of his fear of youth, but he is unsuspecting when three pronounced, dramatic knocks announce the arrival of Hilde Wangel. She has come to claim the promise that he made to her ten years previously when she was a child and he kissed her, that he would build her a kingdom. He has forgotten what was vital to her, but she drags the promise back through his memory.

As Hilde, Joanne Pearce gives a performance which is hauntingly beautiful and disturbing in the complexity of its understanding. Miss Pearce realises the core of Hilde's character – she is both the moth and the flame. She constantly offers lips and body to Solness and withdraws them at the last moment. She feels the excitement of how it must have been to have been taken by a Viking, but she retreats into herself at the realisation of what she has said, and all the time she leaves the chair rocking and measures the room with the playful steps of a child.

Solness is drawn to her because he cannot live without joy and because she awakens visions of castles in the air on a true foundation. She awakens too the awareness of the trolls and the demons that gnaw inside him and the awareness of the price he has paid for his creative ability as an artist; but the

9. John Wood as Solness, Joanne Pearce as Hilde – the moth and the flame – in The Master Builder.

price he has paid is, in fact, the human happiness of others. His ultimate despair, shouted out in agonisingly fatal tones, is that his life, his career, has added up to 'nothing, nothing, nothing'.

Hilde persuades him to put aside his fear of heights and to climb to the top of the tower of his new creation and there converse with God. He goes to his death while Hilde waves her flag of dreams.

John Wood's Solness is a rare achievement, for it is a physical and intellectual masterpiece. He is ever haunted by his demons, but ever eager for the joy in life. He fears that his luck is coming to an end, but he welcomes Hilde both as renewal and retribution. Rarely has one seen an actor by his every gesture, expression and inflection convey a character so completely. We are left with a clarity of perception which is almost frightening in its power. The success of the performance is enhanced in that it is not conducted in isolation but is interwoven with Joanne Pearce's Hilde and with an excellent supporting cast: Geraldine Alexander, the young, impressionable book-keeper, ensnared by Solness;

Duncan Bell, the ambitious and frustrated young architect; and Alfred Burke, his broken father.

Of Joanne Pearce, it must be added that this performance brings her to the front rank of young actresses.

Adrian Noble's direction has an intelligence and intensity of emotion and understanding that make *The Master Builder* one of the great theatrical events of the year, and indeed of all time.

Mary and Lizzie (1989)
FRANK McGUINESS

The Pit from 27 September 1989

A rich and strange comic fantasy about two Irish sisters, Mary and Lizzie Burns, who lived with Frederick Engels.

Mary Burns **Maureen Beattie**
Lizzie Burns **Lesley Sharp**
Pregnant Girl **Cate Hamer**
Old Woman/Mother Ireland **Pip Hinton**
Magical Priest, her son **Nicholas Woodeson**
Mother Burns **Darlene Johnson**
Father Burns/Pig **Robert Demeger**
Queen Victoria **Nicholas Woodeson**
Karl Marx **Simon Dormandy**
Frederick Engels **Simon Russell Beale**
Jenny Marx **Katy Behean**
Boy **Timothy Stark**
Women **Kate Byers, Maggie Carr, Jane Cox, Candida Gubbins, Caroline Harding and Louise Kerr**

Design **Ultz**
Lighting **Geraint Pughe**
Music **Shaun Davey**
Musical Director **Peter Washtell**
Director **Sarah Pia Anderson**

10. Mary and Lizzie by Frank McGuiness: Marxism and Irish history and legend. Lesley Sharp as Lizzie and Simon Russell Beale as Engels.

McGuiness sends his characters on a journey through space and time in what Milton Shulman described as 'a weird and puzzling dramatic experience'. Communism, Irish history and mythology and the private life of Engels jostle each other throughout the play.

In the autumn, the Royal Shakespeare Company again presented a season at the Almeida Theatre in Islington. As well as three major productions, there were seven late night shows of work by Ionesco, O'Neill and others, and 13 lunch-time performances ranging from Mamet and Rudkin to David Holman and James Pettifer.

King Lear (1605)
WILLIAM SHAKESPEARE

Almeida Theatre 14 September–28 October 1989

Earl of Kent **Colin McCormack**
Earl of Gloucester **Desmond Barrit**
Edmund **Patrick Robinson**
Lear **Richard Haddon Haines**
Goneril **Marie Mullen**
Duke of Albany **Peter Lennon**
Regan **Jill Spurrier**
Duke of Cornwall **David Acton**
Cordelia **Amanda Root**
Duke of Burgundy/Servant/Doctor/
Old Man **Stephen Gordon**
King of France/Oswald **Paul Hargreaves**
Edgar **James Purefoy**

Cicely Berry, the RSC voice coach, made it clear that her approach to the play was 'by speaking it, finding the movement and texture of the language, its rhetoric, listening to what it says to us and coming to conclusions about character and relationships afterwards'. The result was a production that focused as much on Edgar's rise as on Lear's fall, brought some strong performances from supporting actors and, for most, was a good production of a great play.

Fool **Patrick Miller**
Gentleman/Captain **Ken Shorter**

Design **Chris Dyer**
Lighting **Robert A Jones**

Sound **Tim Oliver**
Choreographer **Lesley Hutchinson**
Director **Cicely Berry**

Kissing the Pope (1989)
NICK DARKE

Almeida Theatre 21 September–26 October 1989

Heck **Edward Peel**
Pedro/Edwin **Jason Watkins**
Cascabel/Rico **Kevin Doyle**

Nick Darke's play is about Nicaragua and the conflict between Contras and Sandinistas. It depicts the problems as arising directly from American intervention.

Julio/Skinny Girl **Julia Tarnosky**
Louisa/Juanita **Vivienne Rochester**
Sanchez **Mark Hadfield**
Emilio **Christian Dixon**
Josue/Vulture/Miguel **Jack James**

Chico/Pablo **Paul Sykes**
Eco **Dominic Rickhards**
Aldo/Hernandez **Richard Bremner**

Design **Eryl Ellis and Kenny**

MacLellan
Costume **Allan Watkins**
Lighting **Stanley Osborne-White**
Director **Roger Michell**

H.I.D. (Hess is Dead) (1989)
HOWARD BRENTON

Almeida Theatre 28 September–24 October 1989

Larry Palmer **David Calder**
Charity Luber **Polly Walker**
Officer **Mark Strong**
Professor Nicole D'Arcy **Diane Fletcher**
Professor Raymond Trace **Pip Donaghy**

Taking as its starting-point the identity of the man who committed suicide in Spandau prison in 1987, and indeed questioning whether or not it was suicide, Howard Brenton has written a play which raises the debate about rewriting history and obliterating memories of Nazi atrocities to suit present political convenience.

Design **Eryl Ellis and Kenny MacLellan**

Lighting **Geraint Pughe**
Choreographer **Gaby Agis**

Music **Lodewijk De Boer**
Director **Danny Boyle**

In an exceptionally busy year for the RSC, *Coriolanus*, with Charles Dance in the title role, joined the repertoire at the Royal Shakespeare Theatre in December. At the same time, Harriet Walter opened as the Duchess of Malfi at The Swan. *All's Well That Ends Well*, directed by Barry Kyle, opened at the main Stratford theatre in October, and *Singer* followed *Pericles* at The Swan.

A Midsummer Night's Dream and *Romeo and Juliet* each toured nine centres in the autumn, and a co-production with Opera North of *Show Boat* is scheduled both for Stratford and for a national tour in 1990. *Hamlet* and *A Midsummer Night's Dream* are transferring to the Barbican in November, and a production of *A Clockwork Orange* is planned for the New Year. The Pit will welcome *Dr Faustus* and *Romeo and Juliet* from The Swan, and there will be new productions of Poliakoff's *Playing with Trains*, starring Michael Pennington, and of Julius Hay's *Have*.

It concludes a good year for the RSC. In 1988, *The Plantagenets* seemed to suggest that a bleak period was at an end. The work in 1989 has confirmed that feeling. *The Master Builder* was among the outstanding productions of the year as were *Othello* and Caird's *A Midsummer Night's Dream.*

With the help of the generous sponsorship from Royal Insurance and from other sponsors, grants and incentive funding, the accumulated deficit which weighed so heavily on the RSC has now been cleared. There is a generally healthier atmosphere about the whole company. The significant news was, of course, that Terry Hands is to leave the RSC. At the time of going to press, the question as to who would succeed him was one of the main talking points in the theatre world. Adrian Noble is obviously a strong contender, and David Thacker is one of the outsiders who has been mentioned.

One of the happiest aspects of dealing with the RSC in 1989 was contact with the courteous, helpful and effective public and press relations office under Caro Newling and Zoe Mylchreest. Any theatre that puts you in a good mood and makes you feel wanted before you get there is doing its job well.

SECTION FOUR

Outer London, Fringe and Theatre Clubs

1. Ian Hughes and Pamela Nomvete in Daniel Scott's Below the Belt, *one of five new plays by young writers presented in repertoire at the Soho Poly Theatre.*

Almeida Theatre

ALMEIDA STREET, ISLINGTON, LONDON N1
01-359-4404

Anything for a Quiet Life (1988)
devised by THEATRE DE COMPLICITÉ

11–21 January 1989

with **Annabel Arden, Celia Gore Booth, Kathryn Hunter, Marcello Magni, Myra McFadyen, Stefan Metz and Boris Ostan**

Design **Jan Pienkowski**
Lighting **Jon Linstrum**

In this work, Theatre de Complicité invents a farcical scenario of office life. The scenes include a board meeting and an office party. Critics were unanimous as to the brilliance of the company. Words of praise ranged from 'the most dazzling show in the repertoire' to Michael Coveney's 'sheer magic'.

Director **Simon McBurney**

The Vinegar Works (1989)
EDWARD GOREY

24–8 January 1989

with **Julia Bardsley, Richard Edwards, Martin Gent, Rosalind Knight, Phelim McDermott, Ross Muir, Lee Simpson, and students from West Sussex Theatre Studios**

Design **Phelim McDermott**
Costume **Cinzia Friedlander and**
Hilary Niederer
Lighting **Christopher Toulmin**
Music **John Winfield**

Three volumes of moral instruction, *The Gashleycrumb Tinies*, *The Insect God* and *The West Wing*, formed the centre-piece of the Eleventh London Mime Festival. Edward Gorey is an American illustrator and writer of Gothic stories, and Gothic cautionary humour was the tone of this offering.

Director **Julia Bardsley and Phelim McDermott**

Polygraph (1988)

ROBERT LE PAGE and MARIE BRASSARD, with
PIERRE-PHILIPPE GUAY translated by Gillian Raby

23 February–4 March 1989

Lucie Champagne **Marie Brassard**
Antoine Le Breton **Robert Le Page**
Francois **Pierre-Philippe Guay**

Design **Robert Le Page**
Lighting **Eric Fauque**
Music **Janintors Animated**
Director **Robert Le Page**

A fictional reproduction of a true story and presented by a French-Canadian company, *Polygraph* describes the impact of the murder of a 22-year-old girl on a pathologist, an actress and a waiter whose lives are connected with the girl and with each other. Neither killer nor victim appears. It was described as a most inventive piece of theatre.

Indigo (1987)

HEIDI THOMAS

9 March–1 April 1989

Ide **Hakeem Kae-Kazim**
Mamila **Caroline Lee Johnson**
Mobote **Carlton Chance**
Amda **John Adewole**
William Randall **Dougray Scott**
Samuel Randall **P J Davidson**
Pearson **Brian Protheroe**
Barney **Charlie Creed-Miles**
Pluto **Darren Cudjoe**

First produced by the RSC at The Other Place in 1987, *Indigo* is set in the 18th century and spans two continents. It tells the story of two young men in revolt against their fathers: William Randall, whose father is a slave-trader; and Ide, an African prince.

Design **Catherine Armstrong**
Lighting **Sam Garwood**

Music **Jonathan Whitehead**
Director **Keith Boak**

Mozart and Salieri (1830)

ALEXANDER PUSHKIN translated by Lore Brunner and Tilda Swinton, and adapted by Manfred Karge

Mozart **Tilda Swinton**
Salieri **Lore Brunner**
Blind Violinist **Barbara Schmidt**

Design **Manfred Karge**
Music **Mozart**
Director **Manfred Karge**

7 April–6 May 1989

Pushkin's 50-minute play anticipated Shaffer's *Amadeus* by more than 130 years and is generally regarded as rather lightweight. This production with an all-female cast was in conjunction with theatres in Berlin and Vienna.

The Georgian Film Actors' Studio from Tblisi presented their adaption of Molière's *Don Juan* from 16 to 27 May 1989.

The Studio Celavek, Moscow, offered *Cinzano* by Ludmila Petrushevska from 10 to 15 July; and the second presentation in the London International Festival of Theatre was *Fallen Angels and The Devil Concubine*, written by Pat Cumper and performed by the Groundwork Theatre Company of Jamaica.

The Royal Shakespeare Theatre Company's productions at the Almeida will be found in the RSC section.

Beck Theatre

GRANGE ROAD, HAYES, MIDDLESEX
01-561-8371

While the Beck Theatre, concerned mainly with music, dance and cinema, does not fall strictly within the province of this section, it would be ungracious to omit mention of a place which is eager, enthusiastic and forthcoming in communication, being particularly generous in its press releases.

Charlie Drake and Lynda Baron starred in the Christmas pantomime, *Jack and the Beanstalk*; and Frankie Howerd and Honor Blackman were others to appear there early in the year.

Fenton Gray and Stephanie Prince in Steven Berkoff's *Decadence*; the *Meg and Mog Show*; the touring production of *And Then There Were None*; Paul Darrow in *Alibi for Murder*; the Argosy Players' production of *The Three Sisters*; the New Vic's *Robin Hood*; Bernie Winters and Richard Whitmore in *Underneath the Arches*; *The Business of Murder* with Richard Todd, Peter Byrne and Sandra Paine; and *Doctor on the Boil* were among the professional theatre productions to be staged during the year. Jan Harvey, Stephen Yardley and Peter Simon will star in the 1989–90 Christmas pantomime, *Babes in the Wood*.

Bloomsbury Theatre

15 GORDON STREET, LONDON WC1H 0AH
01-387-9629

Director **Andy Arnold**

La Gran Scena Opera Co

7–18 February 1989

Vera Galupe-Borszkh **Ira Siff**
Fodor Szedan/Gabriella Tonnozitti-Casseruola **Keith Jurosko**
Philene Wannelle **Philip Koch**
Sylvia Bills **Bruce Hopkins**
The Brothers Atillanbuccanegra **Carlo Thomas**
Alfredo Sorta-Pudgi **Charles Walker**
Ensemble **David Michael Sabella**
Daniela della Scarpone **Daniel Gundlach**
Maestro Coglioni **Ross Barentyne**

'Inspired visual lunacy in the great tradition of the Marx Brothers and Mel Brooks' was Rodney Milnes's description of this group of men from New York who offer alternative versions of great opera and a peep behind the scenes. They were universally acclaimed as very funny and highly professional iconoclasts.

Design **Cobalt Studios**
Costume **Kenneth M Yount**
Lighting **Richard Coumbs**

Musical Director **Ross Barentyne**
Director **Jane Whitehill, Peter Schlosser and Ira Siff**

Cold Turkey (1989)

devised by BLOOMSBURY THEATRE COMPANY

4–15 April 1989

Toby **Phil Nice**
Mikhail **Paul Mark Elliott**
Bobby **Jenny Lecoat**
Humper **Andy Smart**
Miranda **Maria Callous**

The Bloomsbury Theatre Company, formed by performers from the London cabaret circuit, gave *Cold Turkey* as their first production. The play finds five social outcasts spending New Year's Eve in a DSS hotel. They have little in common and hardly any drink, but they are determined to make what they can of the evening.

Design **Mini Grey**

Lighting **Elaine Grimes**

Director **Nick Broadhurst**

The all-black production of *The Importance of Being Earnest* from the Tyne Theatre, Newcastle, under which details will be found, ran 16–27 May 1989. Donna and Kebab in *Acropolis Now!*, an amusing and sharp observation of everything Greek, played at the Bloomsbury in June, and the National Youth Theatre performed Arnold Wesker's *The Kitchen* in August.

Bush Theatre

SHEPHERDS BUSH GREEN, LONDON W12 8QD
01-743-3388

Artistic Directors **Nicky Pallot and Brian Stirner**

Utopia (1989)
CLAIRE MacDONALD

31 January–25 February 1989

with **Richard Hawley and Jan Pearson**

Design **Simon Vincenzi**
Music **Jocelyn Pook**
Director **Pete Brooks**

The co-founders of Impact Theatre Co-operative have developed a three-act play which uses 'sound as structure and where ritualistic drama powers the interplay of a man and a woman'. The couple create a fantasy world, and the performances of Richard Hawley and Jan Pearson were highly praised in this piece of welcome experimental drama.

Bush Theatre was also in operation at the Riverside Studios, where Brian Stirner directed *The Fatherland*.

The One-Sided Wall (1989)
JANET CRESSWELL and NIKI JOHNSON

28 February–25 March 1989

Theresa Seymour **Cindy Oswin**

Design **Simon Vincenzi**
Music **Andrew Poppy**
Director **Niki Johnson**

Janet Cresswell has been an inmate of Broadmoor since 1976 and although she offers this monologue as a work of fiction, it is apparent that it has a strong autobiographical basis. The patient, having been sexually abused by a general practitioner, is recommended for forced psychiatric treatment by her abuser. So begins the train of events which leads to her incarceration. The play represents the patient's case for release to a mental tribunal, and it was received with great sympathy.

The Way South (1988)
JACQUELINE HOLBOROUGH

5 April–7 May 1989

Commissioned by the National Theatre Studio and performed

Casey **Annette Crosby**
Jo **Sharon Duce**
Liam **Robert Hines**

Design **Alison Chitty**
Lighting **Ben Ormerod**
Sound **Rachel Gray**
Director **John Burgess**

to an invited audience there in December 1988, *The Way South* is a further exploration of issues concerning women and the law by Jacqueline Holborough. It is based on her own experience of the system. Some saw the fact that we are not told why Jo is serving a hard sentence as being a weakness, but it was generally considered to be compelling theatre.

The Marshalling Yard (1989)

TED MOORE

24 May–8 July 1989

Taller **Paul Dalton**
Ken **Tom Georgeson**
Rooney **Tom Mannion**
Vera **Sheila Reid**

Design **Robin Don**
Lighting **Rick Fisher**
Sound **Colin Brown**
Location Sound **Nicholas Fischtel**
Director **Brian Stirner**

An inspiring set with a vast expanse of railway lines in the background and a staff hut/kitchen in the foreground set the mood for Ted Moore's first stage play. Ken is an ageing workman whose wife, Vera – 'condemned to live in a coal hole with a man who doesn't love me' – is suffering from a nervous breakdown. Ken used to act as a surrogate father to the ambitious and self-improving Taller, who is now the marshalling yard foreman. Taller has been replaced in Ken's life by Rooney, a shiftless ex-mercenary who becomes the old man's protector and centre of affection. This is a

2. Sheila Reid and Tom Georgeson – sensitive performances in The Marshalling Yard *at the Bush Theatre.*

3. Tom Mannion in The Marshalling Yard *at the Bush Theatre.*

claustrophobic world, a masculine society with a latent homosexuality beneath the daily grind of physical work. Vera has been driven to her condition by her isolation from this masculine world, but there is a tender scene of reconciliation and hope when Ken courts her for a second time in hospital.

We are never told much about the work which enslaves and unites the men and there is little dramatic action, but there is some fine writing here. Ted Moore has written several radio plays, has worked on the railways and has been a physiotherapist. He draws on his experiences for *The Marshalling Yard*, and the result is a very good first play for the theatre and, more importantly, a promise of better to come. Having said this, one must add that no playwright could have been better served by designer, director, sound designer and cast than Ted Moore.

Tom Georgeson was a greying, wilting Ken, breathing defeat and impotence. Paul Dalton was eagerly mobile; and Tom Mannion had the right blend of surliness, good nature, mystery and aggression in a splendid piece of characterisation. Sheila Reid's Vera had the right air of detachment, vulnerability and suffering in a performance that was delicate and moving.

Songs of Soweto

11–23 July 1989

with **Cleo Dorcas, Eddie Thengani and Charmaine Holder**

Musicians **Peter Goodwin (bass), Alan Hughes (percussion), Keith Holden (harmonica), Simon Bild (guitar) and Andrew Harrod (piano)**

An evening of South African music led by Cleo Dorcas, who was born in Soweto and began singing in the townships at an early age. The evening was so popular that *Songs of Soweto* returned to the Bush in September and October.

Looking At You (Revived) Again played at the Bush from 26 July to 20 August. It was a Haymarket Theatre, Leicester, production and details will be found under that theatre.

Boys Mean Business (1989)
CATHERINE JOHNSON

13 September–28 October 1989

Natalie **Adie Allen**
Will **Paul Brightwell**
Gary **Reece Dinsdale**
Elvis **Richard Graham**
Dawn **Melissa Wilson**

Design **Michael Taylor**
Lighting **Paul J Need**
Sound **Colin Brown**
Director **Brian Stirner**

Brothers Gary and Will, one-time members of a defunct punk band, eke out a meagre living in Weston-super-Mare. Will is homeless and sleeps in a hut. He dresses in an animal suit and poses with children while Gary takes photos. The rivalry and ambitions of the brothers are the centre of the comedy, and Catherine Johnson's delineation of her characters was particularly well received.

Billy Roche's new play, *Poor Beast in the Rain*, opened on 8 November 1989. It is set in a betting shop in Wexford on the eve of the all-Ireland hurling final.

DOC Theatre Club

DUKE OF CAMBRIDGE, 64 LAWFORD ROAD, KENTISH TOWN, LONDON NW5 2LN
01-485-4303

Washday (1988)

F C DELIUS translated by Vera Fuchs

11 July–5 August 1989

Willmers **Kim Fenton**
Keller **Stephen Gough**
Gatow **Robin Malyon**
Uhlendorff **Tom Skippings**

Design **Tahra Kharibian**
Costume **Tracey Smith**

Four high-ranking Nazi officers are sentenced to varying terms of imprisonment in Spandau. On Mondays they meet for washday. One by one they are released until only Keller (Hess) is left. This black comedy caused much stir in Germany and was warmly received in its English translation at the DOC.

Lighting **Guy Retallack**   Director **Olivia Fuchs**

Edge (1989)

JOHN CASSON

22 August–9 September 1989

Johnny Cheevers **Michael Goldie**
Charlie **Tom Knight**
Jeannie **Hilary Townley**

Design **Naomi Wilkinson**
Director **Leona Heimfeld**

Set in the derelict basement of a swimming baths on the night of a boxing promotion, *Edge* is a raw and often moving play about the life of a small-time boxer, his manager and his wife. Like the earlier presentation at the DOC, it was well received.

Hard Feelings (1982)

DOUG LUCIE

10 October–4 November 1989

Viv **Monica Lowenberg**
Jane **Yvonne Ramos-Gonzalez**
Baz **Stephen Pallister**

Set in 1981 at the time of the Brixton riots, *Hard Feelings* features a group of Oxford graduates who are privileged, self-indulgent and insensitive to the world outside. It is typical

Tone **Robin Olett**
Anne **Liz Greenaway**
Rusty **Michael Ashby**

Director **Sam Kogan**

of Lucie's attacks on the contemporary hard, uncaring lifestyle.

Drill Hall

16 CHENIES STREET, LONDON WC1E 7ET
01-637-8270

What is Seized (1988)

POLLY TEALE from a story by Lorrie Moore

12–28 January 1989

with **Julianne Mason**

Design **Andrea Carr**
Lighting **Ace McCarron**
Director **Polly Teale**

Originally presented at the National Theatre Studio, Polly Teale's play is an amusing and painful evocation of an American childhood.

A Vision of Love Revealed in Sleep (1987)

NEIL BARTLETT from the book by Simeon Solomon

2–18 March 1989

with **Neil Bartlett, Bette Bourne, Ivan Cartwright and Regina Fong**

Design **Robin Whitmore**
Costume **Juliet Hamilton**
Lighting **David Kavanagh and Neil Bartlett**

Described as an evening of gay pride and prejudice, Neil Bartlett's play is a tribute to Simeon Solomon, who was imprisoned for homosexual practice in 1873 and died in a workhouse where Centre Point now stands. Bartlett takes a tour of Solomon's life in a piece which was very well received.

Musical Director **Nicolas Bloomfield**

Next To You I Lie occupied the theatre from 20 April to 6 May 1989.

Plague of Innocence (1988)

NOEL GREIG

11–27 May 1989

Winston **Mark Crowshaw**
Julie/Sarah **Mendinah Grae**
Gerald **Damian Myerscough**
Spider **Jenni Myhill**

Design **Ali Allen and Marise Rose**

Originally produced at the Crucible Theatre, Sheffield, *Plague of Innocence* is set in the not-too-distant future. It is a fantasy of politically motivated fear and oppression.

Lighting **Kim Nichols**   Director **Alan Dix**
Music **Lawrie Wright**

Mother Poem (1989)

EDWARD KAMAU BRAITHWAITE

30 May–17 June 1989

with **Josette Bushell-Mingo, Andrie Reid and Joan Carol Williams**

Design **Vonnie Roudette**
Lighting **Paul Armstrong**
Choreographer and Musical Director

Temba Theatre Company's touring production of Braithwaite's celebration of his native island, Barbados. This was followed, 6–22 July, by Staunch Poets and Players presentation of *Tim Tim*, devised and performed by George Alphonse.

'H' Patten   Director **Alby James**

Little Women: The Tragedy (1988)

DEBORAH MARGOLIN with additional material by Peggy Shaw and Louisa M Alcott

5–30 September 1989

with **Peg Healey, Peggy Shaw and Lois Weaver**

Design **Susan Young**
Director **Lois Weaver**

The American feminist group Split Britches's ramble round Louisa M Alcott's life and most famous work in an irreverent manner.

5–22 October 1989, at the Drill Hall the Gay Sweatshop Theatre Company were in Noel Greig's *Paradise Now and Then*.

Gate Theatre Club

ABOVE PRINCE ALBERT PUB, 11 PEMBRIDGE ROAD, NOTTING HILL, LONDON W11
01-229-0706

Artistic Director **Giles Croft**

The Infant (1783)

DENIS IVANOVICH FONVIZIN translated by Joshua Cooper

3–28 January 1989

Mrs Simple **Flip Webster**
Trishka/Boschmann **James Castle**
Mitrofan **Adam Ray**
Simple **Jeremy Rawlinson**
Beast **Steven Wickham**
Mrs Jeremy **Deva Palmier**
Sophia **Kate Byers**
Trueman **Richard Bates**
Milo **Matthew Byam Shaw**
Priestling **Guy Moore**
Figgures **Peter Wear**
Oldwise **George Pensotti**

Design **Camilla Bates**
Lighting **Jon Linstrom**
Director **Giles Croft**

The Gate Theatre embarked on its tenth anniversary season with a series of productions of unjustly neglected international plays. *The Infant*, written by a favourite at the court of Catherine the Great, is about Mrs Simple, a farmer's wife, who rules her household in a tyrannous manner and dotes on her ignorant son. The Simples' illegal ward, Sophia, suddenly becomes an heiress, and Mrs Simple abandons her plan to marry Sophia to her pig-loving brother and reselects Master Simple as her husband to be. It is a mixture of comedy and morality, and this vigorous, well-acted production was warmly received for its enterprise and quality.

4. Adam Ray and Flip Webster in the most interesting revival of The Infant *at the Gate.*

Thunder in the Air (1907)

AUGUST STRINDBERG translated by Eivor Martinus

1–25 February 1989

The Man **Derek Smith**
Louise **Rebecca Saire**
Mr Starck **Joseph Brady**
Karl Fredrik **George Pensotti**
Mr Fischer **Mark Jennings**
Agnes **Maria Brown**
Gerda **Kim Thomson**

Design **Alex Clarke**
Costume **Jean Kelly**
Lighting **Chris Davies**
Sound **Charlotta Martinus**
Director **Derek Martinus**

'London's most adventurous Fringe theatre' is how Michael Billington described the Gate after their staging of the late Strindberg play, *Thunder in the Air*. It is a play about loneliness and the imprisonment of oneself within one's own skin. The hero discovers that his young ex-wife is living in the flat above with their daughter. The knowledge and their meeting brings momentary chaos before the old man returns to his slow march towards death. It is a calmer work than much of Strindberg, and it was rapturously acclaimed in this production and translation. Kim Thomson and Derek Smith gave very fine performances in a strong cast.

The Colony (1750)

PIERRE CARLET DE CHAMBLAIN DE MARIVAUX
translated by Peter Kenvyn

28 February–25 March 1989

Arthenice **Beverley Foster**
Madame Sorbin **Anne Chauveau**
Timagene **Michael Charlesworth**
Monsieur Sorbin **Peter Kenvyn**
Persinet **Mark Ravina**
Lina **Rebecca Clay**

Deputy **Marie-Christine Guillois**
Women in Attendance and Singers
Lilian Evans, Tina Dean, Sarah-Jane Lovett, Clea Friend, Alexandra Boyd and Cheryl Anne Burt
Hemocrate **Richard Bates**

Cellists **Clea Friend and Nicola Marks**

Music **Peter Kenvyn**
Director **Maggi Law**

Island of Slaves (1729)

PIERRE CARLET DE CHAMBLAIN DE MARIVAUX
translated by Peter Kenvyn

28 February–25 March 1989

Iphicrate **Michael Charlesworth**
Arlequin **Mark Ravina**
Trivelin **Richard Bates**

Both plays are set on desert islands and wittily explore the question of equality and of women's place in society. The two plays provided an excellent finale to the Gate's international season.

Islanders **Anne Chauveau and Rebecca Clay**
Cleanthis **Lilian Evans**

Euphrosine **Sarah-Jane Lovett**

Design **Louise Bone**

Lighting **Jeanine Davies**
Director **Astrid Hilne**

Teaser (1984)

MICK YATES

28 March–1 April 1989

Julie **Katherine Fry**

Design **Neil Richardson**
Director **Amanda Parker**

Julie, a single parent deserted by her footballer boyfriend, earns her keep as Ravishing Rita, the stripping traffic warden. Mick Yates's play, first performed at the New End, allows Julie to share with us some of the more ridiculous and more troublesome moments of her life.

The Turn of the Screw (1988)

THE SHADOW SYNDICATE from the story by Henry James

4–15 April 1989

Douglas **Charlie Balfour**
Governess **Beatrice Comins**
Flora **Fiona Kane**
Miles **David Young**
Mrs Grose **Steph Bramwell**

Design **Ali Maclaurin**
Lighting **Charlie Balfour**

A fine adaptation and presentation of the famous ghost story concerning a governess and two children, the Shadow Syndicate's version won a first award at the Edinburgh Fringe in 1988.

Films **Martin Gammon and David Young**
Music **Adrian Johnston**

Director **Jon Pope**

Hawk Moon (1986)

SAM SHEPPARD

18 April–6 May 1989

Billie Joe **Robert Clare**

Design **Michael McLoughlin**
Lighting **Gillian McBride**

Sam Sheppard's monologue of a rodeo bull-rider's life and loneliness.

Sound **Rosalind Ellman**

5. Ian Saville, *the socialist conjuror*, Getting Nowhere – Again *at the Gate.*

Getting Nowhere – Again (1989)

9–27 May 1989

Ian Saville, the socialist conjuror, takes a journey through time and space looking at socialist heroes, comedy and culture and trying to visualise what a socialist Utopia would look like. Ian Saville was a *Time Out* award winner in 1987.

Mercedes (1984)

THOMAS BRASCH translated by Emily King

30 May–17 June 1989

The British première of a play written by Thomas Brasch, who

6. Vincent Pickering in Mercedes.

Sakko **Vincent Pickering**
Oi **Emily King**
Voice of Man in Car **Don Fellows**

Design **Rose Garrard**
Lighting **Kate Carrol**
Director **Julia Pascal**

was expelled from East Germany in 1976. *Mercedes* is set in a scrap-yard, and features two characters who are unemployed and a dummy. It is a piece of expressionist drama using Mercedes as a metaphor for modern Germany.

The Task (1980)

HEINER MULLER translated by Carl Weber

20 June–8 July 1989

The Red Shift Theatre Company and the Gate Theatre combined to present Theatre of Resistance in Muller's

Galloudec **Mike Packer**
Debuisson **Robin Brooks**
Sasportas **Carlton Chance**
First Love **Niki Johnson**

Design **Carmel Said**
Costume **Donatella Barbieri**
Lighting **Jonathan Holloway**
Music **Steve Martland**

'memory of a revolution'. The revolution in question is the French one; the year in question is 1794, when three men are sent by the French Assembly to stir up rebellion in the Antilles. Muller's thesis is that the French Revolution was a theatrical spectacle, but most critics found the play heavy in rhetoric, showing only flashes of political illumination.

Director **Robert Rae**

Vera Baxter (1972)

MARGUERITE DURAS translated by Philippa Wehle

11–19 July 1989

Vera Baxter **Anne Bernardi**
Stranger **Brian Deacon**
Monique Combes **Ruth Vaughan**
Michel Cayre **Owen Scott**
Bartender **Martin Waller**

Design **Cathy Ryan**
Lighting **Gillian McBride**
Director **Peter Moffat**

Aphra Behn Theatre Company gave the first production in Great Britain of what Marguerite Duras has described as her most exact and truthful work. Vera Baxter is a lonely woman who has been faithful to a philandering, gambling husband. There is a confessional conversation between Vera and one of her husband's mistresses, and there is the elusive revelation of Vera's character. It is accepted that this is not one of Duras's best plays, but – following on Foco Novo's wonderful production of *Savannah Bay* in 1988 – one hopes that there will be a revival of interest in this writer's work.

The Jury Will Ignore That Last Remark (1989)

presented by **NOT THE EDINBURGH FRINGE FESTIVAL**

4–26 August 1989

with **Peter Wear, Niall Ashdown, Cuthbert Clarke, Joe Hobbs and Lee Simpson**

So popular was this improvised satire of court room drama and the law that it returned for eight more performances in September. The audience was asked to provide locations, objects and events; from these the cast contrived a case.

The Wonder (1714)

SUSANNAH CENTLIVRE

30 August–23 September 1989

Don Lopez **Victor Whelan**
Isabella **Anna Mazzotti**
Don Felix **Christopher Eccleston**
Violante **Sue Flack**
Don Pedro **Roy Spencer**
Frederick **Ricky Clark**
Colonel Briton **Harry Burton**
Gibby **Robin Cameron**
Vasquez **Danny Miller**
Flora **Evelyn Doggart**
Lissardo **Kevin O'Donohoe**
Jinis **Barbara Penny**

Design **Damian Doran**
Lighting **Ace McCarrow**
Choreographer **Frances**

A masculine looking English actress and dramatist who delighted in playing men's parts, Susannah Centlivre had two unhappy marriages before settling down happily with Joseph Centlivre, cook to Queen Anne. *The Wonder* or *A Woman Keeps a Secret* is set in Portugal, where one grandee is planning to marry his daughter to a rich old man, and another is planning to send his into a convent. There is also a British colonel in the action. After many intrigues, lovers are united and all ends happily. David Garrick enjoyed great success as Don Felix and Anne Oldfield as Violante in the 18th century, when the play was highly popular. The Gate and the Escapade Theatre Company are to be congratulated in giving people an opportunity to see this play in what was hailed as a vibrant production.

Director **Caroline Lynch**

The Struggle (1989)

ROBERT ROYSTON

26 September–21 October 1989

Ruth **Carol Been**
Pietrus Van Zyl **Saul Reichlin**
Gumede **Osei Bentil**
Tim **Ilario Bisi-Pedro**
Al **Alfred Hoffman**
Newsreader **Peter Cartwright**

Design **Cathy Ryan**

Set in the 1990s, Robert Royston's play predicts increasing violent conflict in his native South Africa. Most critics felt that the play tried to say too much and was talking to the committed.

Lighting **Gillian McBride**   Director **Penny Ciniewicz**
Sound **Steve Lillywhite**

The English language première of Arthur Schnitzler's *Summer Breeze* with Glynis Barber played from 24 October to 18 November and was followed by Bulgarkov's *Adam and Eve*. Strindberg's *The Pelican* was scheduled to begin the 1990 season in this active and enterprising theatre.

Greenwich Theatre

CROOMS HILL, LONDON SE10
01-858-7755

Artistic Director **Sue Dunderdale** (resigned October 1989)

The Last Waltz (1986)
GILLIAN RICHMOND

30 January–4 February 1989

Christine Atkins **Cathryn Bradshaw**
Denise Brown **Amanda Redman**

Design **Simon Higlett**
Lighting **Kevin Sleep**
Sound **Steve Huttly**

Two army wives are dependent on each other, but the fact that the husband of one is soon to take a commission will inevitably bring a social divide between them. The play was first seen at the Soho Poly.

Director **Sue Wilson**

Othello (1604)
WILLIAM SHAKESPEARE

14 March–21 April 1989

Roderigo **Daniel Hill**
Iago **Paul Barber**
Brabantio/Policeman/Soldier **Carl Picton**
Othello **Clarke Peters**
Cassio **James Larkin**
Duke of Venice/ Lodovico **David Mallinson**
Senor/Montano **Zeh Prado**
Desdemona **Emily Morgan**

The directors tried to offer a modern colonialist interpretation of *Othello*, but the production was not well received. Only Emily Morgan, Dona Croll and Rita Wolf consistently won praise.

Emilia **Dona Croll**
Clown/Bianca **Rita Wolf**
Cypriot Soldier **Andrew Johnson**

Design **Henk Schut**

Lighting **Chic Reid**
Music **Andrea Hess**
Director **Sue Dunderdale and Hugh Quarshie**

Apocalyptic Butterflies (1988)
WENDY MacLEOD

2 May–3 June 1989

Inspired by the true story of a man who gave his son $4,000

Hank Tater **Brian Protheroe**
Muriel **Julia Swift**
Dick **Ian Thompson**
Francine **Barbara Lott**
Trudi **Amanda Donohoe**

worth of totem poles for his garden, this was described as a dismal American import.

Design **Penny Brown**
Lighting **Paul Need**

Sound **Steve Huttly**
Director **Sue Dunderdale**

The City Wives' Confederacy (1705)
SIR JOHN VANBRUGH

9 June–15 July 1989

Mrs Amlet **Julia Foster**
Mrs Cloggit/Jessamin/Clip **Peter Aubrey**
Brass **Mark Williams**
Dick **Christopher Fulford**
Flippanta **Dona Croll**
Clarissa **Emma Piper**
Araminta **Susan Kyd**
Corinna **Arkie Whiteley**

A very courageous revival of a long-neglected Vanbrugh comedy revolving around the favourite Restoration themes of marital disharmony, social snobbery and pretence. Julia Foster and Emma Piper won particular praise.

Moneytrap **Philip Lowrie**
Gripe **Bill Stewart**

Design **Norman Coates**

Lighting **Spike Gaden**
Director **Jonathan Myerson**

The Piggy Bank (1864)
EUGENE LABICHE adapted by C P Taylor from *La Cagnotte*

3 August–16 September 1989

Champbourcy **Bernard Lloyd**
Colladin **Robert Austin**
Cordenbois **Barry McCarthy**
Leonide/Madame Lea **Susan Colverd**
Blanche/Fifi **Katharine Rogers**
Felix/Cocarel **David Westhead**
Hotel Clerk **Liam Halligan**
Philippe Pareil **Jem Wall**
Trioche/Policeman **Colin Tarrant**
Bechut **Ric Morgan**

Design **Ruari Murchison**

A production of Labiche's farce in C P Taylor's adaptation which originated at the Derby Playhouse, *The Piggy Bank* tells of a group from the provinces who smash a piggy bank and decide to go to Paris for a trip on the money that emerges. They are seeking a variety of things – a corset, a lover, a new lover – and Colladin, a farmer, will only go if he can take a pig with him. The pig disgraces itself in a restaurant and the trippers refuse to pay the bill. They are flung into prison, escape and are pursued through the streets. They end up by hiding in an unfinished building.

Lighting **Nick Beadle**
Sound **Alan Jackson**

Director **Susan Todd**

An Evening with Queen Victoria

devised by KATRINA HENDREY

25–30 September 1989

Queen Victoria **Prunella Scales**

with **Ian Partridge** (tenor) **and Richard Burnett** (piano)
Director **Katrina Hendrey**

Prunella Scales's one-woman show of a portrait of Queen Victoria told through her own words which this fine actress has been touring for nearly two years.

Come for the Ride

2–7 October 1989

Patricia Routledge, with Chuck Mallett at the piano, provided another one-woman show. It included Miss Routledge's memorable portrayal of the poison-pen letter-writer from Alan Bennett's *Talking Heads*.

Talk of the Steamie (1985)

TONY ROPER

16 October–4 November 1989

Mrs Culfeathers **Julia McCarthy**
Margrit **Judy Sweeney**
Doreen **Emma Dingwall**
Dolly **Myra McFadyen**
Andy **Graham de Banzie**

Design **Sally Crabb**
Lighting **Tina MacHugh**
Sound **Matt McKenzie and Steve Huttly**
Music and Songs **David Anderson**

The title of the play has enlarged since it was performed in Nottingham in 1988 and, originally, at the Mayfest, but the plot remains the same – four women talking in a Glasgow Corporation laundry on New Year's Eve in the 1950s. It is an amiable tribute to the togetherness of the working class and was much admired in Alex Norton's production.

Musical Director **Bruce Ogston**
Director **Alex Norton**

Half Moon Theatre

213 MILE END ROAD, LONDON E1 4AA
01-790-4000

Artistic Director **John Turner**

A Common Woman (1983)

DARIO FO and FRANCA RAME translated by Gillian Hanna

7 February–4 March 1989

with **Gillian Hanna**

Design **Andrea Montag**
Lighting **Jon Linstrum**
Director **Sharon Miller**

Bless Me Father for I Have Sinned, *The Rape* and *Coming Home* are the three plays which comprise *A Common Woman*, a mixture of the hilarious, grotesque and tragic. Gillian Hanna, a founder member of Monstrous Regiment, translated and performed the plays.

Red Is the Colour of Night (1989)

PETER STORFER

8–25 March 1989

Ruth **Lawmary Champion**
Nurse Bellamy **Helen Griffin**
Sandy **Dave Kent**
Dr Kelly **Hamish McDonald**
Marte **Caroline Parker**

Design **Helen Turner**
Lighting **Liz Poulter**
Music **Dominique Le Gendre**
Director **Nic Fine**

Double Exposure Theatre Company is the only professional group in the country which integrates performers with and without disabilities. They won the highest praise for this piece, which is about Marte, diagnosed as autistic and institutionalised by her parents. She forms a friendship with Nurse Bellamy which is the only thing that can save her from the blind prejudice that has stifled her. Catherine Wearing wrote in *What's On*, 'the ensemble power of spoken text, sign language and music combine to create a theatre of clarity and communication'.

All Sewn Up (1989)

SU-LIN LOOI and BETH PORTER

18–29 March 1989

Ya Nan/Karen/Woman **Jacqui Chan**
Air Stewardess/Joanna **Leah Bracknell**

The Eastern Actors' Studio touring production about the relationship between three women, explored around the theme of making a new life in England when the older

Woman/Xiad Xue/Susie/Air Stewardess **Su-Lin Looi**
Hugh/Businessman/Immigration Officer/Uncle Sam **Paul Courtenay**

members of the family insist on keeping to the customs of the former homeland.

Lighting **Naomi Arnold**

Director **Beth Porter**

Regeneration (1989)

JONATHAN MOORE

17 April–20 May 1989

Miles **Michael Kingsbury**
Cranley **Jim Dunk**
Mick **James Harkishin**
Meadows **David Glover**
Peter **Tony Collins**
Judy **Sharon Cheyne**

Design **David Blight**
Lighting **Kevin Sleep**
Music **Test Department**
Director **Jonathan Moore**

Regeneration is a new play about the Docklands, regenerated for developers and money-makers rather than for those who once lived there.

Half Moon announced this as an appropriate title for a theatre which was setting out to reclaim its position as the true home of contemporary drama, music theatre and challenging entertainment. 'The Half Moon's resurgence is underway!' Unfortunately, no further communication was received from them for the rest of the year.

Blood Wedding (1932)

FEDERICO GARCIA LORCA translated by Jonathan Martin and Mary Ann Vargas

5–21 October 1989

Mother **Mona Hammond**
Bridegroom **Paul Bhattacharjee**
Neighbour/Beggarwoman **Jacqui Chan**
Mother in Law/Servant **Peggy Phango**
Wife **Meera Syal**
Leonardo **Okon Jones**
Little Girl **Tracy Harper**
Father/Woodcutter **Badi Uzzaman**
Bride **Janet Steel**

The Asian Co-operative Theatre's production of Lorca's powerful poetic drama of vendetta and elopement.

Girl/Moon **Sayan Akkadas**
Youths/Woodcutters **Yogesh Bhatt/David Mishra**

Design **Ashley Martin Davies and Nikki Gillibrand**

Lighting **Stephen Watson**
Choreographer **Shobaba Jeyasingh**
Music **Akintayo Akinbode**
Director **Jonathan Martin**

# Hampstead Theatre

SWISS COTTAGE CENTRE, LONDON NW3
01-722-9301

Artistic Director **Jenny Topper**

Valued Friends (1989)

STEPHEN JEFFREYS

9 February–1 April 1989

Sherry **Jane Horrocks**
Howard **Peter Capaldi**
Paul **Tim McInnery**
Marion **Serena Gordon**
Scott **Martin Clunes**
Stewart **Peter Caffrey**

Design **Sue Plummer**
Lighting **Gerry Jenkinson**
Director **Robin Lefevre**

Mike Leigh's *Smelling a Rat* being extended until 4 February, *Valued Friends* was Hampstead's first production of 1989. Four people rent a basement flat in Earl's Court. A property speculator offers each of them a considerable amount of money to move out so that he can sell the house at a substantial profit. His offer causes problems within their relationships and raises questions about contemporary values. The play was welcomed as an excellent and meaningful comedy, and performances and direction were highly praised.

Amongst Barbarians from the Royal Exchange, Manchester – under which details will be found – played from 7 April to 6 May 1989.

8–13 May 1989, *A Room of One's Own*, with Eileen Atkins as Virginia Woolf, was performed. It transferred to the Playhouse Theatre, London, under which details will be found.

The Debutante Ball (1988)

BETH HENLEY

23 May–1 July 1989

Violet Moon **Valerie Buchanan**
Jen Dugan Parker Turner **Sheila Gish**
Bliss White **Suzannah Harker**
Teddy Parker **Jane Horrocks**
Frances Walker **Caroline Parker**
Hank Turner **Duncan Preston**
Brighton Parker **Ronan Vibert**

Beth Henley has been welcomed as having restored the Southern voice to the American theatre. Her latest play to reach London, directed – like its predecessors – by Simon Stokes, is set in a mansion in Mississippi. Teddy is preparing for her coming-out party, but she is already pregnant by an elevator-man. Her mother has just escaped conviction for beating her first husband to death and has taken a rich man as

Design **Dermot Hayes**
Costume **Sharon Lewis**
Lighting **Paul Denby**
Director **Simon Stokes**

her second husband. She is a bizarre character, as are all those who assemble for the party in this play, the style of which was described as 'Southern Gothic'. Very well acted and designed, it was considered inferior to Miss Henley's earlier work, but was still entertaining and amusing.

Carthaginians (1988)

FRANK McGUINNESS

6 July–12 August 1989

Maela **Sorcha Cusack**
Greta **Stephanie Fayerman**
Sarah **Patricia Kerrigan**
Seph **John Keegan**
Dido **David Herlihy**
Hark **Ian McIlhenney**
Paul **Garrett Keogh**

Design **Wendy Shea**
Costume **Sheelagh Killeen**
Lighting **Paul Denby**
Music **Ilona Sekacz and John Leonard**

First performed at the Abbey Theatre, Dublin, Frank McGuinness's play is about the effect of Bloody Sunday (January 1972) on the people of Derry. There is the note of hope in that life must go on, but the theme of the play is McGuinness's assertion that there is no other memory than the memory of wounds. Michael Billington saw the play as 'literate, witty, allusive' and, in naming those who were killed on Bloody Sunday at the end of the play, McGuinness achieves a 'forceful simplicity'.

Director **Sarah Pia Anderson**

The Water Engine (1977)

DAVID MAMET

21 August–14 October 1989

Dave Murray **Stephen Boxer**
Lawrence Oberman **Nick Dunning**
Bernie **Aiden Gillen**
Morton Gross **Peter Jonfield**
Rita **Mary Maddox**
Mrs Varec **Michelle Newell**
Mr Wallace **Malcolm Terris**
Charles Lang **Peter Whitman**
Chain Letter **David Healey**

A short work by Mamet which is set in Chicago in 1934, *The Water Engine* is about man's fight against the institution. A young inventor creates an engine that will run on distilled water, but he is eventually murdered by those who want the invention suppressed.

Design **Robin Don**
Lighting **Nick Chelton**
Sound **John Leonard**

Music **Stephen Boxer**
Director **Robin Lefevre**

The Big Sweep (1989)

From 25 October 1989

with **Charlie Dore, Alan Hill, George Kahn, Mark Long, Jeff Nuttall and Chahine Yavroyan**

The People Show No. 95
A return of the company of iconoclasts who have consistently earned high praise for their Marx Brothers-like humour.

ICA Theatre

THE MALL, LONDON SW1
01-930-3647

Artistic Director **Michael Morris**

200% and Bloody Thirsty (1989)

devised and performed by FORCED ENTERTAINMENT

7–18 February 1989

with **Robin Arthur, Richard Lowdon and Cathy Naden**

Music **John Avery**
Director **Tim Etchells and Terry O'Connor**

Three friends enact and re-enact 'a hectic ritual of birth and death'. Forced Entertainment perform with a balanced blend of language, sound, music and design, and they have their champions.

Alexandra Kollontai (1989)

BARBARA EWING

4–22 April 1989

with **Barbara Ewing**

Lighting **Martin Hazlewood**
Director **Anthony Tuckey**

A theatrical biography pieced together from Kollontai's diaries, of the Russian woman who campaigned vigorously for maternity provision and state nurseries and who was the first woman to be a member of a government.

9–13 May, the Mamu Players in conjunction with the Market Theatre, Johannesburg, presented *Township Boy*; and 20–4 June, Nan Goldin gave her slide show with music – her life and friends in photographs she has taken – *The Ballad of Sexual Dependency*. Two days later, from Holland, came Christopher Anders and Ursula Balser with their *Krieg*, some 50 minutes on the barbarity of war.

Sons of Bitumen (1989)

devised and presented by DOGS IN HONEY

29 June–1 July 1989

with **Stephen Jones, Graham Wrench, Huw Chadbourn and Phillip Hughes**

Director **Sarah Tutt**

First performed in Nottingham and then at the ICA earlier in the year, *Sons of Bitumen* returned briefly in the summer. Set in a gents' public lavatory after a nuclear holocaust, it depicts four friends who reflect on a number of things – including films of the past and the theatre.

Reduta Deux of New York, and Derevo from Leningrad appeared at the ICA in July as part of the London International Festival of Theatre.

King's Head Theatre Club

115 UPPER STREET, ISLINGTON, LONDON N1
01-226-1916

Artistic Director **Dan Crawford**

Poor Nanny (1989)

SEAN MATHIAS

13 March–9 April 1989

Angus/Uncle Frederick **John Barron**
Anne **Jill Bennett**
Uncle Jonathan **Hugh Paddick**
Mrs Pitchley **Heather Eames**

A splendid cast was assembled for this black comedy which tells of an unhappy family and their house guests over a fateful week-end. The characters were seen as comic grotesques, and the writing as a mixture of Coward and Chekhov. This hint of other people's writing and a weakness of plot disturbed the

Anthony **Jonathan Cecil**
Antonia **Susie Blake**
Andrew **John Hudson**
Giles Fox **Neil Daglish**
Gilliane Fox **Katie Randall**

critics, but there were those who admitted, in spite of their prejudices, that they found it very funny.

Design **Michael Vale**
Costume **Tracy Klyne**
Music **Tracy Williams**
Director **Sean Mathias**

Peace in Our Time (1947)

NOEL COWARD

24 May–18 June 1989

Alma Boughton **Amanda Windsor**
Fred Shatlock **Eamonn Bohan**
Janet Braid **Maureen Allan**
Doris Shatlock **Tricia Schulten**
Mr Grainger/Herr Hubermann **James George**
Mrs Grainger/Frau Hubermann **Ann Courtney**
Nora Shatlock **Victoria McFarlane**
Lydia Vivian **Candida Beveridge**
George Bourne **Paul Gilmore**
Chorley Bannister **Matthew Townshend**
Bobby Paxton/Gestapo Officer/Singer **Gary Clasby**
Albrecht Richter **Derek Bell**
Phyllis Mere **Jennifer Rhule**
Gladys Mott **Linda Miles**
Alfie Blake **John Duggan**
German Soldier/Singer/Mr Lawrence **Patrick Walsh**
SS Guard/Kurt Foster/Singer **David Borrows**
Billy Grainger **Christopher Rickwood**
Dr Venning **Jim Boylan**
Lily Blake **Vivienne Race**
Stevie **Alex Rose**
Singer **Valda Aviks**

The Acting Company is a group comprised of members of the Arts Educational Schools' post-graduate course, actors and actresses who are working in the professional theatre but who are still honing their craft. Under the direction of David Harris, they produced one of the most fascinating revivals of the year, Noel Coward's *Peace in Our Time*, a view of England under German occupation.

One remembers the hostility with which this play was greeted when it was produced. Still smarting from the agonies of war, people were angered by the suggestion that Britain could ever have been occupied by the Germans and that there would have been British collaborators. *Peace in Our Time*, coupled with his song *Don't Let's Be Beastly to the Germans*, made Coward less than popular in some quarters for a short while. The play has seldom been revived since, and this

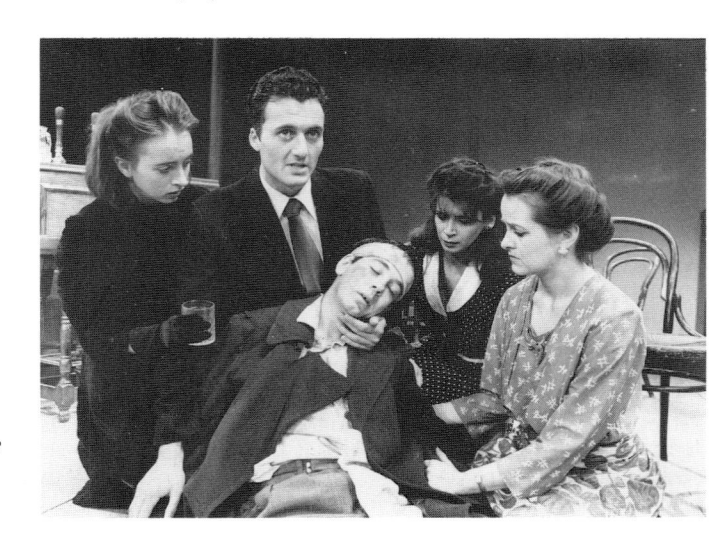

7. *Noel Coward's* Peace in Our Time, *a fascinating revival at the King's Head. A most talented cast with Victoria McFarlane as Nora Shacklock on the right.*

Design **Michael Vale**
Musical Director **Geoffrey Osborn**
Director **David Harris**

exhilarating production at the King's Head (earlier at the Jeanetta Cochrane) was of interest both historically and for the lively talents it displayed.

The scene is the saloon bar of a pub in Knightsbridge, and the tone is captured from the outset by a most able quartet led by Valda Aviks who sing *Let The People Sing* and punctuate the action with songs from the forties, both English and German. The story itself is simple enough, with the resistance, the escaped prisoner-of-war son of the licensees and the ultimate note of optimism that Britain will never be defeated and will throw off these conquerors. It is closer to *This Happy Breed* than to any other of Coward's plays, but it is far less sentimental and cloying than the earlier play and far more plausible.

The strength of the production was not only its pace, but the exactitude of atmosphere, time and place, and the quality of the playing. Derek Bell was a superbly controlled Nazi, suave and sinister, and there were excellent performances from Maureen Allan, Eamonn Bohan and a host of others. It is perhaps unfair to single out any individual in such a company, all of whom showed total commitment, but Victoria McFarlane's portrayal of Nora Shatlock, the landlady of the pub, deserves special praise. Here is an actress capable of transcending the years into middle age and remaining convincing. She is also an actress with the capacity to move an audience. Hers is a rare talent.

Perhaps *Peace in Our Time* revolves around a dated and illogical patriotism, but in the hands of David Harris and his company it was excellent theatre. It was pleasant to see that Elspeth March – who starred with Bernard Lee, Alan Badel, Dora Bryan and Kenneth More in the original production – was a member of the first-night audience at the King's Head.

Days of Cavafy (1989)

GERALD KILLINGWORTH

20 June–8 July 1989

Constantine Cavafy **Tim Hardy**
Haricleia Cavafy **Carol Macready**
Paul Cavafy/Stephanos **William Relton**
Mohammed El Said **Ashley Russell**
Ibrahim Mukhtar/Vassili **Ben Wheatley**

Gerald Killingworth's play about the Greek poet who lived and worked in Alexandria at the turn of the century was first performed at the Finborough Theatre Club in May. Cavafy is at his desk binding copies of his poems and reminiscing. As he speaks, characters, real and imaginary, are recalled – his fat, foolish mother (a beautifully judged performance by Carol Macready); his elegant brother; E M Forster (one of the less satisfying episodes in the play); and the people with whom he lived and worked. His homosexuality is depicted when he takes a male prostitute to his room; and we see him as a man working subserviently in the Ministry of Public Works, bullying and often humiliating those below him. He is prissy and precise, the poet inside the body of a clerk.

If the play does not work totally as a piece of theatre, it nevertheless contains some very fine writing. We are left with a sense of the fragrance of Alexandria in the early part of this century, and of a man moving in his own academic and sexual dreams yet capable of writing *Ithaca* and *Waiting for the Barbarians*. In short, Gerald Killingworth has created a wonderfully theatrical character rather than a piece of theatre. Tim Hardy's interpretation does justice to the quality of the writing. He is fussy and pedantic, but vulnerable, moving and totally convincing in a delicate, sensitive performance. Alison Skilbeck's direction is equally sensitive.

I have a love for Cavafy's poetry and for Lawrence Durrell's Alexandrian quartet, which the 'poet of the city' constantly haunts. Both are evoked by a play which, with all its limitations, deserves a further showing and a wider audience.

8. Tim Hardy – a totally convincing Cavafy in Gerald Killingworth's play at the King's Head.

Hamid/Dimitri **Rodney Matthew**
E M Forster/Pericles **James Woolley**

Alexander **Ashley Russell**
The Young Man **Mark Frankel**

Design **Rachel Lawson**
Music and Sound **Mark Greaves**
Director **Alison Skilbeck**

Comus (1634)

JOHN MILTON adapted by Douglas Slater

10–23 July 1989

Attendant Spirit/Henry Lawes **Nigel Campbell**
Comus/Paul Viner **Adam Fahey**
The Lady/Lady Alice Egerton **Rosamund Burton**
Elder Brother/John, Viscount Brackley **Tom Melly**
Second Brother/Lady Thomasina Egerton **Kathleen Campbell**
Sabrina/Constance Bridgewater **Penny Bunton**

Since 1984, Syllabub have explored new ways of bringing old theatrical forms to modern audiences. On this occasion, Douglas Slater chose to provide a fictional parallel, placed in 1934, for Milton's masque. Milton's piece is a fiery defence of chastity presented in heightened poetic language and with a strong moral tone. Adam Fahey's demonic Comus was singled out for special praise.

Design **Kathryn Challis, Cathy Cooper, Michele Nurnberger and Nigel Wimborne**
Lighting **David Horn**

Choreographer **Louisa McAlpine**
Music **Tom Mohan**
Director **Robin Brooks**

A Slice of Saturday Night, 1–26 August, later transferred to the Arts Theatre Club, London, under which details will be found.

The Lady and the Clarinet (1979)

MICHAEL CRISTOFER

13 September–7 October 1989

The Clarinet Player **Derek Cornhill**
Luba **Imelda Staunton**
Paul **David Thewlis**
Jack **Dan Mullane**
George **Bill Thomas**

Design **Janet Scarfe**
Costume **Sue Ellen Rohrer**
Lighting **Dan Crawford**

A middle-aged lady from Manhattan looks back over the three great loves of her life with the aid of a clarinet player. This Off-Broadway comedy provided a magnificent vehicle for the talents of Imelda Staunton. She won universal acclaim for her performance as Luba, who looks back in anger, wit and fondness.

Music **Stanley Silverman**
Director **Rob Mulholland**

The King's Head is engaged in trying to raise £50,000 to complete the work necessary for essential fire precaution and safety. The capacity of the theatre will be increased by 35% and we are promised greater comfort.

Dan Crawford's energetic theatre is always welcoming and it celebrates its 20th birthday in 1990. It deserves to thrive and prosper. One hopes that it will improve its press relations and information service.

Latchmere Theatre Club

503 BATTERSEA PARK ROAD, LONDON SW11 3BW
01-228-2620

Theatre Director **Chris Fisher**

Meatball (1988)

NICK HERRET and TIM ROLT

5–28 January 1989

performed by **Nick Herret**

Nick Herret's acclaimed solo performance as the 'archetype of the Premium Lager lout' who discourses volubly on life's major events, 'growing up, marriage and being a prick'. The show is constantly updated.

Shakers (1986)
JOHN GODBER and JANE THORNTON

31 January–18 February 1989

The female counterpart to *Bouncers* presented by the Own Boss Theatre Company and originally playing at The Duke's Head, Richmond.

Happy Family
GILES COOPER

20 February–11 March 1989

A black comedy which was presented by G4 Productions. It revolves around Suzanne's introduction of Gregory, her fiancé, to her family – her retarded sister and her stockbroker brother.

Duet for One (1983)
TOM KEMPINSKI

13 March–1 April 1989

Dr Feldman **John Solomon-Clarke**
The Woman **Anna-Luisa De Cavilla**

Presented by the Botticelli Theatre Company, *Duet for One* has proved to be a durable and moving play. Believed to have been inspired by the events which brought a premature death to Jacqueline du Pré, it is set in the consulting room of Dr Feldman and ranges over six psychiatric sessions. It tells of the anguish of a concert violinist who is suffering from multiple sclerosis, and covers the fluctuating moods and emotions that she endures in response to her illness and to the knowledge that her career is at an end.

Frankenstein (1989)

APRIL DE ANGELIS from the novel by Mary Shelley

4–29 April 1989

Capt. Walton/Frankenstein senior/Safie/Monster **Bill Cashmore**
Young Elizabeth/Sydney Flynn/William/Blind Father/Monster/Audrey/Justine **Angela Clerkin**
Young Victor/Harry Tipstaff/Henry Clerval/Monster **John Davitt**
Mr Smith/Victor Frankenstein/Felix **Nick Kemp**
John Evans/Elizabeth/Agatha **Anastasia Mainoff**

Violinist **Emma Peters**
Design **Paul Wilkins**
Lighting **Mark Rider**
Music **Emma Peters and Kjartan Poskitt**
Director **Chris Fisher**

A new working of the Mary Shelley novel by the London Actors Theatre Company, the resident company at the Latchmere, *Frankenstein* was greeted with horror by *Time Out* and *City Limits* and welcomed by *What's On*, which found the interpretation imaginatively daring.

The Malcontent (1604)

JOHN MARSTON

1–20 May 1989

Giovanni Altofronto **Liz Dickinson**
Pietro Iacomo **Billie Reynolds**
Mendoza **Anna Koutelieri**
Celso/Page **Pooky Quesnel**
Bilioso **Ellie Dickens**
Ferneze/Captain of the Citadel **Caroline Bond**
Aurelia **Adam Fahey**
Maria/Emilia **Mark Inman**
Maquerelle **Charles Daish**
Bianca **Forrest Wentworth**

Design **Vicki Mortimer**
Lighting **Maryjane Stevens**
Choreographer **Ian Potter**
Musical Director **Colin Good**
Director **Ramin Gray**

Ramin Gray observed that when *The Malcontent* was first performed it was played by boy actors, and seeing innocent children imitate the cruel Machiavellians and sexually motivated amoralists at work must have had a strong effect upon the audience. In an attempt to recapture some of this original power, Gray took the unusual step of casting men in the women's roles and women in the men's roles.

The deposed Duke of Genoa, Altofronto, returns to his court disguised as Malevole, a malcontent and a sceptic jester. Indulged by the usurper Pietro Iacomo, he is able to scream invective at the court and cut the courtiers with his biting satire until he finally obtains his revenge. As the play moves through a world of fetid deception and disguise, the sexual cross-casting is remarkably successful. The production was received with warmth for its imagination and enterprise, although some found it rather low key and ultimately only partially satisfying.

The Importance of Being Earnest (1895)

OSCAR WILDE

23 May–17 June 1989

John Worthing **Jonathan Poland**
Algernon Moncrieff **Dominic Gray**
Rev. Canon Chasuble **John Samson**
Merriman/Lane **Kevin Land**
Lady Bracknell **Adrienne Johns**
Hon. Gwendolen Fairfax **Francine Brody**
Cecily Cardew **Chloe Annett**
Miss Prism **Hilda Schroeder**

Director **Patrick Duncan**

The fourth Wilde play to be staged at the Latchmere inside two years, *The Importance of Being Earnest*, performed by Voices Theatre Company, was received as a worthy production.

Kennedy's Children (1976)

ROBERT PATRICK

3–22 July 1989

Wanda **Claire Toeman**
Sparger **Kevin Owers**
Rona **Caroline Wildi**
Mark **Zane Stanley**
Carla **Helen Anderson**

Design **Rose Long**
Costume **Helen McCabe**
Lighting **Penny Fitzgerald**
Director **Michael Eriera**

Kennedy's Children has become something of a cult play. It has rich offerings for audition candidates and excites the young, yet it is hardly a play. Five people sit in a New York bar in 1974 and, through monologues, re-create the experiences of the sixties and the attendant traumas. The characters never interact, nor do they even acknowledge each other's presence. Wanda is the idealist who has endowed Kennedy with divine-like qualities, measures her life from the day of his death and has thrown up a lucrative job in journalism to become a teacher, a more worthwhile profession. Mark is a Vietnam war veteran penning his memories of massacres and drug orgies. Rona is the hippy leftover from the sixties remembering beauties of things past. Sparger is a gay actor in alternative theatre, descriptions of which are less than compelling; and Carla, the glamour girl with aspirations to stardom, completes the quintet.

It is a recital of disillusionment, and the disillusionment is most clear in the monologues of Rona who, though clinging to the past, paints a picture of an era, often romanticised, that was squalid and morally indefensible and declined year by year.

The format does not make for compelling drama, but Michael Eriera's direction, Rose Long's intelligent set and some controlled and thoughtful performances, particularly from Helen Anderson, served the play well.

Bird of Prey (1989)

STEVE TASANE and CARL DREYFUSS

24 July–12 August 1989

Danielle **Steve Tasane**

Director **Carl Dreyfuss**

Danielle has been sexually abused both as child and woman, and the monologue, which has 'a raw energy that is almost overwhelming', tells of her pain, feelings of guilt and eventual determination to fight back. Accepted as a powerful and vitally important piece of writing, *Bird of Prey* was criticised for laying all the blame squarely on the shoulders of the male half of the population rather than following the reasoning as to what makes people behave as they do. It was also felt that to have a man play the part of Danielle in an attempt to avoid prejudice was not a success.

Leonardo's Last Supper (1969)

PETER BARNES

4–23 September 1989

Leonardo **Terence Brown**
Alphonso **James Castle**
Angelo **Ian Hurley**
Maria **Malindi O'Rorke**

Design **Peter Dineen and Ian Hurley**
Director **Peter Dineen**

Set in a French charnel house in 1519, this black comedy tells of how a family of undertakers are delighted when they are contracted to bury Leonardo da Vinci. His resurrection, however, unleashes the comedy and the central theme of the play – now more relevant than it was 20 years ago – the artist's struggle for survival in a materialist society. Bawdy and baroque, the play has a message for the Minister for the Arts and the Arts Council. Peter Dineen's production was welcomed as energetic and fast moving.

What Are You Afraid Of? (1989)

RON PHILLIPS

25 September–14 October 1989

with **Christopher Toba, Steven Dougherty, Peter Hamilton, Jackie Stirling and Liz Steer**

Lighting **Stan Johnson**
Director **Michael Futcher**

Three short plays which examine different aspects of fear. The first piece is set in Brazil where the rich play with death for amusement; the second takes place in a world where 'reason is distorted and lunacy is emperor of the soul'; and the third is an examination of the terror of losing a loved one.

Kissing Rough, a new play by Liverpool playwright Howard Kay, followed *What Are You Afraid Of?* and *Romeo and Juliet* in a modern version replaced the originally advertised American Theatre Festival première. The London Actors Theatre Company's Christmas show was *Dr Jekyll and Mr Bumble*.

The production of *Frankenstein* which played at the Latchmere in April had a national tour in the autumn. It began at Darlington in October and ended at Sudbury in December.

New End Hampstead

27 NEW END, HAMPSTEAD, LONDON NW3
01-794-0022

The Pleasure Principle (1989)

JOHN COOPER

17 January–12 February 1989

with **Marcus Gilbert, Claire King, Diane Hart, Joseph Peters and Deborah Shipley**

Director **Tom Leatherbarrow**

The delicate psychology of human relationships among an artistic set in Hampstead is the basis of this play by the author of *Notes From London's Underground*, which was very successful in 1987.

Underwater Swimming (1989)

STEPHEN MAY

14 February–19 March 1989

Psychic **Shyro**
Kik **Neil McKinven**
The Punk **Stephen May**
The Girl **Abigail Cruttenden**

Design **Mini Grey**
Lighting **Andrew Stickland**

Stephen May's first play set in a basement in Notting Hill drew general approval for its vigour and inventiveness. Isabel Arro in *What's On* wrote, '*Underwater Swimming* is poetic and very funny. It's beautifully written, directed like a dream and performed with a brand of comic passion that I didn't know existed until I saw it done.'

Director **Oliver Parker**

The Lady From the Sea (1888)

HENRIK IBSEN

22 March–18 April 1989

Ellida **Aletta Lawson**
Dr Wangel **Jeremy Wilkin**
Boletta **Justine Glenton**
Hilda **Joanne Ridley**
Arnholm **James Hunter**
Lyngstrand **Paul Caisimir**
Ballested **Richard Winch**

A commendable revival of Ibsen's drama about Ellida, emotionally imprisoned in herself, who calls from the sea a mysterious, vanished past love.

The Stranger **Peter Tate**

Lighting **Gordon Fudge**
Director **Tom Scott**

Design **Jennifer Siley**

O Architect (1989)

CHERYL ROBSON

20 April–14 May 1989

with **Wilkie Collins, Peter Ellis, Valerie Sarruf and others**

Design **Kerry Skinner**
Music **Test Department**

The Mafia, international banking, freemasonry and the Vatican all form part of Cheryl Robson's interesting play based on the Calvi affair.

Director **Catherine Carnie**

Creditors (1888)

AUGUST STRINDBERG

18 May–10 June 1989

Adolf **Howard Samuels**
Gustav **Michael Malnick**

Tekla **Karen Cooper**

Latin (1980)

STEPHEN FRY

18 May–10 June 1989

An unusual coupling of two one-act plays. *Latin* is a comedy about a Latin master who, thwarted in his hopes of promotion and of marriage to the headmaster's daughter, runs off with his favourite boy pupil to Tangier where all that they will have is 'money, sun and sensual pleasure'.

Mr Clarke **Howard Samuels**
Mr Brookshaw **Michael Malnick**

Design **Andy Edwards**
Director **Robert Gillespie**

In contrast, *Creditors* sees a more stern schoolmaster breaking up the marriage of his ex-wife to a crippled sculptor.

Rissoles (1989)
RICHARD EDMUNDS

13 June–9 July 1989

Micky **Simon Pearsall**
Ruth **Pamela Nomvete**
Lindy **Janet Dibley**
Norman **Jim Kirby**

Design **Mark Dakin**

Green Light Productions has been formed to forward Green issues, and *Rissoles* is a comedy set in a wholefood restaurant in Bury St Edmunds.

Lighting **Rick Fisher**
Music **Simon Webb**

Director **Nigel Hughes**

On the Road to Jerusalem (1989)
NOMI SHARRON

13 July–6 August 1989

Kenan **Keith Drinkel**
Anna **Yvonne Nicholson**
Issam **Anton Alexander**
Uri **James Bowers**
Tamar **Tricia Hawkins**
Najwa **Nadia Carina**
Lisa **Christine Edmonds**

Set in modern Israel, *On the Road to Jerusalem* shows a balanced view of that country and weds political liberalism to a love story.

Design **Andrea Carr**
Lighting **Stephen Webber**
Director **Chrys Salt**

The Morticians' Tea Party (1989)
HUGH ELLIS

Jed Miller, old **Peter Ellis**
Jed Miller, young **Hugh Ellis**
Will Miller **David Barnes**
Ma Miller **Georgina Griffiths**

Musical Director **Chris Ellis**

6 September–1 October 1989

A macabre black comedy from the Blood Thunder Theatre Company which tells of the Miller brothers, north country undertakers. Jed is a businessman; Will is an artist. Their conflicting attitudes are at the heart of the play.

The Devil and Stepashka (1989)

CLAIRE BOOKER

4 October–5 November 1989

Zhenya **Terence Budd**
Boris **David Beckett**
Stepashka **Miriam Cooper**
Lisa **Susie Jenkinson**
Dasha **Penelope Asquith**

Design **Barney, David Gillies and Sally Campbell**
Lighting **John Rudin**

First performed on the Edinburgh Fringe, Claire Booker's play is loosely adapted from a Tolstoy story about Zhenya, an aristocrat, who has murdered Stepashka, a serf. It was well performed, with Terence Budd drawing praise as Zhenya and the admirable David Beckett scoring well as the defence lawyer.

Director **David Gillies**

Old Red Lion

418 ST JOHN'S STREET, ISLINGTON, LONDON EC1
01-837-7816

Strangers (1989)

ANDREW HOLMES adapted from Ian McEwan's novel *The Comfort of Strangers*

5–28 January 1989

Colin **Tim Shoesmith**
Mary **Caroline Payne**
Robert **Chris Lailey**
Caroline **Kathleen Campbell**

Design **Donatella Barbieri**
Director **Andrew Holmes**

Empty Space Theatre Company specialise in new work, but they have tended to rely on adaptations of novels. Set in Venice, *Strangers* brings a young English couple into contact with a frightening masochistic Italian couple. It is a sinister, menacing, chilly tale and very difficult to transfer to the theatre.

The Assignment (1989)

JOHN CHAMBERS and MAGGIE NORRIS

31 January–25 February 1989

Dawn **Linda Davidson**

The Assignment explores the relationship between two sisters,

Alex **Gina Landor**

Director **Matthew Blakstad**

one who rushes to stardom through a Coca Cola advert and the other who is a photographer of wild flowers. The seductive powers of materialism are in evidence.

Come and Make Eyes at Me (1989)
SHAUN PRENDERGAST

21 February–11 March 1989

Steph **Janet Amsden**
Walter **Johnson Willis**
Annie **Marcia Tucker**

Design **Anthony Dean**

Inner City Theatre Company's production of a new play which examines the use and abuse of alcohol in contemporary society.

Director **Adrian Bean**

Welcome Home (1983)
TONY MARCHANT

16 March–8 April 1989

with **Garry Cooper, Perry Fenwick, Aaron Harris, Wayne Norman** and **Steve Sweeney**

Lighting **Ron Hollis**
Director **Robert Pugh**

A revival of the play about four soldiers returning from the Falklands War by one of the most talented of young playwrights, *Welcome Home* has lost none of the powerful impact it had six years ago. Georgina Brown in *The Independent* described this as 'Fringe theatre at its scalding best'.

In March and April, at the Old Red Lion and later at the King's Head, Peter Burton presented his play *Leaving It All Behind*, which was inspired by the early life of Christopher Isherwood. This was a lunch-time production.

Glen Hoddle, Glen Madeiros (1989)
RUSSELL LEWIS

11–27 May 1989

Kelly **Amanda Aspinall**
Chantal **Kendal Travis**
Roger **Russell Lewis**

Smooth salesman Roger attempts to seduce the two secretaries, but his plans go astray in this light comedy.

Director **Kevin Allen**

Judgement Day (1936)

ODON VON HORVATH translated by Martin and Renata Esslin

31 May–24 June 1989

Forestry Worker **Tim Barlow**
Porkorny/Kohut/Customer/
Salesman **Brendan Coyle**
Mrs Leimgrubber **Merelina Kendall**
Mrs Hudetz **Anny Tobin**
Alfons **Stephen Tindall**
Anna **Matilda Zeigler**
Ferdinand **Delaval Astley**
Hudetz **Stephen Boxer**
Landlord **Robin Polley**
Leni **Anne Kavanagh**
Policeman **Sean Munro**
Inspector **Daniel Kruyer**
Child **Chloe Sutcliffe**

This was a great event for the Old Red Lion in that Filthy Lucre Productions gave the British première of Horvath's exploration of moral guilt. Hudetz, a station master, is temporarily diverted from his duty by a kiss from Anna. He fails to change signals and causes a train crash in which 18 people are killed. At the subsequent enquiry, Anna lies and is believed, but Hudetz's wife has seen the incident, tells the truth and is reviled. Hudetz is released from custody and given a hero's welcome home, but Anna is tortured by guilt and arranges a meeting with him which proves fatal to both of them. The production at the Old Red Lion was received with great enthusiasm.

Design **Claudia Mayer and Mini Grey**
Lighting **David Lawrence**
Musical Directors **Stephen Warbeck and Rory Allam**
Director **Stephen Daldry**

Who's Left? (1986)

BARRY McCARTHY

3–27 August 1989

Trish **Emma Wray**
Chrissie **Kathy Burke**
Alice **Tilly Vosburgh**

Director **John Moulton-Reid**

Three women who were at university together leave their partners and set up home together in a dingy flat. The play is about 'women coming to terms with the awfulness of men', but it was not just the male reviewers who did not like it.

The Increased Difficulty of Concentration (1968)

VACLAV HAVEL

26 September–21 October 1989

Dr Huml **Roland Curram**
His Mistress **Sally Mortemore**

Dr Huml is a lecherous professor of social science who becomes involved in an experiment to create the unique

His Wife **Julia Righton**
Blanka **Saskia Wickham**
with **Andy Serkis, Caroline O'Neill, Bill Radmall and Adam Ray**

Design **Narelle Sissons**
Director **Tamsin Oglesby**

personality of the future. He is also wearying of both his wife and his mistress and dictating lectures on the nature of happiness and social values. Basically, the work of the Czech dissident dramatist Vaclav Havel is a sexual comedy, but, inevitably, it is a political satire.

Buster Theatre's bizarre comedy of the dark mysteries of the occult world, *Talk of the Devil*, was scheduled to play at the Old Red Lion, 21 November–16 December 1989.

Orange Tree Theatre

45 KEW ROAD, RICHMOND, SURREY
01-940-3633

Artistic Director **Sam Walters**

Les Parents Terribles (1938)

JEAN COCTEAU

3 February–7 March 1989

George **Roland Curram**
Yvonne **Elizabeth Shepherd**
Leo **Caroline Blakiston**
Michael **Samuel West**
Madeleine **Sally Cookson**

Design **Anne Gruenberg**
Director **Derek Goldby**

No longer as fashionable or as shocking as he was 50 years ago, Cocteau still has his admirers. An excellent production of *Les Parents Terribles* at the Orange Tree clearly depicted the Cocteau theme of the claustrophobic effects of family life delineated by the incestuous relationships. The acting in Derek Goldby's production won much applause. 'They perform with an emotion that blazes like a forest fire', wrote Michael Billington.

Situation Vacant (1972)

MICHAEL VINAVER translated by John Burgess

17 March–8 April 1989

Wallace **Gareth Armstrong**
Fage **Paul Moriarty**
Louise **Auriol Smith**

La Demande d'Emploi concerns a family crisis in the life of a middle-aged man who has just lost his job and is seeking another. He is subjected to humiliating interviews by a

Nathalie **Emma D'Inverno**

Director **Sam Walters**

recruitment director from a travel firm. His 16-year-old daughter is pregnant and must go to England for an abortion. The play has as many as 30 scenes, which tend to prolong the action, but it was a worthy production of an interesting play which had waited 17 years for a British première.

The Bourgeois Gentilhomme (1671)

MOLIÈRE translated by John Wood

21 April–20 May 1989

Monsieur Jourdain **David Timson**
Madame Jourdain **Auriol Smith**
Lucille **Oona Beeson**
Nicole **Saira Todd**
Cleonte **Philippe Giraudeau**
Covielle **Robert Daws**
Dorante **Andrew Branch**
Countess Dorimene **Tilly Tremayne**

The Orange Tree continued its international season with Molière's gentle mockery of a solid middle-class man who has delusions of grandeur.

Design **Anne Gruenberg**
Choreographers **Oona Beeson and Philippe Giraudeau**

Music **Andrew Branch and David Timson**
Director **Sam Walters**

The Queen of Spades and I (1989)

SYLVIA FREEDMAN

26 May–17 June 1989

Pushkin/Tomsky **Richard Rees**
Raevsky/Hermann **Michael Keating**
Natalia/Princess **Natalie Slater**
Mrs Goncharov/Countess **Sheila Mitchell**
Catherine/Lisa **Gillian Bush Bailey**
Baron/Namurov **Mark Payton**

Sylvia Freedman's second play interweaves the story of Pushkin's life with one of his most famous and sinister stories, *The Queen of Spades*. It was welcomed as showing great promise.

Design **Anne Gruenberg**
Choreographer **Oona Beeson**

Director **Andrew Harmon**

Mrs Warren's Profession (1893)

GEORGE BERNARD SHAW

8 September–7 October 1989

Vivie **Irina Brook**
Praed **Robert Langdon Lloyd**
Mrs Warren **Natasha Parry**

Having directed the Moscow Art Theatre School in *The Crucible*, which played at the Riverside Studios, Brian Cox turned his attention to Shaw's play about the 'new' woman of

Sir George Crofts **Richard Owens**
Frank Gardner **Stephen Marchant**
Rev. Samuel Gardner **Ben Aris**

Design **Tom Piper**
Director **Brian Cox**

the late 19th century whose mother had provided her with education and social standing from her profits as a brothel owner. The play is also about mother–daughter relationships, and, via the mouth of Crofts, the arch-Tory, Shaw puts one of his finest pleas for socialism. The play is as sharp today as it ever was, and Brian Cox's production was welcomed as doing it full justice.

Play with Repeats (1989)

MARTIN CRIMP

13 October–11 November 1989

Anthony Steadman **Thomas Wheatley**
Nick/Terry **Stephen Marchant**
Kate/Franky **Caroline Gruber**
Mouhamed Lamine/Marc/Man in Launderette **Ben Onwukwe**
Mrs Dent/Woman at Bus Stop/Barbara **Vivien Heilbron**

Written while Martin Crimp was Thames TV Writer-in-Residence at the Orange Tree, *Play with Repeats* begins with the lone Anthony Steadman meeting a couple in a pub and, after a series of bizarre escapades, ends when he is stabbed in a slight dispute in another pub. Like Crimp's earlier plays, it explores the waste of potential in human beings.

Design **Anne Gruenberg**   Director **Sam Walters**

Alexander Gelman's *We, The Undersigned* was scheduled at the Orange Tree for 17 November to 9 December. This enterprising and exciting theatre is raising funds for a new theatre opposite to where the present one now stands.

Riverside Studios

CRISP ROAD, HAMMERSMITH, LONDON W6 9RJ
01-748-3354

The Fatherland (1987)

MURRAY WATTS

20 January–18 February 1989

Lefty Mabhena **Jude Akuwudike**
Mattea Mabhena **Cleo Dorcas**

The first large-scale production presented by the Bush Theatre outside its own home, *The Fatherland* was the winner of the

Peggy **Jeillo Edwards**
Reuben Mabhena **Geff Francis**
Nunu **Valerie Hunkins**
Electricity **Jabu Mbalo**
Fritz Mabhena **Ade Sapara**
Freddie **Eddie Thengani**
Zulu **Reggie Tsiboe**
Mfundisi/Sangoma **Rudolph Walker**
Maki Mabhena **Natasha Williams**

Design **Michael Taylor**
Costume **Sue Born Thompson**

LWT Plays on Stage competition in 1987. Murray Watts, who has worked in Soweto, centres his play on the Mabhena family, whose father is in a prison hospital. One son, Reuben, is a star footballer; another, Lefty, is the black sheep of the family; the third, Fritz, carries on his father's work for the ANC. Andy Lavender in *City Limits* described *The Fatherland* as a 'deeply humanist play which remembers how to laugh and which is at the same time polemical'.

Lighting **Rick Fisher**
Choreographer **Jabu Mbalo**
Sound **Colin Brown**

Musical Director **Cleo Dorcas**
Director **Brian Stirner**

Dr Faustus (1590)
CHRISTOPHER MARLOWE

6–11 March 1989

Dr Faustus **Neil Salvage**
with **The Medieval Players**

Design **Phil Daniels**

Often carrying echoes of the circus, this was a highly individual and comic presentation of Marlowe's play.

Director **Carl Heap**

Irish Week

23–9 April 1989

I Am of Ireland (1989)
A tribute to W B Yeats performed by Bosco Hagan and written by Edward Callan.

Shades of the Jelly Woman (1989)
Written by Peter Sheridan and performed by Jean Doyle.

The Watchman (1989)
Sean Lawlor's play was performed by Johnny Murphy and directed by Sean Lawlor.

Bat the Father, Rabbit the Son (1989
Written and performed by Donal O'Kelly, and directed by Decland Hughes.

Piers the Plowman (1989)

CARL HEAP and JAMES PETTIFER from the poem by William Langland

30 May–3 June 1989

The Medieval Players' touring production of their version of Langland's poem was seen as worthy for the 'physical enthusiasm' of its cast and the versatility which they displayed.

Lady Lucre/Repentance/Lady/World/Hope (Moses)/Death/Mercy **Paul Bingham**
Angel/Fraud/Minstrel/Conscience/Lechery/Wrath/Piers the Plowman/Jesus/Charity/Old Age/Satan **Nicholas Collett**
Holy Church/Officer/Peace/Pride/Envy/Beggar/Conscience/Flesh/Mob/Corpse/Longinus/Righteousness **Joanne Howarth**

William/Reason/Peace/Free Will **Paul Kirk**
Lucifer/Liar/Judge/Crime/Sloth/Hunger/Mrs Gluttony/Pilgrim/Imagination **Patricia Martinelli**
King/Sir Civil Law/Friar/Avarice/Faith/Gluttony/Knight/Haukin/Truth/

Corpse **Steven Speirs**

Design **Andrew Feest**
Costume and Lighting **Anthony Matheson**
Musical Director **Andrew Watts**
Director **Carl Heap**

The Pornography of Performance (1988)

THE SYDNEY FRONT from texts by Peter Weiss, Heiner Muller, Oscar Wilde, Aeschylus, Euripides, Baudelaire, Robert Lowell and the Marquis de Sade

24 August–2 September 1989

Polyxena **Elise Ahamnos**
Electra **Andrea Aloise**
Not Hamlet **John Baylis**
Ophelia on the Phone **Clare Bucknall**
Sade in the Bath **Nigel Kellaway**
Natural Woman **Christopher Ryan**

Lighting **Simon Wise and Geoff Cobham**

From 3 to 15 July, El Gran Circo Teatro from Chile presented *La Negra Ester* by Roberto Parra as part of the London International Festival of Theatre. In August, The Sydney Front offered *The Pornography of Performance*, which had first been performed at the Adelaide Fringe. Betty Caplen in *The Guardian* suggested that by the end of the evening there was nothing left to subvert.

Continuing with their international flavour, the Riverside presented the Moscow Art Theatre School's production of *The Crucible* from 5 to 16 September. It had previously been presented at the Edinburgh Fringe Festival.

Shylock (1976)

ARNOLD WESKER

16–22 October 1989

Shylock Kolner **Oded Teomi**
Jessica **Julia Lane**
Rivka **Anna Korwin**
Tubal di Ponti/Moses **Michael Poole**
Antonio Querini **Frank Barrie**
Bassanio Visconti **Pip Torrens**
Lorenzo Pisani **Richard Lintern**
Graziano Sanudo **Hugh Simon**
Portia Contarini **Julie Legrand**
Nerissa **Jan Shand**
Solomon Usque **Mark Sproston**
Rodrigues de Cunha **Brian Mitchell**
Rebecca de Mendes **Kate Percival**
Girolamo Priuli **Michael Cronin**

Lighting **Konrad Watson**
Director **Arnold Wesker**

Arnold Wesker is not alone in feeling that *The Merchant of Venice* is neither a very good nor a very pleasant play. He reacted to it by writing *The Merchant*, later renamed *Shylock*, which has had a chequered career in England and America. It arrived at the Riverside Studios in October as a rehearsed reading with the leading Israeli actor Oded Teomi in the title role.

Wesker's *Shylock* is the result of extensive research into the true plight and position of the Jews in Venice in the 16th century. Shylock is a collector of books who shares his passion with his friend Antonio, a merchant and a Gentile who has no joy in a bargain and who is weary of buying and selling goods that he never sees. It is the friendship of these two men which is at the heart of the play, and the warmth and sensitivity with which the characters are played by Teomi and Frank Barrie is both appealing and moving.

Into the friendship of these two men stumbles Antonio's godson, Bassanio, a cold, unloving man who has inherited bigotry and wants 3,000 ducats from his godfather so that he may woo the wealthy Portia. Antonio borrows the money from Shylock, and the bond that they draw up between them is a mockery of the law. Antonio and Shylock are joined in their love of knowledge, but separated by the curfew that restricts the Jew to the ghetto and the yellow hat that he must wear as a leper wears a bell.

The ghetto is inhabited by 1,400 Jews; it has just three water-holes, and a proclivity for fire and exploitation by the Christians.

Shylock has raised his daughter Jessica as an independent spirit, but she cries for a world outside the cover of a book and would 'escape from oppressive expectation'. The part is played with vigorous clarity by Julia Lane. Jessica deserts her father and elopes with the pseudo-poet Lorenzo, who is arrogant and envious. Jessica has been seduced by the superficial and, with Lorenzo, she flies to Belmont where Portia, exuberantly played by Julie Legrand, is repairing the estate her father left in decay.

Portia sees Lorenzo and Bassanio for what they are and will bow the knee to no man. It is she who has the wit to unravel the bond that threatens the lives of both Shylock and Antonio, but she cannot save Shylock from losing all but his dignity.

She returns to Belmont where she will continue her quest for knowledge. She will honour her father's wishes by marrying 'the man who chose lead', but he will find his place or leave. Nerissa, who has acted as narrator, brings the young 'heroes' a drink as they celebrate their victory, which has destroyed a man and a friendship. Shylock's Venice is but a few paces from Hitler's Germany.

Shylock was presented as a reading, hopefully as a prelude to a full-scale West End production. Three scenes of political, historical and religious debate at the end of the first act would suggest that some restructuring is needed before this comes about, but this is a wonderfully intelligent play with witty

9. Julie Legrand, an exuberant and intelligent Portia in Wesker's Shylock *at the Riverside. Jan Shand is a thoughtful Nerissa.*

10. Oded Teomi as Shylock and Frank Barrie as Antonio in Arnold Wesker's thought-provoking and entertaining Shylock.

dialogue and interesting characterisation. It is challenging and compelling, and it engages us intellectually and emotionally. We have not had so many plays of this quality that we should neglect it.

The Gods Are Not To Blame (1968)
OLA ROTIMI

1–25 November 1989

Narrator **Susan Aderin**
Ogun Priest **Carlton Chance**
Adetusa/Aderopo **Tyrone Huggins**
Queen Ojuola **Leonie Forbes**
Baba Fakunle/Alaka **Jason Rose (Peter Badejo)**
Boy/Oyeyemi **Faith Edwards**
Chief Balogun **Ian Roberts**
Chief Otun **Delmozene Morris**

King Odewale **Jeffrey Kissoon**
Iya Aburo/Abero **Sandra Yaw**
Gbonka/Agidi **Taiwo Payne**
Labata **Mo Sesay**

Design **Ellen Cairns**
Lighting **Larry Coke**
Director **Yvonne Brewster**

The Gods Are Not To Blame is a powerful reworking of the Oedipus legend set in 15th-century Nigeria. It was presented by the Talawa Theatre Company in conjunction with the Everyman Theatre, Liverpool.

11. *Jeffrey Kissoon as King Odewale in* The Gods Are Not to Blame, *a powerful reworking of the Oedipus legend.*

Soho Poly Theatre

16 RIDING HOUSE STREET, LONDON W1
01-636-9050

Artistic Director **Tony Craze**

On 19 January 1989, in the Lord Mayor's parlour of Westminster City Hall, the Soho Poly Theatre launched its Move Ahead Fund. Such has been the success of the Soho Poly Theatre and so exciting the standard of performances and quality of productions that the theatre now seeks a larger home. At present, plans are being considered to move to a new base, a development on the Rialto site, in Coventry Street. The Move Ahead Fund is the programme and appeal by which this move will be made possible. Westminster City Council has offered to match money raised by sponsorship and from private sources.

Soho Theatre Company was founded in New Compton Street in 1969 and moved to Riding House Street in 1972. In the past 20 years the Soho Poly Theatre has been responsible for forwarding the talents of new British playwrights. It remains committed to original work, but it no longer restricts its productions to British plays. It is an energetic and exciting theatre demanding and obtaining high standards. Its proposed move to larger premises will be one of the major theatrical events of the next few years.

Improbabilities (1988)

ALEX BARR, LUCINDA COXON, CHRISTINA KATIC, VINCENT O'CONNELL, NICK PERRY and HOWARD RUSSELL

11 January–4 February 1989

Loose Exchange, a national touring company, presented *Improbabilities*, which is 16 short theatre pieces fused into a single performance. It is a constantly changing programme. It sprang from a 12-hour marathon of continuous writing and performing carried out in September 1988. Some of the plays are even written as the performance is taking place. Paul Taylor in *The Independent* felt that 'despite some sharp, comic acting from a talented cast, too many of the plays come across

Actors **Helen Anderson, Pete Bailie, Barbara Barnes, Nina Bell, Liz Dickinson, Clive Kneller, James Lailey, Alex Paterson, Steve Tindall and Philippa Williams**

as though they are lovingly preserved minutes of an improvisation act'. James Christopher, however, found the plays 'brutally honest'.

Director **Nigel Halton and Vincent O'Connell**

12. Chris Halliday, Ian Hartley and Steve Sangster in State of Play, *boisterous cricket at the Soho Poly.*

State of Play (1988)

IAN HARTLEY and TOBY SWIFT

10–25 February 1989

Minty **Chris Halliday**
Wesley Barraclough **Ian Hartley**
JC **Steve Sangster**
Kath **Kathryne Dow**

Director **Ian Hartley**

Wesley Barraclough drives his new girl-friend, Kath, to watch him play cricket for the local Yorkshire league team. On the way they meet Minty and the overweight, aggressive captain of the side, JC. At the ground, Kath is banished to the pavilion with other wives and girl-friends to prepare tea. As in *Bouncers*, the men don aprons and play a multitude of parts. It is a zestful, very funny play peppered with couplets and music which questions the male, and female, ego as the players in the match act out their adolescent fantasies. The play was presented by the Yorkshire Theatre Company. It was very highly acclaimed and had an extensive national tour.

Cardboard City (1989)

TIM FIRTH

28 February–18 March 1989

Bernie **Chris Higgins**
Matt **Rob Humphreys**
Hermione **Jenny Dee**
Alan **John Hodgkinson**
Charlie **John Edmondson**
Marian **Sarah Dudman**

Design **Tom Piper**
Lighting **Luke Tunmer**
Director **Sam Mendes**

Tim Firth's play depicts life in the cardboard city of the Waterloo Underpass where men and women, casualties of a state in which there is now little welfare, pass their nights. The Works Theatre Co-operative spoke to the real inhabitants of cardboard city, and the result is a play that has an element of the social documentary. Irving Wardle in *The Times* felt that Sam Mendes's production scored a rare success in that it turned 'a low-spirited subject into a high-energy performance'.

Ladies in the Lift (1988)

HELEN EDMUNDSON

21 March–8 April 1989

Lisa **Henrietta Whitsun-Jones**
Sarah **Amelia Bullmore**
Annie **Joan Linder**

Design **Mhairi Fraser**
Music **Helen Edmundson**
Songs arranged by **Carol Donaldson and Kathryn Turner**
Musician **Carol Donaldson**

The Manchester-based Red Stockings Theatre Company, founded in 1985, offered a highly entertaining, funny and tender musical about three ladies trapped in a lift. The women, from different walks of life, are suspicious of each other and worried about themselves. Claire Armitstead in *The Financial Times* found it 'bizarrely funny and really rather profound'.

Director **Polly Teale**

Workstage (1989)

12–19 April 1989

This was a programme of five new plays by young writers which were performed in repertoire by an ensemble company of actors. It was the first of what is promised as an annual event.

In His Name
NIKKI FOULDS

Glennis **Katharine Page**
Pastor **Dhirendra**
Richard **Patrick Keeley**
Trish **Jaqueline de Peza**

A play that deals with the effect of the evangelical church on a desperate young man.

Director **Francesca Joseph**

Below the Belt
DANIEL SCOTT

Bron **Pamela Nomvete**
Charlie **Ian Hughes**

Director **Ruth Garnault**

Described as a 'yuppy morality tale', *Below the Belt* deals with a successful television presenter and a frustrated film director who meet and fall in love

Redefining the Whore
DEI TREANOR

Artemesia Gentileschi **Emer Gillespie**
Quorly/Orazio **Oengus MacNamara**
Susanna/Tutia **Pamela Nomvete**
Tassi **Ian Hughes**

Director **Mark Ravenhill**

Considered in the 17th century as a painter of exceptional talent, Artemesia Gentileschi was raped by her tutor, Tassi. In consequence, she was tortured to prove her innocence and later branded a whore and banished from Rome, having been married to a stranger, even though Tassi had been found guilty. Dei Treanor's play, which deals with the period up to the rape, redefines the circumstances and repercussions of the event.

Last of the Irish Indians
MARK WATTERS

Kitty **Jaqueline de Peza**
Old Man/Sean **Oengus MacNamara**
Pat **Dhirendra**
Tom **Patrick Keeley**

Mark Watters explores the corruption of Irish identity by American culture in a play set in the West of Ireland in 1962.

Director **Susan Croft**

Wush Way

RUFUS ORISHAYOMI

Evans **Ian Hughes**
Security Guard **Rufus Orishayomi**
Sharon **Emer Gillespie**
Steve **Dhirendra**
Newsagent **Pamela Nomvete**

An examination of the frustrations, ambiguities and biases of Afro-Caribbean immigrants in Britain.

Director **Rufus Orishayomi**

Caving In (1989)

AYSHE RAIF

4–27 May 1989

Maggie **Diane Bull**
Dave **Simon Wright**
Jack **Phillip Joseph**
June **Mona Bruce**

Design **Amanda Fisk**
Lighting **Dee Kyne**
Sound **Colin Brown**
Director **Claire Grove**

Ayshe Raif's play tells of Maggie, whose husband has been imprisoned for fraud. She is 38 and desperate for a baby. She finds herself loved by a good-natured sociologist, Dave, and forces herself to tell the man she still loves that she wants a divorce. Jeremy Kingston in *The Times* considered Diane Bull's performance to be one of the few truly moving performances to be seen in London at the time. Phillip Joseph, on stage throughout as the imprisoned husband ever in Maggie's thoughts, characterised the part with a 'rough tenderness'.

Abingdon Square (1987)

MARIA IRENE FORNES

2 June–1 July 1989

Marion **Annabelle Apsion**
Juster **Philip Voss**
Michael **Pearce Quigley**
Minnie **Helen Blatch**
Mary **Veronica Smart**
Frank **Christopher Eccleston**

Design **Lucy Weller**
Lighting **Tina MacHugh**
Sound **Colin Brown**
Director **Nancy Meckler**

Maria Irene Fornes, born in Havana in 1930, emigrated to the United States in 1945. Originally a painter, she became a playwright in 1963 and has now written some two dozen plays. She has gained a considerable reputation Off-Broadway – on the strength of *Abingdon Square*, ambitiously and thankfully brought to London by Shared Experience and the Soho Poly Theatre, it is easy to understand why. This is an exquisite play, and it was exquisitely produced and acted and intelligently and imaginatively designed. The Soho Poly basement was transformed by whiteness, by clumps of flowers and by shafts of sunlight. There is an initial feeling of youthful happiness and innocence. Marion, a lovely 15-year-old girl, is

13. Diane Bull, Phillip Joseph and Simon Wright in Ayshe Raif's moving drama Caving In *at the Soho Poly.*

romping with a handsome young man, Michael; he is not her lover, but a step-son to be. Set in the years before the First World War and in the years of the war, *Abingdon Square* has a haunting Jamesian quality. It tells of Marion and her marriage to a wealthy 50-year-old widower. Underlying the episodes of innocence and tranquillity is a growing sexuality which is to culminate in adultery. Juster reads to his son and his new wife about the pollination of plants. Marion holds on to a post in her bedroom as she recites her lesson. She grips like a mariner tossed in a storm as the passion rages within her. These are scenes of lyrical beauty and theatrical magic. Subconsciously

14. *One of the year's greatest delights,* Abingdon Square *at the Soho Poly. Philip Voss as Juster dances with his young wife Marion (Annabelle Apsion) while Michael (Pearce Quigley) looks on.*

they prepare us for the violent break and tender reconciliation that are to come. As Juster, the ageing businessman, Philip Voss confirmed his stature as an actor of outstanding talent as he moved from controlled, dry, but always sympathetic rectitude to a vicious loss of demeanour. In voice and gesture he missed nothing. Annabelle Apsion's Marion was equally fine as she grew from girlhood to womanhood, from innocence to knowledge, motivated by feelings and desires for which she had never been truly prepared. The rest of the cast gave strong support in a play in which the painter's eye was clearly apparent. Thanks are due to Mr Voss, Miss Apsion, Shared Experience and the Soho Poly for giving us one of the great delights of 1989.

Nearly Siberia (1989)

CAROL RUMENS

29 September–21 October 1989

Katherine Cavendish **Geraldine Hinds**
Slava **Peter Silverleaf**
Misha **Metin Yenal**
Nadya **Juliet Dante**

Design **Michael Vale**

Nearly Siberia replaced the originally advertised *Piano Play*. The play explores East–West relations in the age of *glasnost*, and the effect of *perestroika* on exiled Russians. The play later had a brief tour.

Lighting **Graham Russell**
Director **Julia Pascall**

Leaf Storm (1989)

ANDREW HOLMES adapted from the story by Gabriel Garcia Marquez

25 October–18 November 1989

Boy **Gina Landor**
Isabel **Ruth Mitchell**
Colonel **Martin Poole**
Doctor **Tim Pemberton**

Design **Madeleine Adams**
Lighting **Ron Hollis**
Music **Richard Heacock**
Director **Andrew Holmes**

A doctor, a man with no name, arrives in a town, lives there for many years and dies with none but a colonel and his family willing to bury him. The hostility that has grown up against the doctor is due to his apathy towards and even rejection of Macondo (the town) and its people. He is something of a bringer of doom, death and bad luck, for the prosperity of the town, brought about by the exploitation of the land by big business, declines while he is there.

Once again Empty Space have turned to literature for their inspiration. Although *Leaf Storm* is played with tremendous vigour by a company of four and has moments of lyrical beauty, it remains something of a perplexing experience. The four actors take on a multiplicity of roles as we move backwards and forwards in time, and within a few seconds two actors can be playing the same character. The cast copes splendidly, and very special mention should be made of Gina Landor – but confusion is a dominant response.

15. *Martin Poole and Ruth Mitchell (front) and Tim Pemberton and Gina Landor (rear) in Empty Space's* Leaf Storm *at the Soho Poly.*

Soho Poly plan to stage *The Vanek Plays* by Vaclav Havel in November–December. This is a wonderfully vigorous theatre with some dynamic marketing and publicity by Undine Marshfield to match the quality of work.

Stratford East Theatre Royal

GERRY RAFFLES SQUARE, NEWHAM, LONDON E15 1BN
01-534-0310

Artistic Director **Philip Hedley**

Just Frank (1989)

VINCE FOXALL

26 January–21 February 1989

Specially commissioned by Philip Hedley, *Just Frank* is the true story of Frank Gilchrist, who joined the army to get away from dead-end jobs, served in the Falklands, was injured and put on morphine, and became an addict when he was discharged. He served a prison sentence and was later diagnosed as having AIDS. Reception to the play was mixed, but some found it a life-enhancing evening.

Frank Gilchrist **Calum Shaw**
Loz/Chap/Radio/Watt/Jimmy/Gaz/Dave/Trev/Photographer **William Blair**
Headmaster/Officer/Signals Officer/Willie/Harry/Stuart/Doctor 3 **Michael Bertenshaw**
Trudie/Sue/Penguin Spotter/Visitor/Kate/Tracey **Sheri Graubert**
Judy/The Goodbye Girl/Princess/Jill/Penguin Spotter/Sister/Sheep/Stacey/Madeline/Steff/Woman at Funeral **Kathryn Howden**
Neil/Guard/Chap/Medic/Dick/Graham/Baz/Tim **John Lawrence**
Father/Officer/Medic/Shrink/Ben/

Bobby **Michael McKevitt**
Special School Teacher/Sgt George/Officer/Mick/Alan/Kenny/Doctor 4 **Louis Mellis**
Ian/Officer/Chap/Radio/Rick/Stevie/Doctor 1/Ray/Jon/Reporter **Nigel Pivaro**

Mother/Doctor 2/Helen **Kate Williams**

Design **Jenny Tiramani**
Lighting **Stephen Watson**
Choreographer **John Halstead**
Music **Tom Robinson**
Director **Philip Hedley**

My Girl (1989)

BARRIE KEEFFE

6 March–1 April 1989

A new play about a social worker and his wife and the desperation of having to live on a pittance in Thatcher's Britain. The play is located in the borough of Newham and punctuated by Otis Reading songs. It was welcomed as a little gem, and production and performance were highly praised.

Sam **Karl Howman**
Anita **Meera Syal**

Design **Jenny Tiramani**
Lighting **Stephen Watson**
Director **Philip Hedley and Barrie Keeffe**

The Wicked World of Bel Ami (1989)

KEN HILL from the novel by Guy de Maupassant

13 April–13 May 1989

Georges Duroy **Haluk Bilginer**
Charles Forestier/Fencer/Priest/
Count Latour-Yvelin/Delorme
Anthony Pedley
Jacques Rival **Peter Straker**
Norbert de Varenne/Dr Le Brument
Ian Steele
Rachel/Mrs Bougereaux **Toni Palmer**
Heloise/Suzanne Walter **Shona Lindsay**
Clotilde de Marelle **Vivien Parry**
Virginie Walter **Judith Bruce**
Madeleine Forestier **Fiona Hendley**

A musical version of de Maupassant's 19th-century story of rags to riches in Paris, in which Georges Duroy (Bel Ami) is the lovable rogue. Most saw this as a zestful, well-acted version of a famous novel in which the darker side of life is never far away.

Walter **Freddie Earlle**
Laurine de Marelle **Nicola Khosandion/Kate Crego**
Count de Vaudred/Saint-Potin/De Marelle **Steve Bennion**
Montelin/Foucart **Richard Shilling**
Rose Walter **Emily Perkins/Lynsey Sugarman**

Design **Jenny Tiramani**
Costume **Andrea Montag**
Lighting **Vic Lockwood**
Music **Jacques Offenbach**
Musical Director **Millie Taylor**
Director **Ken Hill**

Down Every Street (1989)

VINCE FOXALL

22 May–3 June 1989

Ruth **Miriam Karlin**
Tina **Susan Tully**
Marilyn **Barbara Assiin**
Beena **Zohra Segal**
Lil **Barbara Keogh**

Vince Foxall's second play of the year at the Theatre Royal was about the disappearing East End community.

Design **Jenny Tiramani**
Lighting **Stephen Watson**

Director **Jeff Teare**

Theatre Royal's summer programme was predominantly musical, but there was a third version of *World Story Time*, folk tales from round the world. The Flying Pickets occupied the theatre for the second half of September and the first half of October with their celebration and condemnation of work, *The Late Shift*.

Tabard Theatre

2 BATH ROAD, TURNHAM GREEN, LONDON W4 1LW
01-995-6035

Riverman (1985)
SAM DOWLING

4 January–11 February 1989

First produced at the Tabard in 1985, and now enhanced by the addition of music and songs, *Riverman* is about the sad neglect of painter Walter Greaves. He was a pupil of Whistler's and worshipped the American painter until his death. The new production, like the original, won warm praise – particularly Stephen Bateman's performance as the artist. Michael Darvell in *What's On* described this as 'an exceptionally moving play'.

Walter Greaves **Stephen Bateman**
Tinnie Greaves **Jane Evers**
Augustus John **Robbin John**
William Marchant **Ciaran McIntyre**
Joseph Pennell **Dave Roberts**
Elizabeth Pennell **Catherine McQueen**
Jenny **Vivien Keene**
Sarah Spencer **Julia Nelson**

Design **Paul Dowling**
Lighting **Stephen Thompson**
Musical Director **Jack Raymond**
Music **Jack Raymond and Nicola Warren**
Director **Clarissa Brown and Gabriel Gavin**

Pavane (1987)
SHEILA DEWEY

15 February–25 March 1989

One of the winners in the Warehouse Croydon's 1987 South London Playwriting Festival, *Pavane* concerns a clairvoyant and a musician who let out their attic room to students whom they exploit in a variety of ways. Paula and Dorothy, however, disrupt their plans.

Mim **Patricia Clapton**
Ludo **Jack Raymond**
Paula **Kate Hatch**
Dorothy **Lucy Salter**
Pug **Nicholas Cannon**

Design **Jo Lynch**
Lighting **Steve Thompson**
Music **Jack Raymond**
Director **Sheila Dewey and Ted Craig**

A Cat in the Ghetto (1965)

SIMON WINCELBERG from the novel by Rachmil Bryks

6 April–6 May 1989

Yablonka **Dikran Tulaine**
Krause **John Abbott**
Schnur **Lawrence Werber**
Beryl **Ethan Stone**
Blaustein **Sean Baker**
Esther Blaustein **Roz Clifton**
Hauptmann **Ultan Ely O'Carroll**
Hupert **James Snell**
Madam Hershkovitch **Trudy Weiss**
Anya **Kristin Milward**

A most welcome opportunity to see a neglected play set in a Jewish ghetto in Eastern Europe in the Second World War. The cat becomes a symbol of moral worth, the reaffirmation of the indestructibility of the human spirit. The ending of the play is regarded as weak, but the energy and acting of this production was highly praised.

Design **Tom Piper**
Lighting **Steve Thompson**
Director **Michelle Newell**

Mourning Becomes Electra (1931)

EUGENE O'NEILL

10 May–17 June 1989

Lavinia **Shirley Wardell**
Orin **Westbury King**
Christine **Sarah Case**
Ezra **Victor Whelan**
Brant **Clyde Gatell**
Peter **Peter Taggart**
Hazel **Katharine O'Brien**
Seth/Chantyman **Ben Gaule**
Minnie **Jessica Hawksley**

Sam Dawling and Steve Mills explored a new method of work in producing O'Neill's mighty trilogy, his adaptation of the *Oresteia*. There was no director, but each member of the company put forward ideas as to interpretation so that the production was a corporate affair. This was a brave and bold effort on the part of the Tabard.

Design **Paul Dowling**
Costume **Dylan Stone**
Lighting **Simon Clark**
Director **The Company**

Theatre Museum Theatre

RUSSELL STREET, COVENT GARDEN, LONDON WC2
01-836-2330

Village Wooing (1934)
GEORGE BERNARD SHAW

5–29 January 1989

Z **Charmaine Parsons**　　　　　Deck Steward **Paul Raffield**
A **Robert Daws**

Overruled (1912)
GEORGE BERNARD SHAW

5–29 January 1989

Gregory Lunn **Paul Raffield**
Mrs Juno **Charmaine Parsons**
Sibthorpe Juno **Robert Daws**
Seraphita Lunn **Amanda Drewry**

Design **Phili Josephs**

The London Theatre Company presented two complementary comedies on the themes of courtship and marital infidelity. The productions were highly praised.

Lighting **David I Taylor**　　　　Director **Jim Dunk**
Sound **Mike Furness**

Commonweal's production of *Measure for Measure* played at the Theatre Museum from 22 March to 18 April 1989.

Don't You Know There's A War On? (1989)
JONATHAN CROALL

with **Penelope Dimond, Iain Macrae, Anne Kavanagh, Keith Myers and Nini Pitt**

Design **Rosa Maggiora**
Lighting **Bill Lee**
Director **Jonathan Croall**

25 April–20 May 1989

Jonathan Croall collated testimonies from those living in England during the Second World War. He wrote a book based on these which he has now turned into a play performed by the Real Theatre Company.

Equus (1973)

PETER SHAFFER

4–22 July 1989

Dysart **Paul Gilmore**
Alan **Chris Rickwood**
Hester **Amanda Windsor**
Frank **Eamonn Bohan**

Dora **Maureen Bell**
Jill **Candida Beveridge**
Nurse **Jennifer Rhule**
Horseman/Nugget **Alex Rose**

Horses **Patrick Walsh and Gary Clasby**

Director **Pat O'Toole**

Ghosts (1881)

HENRIK IBSEN

4–22 July 1989

Mrs Alving **Victoria McFarlane**
Oswald Alving **David Borrows**

Pastor Manders **Jim Boylan**
Engstrand **John Duggan**

Regina Engstrand **Linda Miles**

Director **Valda Aviks**

She Stoops To Conquer (1773)

OLIVER GOLDSMITH

4–22 July 1989

Prologue/Jack Slang/Diggery **Gary Clasby**
Mrs Hardcastle **Vivienne Race**
Mr Hardcastle **Matthew Townshend**
Tony Lumpkin **James George**
Kate Hardcastle **Ann Courteney**
Constance Neville **Tricia Shulten**
Dick Muggins/Roger **Eamonn Bohan**
Stingo/Sir Charles Marlow **Derek Bell**
Young Marlow **Alex Rose**
Hastings **Patrick Walsh**
Pimple **Jennifer Rhule**

Director **M J Coldiron**

Following their great success at the King's Head with *Peace in Our Time*, the Acting Company presented a summer season at the Theatre Museum, which had earlier seen First Light's *The Two Gentlemen of Verona*. *Equus* provided a good vehicle for a young cast who were also happy to romp through *She Stoops To Conquer*. *Ghosts* presented greater problems. Director Valda Aviks never seemed able to come to terms with the thrust stage at the Theatre Museum, with the result that much of the action was played at such a distance from the audience as to render it obscure – and sometimes it was obscured by furniture or other members of the cast. Nevertheless, the production had its good points, mainly in the performance of Victoria McFarlane as Mrs Alving. After an uncertain start, this young actress again revealed an immense talent, a potential which one hopes will soon be realised to the full on the British stage. There was adequate support from David Borrows and Jim Boylan, but John Duggan's Engstrand, a limping cockney wide boy, was an unfortunate piece of characterisation.

White Liars (1967)
Black Comedy (1965)
PETER SHAFFER

7–30 September 1989

with **Shirley-Anne Field, Kathryn Apanowicz, John Atterbury, Pamela Binns, Kenneth Bryers, Alexa Jago, Robert Lankesheer, Richard Linford and Iwan Thomas**

Director **David Evans Rees**

Argyle Productions offered a Peter Shaffer double-bill. *White Liars* is set in a fortune-teller's parlour and concerns self-deceit and insecurity; *Black Comedy* is a light-hearted play about what happens when the lights fail.

One of the great problems with regard to the Theatre Museum is to find out what is actually going on there. Publicity and communication are close to non-existent.

Warehouse Theatre Croydon

62 DINGWALL ROAD, CROYDON, SURREY CR0 2NF
01-680-4060

Artistic Director **Ted Craig**

Island Life (1988)
JENNY McLEOD

26 February–12 March 1989

Sophia **Joanna Field**
Emmy **Joan Hooley**
Vera **Stella Tanner**
Kate **Irma Innis**

Design **Iona McLeish**
Lighting **Dee Kyne**
Director **Jane Collins**

The Warehouse opened the year with the London Shakespeare Group's production of *Romeo and Juliet*, directed by Delena Kidd and starring Paul Rattigan and Rachel Fielding. This was followed by Red Shift's *Timon of Athens*, details of which can be found in the section dealing with touring companies. Monstrous Regiment's *Island Life* succeeded *Timon of Athens*.

Island Life was first presented in Nottingham in 1988 by one of the most renowned of women's theatre companies. Three ageing women in an old people's home, Sophia, Emmy and Vera, are visited by Kate. She seeks to destroy the dreams and illusions by which they live and confront them with reality. Ann McFerran, in *Time Out*, felt that Jenny McLeod wrote with 'empathy and insight for her characters' and that the production was fluent and the acting of high quality, but other critics were far less enthusiastic.

The play was also performed at the Drill Hall in February.

Dinner (1989)

MARK BUNYAN

17 March–16 April 1989

Elizabeth/Phillida **Pamela Moiseiwitsch**
Robert/Guy **Jonathan Hackett**
Clifford/David **Paul Gregory**
Arabella/Mary **Sally Faulkner**

Design **Michael Pavelka**
Lighting **Chris Corner**
Sound **Tim Carr**
Director **Ted Craig**

Dinner was the winner of the Warehouse's 1988 South London Playwriting Festival. Mark Bunyan, best known as a cabaret entertainer, has produced a play which involves four couples of different political persuasions and different social classes. A fine cast supported a play which showed that, with his witty lines and acute observation, the author has much promise and a sense of theatre which will hopefully be seen to good effect in the future.

16. Jonathan Hackett, Paul Gregory, Pamela Moiseiwitsch and Sally Faulkner in Dinner, Warehouse Croydon.

Factory Follies (1989)

TASHA FAIRBANKS

21 April–14 May 1989

Margery **Mandy Short**
Sharon **Rebecca Clow**
Annie **Katrina Buchanan**

Based on an original idea by the Hot Doris Band, *Factory Follies* tells of four women from diverse backgrounds who work in Hand Maid Sequins factory. The factory is threatened

Ria **Sayan Akkadas**

Design **Jacqueline Gunn**
Lighting **Bill Deverson**
Music **Sayan Akkadas, Colin Sell and Juliet Hill**
Musical Director **Juliet Hill**
Choreographer **Sue Colgrave**

with closure, and they are faced with the loss of their jobs. They resort to stealing ball-gowns from contestants in 'Come Dancing' and going to Paris to convince the French that sequins are the rage. The musical was welcomed for its vitality and zany moments, and Jacqueline Gunn's set was warmly applauded.

Director **Sue Colgrave**

Take Back What's Yours (1989)
JACQUELINE RUDET

19 May–11 June 1989

Apa **Allister Bain**
Jimmy **Alan Cooke**
Stan Man **Tommy Eytle**
Jenny **Irma Innis**
Steve **Robert McKewley**
Beatie **Cecilia Noble**
Fishboy **Mo Sesay**
Ama **Cleo Sylvestre**

Established as a sharp observer of black life in Britain, Jacqueline Rudet chose to make a faithful adaptation of Wesker's *Roots* for her latest play. Beatie returns to Dominica to break the news of her forthcoming marriage to Ronnie, but she is drawn into confrontation with her family and with her native island.

Design **Michael Pavelka**
Costume **Jessica Rufus**

Lighting **Chris Corner**
Director **Anthony Cornish**

The Harlot's Curse (1988)
RODNEY ARCHER and POWELL JONES

16 June–16 July 1989

Mary Kelly/Minnie/Margaret **Louise Bangay**
Edward/Clergyman **P J Cassell**
The Wife/Mazeppa/Streetwalker **Christine Hoodith**
Dickie/Brothel MC/Husband/Patient **John Hoye**
Mrs Berkeley/Lushing Loo **Heather Page**
Lord Esme Asterisk **Barry Shannon**
Mrs Berkeley's Horse/Surgeon **Kevin Squelch**
Journalist/Mazeppa's Father/Reggie **Prince Albert Tucker**
He Who Gets Spanked/Crippled Boy **Paul Viragh**

The Operating Theatre Company's production of an LWT award-winning play, *The Harlot's Curse*, is presented in documentary fashion. It tells of Mary Kelly, who was murdered by Jack the Ripper. Inevitably, it had a mixed reception, but Kate Kellaway in the *Observer* felt it was 'shocking, restrained and well researched'.

Design **Michael Pavelka**
Lighting **Barry Shannon**
Music **Marc Fraser**
Director **Rodney Archer and Powell Jones**

17. The Operating Theatre Company in The Harlot's Curse, *Warehouse Croydon.*

The Sweet Shop Owner (1989)

PHELIM McDERMOTT from the novel by Graham Swift

18–30 July 1989

with **Joanna Field, Michael Hadley, Johanna Kirby, Helen McGregor and Lee Simpson**

Design **Julia Bardsley**

Devised by Phelim McDermott and the company and based on Graham Swift's novel, *The Sweet Shop Owner* was commissioned by the Warehouse Theatre Croydon and by the Watermans Arts Centre, Brentford, where it played in June. It had earlier been seen at Mayfest. It is a melancholic, reflective

Lighting **Jon Linstrum**
Director **Phelim McDermott**

piece about a sweet shop owner and his beautiful, but sickly, wife. It spans a period of 40 years and tells of his constant desire for peace and the avoidance of family argument.

Gulliver's Travels (1988)

ALAN LEIGH from the book by Jonathan Swift

26 September–8 October 1989

Lemuel Gulliver **David Ford**
all other parts **Alan Leigh**

Music **Colin Good**

The Warehouse began their autumn season with Red Shift's *Frida and Diego* and had cause for celebration at the revival of Ted Craig's production of *The Astronomer's Garden* at the Royal Court Upstairs. The Lords of Misrule's version of *Gulliver's Travels* was originally presented at the Edinburgh Fringe in 1988 and won a First. It was recognised as being 'full of theatrical invention and flourish, and expertly performed by the cast of two'.

18. David Ford and Alan Leigh in Gulliver's Travels, *Warehouse Croydon.*

Sleepie Nightie (1989)

VICTORIA HARDIE

13 October–12 November 1989

with **Louise Jameson, Serena Gordon, Ray Jewers and Michael Garner**

Director **Terry Johnson**

A co-production with the Royal Court Theatre, *Sleepie Nightie* explores eroticism, rivalry and maternal passion through the eyes of two sisters who share a childhood secret. It was to transfer for November–December.

19. Warehouse Croydon and the Royal Court Theatre combined to present Victoria Hardie's Sleepie Nightie *with Serena Gordon and Louise Jameson.*

Gary, performed by a majority deaf and partially hearing company, is the story of a partially deaf boy who becomes the class clown in a comprehensive school. It was scheduled to play at the Warehouse from 15 to 26 November, prior to a national tour.

New seating and a vigorous approach to marketing and publicity since the arrival of Amanda Malpass from Chichester make the Warehouse a most entertaining and hospitable venue.

SECTION FIVE
Regional Theatre

1. Stepping Out *at the Palace Theatre, Westcliff.*

BAGNOR

Watermill Theatre

BAGNOR, NEWBURY, BERKSHIRE RG16 8AE
0635-46044

Artistic Director **Jill Fraser**

Pack of Lies (1983)

HUGH WHITEMORE

11 April–13 May 1989

The 22nd professional season at the Watermill began with Hugh Whitemore's compelling and moving play about the Krogers. The play centres on the spies' friendship with their neighbours and the effect that their capture and publicity has on them.

Stewart **Peter Cartwright**
Thelma **Cordelia Ditton**
Helen **Jane Lowe**
Peter **Geoff Oldham**
Barbara **Lill Roughley**
Bob **Christopher Scoular**
Sally **Stephanie Sirr**
Julie **Carol Starks**

Design **Stephen Howell**
Lighting **Brian Harris**
Director **Graham Callan**

2. Geoff Oldham and Lill Roughley in Pack of Lies at the Watermill.

Just So (1989)

GEORGE STILES and ANTHONY DREWE

18 May–17 June 1989

Zebra **Julie Armstrong**
Elephant Child **Anthony Barclay**
Kangaroo **Simon Bowman**
Parsee **Eric Ray Evans**
Leopard **Paul Gyngell**
Ethiopian **Okon Jones**
Strorks the Rhino **Charles Millham**
Kipling/Eldest Magician/Crocodile **Martin Smith**
Giraffe **Dawn Spence**
Kolo Kolo Bird **Sally Ann Triplet**
Dingo **Alexandra Worrall**

Design **Mark Thompson**

A revision of a musical inspired by the writings of Rudyard Kipling, *Just So* had its first staging in its new form at the Watermill. The earlier version was first performed in 1985 when it won the Vivian Ellis Prize. Under the direction of Julia McKenzie and with Cameron Mackintosh evidently enthusiastic about it, the production at the Watermill was well received. Michael Coveney in *The Financial Times* praised a cast that was 'uniformly good, from Charles Millham's bombastic rhino to Simon Bowman's cool, moon-walking kanga'.

Lighting **Howard Harrison**
Choreographer **Lea Anderson**
Sound **Julian Beech (Autograph)**

Musical Director **Kate Young**
Director **Julia McKenzie**

I Wish I Wish (1989)

TERENCE BRADY and CHARLOTTE BINGHAM

20 June–22 July 1989

William Dunster **Christopher Blake**
Georgina Burrell **Nell Conway**
Dulcie **Fiona Curtis**
Mrs William Dunster **Cheryl Kennedy**
Maid **Stephanie Sirr**

Design **Saul Radomsky**
Lighting **Brian Harris and Lawrence Doyle**

The Watermill prides itself that each year it tries to stage at least one world première. In 1989, a new comedy by Terence Brady and Charlotte Bingham had its first outing at Bagnor. To celebrate their 20th wedding anniversary, the Dunsters, William and Dulcie, return to the hotel where they spent their honeymoon – but events do not go quite as they had planned.

Director **Graham Callan**

Caste (1867)

T W ROBERTSON

25 July–26 August 1989

Historically, Tom Robertson stands as one of the most

3. Helen Patrick, Valentine Pelka and Kazia Pelka in the Watermill's worthy revival of Caste.

Marquise de St Maur **Yvonne Bonnamy**
Captain Hawtree **Paul Clayton**
Eccles **Barry Ewart**
Esther Eccles **Helen Patrick**
Polly Eccles **Kazia Pelka**
Sam Gerridge **Valentine Pelka**
Hon. George d'Alroy **Lucien Taylor**

Design **Jane Green**
Lighting **Ian Gibson**
Director **Euan Smith**

important figures in British drama, the founder of 'the cup-and-saucer-drama', the father of realism, yet his plays are all too seldom performed today. *Caste* was a play of deep social significance. George d'Alroy wants to marry Esther. He is an aristocrat; she is a variety girl. George goes off to fight in India, puts down the natives and is believed to have perished; but he returns to claim his bride and overcome the objections of his mother. Today it seems a mixture of melodrama and sentimentality, but it was given a rattling production at the Watermill. Helen Patrick provided a performance of note; Barry Ewart made 'a sly old dog Eccles'; and Yvonne Bonnamy gave 'a formidable stance in black glitter'.

84 Charing Cross Road (1981)

HÉLÈNE HANFF adapted for the stage by James Roose-Evans

29 August–30 September 1989

Frank Doel **Derek Anders**
Mrs Todd **Yvonne Bonnamy**
William **Paul Clayton**
Mr Martin **Barry Ewart**
Helen **Helen Patrick**
Maxine/Megan **Kazia Pelka**
Cecily **Stephanie Sirr**

Shortly after the Second World War, an American writer, Hélène Hanff, began a correspondence with a second-hand bookshop in Charing Cross Road. A strong transatlantic friendship developed, cemented by a love of literature. Surprisingly, the collection of letters was translated into remarkably charming and entertaining theatre.

Design **Geoffrey Scott**   Director **Euan Smith**
Lighting **Ian Gibson**

Old Herbaceous

ALFRED SHAUGHNESSY from the book by Reginald Arkell

2–7 October 1989

The one-man play about the head gardener who tells of his life at the manor house. It has been performed before the Queen Mother, and Roger Hume has been touring with the play for several years.

Old Herbaceous **Roger Hume**

11–25 November 1989, Old Time Music Hall, presented for the third year in succession by the exuberant and talented comedienne Helen Watson, who directs the show. This is something of a festival occasion for the Watermill, for the audience are encouraged to dress up in period costume and prizes are awarded to those wearing the most outlandish costumes.

King Rollo Space Crusader was to be the Watermill's Christmas show.

In 1965, the mill was converted into a 113-seat theatre in which there were occasional amateur performances. The first professional productions were staged the following year. In 1971, the auditorium was rebuilt and the capacity increased to 170. Further extensions and refurbishments have continued at this beautiful theatre with its pleasant restaurant. Enterprising and energetic, it is a theatrical equivalent of opera's Glyndebourne in its beauty and setting.

BELFAST

Lyric Theatre

55 RIDGEWAY STREET, STRANMILLS, BELFAST,
NORTHERN IRELAND BT9 5FB
0232-381081

Artistic Director **Roland Jaquarello**

After the Fall (1964)
ARTHUR MILLER

11 January–4 February 1989

Quentin **Tim Woodward**
Maggie **Claire Hackett**
Mother **Trudy Kelly**

Design **James Helps**
Lighting **Gerry Jenkinson**
Director **Roland Jaquarello**

Miller's powerful drama, allegedly based on his life with Marilyn Monroe, shows how a man battles through personal trials, slights and persecutions and the failure of personal relationships. In Roland Jaquarello's highly praised production, Ray Rosenfield in *The Stage* felt that Tim Woodward, as Quentin, never lost his magnetic hold and that Claire Hackett created 'a character of vulnerability and innocence, lost in loneliness of spirit and hysteric neurosis'.

Waiting for Godot (1953)
SAMUEL BECKETT

8 February–4 March 1989

with **Steve Martin and Robin Williams**

Design **Laura Pritchard**
Lighting **Patrick Dalgety**

The production was sponsored by Ulster Television, a reminder that Beckett is a major Irish playwright.

Director **Tim Webb**

Comedians (1975)
TREVOR GRIFFITHS

8 March–1 April 1989

Design **James Helps**
Lighting **Roger Simonsz**
Director **Brian Croucher**

The Northern Irish première of Trevor Griffiths's challenging play about a night class for would-be stand-up comedians.

Threshold (1980)

ALEXEI DUDAREV translated by Nina Fround, adapted by Derek Mahon

7–29 April 1989

Andrei Buslai **B J Hogg**
Alina **Marianne Wilson**
Sasha **Sean Kearns**
Mother **Trudy Kelly**
Father **Birdy Sweeney**
Nikolai **Noel McGee**
Krasovsky **Stephen Bent**
Nina **Lindy Whiteford**
Shargaev **Alan Devlin**
Policeman **Dan Gordon**
Grisha **Christopher Porter/ Andrew Carlisle**

Design **Boris Gerlovan**
Lighting **Roger Simonsz**

Threshold was very much a coup for the Belfast Lyric in that this was the first English production of a play which has been immensely popular in Russia. Directed and designed by leading figures in the Soviet theatre, the play is about Buslai, an alcoholic, who is rescued from freezing to death on the roadside by a famous writer. There is a sharp contrast between the writer's flat and the home of Buslai's parents, which is harsh and rural. The contrasts in Soviet life occupy Buslai's thoughts, and he is further distressed when he learns that a body, believed to be his, has been found and buried under his name. He returns home to find most people untroubled by his 'death'.

Music **Alexander Renanski**   Director **Valery Raevsky**

The Belle of the Belfast City (1989)

CHRISTINA REID

3–27 May 1989

Design **James Helps**
Lighting **Patrick Dalgety**
Director **Tim Luscombe**

A world première of a play in which three generations of a Northern Irish family are reunited during the week of an anti-Anglo–Irish Agreement rally.

Spokesong (1975)

STEWART PARKER

7–30 September 1989

Frank **Malcolm Douglas**
Daisy Bell **Ann Hasson**
with **Sean Caffrey and Fay Howard**

Design **James Helps**

The early and lamented death of Stewart Parker was marked by a revival of his first play. Set in a bicycle shop in Belfast, it traces the evolution of the bicycle against the threats of the car, the terrorists and the redevelopers. Frank battles to maintain the family bicycle shop and to win Daisy. It is she who finally rescues him from defeat and despair. Effectively allied to

Lighting **Roger Simonsz**
Director **Helena Kaut-Howson**

music, the play charts the survival of the individual against violence and bureaucracy. The production, with a most imaginative set, was highly acclaimed. Ray Rosenfield saw Malcolm Douglas as 'a sheer delight as Frank, both in his moments of ebullience and geniality and in unwonted despair'.

Tartuffe Today (1664)

MOLIÈRE adapted by John D Stewart

5–28 October 1989

with **Ann Hasson, Stella McGibbon and Malcolm Douglas**

Director **Jonathan Myerson**

Jonathan Myerson updated John D Stewart's 1971 adaptation of Molière's exposure of religious cant and hypocrisy. It was, perhaps, a little too brutal for the Northern Ireland public of today.

Charlie Gorilla (1989)

JOHN McCLELLAND

9–28 November 1989

Design **Alison Bockh**
Lighting **Roger Simonsz**
Director **Roland Jaquarello**

The Lyric's contribution to the Belfast Festival was the world première of a first play by a new Ulster writer. The play is set in a zoo and the central character is a gorilla.

The Little Shop of Horrors was planned as the Christmas–New Year production. An ambitious staging of Eugene O'Neill's *The Iceman Cometh* was scheduled for January and February, to be followed by *Ghosts* and *Sandy Deserts Snowy Mountains*.

BIRMINGHAM

Birmingham Repertory Theatre

BROAD STREET, BIRMINGHAM B1 2EP
021-236-4455

Artistic Director **John Adams**

Who's Afraid of Virginia Woolf? (1962)

EDWARD ALBEE

6–25 February 1989

Martha **Sylvia Syms**
George **James Bolam**
Nick **Jerome Flynn**
Honey **Beatie Edney**

Design **Roger Butlin**
Lighting **Paul Pyant**
Director **John Adams**

Albee's bitter and witty play about a college professor and his wife and the young couple whom they invite back for a drink after a party. The elder, childless couple play sado-masochistic games and the youngsters are caught up in the crossfire. This is a powerful, often harrowing, study of marital emotional agony; and the Birmingham Repertory production did the play justice, with Sylvia Syms and James Bolam as the fantasising, warring couple. The exchanges between Sylvia Syms and Beatie Edney (her daughter in real life) as Honey won special mention.

On the Verge (1988)

ERIC OVERMEYER

Studio 4–18 March 1989

Mary **Paola Dionisotti**
Fanny **Juliet Stevenson**
Alex **Gerda Stevenson**
Alphonse/Grover/The Gorge Troll/
Gus/The Yeti/Madame Nhu/Mr
Coffee/Nicky Paradise **George Irving**

Design **Kate Owen**
Lighting **Gerry Jenkinson**
Music **Caroline Humphris**
Director **Anna Furse**

Three Victorian ladies take a journey into *terra incognita*. They travel in space and time in what the author describes as the geography of yearning. This Birmingham Rep/Free Fall production was a British première of Overmeyer's play. Overmeyer has been one of the script writers for 'St Elsewhere'. Michael Ratcliffe found that the humour was 'always unpredictable and the whimsy refines into gentle anarchy and charm'. The play transferred to the Lilian Baylis Theatre, and the National Theatre schedule for *Hedda Gabler* was disrupted so that Juliet Stevenson could appear in *On the Verge*.

Our Ellen (1989)

RICHARD OSBORNE

Studio 11–22 April 1989

Ellen Terry **Tina Gray**

Design **Trudy Marklew**
Music **Nikola Chivers**
Director **Richard Osborne**

A highly successful one-woman show about the great actress, who was born in Coventry. We meet Ellen Terry in 1906 on the eve of her 50th anniversary on the stage. John Gross in the *Sunday Telegraph* described *Our Ellen* as 'not only entertaining, in fact, but also a vivid lesson in theatrical history'. The show toured and was at the Battersea Arts Centre and the Edinburgh Fringe.

The Importance of Being Earnest (1895)

OSCAR WILDE

10 March–15 April 1989

Jack Worthing **Rodney Cottam**
Algernon **Nigel Leach**
Gwendolen **Zelah Clarke**
Miss Prism **Jane Freeman**
Lady Bracknell **Kathy Staff**
Canon Chasuble **Peter Miles**

Having been associate director at the Birmingham Rep for four years, Derek Nicholls left to become artistic director at the York Theatre Royal. His last production at Birmingham was an exuberant staging of Wilde's most famous comedy.

Design **Terry Parsons**   Director **Derek Nicholls**

On the Plastic (1986)

JULIE WILKINSON

Studio 20–5 March 1989

with **Sally Armstrong, Janys Chambers, Dougal Lee and Royce Ullah**

Design **Jane Linz-Roberts**
Musical Director **Paul Herbert**
Director **Gwenda Hughes**

A Birmingham Rep touring production, *On the Plastic* is a comedy about the topical subject of living on credit. With her fiancé on the dole, Alexis is seduced by the glitter of the department store and uses her credit card to the full. Ruby, on the other hand, is thrifty – but her husband, Sid, is not.

Women Beware Women (1621)
THOMAS MIDDLETON

21 April–13 May 1989

Widow **Brenda Dowsett**
Laentio **Mark Jax**
Bianca **Judy Damas**
Guardiano **Nicholas Denney**
Fabritio **Alexander John**
Livia **Patricia Quinn**
Isabella **Alyson Spiro**
Hippolito **Renny Krupinski**
The Ward **Joe Dixon**
Sordido **Paul Henry**
Duke of Florence **Ian Barritt**
Lord Cardinal **Wyllie Longmore**

John Adams took *Women Beware Women* out of the Jacobean period and showed it to us with the aid of a Victorian Master of Ceremonies. The play depicts the corruption of two innocents, Bianca and Laentio. It displays a world of fetid evil which is motivated by lust, in which there are no heroes or heroines and where most end up dead. This was an imaginative production that was generally well received.

Master of Ceremonies **David Moylan**
Design **Paul Brown**
Lighting **Robert Ombo**
Director **John Adams**

A Small Family Business (1987)
ALAN AYCKBOURN

19 May–10 June 1989

with **Patricia Quinn, Renny Krupinski, Peter Laird, Terence Longdon, Judy Damas, Linda Gardner, Nicholas Law, Harriet Ashcroft, Ian Barritt, Leda Hodgson, Brenda Dowsett, Christopher Baines and Patrick Toomey**

One of Ayckbourn's more bitter comedies, *A Small Family Business* shows us drugs, murder, shop-lifting and the Mafia. A highly successful production with Douglas Heap's set design winning the highest praise.

Design **Douglas Heap**
Director **Helena Kaut-Howson**

Our Day Out (1983)
WILLY RUSSELL

16 June–8 July 1989

with **Edward Clayton, Beth Morris, Adjoa Andoh, Guy Moore, Tayo Akinbode, David Williams, Rachel Harvey, Victoria Bourne and Anthony Ryan**

Written first for television, *Our Day Out* is simply the story of a coach load of 14-year-olds from the city who are given a day out in the country, including a visit to the zoo, as a school trip. It is gloriously human, funny and sad; and it is full of vitality, with singing and dancing. Local schoolchildren played an

Design **Simon Higlett**
Director **Peter Oyston**

important part in the production, and much work was done with schoolchildren during the summer break when this community project was in full operation.

Punch and Judy The Real Story! (1989)

DEBBIE ISITT

Studio 18–20 September 1989

An award winner at the Edinburgh Fringe, *Punch and Judy* is an exciting piece of theatre which examines the horrors of domestic violence. Judy realises she must get away and take her revenge, for the sake of Judies everywhere.

Damn Yankees (1955)

18 September–14 October 1989

Lola **Caroline O'Connor**
Joe **Dursley McLinden**
with **Ian Burford, Geraldine Fitzgerald, Meg Johnson, Bill Bradley, Claude Close, Christopher Colby, Amanda Dainty, Kieran Daniels, Peter Edbrook, Michelle Fine, James Gavin, Dominic Gray, Doreen Hermitage, Cornell John, Stephanie Johns, Berwick Kayler, David Kort, Alan Mosley, David Needham and Jason Webb**

One of the most successful of musicals in America but only modestly successful at the Coliseum in 1957, *Damn Yankees* is based on the Faust legend. In the musical, a middle-aged baseball fan sells his soul to the devil in order to become a star player. Berwick Kayler was credited with giving an excellent comic performance as the Mephistophelian Mr Applegate in a brave production.

Words and Music **Richard Adler and Jerry Ross**
Book **George Abbott and Douglass Wallop**, based on Douglass Wallop's novel, *The Year the Yankees Lost the Pennant*

Design **Martin Johns**
Lighting **Mark Pritchard**
Costume **Charles Cusack Smith**
Musical Director **David Beer**
Orchestration **Julian Kelly**
Director **Paul Kerryson**

Hitler's Women, Foursight Theatre Company's vision of a war-shattered world through the eyes of Eva Braun and Unity Mitford, ran in the Studio from 21 to 23 September, and was followed by The Young Vic's *Can't Pay? Won't Pay! The Gun*, the Vox Theatre Company's production of *The Revenger's Tragedy*, and the Birmingham Rep's Touring Company production of *Stamping, Shouting and Singing Home* were among other pieces to be mounted in the Studio in the autumn.

Heartlanders (1989)

STEPHEN BILL, ANNE DEVLIN and DAVID EDGAR

19–28 October 1989

Design **Gavin Davies**
Costume **Anne Curry**
Lighting **Gerry Jenkinson**
Choreographers **Chitraleka and Nicola Davies**
Musical Directors **Peter Grahame and Stephen Rose**
Director **Chris Parr**

A celebratory play for the centenary of the city of Birmingham with a cast drawn entirely from the city's population.

Tom from Wales, Margaret from Oswestry and Aan from India come to Birmingham in search of different things. They meet at Digbeth bus station and journey through the city in this full-scale community project. Claire Armistead in *The Financial Times* called it 'courageous, colourful and occasionally awe-inspiring'.

Twelfth Night (1602)

WILLIAM SHAKESPEARE

3–25 November 1989

Maria **Judith Jacob**
Count Orsino **Thomas Baptiste**
Sir Toby Belch **Joseph Marcell**
Olivia **Ellen Thomas**
Feste **Jim Findlay**
Viola **Jan Ravens**
Sir Andrew Aguecheek **Matthew Kelly**
Malvolio **Joseph Charles**
Sebastian **Craig Stevenson**
Antonio **Anthony Wellington**
Fabian **Chris Tajah**
Courtier etc. **Trevor Butler**
Design **Jacqueline Gunn**
Music **Eugene Romain**
Director **Pip Broughton**

Set on a Caribbean island, Birmingham's production of *Twelfth Night* had distinctly Caribbean music and a mainly black cast. The shipwrecked Viola and Sebastian and Sir Andrew Aguecheek were the only characters played by white actors in this highly imaginative production.

Ron Pember's musical version of *A Christmas Carol* was the scheduled Christmas–New Year show; and *Summer of the Seventeenth Doll* and *The Seagull* were to follow. *The Seagull* was to be directed by Anthony Clark, being his first work since joining the Birmingham Rep.

BRISTOL

Bristol Old Vic

KING STREET, BRISTOL BS1 4ED
0272-250250

Artistic Director **Paul Unwin**

Abolition (1989)

GABRIEL GBADAMOSI

New Vic Studio 15 March–8 April 1989

Fox/Bosun **David Barrass**
Jake/Shantyman **Osei Bentil**
Surgeon/Balziel/Tarleton **Richard Durden**
Jenny/Cabin Boy **Julia Lane**
Tom/Pitt **Richard Lintern**
Knox/Wilberforce **Martyn Read**

Design **Sally Crabb**

Presented in conjunction with Paines Plough and later performed in Birmingham, at The Young Vic and elsewhere. Much of the action takes place on an overloaded slave ship bound for America. Concerned, as the title suggests, with the abolition of slavery, the play was felt by many critics to be too heavily weighted with too many themes and facts.

Lighting **Tim Mitchell**
Sound **David Redmayne**

Musical Director **Mark Vibrans**
Director **Debbie Seymour**

The Misanthrope (1666)

MOLIÈRE in a version by Tony Harrison

16 March–8 April 1989

Alceste **Edward Petherbridge**
Philinte **David Horovitch**
Oronte **Donald Pickering**
Célimène **Sian Thomas**
Eliante **Ingrid Craigie**
Arsinoé **Sheila Ballantine**
Acaste **Malcolm Sinclair**
Clitandre **Brian Pettifer**
Basque **Matthew Byam Shaw**
An Official of the Academie Française **Guy Nicholls**
Dubois **Peter Gunn**
Guests **Stephen Gray** and **Margaret Shade**
Keyboard **Laurie Stras/Linda Mayle**

A co-production between the Bristol Old Vic and the National Theatre, *The Misanthrope* later toured and played at the Lyttleton Theatre. The version of Molière's disturbing comedy – about Alceste, who becomes cut off from mankind because of his insistence on telling the truth – is that which was used in the Old Vic–National Theatre production in 1973. This is a sharp, witty translation using rhyming couplets. It sets the play in De Gaulle's France, a fact which, 16 years on, has lost some of its immediacy. Nevertheless, this remained a most stylish, often chilling production. Played on a severely raked stage which had the effect of telescoping Alceste's increasing isolation, it was acted with polish. Edward Petherbridge, if missing some of the pathos, was wonderfully disenchanted as he retreated further and further into himself and away from the hypocrisy that surrounded him. The support was excellent in style and characterisation.

Design **Richard Hudson**
Lighting **Laurence Clayton**

Sound **David Redmayne**
Music **Terry Davies**

Director **Paul Unwin**

4. The Bristol Old Vic/National Theatre production of The Misanthrope. Edward Petherbridge as Alceste and Sian Thomas as Celimente.

Joe **John Hannah**
Minnie **Ruth Mitchell**
Mrs Gascoigne **June Barrie**
Luther **Neil Dudgeon**

The Daughter-in-Law (1912)

D H LAWRENCE

New Vic Studio 12 April–6 May 1989

Lawrence's work for the theatre was unearthed by the English Stage Company in the sixties, but it has suffered an unwarranted neglect since. *The Daughter-in-Law* explores a favourite Lawrentian theme, the rival influences on a man

Mrs Purdy **Maureen Morris**

Design **Lez Brotherston**
Lighting **Tim Streader**
Sound **David Redmayne**
Director **Jenny Killick**

(Luther) of his wife (Minnie) and his mother (Mrs Gascoigne). B A Young was fulsome in his praise in *The Financial Times*: 'Jenny Killick's production of this splendid play is well-nigh perfect.' In a cast which was consistently good, Ruth Mitchell won special praise.

A Streetcar Named Desire (1947)

TENNESSEE WILLIAMS

13 April–6 May 1989

Blanche DuBois **Eleanor David**
Stella Kowalski **Claire Hackett**
Stanley Kowalski **Robert Pugh**
Harold Mitchell **Nicholas Colicos**
Eunice Hubbel **Deena Gornick**
Steve Hubbel **Simon Cook**
Pablo Gonzales/Sailor **Christopher Eccleston**
Woman/Nurse **Flaminia Cinque**

Young Collector/Street Vendor **Tim Crouch**

Design **Anthony Ward**

Lighting **Tim Mitchell**
Sound **Paul Arditti**
Music **Gary Yershon**
Director **Phyllida Lloyd**

A highly commended production which showed great imagination in design, lighting and music, creating a total atmosphere apposite to the play. The acting was universally praised, confirming the high standards of the Bristol Old Vic.

Knickers (1910)

CARL STERNHEIM translated by Eric Bentley

11 May–3 June 1989

Theobald Maske **Bruce Alexander**
Luise Maske **Julia Ford**
Gertrud Deuter **Jenny Galloway**
Frank Scarron **Alan Cumming**
Benjamin Mandelstam **Martyn Hesford/Mark Drewry**
A Stranger **Gary Yershon**

Design **Sally Crabb**
Lighting **David Redmayne**
Sound **Bill Ward**
Music **Gary Yershon**
Director **Stephen Unwin**

The Bristol Old Vic's major contribution to the Bath Festival was a most adventurous offering of the rarely seen *Die Hose* (or *Heroic Scenes from the Middle Classes*), a German comedy dating from before the First World War. Luise is young and beautiful and much admired, but there is a threat of a loss of reputation for her and her husband when her knickers fall down in public. She has three men in her life, a husband and two rival lovers, all of whom are affected by her embarrassment. She has other more pressing problems to worry about. 'An excellent company' under Stephen Unwin's direction adopted a style of over-playing which, according to Jeremy Brien, was the best method of coping with Sternheim's comment on the middle class of his time. Jenny Galloway's performance as the gossiping neighbour was warmly praised.

5. Patrick Malahide in Nick Dear's In the Ruins, a play and performance of immense power to end the season at the New Vic Studio, whose future is uncertain.

In the Ruins (1989)

NICK DEAR

New Vic Studio 22 May–3 June 1989

King George III **Patrick Malahide**
Page **James Brereton/Ben Wiles**

Design **Annabel Temple**
Lighting **Tim Streader and Lorraine Laybourne**
Sound **Bill Ward**
Music **Gary Yershon**
Director **Paul Unwin**

The last production of the year in the studio, before cuts forced this exciting theatrical venue to close. George III is a prisoner at Windsor in the closing years of his life. He is blind, deaf and devout. He is tortured by his doctors, abandoned by his people, scornful of republicanism, ruminative and reactionary. Learned in two weeks by Patrick Malahide as he wished to bless the New Vic studio with this 90-minute play before it went dark indefinitely, *In the Ruins* was welcomed as a brilliant piece, with Patrick Malahide giving a masterly and compelling performance.

Plaza Suite (1968)

NEIL SIMON

14 September–7 October 1989

Visitor from Mamaroneck

Karen Nash **Marcia Warren**
Sam Nash **Davyd Harries**
Bellhop **Adrian Scarborough**
Waiter **Matthew Roberton**
Jean McCormack **Jane Annesley**

Visitor from Hollywood

Waiter **Matthew Roberton**
Jesse Klipinger **Davyd Harries**
Muriel Tate **Marcia Warren**

Visitor from Forest Hills

Norma Hubley **Marcia Warren**
Roy Hubley **Davyd Harries**
Borden Eisler **Adrian Scarborough**
Mimsey Hubley **Jane Annesley**

Design **Louise Belson**
Lighting **Tim Streader**

The most famous of Neil Simon's social comedies is, in fact, three plays set in a New York hotel. It deals with the difficulties of growing older, apprehension about marriage and much else. The excellent Bristol production starred the delectable Marcia Warren.

Sound **Christopher Johns**

Director **Chris Harris**

Dona Rosita (1935)

FEDERICO GARCIA LORCA translated by Gwynne Edwards

12 October–4 November 1989

Dona Rosita **Susan Curnow**
The Housekeeper **Sandra Voe**
The Aunt **Eve Pearce**
The Uncle **Michael Turner**
Spinster/Manola **Michelle Butt**
Spinster **Petronilla Whitfield**
Spinster/Manola **Lucinda Smith**
Mother **Laura Cox**
Miss Ayola **Samantha Shaw**
Miss Ayola/Manola **Jane Annesley**
Nephew **Chris Eccleston**
Youth/Teacher of Political Economy
Adrian Scarborough
Don Martin **Peter Russell**

Design **Anthony Ward**

'The outwardly calm but inwardly passionate life of a young woman of Granada who slowly becomes that most grotesque and moving of Spanish spectacles: a spinster' – so Lorca described *Dona Rosita*, which, astoundingly, received its British première at Bristol in October. A picturesque production captured the richness of the poetry and of the symbolism. Nicholas de Jongh in *The Guardian* commented that Phyllida Lloyd's production sensibly allowed the play to escape from realism. This was aided by 'the superlative atmospherics of Anthony Ward's design and Tim Mitchell's lighting schemes with its sudden pink and blue hues'. A most courageous addition to the repertoire.

Lighting **Tim Mitchell**
Sound **Christopher Johns**
Choreographer **Petronilla Whitfield**
Music **Gary Yershon**
Director **Phyllida Lloyd**

6. *Sandra Voe in* Dona Rosita *by Lorca*.

Timothy West in *The Master Builder*, an adaptation of *Oliver Twist* and a production of *Othello* were planned to take this exciting theatre into the New Year when, one hopes, its quality will be more recognised with better funding and the reopening of the studio.

CHESTER

Gateway Theatre

HAMILTON PLACE, CHESTER CH1 2BH
0244-44238

Artistic Director **Philip Partridge**

21 January–18 February 1989, Alan Ayckbourn's *How the Other Half Loves* (1969) was presented.

Skin Deep (1989)
DAVID PINNER

2–25 March 1989

with **Mark Kingston, Oscar James** and **John Ringham**

The world première of a comedy which is set in Henley-on-Thames. The local school appoints a black headmaster (Oscar James). He wants a mortgage from the bank managed by Bob Woodward (Mark Kingston) so that he can move into the Woodwards' close.

Up 'N' Under (1984)
JOHN GODBER

13 April–6 May 1989

Arthur Hoyle **Andrew Tansey**
Reg Welsh **Geof Atwell**
Frank Rowley **David Barber**
Tony Burtoft **Steven Pinder**
Phil Hopley **Ron Meadows**
Hazel Scott **Ingrid Wells**

Godber's popular comedy was a substitute for the originally scheduled *Elsie and Norm's Macbeth*. It was a resounding success. Hal Wilton in *The Stage* felt that the cast made the most of 'the flimsiest of material'.

Design **Sue Pearce**   Sound **Chris Boneck**
Lighting **Jim Woodley**   Director **Laurence Honeyford**

Serious Money (1987)
CARYL CHURCHILL

12 May–3 June 1989

'A production with the usual Gateway polish', *Serious Money*,

Scilla Todd/Ms Biddulph **Sophie McConnell**
Jake Todd/Frosby/Grevett **Phil Willmot**
Grimes/Billy Corman **John Ashton**
Zackerman **Matthew Line**
Merrison/T.K./Nigel Abjibala **Tyrone Huggins**
Marylou Baines/Dolcie Starr/Mrs

one feels, has been a grossly over-rated play. Popular among the very money-market yuppies it satirises, it is a formless play and self-indulgently obscene.

Etherington **Gina Landor**
Jacinta Condor **Basienka Blake**
Dirkfield/Greville Todd/Duckett/Soat/Gleason **Ron Meadows**

Design **Linda Galvin**
Lighting **Jim Woodley**
Director **Philip Partridge**

The Rivals (1775)
RICHARD BRINSLEY SHERIDAN

14 July–12 August 1989

Mrs Malaprop **Nina Holloway**
Lydia Languish **Sophie McConnell**
Julia **Melanie Walters**
Captain Jack Absolute **Andrew Hall**
Sir Anthony Absolute **Tony Booth**
Faulkland **Bill Homewood**
Acres **David Barber**
Sir Lucius O'Trigger **Ron Meadows**
Lucy **Sandra Maitland**
Fag **Paul Mori**
David/Coachman **Guy Stevens**

Philip Partridge, who has moved into the world of film, ended his career as artistic director of the Gateway with a 'completely delightful' production of *The Rivals*. Lydia loves Jack Absolute only when she thinks he is Ensign Beverly, and Mrs Malaprop will only bless the union as long as she thinks it is not what her niece wants. The play was said to have been cast 'well and wisely' at Chester.

Design **Juliet Watkinson**   Director **Philip Partridge**

Elsie and Norm's Macbeth (1988)
JOHN CHRISTOPHER WOOD

7–30 September 1989

Norman Grimethorpe **Gorden Kaye**
Elsie Grimethorpe **Madge Hindle**

Design **Juliet Watkinson**
Lighting **Wayne Dowdeswell**

Rescheduled from earlier in the year, the play is a northern comedy in which Norman's discovery and editing of *Macbeth* is the heart of the humour.

Director **Andy Jordan**

An ambitious production of *Hamlet*, *The Turn of the Screw*, *Aladdin* and *Stepping Out* feature in the Gateway's autumn programme.

CHICHESTER

Chichester Festival Theatre

OAKLANDS PARK, CHICHESTER, WEST SUSSEX PO19 4AP
0243-781312

Artistic Director **John Gale**

Victory! (1908)

THOMAS HARDY adapted by Patrick Garland from *The Dynasts*

28 April–1 July 1989

This must have been the most courageous effort of the year. Patrick Garland took Thomas Hardy's three-part, 19-act, 139-scene *The Dynasts*, added a spice of humanity from *The Trumpet Major* and condensed it into a stageable play which he called *Victory!* The professional cast was augmented by 100 extras from the local community. Between them they delivered Hardy's epic prose and verse drama of the Napoleonic wars. Most were impressed by the grandeur of the conception and achievement, but Michael Billington got to the heart of the problem of *The Dynasts* when he wrote, 'Despite wonderful passages of lyric verse and some exhilarating spectacle, it gives little sense of how individual lives are shaped by history. It has a vast cast but few real characters.' Nevertheless, this was a mighty achievement. James Bolam was much praised for his Napoleon, 'a man coming to terms with his own helplessness'; and there were excellent performances from David Collings and Phyllida Hancock.

Napoleon **James Bolam**
Nelson/Wellington **David Collings**
The Old Soldier/Collingwood **Brett Forrest**
Dick Dewy **Tim Laycock**
William Dewy/Archbishop/Capt. Hardy/General Heymes/Prince Eugene **Robert Ralph**
Reuben Dewy/Miller Loveday **Terence Conoley**
Mrs Penny/Lady in Prussia/Second Lady at Waterloo **Charmian May**
Lady Susan/Josephine/Marie-Louise/Lady in Prussia/First Lady at Waterloo **Ana Healy**
Sgt.-Maj. Young/Murat/Mulgrave/Russian General **Michael G Jones**
Festus Derriman/Marshal Ney/Scott **Geoff Owen**
Keziar Cantle/Lady in Prussia/Cantiniere/Lady at Waterloo **Sara Weymouth**
Jems Purchess/Michael Mail/Lariboisiere **Craig Stevenson**
Farmer Ledlow/General Mack/Beattie/Duke of Richmond **Michael Bulman**
Duchess of Richmond/Lady in Prussia/Anne Garland **Phyllida Hancock**
Widow Garland/Lady at Waterloo **Dinah Harris**
Penny/Marshal Soult/Old Sailor **Kevin Stoney**
Mrs Maybold/Lady in Prussia/Lady at Waterloo/Sniper **Susan Gott**
Cripplestraw/Pitt/Kutozov **John Rogan**
Spink/Officer at Trafalgar/Imperial Guard **Bill Britten**
Jack Loveday/The Trumpet-Major **Robert Hands**
Bob Loveday/The Midshipman **Roger Moss**
Tommy Leaf/Imperial Guard/Midshipman **Malcolm Browning**
Shiner/Guard/Midshipman **Tim Dutton**

Design **Poppy Mitchell**

Lighting **Mark Pritchard**
Choreographer **Sue Harris**

Sound **Matthew Gale**
Musical Director **David Townsend**

Director **Patrick Garland and Matthew Francis**

The Heiress (1947)

RUTH and **AUGUSTUS GOETZ** from the novel, *Washington Square*, by Henry James

15 May–22 July 1989

Maria **Lois Harvey**
Dr Austin Sloper **Alec McCowen**
Mrs Lavinia Penniman **Phyllis Calvert**
Catherine Sloper **Nichola McAuliffe**
Mrs Elizabeth Almond **Valerie Colgan**
Marian Almond **Debra Beaumont**
Arthur Townsend **Jonathan Drysdale**
Morris Townsend **Ian Buchanan**
Mrs Montgomery **Hilary Tindall**

Ruth and Augustus Goetz turned James's novel into a melodrama which has been staged on numerous occasions throughout the world because it supplies what many see as 'good theatre'. That is doubtful, but it certainly supplies some good acting parts with its stern father, dowdy spinster daughter, silly but well-meaning aunt and mercenary suitor. The heiress herself is jilted when there is no money accompanying her, but she later takes her revenge on the man who has cheated her. Alec McCowen, Nichola McAuliffe and Phyllis Calvert took the opportunities offered to the full.

Design **Saul Radomsky**
Costume **Jane Robinson**

Lighting **Bill Bray**
Director **Vivian Matalon**

Summerfolk (1904)

MAXIM GORKY translated by Michael Robinson, adapted by Botho Strauss and Peter Stein

Minerva Studio 19 May–17 June 1989

Sergei Basov **Chris Hunter**
Varvara **Lesley Sharp**
Kaleria **Kate Duchene**
Vlas Chernov **Sam Graham**
Pyotr Suslov **Dermot Crowley**
Yulia **Caroline Loncq**
Kiril Dudakov **Will Knightley**
Olga **Caroline Webster**
Yaska Shalimov **Peter McEnery**
Pavel Ryumin **Tom Dunn**
Maria Lvovna **Dearbhla Molloy**
Dvoetochie **Stanley Page**
Zamislov **Darren Tunstall**

While studio theatres elsewhere were closing because of lack of funds, Chichester opened its new Minerva Studio. The first production was a revival of Gorky's play about an idle middle class who failed to create a better life as the Russia around them fell into decay and bred revolution. *Summerfolk* was praised for the high quality of its acting, with Lesley Sharp 'excellent as a broody, bookish lawyer's wife seething with quiet fury at these superfluous people'.

Pustobaika **Will Knightley**
Kropikin **Tom Hollander**

Lighting **Steve O'Brien**
Director **Sam Mendes**

Design **Paul Farnsworth**

Culture Vultures (1989)

ROBIN GLENDINNING

Minerva Studio 26 May–22 June 1989

Roly Miller **Roger Moss**
Fergus Roche **Robert Hands**
Deirdre Smith **Anna Healy**
Colonel Miller **Kevin Stoney**
Tommy Doran **John Rogan**
Sarah Ferguson **Sara Weymouth**
Teresa Devlin **Susan Gott**
Imelda O'Hare **Charmian May**
Sam McDowell **Geoff Owen**

The English première of Robin Glendinning's comedy parable. It is set in Ulster, where a Protestant and a Catholic return from university determined on reconciliation and put on a dreadful version of *The Cherry Orchard* with the local dramatic society.

Billy McFarland **Bill Britten**
The Auctioneer **Malcolm Browning**

Lighting **Steve O'Brien**
Director **Matthew Francis**

Design **Emma Fowler**

Warrior (1989)

SHIRLEY GEE

Minerva Studio 23 June–19 July 1989

Hannah **Lois Harvey**
Sculley/Ditch **Tom Hollander**
Mrs Sculley **Valerie Colgan**
Susan **Victoria Scarborough**
Godboll **Chris Hunter**
Drubber/Cumberland **Jonathan Drysdale**
Billy Cuttle **Stanley Page**
Flegg/Dr Kemp **Darren Tunstall**

Design **Paul Farnsworth**
Lighting **Steve O'Brien**

The world première of a play which tells of Hannah Snell who, in the 18th century, disguised herself as a boy and joined the navy. She survived the ravages of war, but, denied a pension, later earned a living as an entertainer. She was eventually sent to a lunatic asylum and diagnosed as mad because she prophesied that a weapon would be invented that could wipe out nations. The story itself is a remarkable one, and Tim Luscombe and his cast were warmly praised for maintaining attention and dramatic suspense until the end.

Musical Director **Corin Buckeridge**   Director **Tim Luscombe**

The Triumph of Love (1732)

PIERRE CARLET DE CHAMBERLAIN DE MARIVAUX
translated by Guy Callan

Minerva Studio 30 June–26 July 1989

Leonide **Kate Duchene**
Corine **Caroline Webster**
Arlequin **Tom Dunn**

In order to secure the love of Agis, Leonide has to persuade his guardians, Hermocrate and Leontine, that she is in love with them. Welcomed as a fine production.

Dimas **Stanley Page**
Agis **Sam Graham**
Leontine **Caroline Loncq**

Hermocrate **Will Knightley**

Design **Vicki Mortimer**

Lighting **Bill Bray**
Musical Director **Corin Buckeridge**
Director **Jeremy Raison**

London Assurance (1841)
DION BOUCICAULT

10 July–29 September 1989

Sir Harcourt Courtly **Paul Eddington**
Cool **Peter Fontaine**
Martin **Carl Oatley**
Charles Courtly **Benedict Taylor**
Richard Dazzle **Billie Brown**
Max Harkaway **Frank Gatliff**
Mr Solomon Isaacs **Jonathan Elsom**
William **John Hodgkinson**
Grace Harkaway **Sarah Woodward**
Pert **Phyllida Hancock**
Mark Meddle **John Rogan**
Jenks **Tim Dutton**
Lady Gay Spanker **Angela Thorne**
Mr Adolphus Spanker **John Warner**

An immense success when revived by the RSC in 1975, *London Assurance* is about the courtship by a young man, heavily in debt, of a cynical country beauty who is at first content to marry a rich old man but then falls in love with his son. The Chichester production, directed by the artistic director of the Minerva Studio, Sam Mendes, was hailed as a great success. There were hopes of taking the play to London, but half the theatres there are permanently cluttered with less engaging pieces.

James **Robert Ralph**
Maid **Susan Gott**
Footmen **Tony Ashton and Malcolm Browning**

Design **Daphne Dare**

Lighting **Bill Bray**
Sound **Matthew Gale**
Music **Peter Hayward**
Director **Sam Mendes**

Cloud Nine (1979)
CARYL CHURCHILL

28 July–22 August 1989

Maud/Betty **Kate Duchene**
Betty/Gerry **Tom Dunn**
Harry Bagley/Martin **Sam Graham**
Joshua/Cathy **Tom Hollander**
Edward/Victoria **Caroline Loncq**
Clive/Gerry **Darren Tunstall**
Ellen/Mrs Saunders/Lin **Caroline Webster**

'A brilliantly funny diptych of British sexuality in two eras', *Cloud Nine* was seen at Chichester as an excellent production of a flawed play.

Design **Vicki Mortimer**
Lighting **Steve O'Brien**

Director **David Leveaux**

7. Dorothy Tutin – an engagingly mature performance in A Little Night Music at Chichester.

A Little Night Music (1973)

31 July–30 September 1989

Madame Armfeldt **Lila Kedrova**
Desirée Armfeldt **Dorothy Tutin**
Fredrika Armfeldt **Debra Beaumont**
Frid **David Hitchen**
Fredrik Egerman **Peter McEnery**
Henrik Egerman **Alexander Hanson**
Anne Egerman **Deborah Poplett**
Petra **Sara Weymouth**
Count Carl Magnus Malcolm **Eric Flynn**

Sondheim always presents a problem: whether he should be performed by actors who are competent singers or by singers for whom acting is of secondary importance. A couple of years ago, the ENO chose the latter course for *Pacific Overtures* with disastrous results; in 1989, the Chichester Festival Theatre opted for the first course with considerable success. *A Little Night Music* has tenuous links with Ingmar Bergman's *Smiles of a Summer Night*, Shakespeare's *A Midsummer Night's Dream* and Woody Allen's *A Midsummer Night's Sex Comedy*; but, set in Sweden at the turn of century, it is unmistakably

Countess Charlotte Malcolm **Susan Hampshire**
The Liebeslieder Singers **Dinah Harris, Hilary Western, Susan Flannery, Michael Bulman and Philip Guy-Bromley**
Malla **Anna Healy**
Osa **Susan Gott**

Music and Lyrics **Stephen Sondheim**
Book **Hugh Wheeler**
Musical Director **Roger Ward**
Design **Mark Thompson**
Lighting **Nick Chelton**
Choreography **Anthony van Laast**
Sound **Matthew Gale**
Director **Ian Judge**

Sondheim with its wistful, often sardonic, view of human relationships.

Fredrik Egerman, a lawyer, has married for the second time. His new bride is much younger than he, and after eleven months the marriage has not been consummated. He takes her to the theatre where they see his former mistress, Desirée Armfeldt, a famous actress. They leave abruptly, but Fredrik returns to speak to Desirée. They renew their love affair until interrupted by Desirée's current lover, Count Carl Magnus Malcolm, a bristling officer. Eventually Fredrik's young wife elopes with his son, both having discovered the joys of love. Fredrik and Desirée, and their daughter Fredrika, are left to find happiness together.

In spite of Ian Judge's witty and sensitive direction, the exquisite design and costume of the piece, the delightful performance from the veteran Lila Kedrova as Desirée's mother and the enchantment of the Liebeslieder Singers, the production began slowly. This was mainly owing to Deborah Poplett's Anne. Miss Poplett's failure to comprehend the inner fear and uncertainty of the character and her presentation of Anne as nothing more than a silly, giggling girl was a grave flaw in an otherwise fine production. The play began to live when Desirée and Fredrik met and sang *You Must Meet My Wife*. From that point, with these two at the centre, it never flagged.

Both Dorothy Tutin – who, like vintage wine, improves with the years – and Peter McEnery gave highly intelligent performances rounded by a sense of the past. They were most ably supported by Susan Hampshire and Eric Flynn as the Malcolms. Miss Hampshire was beautifully at home in the part of the Countess, and it was good to see her being able to use her fine sense of comedy so effectively. It was one of her very best stage performances. Sara Weymouth and Alexander Hanson were equally impressive as rollicking maid and guilt-ridden son. Ian Judge's direction made us keenly aware of the symmetry of the piece.

The Purity Game (1989)

GILLIAN PLOWMAN

Minerva Studio 8–23 September 1989

Eddie **Michael G Jones**
Martha **Hilary Weston**
Eamon **Alex Hanson**

The world première of a soap opera in two episodes. *The Purity Game* is a musical which satirises soap operas. It was harshly received by some critics.

Greg **Roger Moss**
Derek **Tony Ashton**
Diana **Dinah Harris**
Sophie **Debra Beaumont**

Design **Vicki Mortimer**
Lighting **Bill Bray**
Choreographer **Andrea Wray**
Music **Corin Buckeridge**

Director **Will Cohu**

There was also a production of *Love's Labour's Lost* at the Minerva, but communication and press relations are not the theatre's strong point.

The opening of the new studio marks a fine and welcome achievement, but the interior of the main house is in need of a face-lift, and the public relations side as a whole needs a shake up. The pleasant town of Chichester still seems unaware that it hosts a major theatre. Try getting dinner after the show.

COLCHESTER

Mercury Theatre

BALKERNE GATE, COLCHESTER, ESSEX CO1 1PT
0206-573948

Artistic Director **Michael Winter**

16 March–8 April 1989, the touring production of *Gypsy*, by Newpalm Productions.

Brighton Beach Memoirs (1983)

NEIL SIMON

12 April–6 May 1989

Eugene **Christopher Luscombe**
Stanley **Jonathan Donne**
Jack **Paul Maxwell**
Kate **Celestine Randall**
Laurie **Mary Roscoe**
Nora **Teresa McElroy**
Blanche **Tessa Pritchard**

Neil Simon's autobiographical piece was very well received at the Mercury with 'a magnetically watchable performance' from Jonathan Donne, and the cast as a whole was highly praised.

Design **Jessica Bowles**
Costume **Jackie Trousdale**

Lighting **Jim Bowman**
Director **Dilys Hamlet**

Godspell (1971)

JOHN MICHAEL TEBELAK

27 July–26 August 1989

The Colchester production brought *Godspell* 'defiantly into the late eighties, its peace and love theme no less significant when acted and sung in tight leggings, baseball caps and baggy tee shirts instead of clownish post-hippy gear'.

with **Richard Brightiff**, **Karen Chatwin**, **William Cox**, **Hal Fowler**, **Paulette Ivory**, **Tracey-Ann Morris**, **Graham MacDuff**, **Jack Murphy**, **Jean-Paul Orr** and **Sam Torrington**

Design **Jessica Bowles**
Lighting **Jim Bowman**

Choreographer **Sean Walsh**
Music and Lyrics **Stephen Schwartz**
Musical Director **Nick Sexton**
Director **Michael Winter and Sean Walsh**

When I Was a Girl I Used to Scream and Shout (1985)

SHARMAN MacDONALD

30 August–9 September 1989

The exploration of the mother–daughter relationship and of lost youth was a popular choice for repertory companies in 1989, but the play is not wearing well.

Fiona **Liz Brailsford**
Vari **Louise Gold**
Morag **Helen Fraser**
Ewan **Jan Lower**

Design **Jackie Trousdale**

Lighting **Jim Bowman**
Costume **Gilly Crowther**
Director **Elizabeth Gorla**

A Midsummer Night's Dream (1596)

WILLIAM SHAKESPEARE

13–30 September 1989

Lighting transforms a marbled hall into the woods, for Richard Digby Day's *Dream* is set in the 19th century in a production which, according to Liz Mullen in *The Stage*, was 'sure to enrapture audiences'. 'Sexual sparks fly in fairyland and glow more steadily on the mortals.'

Theseus/Oberon **Mark Barratt**
Bottom **Brian Parr**
Philostrate/Puck **Paul Reeves**
Hippolyta/Titania **Susan Edmonstone**
Egeus/Peter Quince **Geoffrey Colville**

Snout **Hal Fowler**
Starveling **Nicholas Haverson**

Snug **Jack Murphy**
Fairy/Flute **Derek Wright**
Helena **Hermione Norris**
Demetrius **Michael Hodgson**

Hermia **Susannah Jupp**
Lysander **Russell Porter**

Design and Costume **India Smith**

Lighting **Jim Bowman**
Music **Nick Sexton**
Director **Richard Digby Day**

Habeas Corpus (1973)
ALAN BENNETT

4–28 October 1989

Dr Wicksteed **Basil Hoskins** with **Janet Hargreaves, Delena Kidd, Patricia Kneale, Tessa Pritchard, Keith Osborn, Nicholas Haverson, Michael Hodgson, Hermione Norris and Brian Parr**

The frustrations and mistakes of a doctor, his family and their friends are the themes of Bennett's comedy.

Design and Costume **Jessica Bowles**
Lighting **Christine Piper**

Sound **Jim Bowman**
Choreographer **Stephanie Carter**
Director **Michael Winter**

In November, the Mercury presented *Siege*, a community project which celebrated the 800 years since Colchester first received its charter. The Christmas–New Year show was *Wind in the Willows*.

COVENTRY

Belgrade Theatre

BELGRADE SQUARE, COVENTRY,
WARWICKSHIRE CV1 1GS
0203-553055

Director **Robert Hamlin**

The Unexpected Guest (1958)
AGATHA CHRISTIE

26 January–18 February 1989

Richard Warwick **John Kelly**
Laura Warwick **Holly de Jong**
Michael Starkwedder **Stephen Hattersley**
Miss Bennet **Katharine Barker**
Jan Warwick **Tim Crouch**

The post-Christmas period hatches a crop of Agatha Christies for commercial reasons, and the Belgrade followed the pattern.

Mrs Warwick **Veda Warwick**
Henry Angell **George Parsons**
Sergeant Cadwallader **Peter Rylands**
Inspector Thomas **Peter Barnes**
Julian Farrar **Christian Roberts**

Design **Trevor Coe**
Costume **Trudy Marklew**

Lighting **Tim Wratten**
Sound **Steve Wilson**

Director **Simon Dunmore**

The Glass Menagerie (1944)
TENNESSEE WILLIAMS

23 February–11 March 1989

Tom **Nicholas Jeune**
Amanda **Tina Gray**
Laura **Phoebe Burridge**
Jim O'Connor **Dominic Hawksley**

Design and Costume **Trudy Marklew**
Sound **Steven Wilson**
Lighting **Tim Wratten**
Director **Robert Hamlin**

'All these huge buildings are always burning with the slow and implacable fires of human desperation', wrote Tennessee Williams in his setting for *The Glass Menagerie*. The talkative, domineering mother, Amanda, tries to bring love for her daughter, but her plans are dashed, just like the glass menagerie which her daughter collects. A play of poetry and memory which Robert Hamlin's sensitive direction and some fine acting distilled with the necessary delicacy.

8. Phoebe Burridge as Laura and Dominic Hawksley as the Gentleman Caller in The Glass Menagerie *at the Belgrade Theatre, Coventry.*

4–22 April 1989, *Return to the Forbidden Planet.* The production transferred to the Cambridge Theatre, London, under which details will be found.

Stiff Options (1982)

JOHN FLANAGAN and ANDREW McCULLOCH

24 April–6 May 1989

Stringer **John Savident**
Sharon **Tracy Brabin**
Edgar **Stephen Hancock**
Clegg **Richard Platt**
Ronnie **Peter Howitt**
Violet **Anne Jameson**

Originally produced at Theatre Royal Stratford E15, *Stiff Options*, a comedy set in a funeral parlour in Lancashire, was a touring production mounted by the Churchill Theatre, Bromley.

Design **Glenn Willoughby** Director **Warren Hooper**
Lighting **Mike Seignior**

Brighton Beach Memoirs (1983)

NEIL SIMON

11–27 May 1989

Eugene Jerome **Gian Sammarco**
Blanche Morton **Amanda Boxer**
Kate Jerome **Joyce Springer**
Laurie Morton **Helen Barrett/ Shelley Simmons**
Nora Morton **Julie Clare**
Stanley Jerome **Hugo E Blick**
Jack Jerome **Carl Forgione**

The semi-autobiographical comedy, essentially human, set in Brooklyn just before the outbreak of the Second World War. Under Robert Hamlin's direction, the Belgrade cast worked hard to clarify Simon's wry recognition of the fallibilities, hopes and dreams of the people around him.

Design **Adrian Rees** Sound **Steve Wilson**
Lighting **Tim Wratten** Director **Robert Hamlin**

Dangerous Obsession (1987)

N J CRISP

5–10 June 1989

Sally Driscoll **Susan Penhaligon**
John Barrett **Simon Ward**
Mark Driscoll **Jeremy Bulloch**

Design **Shelagh Keegan**

Another touring production from the Churchill Theatre Crisp's thriller could not have had a better cast than the three listed here.

Lighting **Chris Boyle** Director **Roger Smith**

Steaming (1981)

NELL DUNN

22 June–8 July 1989

Violet **Jill Graham**
Bill **Stuart McCartney**
Josie **Caroline Gruber**
Dawn **Sunny Ormonde**
Mrs Meadow **Pauline Jefferson**
Nancy **Sara Coward**
Jane **Katharine Barker**

Design **Trudy Marklew**

If the striptease masquerading as women's liberation is now rather outdated, there is still a warmth in the relationships of a group of women made equal by their nudity and united in their opposition to the threatened closure of their Turkish bath. Sue Wilson's production achieved fine teamwork which created a 'sense of shared liberation and naturalness'.

Lighting **Susie Caird**
Sound **Steven Wilson**
Director **Sue Wilson**

Belgrade Theatre/National Theatre production of The Beaux Stratagem, *with Brenda Blethyn as Mrs Sullen and Nicholas Day as Gibbet.*

The Beaux Stratagem (1707)

GEORGE FARQUHAR

25 August–23 September 1989

Boniface **Harold Innocent**
Cherry **Jessica Turner**
Thomas Aimwell **Paul Mooney**
Francis Archer **Stephen Dillon**
Dorinda **Jane Gurnett**

The Belgrade Theatre's event of the year, in that this was a co-production with the National Theatre. It later toured and played at the National. Aimwell and Archer are nearly penniless. Aimwell falls in love with Dorinda, but Archer attempts to seduce Mrs Sullen, whose marriage to the country

Mrs Sullen **Brenda Blethyn**
Squire Sullen **Marc Sinden**
Gibbet **Nicholas Day**
Scrub **Allan Corduner**
Gipsy **Nicola Redmond**
Foigard **John Franklyn-Robbins**
Count Bellair **Peter Darling**
Countrywoman **Rita Davies**
Lady Bountiful **Matyelok Gibbs**
Hounslow **David Annen**
Bagshot **Anthony Renshaw**
Sir Charles Renshaw **Geoffrey**

squire is in decline. What makes the play unique among Restoration comedies is that happiness is brought about by divorce rather than by marriage. Brenda Blethyn's performance was seen as the jewel in a production which was regarded as rather mellow.

Church
Tapster **Jon Croft**
Servant/Fellow **John Holbeck**
Serving Woman **Tacye Nichols**

Design **Peter J Davison**

Costume **Sue Wilmington**
Lighting **Mark Henderson**
Choreographer **David Toguri**
Music **Dominic Muldowney**
Director **Peter Wood**

One for the Road (1976)

WILLY RUSSELL

28 September–21 October 1989

Dennis Cain **Roy Brandon**
Pauline Cain **Diane Whitley**
Roger Fuller **Richard Walker**
Jane Fuller **Lynette Edwards**

Design **John Elvery**
Lighting **Susie Caird**
Sound **Steven Wilson**
Director **Richard Brandon**

One for the Road is the play by Willy Russell which is, perhaps, closest to Ayckbourn in that it deals with middle-class marriage and marital infidelity brought about by boredom.

The Belgrade's programme from October 1989 to March 1990 is *Hold Tight*, a new musical; *Dead of Night*; *Aladdin*; *Noises Off* and *Pack of Lies*.

DERBY

Derby Playhouse

THEATRE WALK, EAGLE CENTRE, DERBY DE1 2NF
0332-363275

Artistic Director **Annie Castledine**

Wicked Old Nellie (1989)

LUCY GANNON

Studio 26 January–11 February 1989

Director **Annie Castledine**

A new play which later had an extensive tour, *Wicked Old Nellie* is about an elderly woman who refuses to conform to society's view of her as helpless and senile. In her own mind she lives in a world of beauty, fantasy and the past.

Entertaining Mr Sloane (1964)
JOE ORTON

10 February–11 March 1989

Sloane **David Harewood**
Kath **Penelope Nice**
Ed **James Tomlinson**
The Dadda **Chris Wilkinson**

Director **Susan Todd**

The arrival of a young, attractive and mysterious lodger has a devastating effect upon the Kemps' household. This black comedy established Orton as a satiriser of the gap that exists between what people consider proper and how they behave. Susan Todd's direction missed none of the irreverence or humour.

Love Games (1895)
ARTHUR SCHNITZLER translated by Charles Osborne from *Liebelei*

17 March–8 April 1989

Hans Weiring/Man **Christopher Wilkinson**
Christine **Jane Gwilliams**
Mizi Schlager **Joy Blakeman**
Katharina Binder/Lady in Black **Mary McCusker**
Lina **Heather Cairney/Phillipa Harris**
Fritz Lobheimer **Ian Fitzgibbon**
Theodore Kaiser **David Westhead**

Design **Anthony Ward**
Lighting **Nick Beadle**

In the elegant, artistic, socially exciting Vienna of the late 19th century, Fritz amuses himself with a relationship with Christine, a lovely young girl who, as the daughter of a poor violinist, is socially his inferior. She comes close to redeeming him, but his past philandering catches up with him and the end is tragic. This is a masterly play, and Susan Todd's production won the highest accolades. Michael Schmidt in *The Daily Telegraph*, having praised an outstanding set and some fine acting, wrote, 'Schnitzler is a major playwright, a fact which we tend to forget between the rare outstanding productions of his work. This is one of them.'

Sound **Alan Jackson**   Director **Susan Todd**

Touched (1977)
STEPHEN LOWE

14 April–6 May 1989

The theme of Lowe's play is the way in which individual lives

Sandra **Sally Edwards**
Joan **Barbara Peirson**
Betty **Tanya Myers**
Mother **Madeline Blakeney**
Pauline **Tiffany Wilkey**
Mary **Fenella Norman**
Keith **Simeon Moore**
Bridie **Charlotte Barker**
Harry **David Lusted**
Johnny **Stefan Escreet**

are touched by national events. It is set in the summer of 1945, in Nottingham, and covers the hundred days between VE Day and VJ Day, by which time two atom bombs have been dropped. 'Derby is fortunate to see acting of this calibre in a production which combines emotional truth with expressive theatricality', was Michael Billington's verdict.

Design **Ruari Murchison**
Lighting **Nick Beadle**

Sound **Alan Jackson**
Director **Annie Castledine**

Noises Off (1982)

MICHAEL FRAYN

19 May–10 June 1989

Director **Annie Castledine**

This was a replacement for the originally intended *The Singular Life of Albert Nobbs*, and, one believes, was a compromise with the Derby public after three brilliant productions which were of a more specialised nature. It was followed by *The Piggy Bank*, 16 June–8 July – which transferred to Greenwich, under which details will be found – and touring productions of *Dangerous Obsession* (see Belgrade, Coventry) and *Joseph and the Amazing Technicolor Dreamcoat*.

This is a wonderfully virile theatre with directors of high quality. One hopes that they get the support that they deserve.

DUNDEE

Dundee Repertory Theatre

TAY SQUARE, DUNDEE, SCOTLAND DD1 1PB
0382-23530

Director **Robert Robertson**

A Man at Yir Back (1989)

GORDON BURNSIDE

19 January–4 February 1989

A new play which revolves around a 72-year-old council flat

Dolly **Irene Sunters**
Social Worker **Joanna Dadd**
and others

Director **Robert Robertson**

tenant – 'a lovable, moving performance from Irene Sunters' – and her dealings with an obtuse and incompetent social worker from Plymouth.

Ruffian on the Stair (1964)
Funeral Games (1968)
JOE ORTON

9 February–4 March 1989

Design **Neil Murray**
Director **Cliff Burnett**

Two Orton plays which began life as television plays.

The Cherry Orchard (1904)
ANTON CHEKHOV translated by Ronald Hingley

9 March–1 April 1989

Madame Ranevskaya **Joanna Lumley**
Lophakin **Cliff Burnett**
Pishchik **Robert Robertson**
Lambent Gayev **Richard Simpson**
Trofimov **Richard Clewes**
Yepikhodov **Robbie MacNab**
Yasha **Ken Dudley**
Varya **Tacye Nichols**

'A handsome production' which Dundee had long been promised, *The Cherry Orchard* was warmly received for the style and consistency of the playing.

Carlotta **Julie T Wallace**
Anya **Polly Pleasence**
Dunyasha **Lucy Ellis**
Firs **Robert McIntosh**

Design **Monika Nisbet**
Lighting **Andre Thames**
Director **Robert Robertson**

The Philanthropist (1970)
CHRISTOPHER HAMPTON

6–29 April 1989

Philip **Robert McIntosh**
Donald **Richard Clewes**
Braham **Kenneth Oxtoby**
Celia **Lisa Tramontin**
Araminta **Tacye Nichols**

Christopher Hampton's black comedy owes a debt to Molière in that its hero, Philip, believes in being pleasant to everyone and agreeing with them and, in keeping to that, causes havoc. Indeed, the play begins with the suicide of a young student whose flawed play he has wrongly praised. There were fine performances from a strong cast, with Robert McIntosh

Design and Director **Neil Murray**

excelling in the lead and Kenneth Oxtoby to the fore as the egotistical and offensive writer, Braham.

The Government Inspector (1836)

NIKOLAI GOGOL in a Scottish version by Andrew McKinnon

17 August–9 September 1989

with **Kenneth Lindsay, Jackie Farrell and others**

A most unhappy attempt to redirect to Scotland Gogol's classic comedy of small-town lives and fear of higher authority.

Director **Robert Robertson**

She Stoops to Conquer (1773)

OLIVER GOLDSMITH

14–30 September 1989

Tony Lumpkin **Gerard Doyle**
Mr Hardcastle **Lewis Cowen**
Marlow **Bernard Wright**
Hastings **Graham McTavish**
Mrs Hardcastle **Maggie Shevlin**
Kate Hardcastle **Rosaleen Pelan**
with **Kenneth Lindsay, Kate O'Connell, Kenneth Bryans and Tony Cownie**

Goldsmith's gentle comedy of the mistakes of a night and of identity won praise for Gerard Doyle, who played Tony Lumpkin with 'an amiable sense of mischief', and for Rosaleen Pelan's 'delicate skill'. The cast as a whole were complimented although the production was felt to be lacking in intimacy.

Design and Director **Neil Murray**

The Playboy of the Western World (1907)

J M SYNGE

5–28 October 1989

Christy Mahon **Paul Boyle**
Pegeen **Kate O'Connell**
Old Mahon **Decland Mulholland**
and others

Director **Robert Robertson**

Synge's play provoked a riot when it was first performed, for its tale of the supposed father-murderer who becomes hero worshipped by the villagers upon whom he stumbles shocked the people of its day. This is a very fine play which gained an honest and praiseworthy production at Dundee.

The Dundee Repertory Theatre's 50th anniversary season continued with productions of *Macbeth, When the Wind Blows, Death of a Salesman, 'Tis Pity She's a Whore* and the return of *A Man at Yir Back*.

EDINBURGH

Royal Lyceum Theatre Company

GRINDLAY STREET, EDINBURGH, SCOTLAND EH3 9AX
031-229-9697

Artistic Director **Ian Woolridge**

Le Bourgeois Gentilhomme (1671)

MOLIÈRE translated and adapted by Hector MacMillan

13 January–4 February 1989

Maister Jourdain **Robert Carr**
Covielle/Music Master/Tailor **Jimmy Chisholm**
Mufti/Musician **Fin Johnstone**
Dorimene **Eliza Langland**
Lucile/Dancing Master **Una Ailsa McNab**
Dorente/Philosopher **Bill Murdoch**
Madame Jourdain **Mary Riggans**
Nicole **Ann-Louise Ross**
Cleonte/Fencing Master **Alexander West**

Molière's humorous observation of the *nouveau riche* attempting to acquire the social graces that would match their wealth was given a Scottish setting. Although the tone and mood of the play transferred well to Scotland, the production was seen as patchy.

with **Gail Donaldson, Fiona Dougal, Vicky Fairfull, Edith Gould, Annabel McWilliam, Ronnie Simon and Robert Cavanah**

Design **Philippe Cherbonnier**
Lighting **Stella Goldie**
Choreographer **Eliza Langland**
Musical Director **Iain Johnstone**
Director **Hamish Glen**

Ghosts (1881)

HENRIK IBSEN

6–21 October 1989

Mrs Alving **Paola Dionisotti**
Oswald Alving **George Anton**
Pastor Manders **Jonathan Hackett**
Engstrand **Kenneth Owens**

One can think of few theatres in Great Britain, indeed the world, which would offer their audiences such a challenging programme as the Royal Lyceum has for 1989–90. It began with *Volpone* and was followed by a production of *Ghosts* which, if

Regina Engstrand **Cara Kelly**

Design **Kenny Miller**
Lighting **Kevin Sleep**

Music **Adrian Johnston**

Director **Robert J Carson**

it had its weaknesses, was commended for Carson's 'careful, text-book direction'.

Othello (1604)

WILLIAM SHAKESPEARE

27 October–18 November 1989

Othello **Burt Caesar**
Brabantio **Alex McAvoy**
Cassio **Paul Spence**
Iago **Bill Leadbitter**
Roderigo **Robin Sneller**
Duke/Gratiano **Derek Anders**
Montano/Senator **Lawrence Douglas**
Lodovico/Senator **Kenneth Owens**
Desdemona **Gerda Stevenson**
Emilia **Ann-Louise Ross**
Bianca **Anne Marie Timoney**
with **Edward Cory and David Roylance**

Design **Gregory Smith**

Lighting **Stella Goldie**
Music **Savourna Stevenson and John Sampson**

Director **Ian Woolridge**

Another impressive production of a classic of the theatre graced the Lyceum stage as the third play in the 1989–90 season. It was to be followed by *The Slab Boys* by John Byrne, *Fitting for Ladies*, a Feydeau farce, *Juno and the Paycock*, *Look Back in Anger* and *The Duchess of Malfi*. This is an impressive programme, but one would expect nothing less from a theatre which is well organised on the business side and jealous of the quality of its productions and of the quality of the plays it presents.

The Royal Lyceum Theatre Company is Scotland's largest producing theatre company. It operates a wide range of activities and presents 12 to 13 classics or new Scottish plays in its repertoire each year as well as taking them on tour.

FARNHAM

The Redgrave Theatre

BRIGHTWELLS, FARNHAM, SURREY GU9 7SB
0252-715301

Artistic Director **Graham Watkins**

The Old Country (1977)

ALAN BENNETT

25 January–11 February 1989

Hilary **Francis Matthews**
Bron **Helen Christie**
Duff **Nigel Davenport**

Alan Bennett's carefully judged and wryly humorous play gained an excellent production at The Redgrave before it embarked on a national tour. It is about a spy in exile on the eve

Veronica **Anne Ridler**
Eric **David Bannerman**
with **Sally Goodman**

Design **Elroy Ashmore**
Director **Graham Watkins**

of repatriation and the barriers of class which exist even when two men have committed the same offence. 'Francis Matthews created a highly polished character study' and Helen Christie was 'serenely composed' as his wife, wrote Peter Tatlow. The serenity is important for that chilling line when she talks of waking in the middle of the night and realising that this is 'happy ever after'.

A Pin to See the Peep Show (1952)

F TENNYSON JESSE and H M HARWOOD adapted from the novel by F Tennyson Jesse, further adapted by Eric Standridge

15 February–11 March 1989

with **Helen Patrick, Rebecca Charles, Norman Eshley, Annette Fraser, Alison Larkin, Gillian Roberts, Desmond Jordan, Di Langford, Damien Thomas, Derek Beard, Lisa Heeley, Ross Kemp, Richard Dyball and Craig James**

Based on the notorious murder case of 1922, the Thompson–Bywaters affair, *A Pin to See the Peep Show* was first a best-selling novel and then a play that was banned by the Lord Chamberlain. A 20-year-old seaman killed his lover's husband. She was a few years older than him, which is what caused the initial stir. With a clever use of mobile scenery and with good ensemble playing, The Redgrave 'presented a production so intense that the audience was stunned into silence at the end' (*The Stage*). The play subsequently toured.

Candida (1897)

GEORGE BERNARD SHAW

15 March–8 April 1989

Candida **Karen Ford**
Marchbanks **Phillip Dupuy**
Burgess **Alan Towner**
Lexy **Lawrence Thornbury**
Miss Proserpine **Poppy Hands**
Morell **William Whymper**

A neatly competent and sensitive production of Shaw's tale of the vicar's wife who must choose between her husband and a young poet.

Design **Clare Southern**   Director **Julia Limer**

Dust-Up In the Attic (1989)

JEANETTE RANGER and CHRISTOPHER LILLICRAP

21 March–8 April 1989

Racket **Robert Hughes**
Mrs Mop **Lucille O'Flanagan**
Tinsel **Annie Wensak**
Dry Rot **Tim Raynham**
Left **Paul Tyrer**
Right **Karl Moffatt**
Woodworms **Jack Jewers, Amy Thomas, Adele Cullen, Eve**

Awdrey, Sam and Gemma Fielding, Zoe Cox and Emma Turner

A tremendously successful afternoon show for children, the 'goodies' being the rejects in the attic and much audience participation.

Music **Marilyn Phillips**
Choreographer **Annie Wensak**
Director **Jeanette Ranger**

The Aspern Papers (1959)

MICHAEL REDGRAVE from the story by Henry James

12 April–6 May 1989

Juliana Bordereau **Anna Wing**
H. J. **Julian Glover**
Tina Bordereau **Ruth Trouncer**
Pasquale **Stuart Powell**
Assunta **Christine Drummond**
Mrs Prest **Ginnette Clarke**

Director **Graham Watkins**

An historic revival of Michael Redgrave's fine adaptation of James's atmospheric and moving tale. An American literary man is determined to obtain from an old woman the love-letters which her lover, a famous poet, wrote to her in her youth.

10 May–3 June 1989, The Redgrave offered Beaumarchais's *The Barber of Seville* (1775).

The Complaisant Lover (1959)

GRAHAM GREENE

7 June–1 July 1989

Victor Rhodes **Ken Farrington**
Mary Rhodes **Christine McKenna**
Clive Root **Peter Sands**
Valet **Bill Angel**

Great novelist though he is, Graham Greene has not written well for the stage, and *The Complaisant Lover* is a mixture of bedroom farce and strong drama. Given its limitations, it was well served by an energetic cast at Farnham.

Dutch Dentist **Peter van Dissel**
Family Friends **David Crosse**,
Francesca Austin and Myrtle Reed
Son **Jack Jewers/Daniel Saxton**

Director **Graham Watkins**

Dial M For Murder (1952)

FREDERICK KNOTT

5 July–5 August 1989

Sheila **Joanna Hole**
Max Halliday **Peter Czajkowski**
Tony Wendice **Ben Robertson**
Captain Lesgate **Jack Power**
Inspector Hubbard **Christopher Birch**

With a Hitchcock season looming on Channel 4 at the time, *Dial M For Murder*, about a woman who is nearly convicted of murder because of her husband's clever plot, was an appropriate choice.

Director **Eric Standidge**

Hay Fever (1925)

NOEL COWARD

9 August–2 September 1989

Judith Bliss **Dora Bryan**
Sorel Bliss **Suzy Aitchison**
Simon Bliss **Simon Butteriss**
David Bliss **Ronald Hines**
Myra Arundel **Lisa Bowerman**
Richard Greatham **Tim Heath**
Sandy Tyrell **Julian Gartside**
Clara **Pamela Vezey**

Coward's caricature of the foibles of an artistic family in the twenties was well performed, capturing mood and manner. 'Dora Bryan led with all the whimsicality of a retired actress fishing for yet another comeback.' Later, the production toured.

Jackie Coryton **Jilly Bond**

Director **Graham Watkins**

Death of a Salesman (1949)

ARTHUR MILLER

6–30 September 1989

Willy Loman **Roy Barraclough**
Linda Loman **Jane Lowe**
Uncle Ben **Alan Bennion**
Charley **Nick Simons**
Biff **Stephen Hattersley**
Happy **Kevin McGowan**
Bernard **Peter Doran**

Having had success with the play at Nottingham in 1988, Richard Frost directed *Death of a Salesman* at Farnham with many of the same cast. Peter Tatlow, in *The Stage*, hailed this production as a triumph, with Roy Barraclough 'stunning' in the part of Willy. This is, of course, one of the great plays of the century. It needs sensitive directing and good acting, and that is what it received at Farnham.

The Woman **Carol Cleveland**
Howard Wagner/Stanley **Glen Kinch**
Jenny/Letta **Annie Cowan**

Miss Forsythe **Samantha Best**

Design **Nigel Hook**
Lighting **Mark Doubleday**

Sound **Gaetan Portal**
Director **Richard Frost**

Macbeth (1606)

WILLIAM SHAKESPEARE

4–28 October 1989

Macbeth **James Bolam**
Lady Macbeth **Susan Jameson**
Banquo **Peter Craze**
Witches **Nick Simons and Jack McKenzie**
Witch/Porter **Robin Hodson**
Malcolm **Robert Hands**

'James Bolam was supreme as Macbeth. He registered in every line, gesture and movement reluctant perfidy stirred up by ambition on a backdrop of conscience, remorse and fear.' (Peter Tatlow, *The Stage*)

Macduff **Stephen Hattersley**
Lady Macduff **Karen Ford**

Director **Graham Watkins**

Cluedo and *Matilda* were the productions scheduled for the end of the year and for early 1990.

GLASGOW

Citizens Theatre

GORBALS, GLASGOW, SCOTLAND G5 9DS
041-429-0022

Artistic Director **Giles Havergal**

The Alchemist (1610)

BEN JONSON

27 January–18 February 1989

Subtle **Peter Jonfield**
Drugger **George Anton**
Lovewitt **Steven Dartnell**
Face **Laurance Rudic**
Dol Common **Anne Myatt**
Epicure Mammon **Ron Donachie**
Surly **Stewart Porter**
Tribulation **Angela Chadfield**

Robert David MacDonald leapt forward in time and placed Jonson's masterpiece in Hollywood in the jazz age. It succeeded in that, as Michael Coveney pointed out, it achieved 'the crucial effect of displacing the real world with a surreal alternative'. It was designed in black and white, excitingly staged and dressed, and it proved to be a most interesting production with some fine performances.

Kastril **Garry Roost**
Ananias **Mark Lewis**
with **Patti Clark, Christopher Gee,**
Wayne Hawrish, Cheryl Innes,
Dennis Knotts, David Mills and
Gavin Mitchell

Design **Stewart Laing**

Lighting **Michael Lancaster**
Director **Robert David MacDonald**

Douglas (1756)
JOHN HOME

24 February–11 March 1989

Lord Randolph **Ron Donachie**
Glenalvon **Mark Lewis**
Norval **George Anton**
Old Norval **Sandy Welch**
Steward **Stewart Porter**
Lady Randolph **Angela Chadfield**
Anna **Anne Myatt**
with **Christopher Gee**

Written by a member of the Church of Scotland – which caused great concern to the elders, who prosecuted any ministers seen at the first performance – *Douglas* is a web of jealousies written in controlled verse. In 1756, a voice from the audience cried in an ecstasy of national fervour, 'Where's yer Wully Shakespeare noo?' A fascinating and highly successful revival.

Design **Stewart Laing**

Lighting **Gerry Jenkinson**

Director **Robert David MacDonald**

A Tale of Two Cities (1989)

CITIZENS THEATRE COMPANY from the novel by Charles Dickens

5 May–10 June 1989

with **Angela Chadfield, Steven Dartnell, Ron Donachie, Alastair Galbraith, Ruth Gemmell, Peter Granger-Taylor, Matthew Green, Patrick Hannaway, Calum Macaninch, Robert David MacDonald, Anne Myatt, Stewart Porter, Tim Potter, Laurance Rudic, Ellen Sheean, Robin Sneller, Ellis Van Maarseveen, Sandy Welch, Colin Wells, Tim Woodward and Tristram Wymark**

A splendid cast was assembled for a lively contribution to the general celebrations concerning the French Revolution, Mayfest and the reopening of the refurbished Citizens Theatre.

Road (1986)
JIM CARTWRIGHT

13 June–1 July 1989

Road was the first play to be produced by David Hayman in his

Scullery **Gerard Kelly**
with **Frank Gallagher, Douglas Henshall, Kathryn Howden, Cara Kelly, Neil McKinven, Alexander Morton, Caroline Paterson and Anne Marie Timoney**

Design **Geoff Rose**

new post as artistic director of 7:84. The production was made possible at the Citizens by special funding from the Strathclyde Regional Council. It was a towering success. Hayman peopled the stage with 'living, breathing community'. This is a wonderful play, a tragedy of our time.

Director **David Hayman**

4–22 July 1989, the Citizens Theatre offered *Harmony Row*, by Peter Arnott and Peter Mullan. This was followed, 26 July–12 August 1989, by *The Appointment*, written by David Anderson and David MacLennan.

The Crucible (1953)
ARTHUR MILLER

25 August–23 September 1989

with **Charon Bourke, James Duke, James Durrell, Alastair Galbraith, Peter Granger-Taylor, Patrick Hannaway, Ashley Jensen, Kate Lonergan, John McGlynn, Eamon Maguire, Sharon Maharaj, Anne Myatt, Irene Sunters, Derwent Watson and Joan Carol Williams**

Miller's powerful drama about witch-hunting with its thinly disguised criticism of McCarthyism opened the autumn season.

Design **Stewart Laing**
Director **Giles Havergal**

Macbeth (1606)
WILLIAM SHAKESPEARE

6–28 October 1989

with **Charon Bourke, James Duke, James Durrell, Alastair Galbraith, Peter Granger-Taylor, Kate Lonergan, Sharon Maharaj, Simon Tyrrell, Derwent Watson and Joan Carol Williams**

Design **Stewart Laing**
Director **Jon Pope**

Travels With My Aunt
GRAHAM GREENE

10–18 November 1989

An adaptation of Greene's amusing novel concluded the

with **Christopher Gee, Patrick Hannaway, Giles Havergal and Derwent Watson**

Design **Stewart Laing**
Director **Giles Havergal and Jon Pope**

autumn season. *The Sorcerer's Apprentice* was scheduled to run from November to January, and the 1990 programme was announced as *Enrico Four*, *The Four Horsemen of the Apocalypse*, *Antony*, *Mother Courage*, *Mrs Warren's Profession*, *The Housekeeper* and *Jane Shore*. Theatre in Scotland is thriving.

HORNCHURCH

The Queen's Theatre

BILLET LANE, HORNCHURCH, ESSEX RM11 1QT
040-24-43333

Artistic Director **Bob Tomson**

Tom Thumb (1988)

LES MILLER and BOB TOMSON from an idea by David Wood

5 December 1988–11 February 1989

Tom Thumb **Richard Gauntlett**
Max/Magnus **Michael Cantwell**
Grandad/Maggotts/Vole **Patch Connolly**
Grandma/Nitwit Newt/Shrew **Nan Kerr**
Mary/Henrietta **Susan-Jane Tanner**
Will/Cyril Woodlouse **Steve Edwin**
Bassett/Toad **Roger Alborough**
Melissa/Tanya **Beth Tuckey**
Mowbray/Cockroach **Stephen Reynolds**
Sergeant Ant/Spider/Centipede **Natasha Langridge**
Garden Insects **local children**

Design **Kate Robertson**

In his fifth year as the Queen's Theatre's first artistic director in its new building, Bob Tomson joined with Les Miller to provide an exuberant, original and entertaining Christmas show.

Costume **John Knowles**
Lighting **Dave Horn**
Music and Sound **Graham Pike**
Musical Director **Graham Pike**
Director **Bob Tomson**

One Careful Owner (1988)

16 February–11 March 1989

Billy Boyle **Joe Brown**
Frankie Boyle **Stephen J Dean**
Ted/Garage Manager **Howard Attfield**
Joey/Policeman **Steven Law**
Customer/Jenny **Pauline Hannah**
Angela **Maggie Carr**

First staged at the Queen's in May 1988, *One Careful Owner* was rewritten and re-presented early in 1989 prior to a national tour and, hopefully, a place in the West End. Set in the East End, it is about a crooked car dealer (Joe Brown) and the crooked landlady of the local pub (Lynda Baron). There are skirmishes with the tax inspector and the police, and contrasts in brothers and sisters. It is a fast moving show.

Big Betty **Lynda Baron**
Joanne **Tessa Burbridge**
Sheila **Deena Payne**

Book **Jim Cammell and Les Miller**

Lyrics **Jim Cammell**
Music **Jim Cammell and Bruce Davis**
Design **Marty Flood**
Lighting **Dave Horn**

Sound **Paul Astbury**
Choreographer **Henry Metcalfe**
Costume **Yvonne Milnes**
Musical Director **Rod Edwards**
Director **Bob Tomson**

Bare Necessities (1988)

ROB BETTINSON

16 March–8 April 1989

Charmain **Carmen Rodriguez**
Mike **Michael Walker**
Marjorie **Wendy Allnutt**
Greg **Roger Martin**
Madge **Hilary Crane**
Charlie **Leslie Randall**
Eddie **Mark Aspinall**
Carola **Celia Blaker**

Staged in 1988 at the Belgrade Theatre, Coventry, where the author was associate director, *Bare Necessities* received its southern première at Hornchurch. Set on a camp site in the Lake District, it is a comedy of marital disputes and adulterous indiscretions.

Design **John Knowles**
Lighting **Dave Horn**

Director **Richard Lewis**

Bouncers (1985)

JOHN GODBER

12 April–6 May 1989

Lucky Eric **Robert Putt**
Judd **Adrian Hood**
Ralph **Peter Chequer**
Les **Steve Edwin**

Design **John Knowles**
Lighting **Dave Horn**

Not the Hull Truck Company's touring version, but the Queen's Theatre's own production of Godber's wonderful play about Saturday night out. It was, said Julie Watterston, a production that never faltered.

Choreographer **Peter Chequer**
Music **Graham Pike**

Director **Richard Lewis**

Hair (1968)

10 May–3 June 1989

Leata **Janet Anderson**
Walter **Matthew Baidoo-Heath**
Hud **Leroy Charlery**
Paul **Joseph Connors**

Bill Kenwright resurrected *Hair*, seemingly so much of the sixties, staged it at Hornchurch and then sent it on a national tour. The show is now heavily nostalgic, but it has taken on a fresh significance with the political and international events of

Berger **Steve Edwin**
Dionne **Shelaagh Ferrell**
Suzannah **Julie Fox**
Jeanie **Jo-Anne Lee**
Angela **Kemi Martins**
Steve **Iain McInnes**
Ron **Stuart Morrison**
Apache **Nick Parmenter**
Claude **John Purcell**
Sheila **Sian Reeves**
Woof **Nigel Richards**

1989. Robert Elms in the *Mail on Sunday* was adamant, 'Anybody who has ever been tempted to get dewy-eyed about those radical, chemical, earth-shattering times should go and see the show.'

Crissy **Claire Woyka**

Book and Lyrics **Gerome Ragni and James Rado**
Music **Galt MacDermot**
Design **Glenn Willoughby**
Lighting **Dave Horn**
Choreographer **Henry Metcalfe**
Musical Director **Rick Lloyd**
Director **Bob Tomson and Bill Kenwright**

Grange Hill – Tucker's Return (1989)

PHIL REDMOND

31 August–23 September 1989

Another Bill Kenwright presentation destined for a national

10. Grange Hill – Tucker's Return at the Queen's Theatre, Hornchurch.

Mr Mitchell **Michael Percival**
Miss 'Ginger' Rogers **Sandra Slinger**
Mr 'Tucker' Jenkins **Todd Carty**
Benny Green **Terry Sue Patt**
Gonch **John McMahon**
Hollo **Bradley Sheppard**
Freddie **Simon Vaughan**
Laura **Fiona Lee-Fraser**
Helen **Ruth Carraway**
Rachel **Joanne Bell**
Imelda **Fleur Taylor**

tour, *Tucker's Return* was the children's television programme transformed into a musical. With one exception, Sandra Slinger, the cast were re-enacting their television roles. Tucker, once the trouble-maker, returns to his old school as games master. Grange Hill contains the usual assortment of bullies and intellectuals.

Mandy **Melanie Hiscock**

Design **Glenn Willoughby**
Choreographer **Sheelagh Dennis**
Music and Lyrics **Gordon Higgins**

and Steve Wright
Musical Director **Graham Pike**
Director **Bob Tomson**

Corpse! (1982)
GERALD MOON

28 September–21 October 1989

Evelyn Farrant **Graham Seed**
Mrs McGee **Brenda Peters**
Major Walter Powell **Paul Imbusch**
Rupert Farrant **Adam Gresche**
(Graham Seed)
Hawkins **Jed Spittle**

Design **John Knowles**
Lighting **Derek Olds**
Director **Kit Thacker**

A comedy thriller set in Soho and Regent's Park in 1936, *Corpse!* revolves around twin brothers, both played by Graham Seed, and a liberality of blood-spattered bodies. The play was first seen in America and has been a huge success all over the world ever since.

11. *Graham Seed in* Corpse *at Hornchurch.*

Fiddler on the Roof (1965)

26 October–25 November 1989

Tevye **Brian Hewlett**
Golde **Jenny Logan**
Tzeitel **Catherine Terry**
Hodel **Lisa Bluthal**
Chava **Abigail Lee**
Shprintze **Nina Kitt/Lisa Kavanagh**
Bielke **Lauren Easter/Rebecca Roche**
Lazar Wolf **David Verrey**
Yente **Amanda Wise**
Motel **Simon Lovat**
Perchik **Felix Medina**
Mordcha **Richard Hallam**
Rabbi **John Scott Martin**
Mendel **Nick Sadler**
Avrahm **Jed Spittle**
Nachum **Phillip Sutton**
Grandma Tzeitel **Peggy Ann Jones**
Fruma-Sarah **Diane Raynor**
Shandel **Maureen Hartley**

Another lively and highly successful revival at the Queen's which may be destined for a longer life elsewhere than its month's run in Hornchurch. Since losing their Arts Council funding, the Queen's has had to think in strict commercial terms, but they raise their sights high and have had a succession of notable revivals. The Christmas–New Year show was *The Wizard of Oz*.

12. Fiddler on the Roof at the Queen's Theatre, Hornchurch.

The Constable **Julian Parkin**
The Fiddler **George Giles**
Fyedka **Patrick Jamieson**
Russians **Matthew Barrett, John Cosgrave, Brian Graves, Ian Smith, Wayne Spring and Graham Turner**

Book **Joseph Stein**
Music **Jerry Block**
Lyrics **Sheldon Harnick**
Based on stories by **Sholem Aleichem**

Design and Costume **Russ Barson**
Lighting **Roger Frith**
Choreographer **Gerry Tebbutt**
Musical Director **James Simpson**
Director **Gerry Tebbutt**

IPSWICH

Wolsey Theatre

CIVIC DRIVE, IPSWICH, SUFFOLK IP1 2AS
0473-53725

Artistic Director **Antony Tuckey**

And Then There Were None (1943)

AGATHA CHRISTIE

1–25 February 1989

Rogers **Steven Fitt**
Narracot **David Verrey**
Mrs Rogers **Josephine Cooper**
Vera Claythorne **Sian Reeves**
Philip Lombard **Nigel Bowden**
Anthony Marston **Mark Bannister**
William Blore **Robert Benfield**
General MacKenzie **Philip Newman**
Emily Brent **Buster Skeggs**
Sir Lawrence Wargrave **David Beale**
Dr Armstrong **Brian Ralph**

Design **India Smith**
Lighting **Geoff Spain**
Sound **Rhys Davies**
Director **Antony Tuckey**

Highly successful in revivals in two West End theatres in 1988, *And Then There Were None* opened the spring season at the Wolsey Theatre and, inevitably, played to good houses.

The Merchant of Venice (1597)

WILLIAM SHAKESPEARE

1–18 March 1989

Portia **Nicola Redmond**
Antonio **David Beale**
Shylock **Brian Ralph**
Bassanio **Nigel Bowden**
Gratiano **Robert Benfield**
Salerio **Edward Arthur**
Solanio **Philip Newman**
Lorenzo **Mark Bannister**
Jessica **Sian Reeves**
Launcelot Gobbo **Lennie James**

Ecstatically received by Alfred Glenn in *The Stage* and declared to be deserving of a wider audience, Wolsey Theatre's production of *The Merchant of Venice* was set in the thirties amid David Knapman's 'towering masterpiece of baroque antiquity'. Brian Ralph's Shylock was 'a beautifully spoken portrayal of cold, reasoned dignity' and there was some delightful comedy from Lennie James in a cast that was consistently strong. This was, indeed, seen as a triumph for the Wolsey Theatre and one of the very best of regional productions.

Old Gobbo **David Verrey**
Prince of Morocco **Lennie James**
Prince of Arragon **Terence Soall**
Duke of Venice **David Verrey**

Nerissa **Sonia Green**
Servant **Josephine Cooper**

Design **David Knapman**

Lighting **Geoff Spain**
Costume **Ann Summers**
Director **Antony Tuckey and Gerry Tebbutt**

Table Manners (1974)
ALAN AYCKBOURN

22 March–1 April 1989

Norman **Nigel Bowden**
Tom **Robert Benfield**
Sarah **Felicity Harrison**
Anne **Felicity Goodson**
Reg **Edward Arthur**
Ruth **Lesley North**

Design **India Smith**
Lighting **Geoff Spain**
Sound **Joanne Hinchliffe**
Director **Gerry Tebbutt**

One of the most delightful of Ayckbourn's sharp comedies and one of the *Norman Conquests*, *Table Manners* was most competently performed and enthusiastically received. It was particularly pleasing to see Felicity Harrison on the stage of the Wolsey Theatre again.

13. A happy return to the stage for Felicity Harrison as Sarah with Felicity Goodson as Anne (crouched apprehensively) in Table Manners *at Ipswich.*

14. Francesca Brill as Jenny and Marcia Warren as Beryl in the world première of Sitting Duck *at Ipswich.*

Sitting Duck (1989)

GILLIAN RICHMOND

5–22 April 1989

Jenny **Francesca Brill**	
Wendy **Sian Webber**	
Beryl **Marcia Warren**	
Adam **Neil Conrich**	
Chalky **Graeme Henderson**	
Len **Philip Newman**	
Extra **Ingrid Wiseman**	

Design **David Knapman**
Lighting **Geoff Spain**

Antony Tuckey offered a world première of Gillian Richmond's latest play, *Sitting Duck*. Jenny, a schoolteacher, is physically attacked, and the attack dramatically changes her life. Her friend and flat-mate Wendy is a policewoman who is used as a decoy to catch the attacker. A very strong cast included the delicious Marcia Warren as a nosey neighbour, and the attractive young ladies at the heart of the action played with conviction and sensitivity.

Sound **Geraint Thomas**   Director **Antony Tuckey**

Stepping Out (1987)

RICHARD HARRIS

26 April–20 May 1989

Mavis **Lesley North**
Mrs Fraser **Sheri Shepstone**
Lynne **Felicity Goodson**

Sheri Shepstone created the role of Mrs Fraser in the original production of *Stepping Out* at the Duke of York's Theatre and toured with the play in the Middle and Far East. She was one of

Dorothy **Diane Raynor**
Maxine **Joan Savage**
Andy **Claire Grogan**
Geoffrey **Teddy Green**
Sylvia **Amanda Wise**
Rose **Elaine Grant**
Vera **Ursula Smith**

Design **David Knapman**
Lighting **Geoff Spain**

the cornerstones of a lively and splendidly performed revival of the comedy at the Wolsey Theatre. Elaine Grant continued in the role of Rose, which she had played on the national tour of Harris's play. Others in an exceptionally strong cast included Ursula Smith, creator of the part of the Duchess of Dene in *Me and My Girl* at the Adelphi, and the enchanting and talented Claire Grogan.

Sound **Geraint Thomas**
Choreographer **Gerry Tebbutt**

Director **Gerry Tebbutt**

Equus (1973)

PETER SHAFFER

24 May–10 June 1989

Martin Dysart **Brian Ralph**
Nurse/Dora Strang **Josephine Cooper**
Frank Strang/Harry Dalton **Malcolm Reid**
Hesther Salomon **Jill Brassington**
Alan Strang **Lucien Taylor**
Young Horseman/Nugget **Adrian Hough**
Jill Mason **Susannah Hitching**
Horses **Josephine Cooper, Ian Lambert, Jill Brassington, Malcolm Reid, Adrian Hough and Robert Palacios**

Design **India Smith**
Lighting **Geoff Spain**
Sound **Geraint Thomas**

That Peter Shaffer's absorbing and disturbing analysis of the reasons that brought a young man to blind six horses has been with us for 16 years is surprising, for the play is as fresh and as dramatically effective as ever. Antony Tuckey's production at the Wolsey Theatre was received with great acclaim. Brian Ralph, who had triumphed as Shylock earlier in the season, returned to play the psychiatrist Dysart. According to *The Stage*, he gave 'a sensitive and masterly performance' of almost unbearable poignancy in the closing scene when, having exorcised his patient, he is left with his own tormented mind. Set and lighting were highly praised, and Tuckey's direction achieved a lucid and balanced continuity. As Alan, the disturbed teenager, Lucien Taylor gave a 'meticulously studied portrayal', and the supporting cast was without weakness in another production which confirmed the very high standards of the Wolsey.

Director **Antony Tuckey**

House Guest (1981)

FRANCIS DURBRIDGE

2–26 August 1989

Vivien Norwood **Rachel Fielding**
Jane Mercer **Claire Grogan**
Stella Drury **Lyndon Hughes**

The tenth anniversary season of the Wolsey Theatre began rather inauspiciously with Francis Durbridge's thriller about two film-stars, kidnapping and double identity. First

Robert Drury **Brian Ralph**
Crozier **Malcolm Reid**
Inspector Burford **Brian Hewlett**
Sgt Clayton **John Hudson**
Dorothy Medway **Nan Kerr**
Philip Henderson **Phil Branar**

performed eight years ago with Susan Hampshire and Gerald Harper, it remains one of the least engaging of Durbridge's plays and a very meagre offering.

Design **David Knapman**
Lighting **John Owens**

Sound **Geraint Thomas**
Director **Gerry Tebbutt**

The Importance of Being Earnest (1895)

OSCAR WILDE

30 August–23 September 1989

Algernon Moncrieff **Rupert Baker**
Lane **Malcolm Reid**
John Worthing, JP **John Hudson**
Lady Bracknell **Nancy Mansfield**
Hon. Gwendolen Fairfax **Philippa Haywood**
Cecily Cardew **Rachel Fielding**
Miss Prism **Nan Kerr**
Rev. Canon Chasuble **Brian Hewlett**
Merriman **Malcolm Reid**

Design **David Knapman**
Lighting **Geoff Spain**
Sound **Geraint Thomas**
Director **Antony Tuckey**

On 19 September 1979, the Wolsey Theatre opened its doors with a production of *The Servant of Two Masters*. In 1989, it celebrated its tenth anniversary with one of the most technically perfect and wittiest of comedies, *The Importance of Being Earnest*. A beautifully dressed and designed production, played with charm and elegance, it proved to be the ideal birthday celebration.

15. Rupert Baker as Algernon and Rachel Fielding as Cecily in the Wolsey Theatre's delightful production of The Importance of Being Earnest.

Driving Miss Daisy (1987)

ALFRED UHRY

26–30 September 1989

Daisy Wertham **Nancy Mansfield**
Boolie Wertham **Brian Hewlett**
Hoke Coleburn **Guy Gregory**

Design **Phillipa Jackson**
Lighting **Geoff Spain**
Sound **Geraint Thomas**
Director **Antony Tuckey**

Produced at the Apollo Theatre, London, in 1988 with Wendy Hiller as Miss Daisy, Alfred Uhry's Pulitzer Prize-winning play tells of the bond that develops between the fiercely independent Jewess, Daisy Wertham, and her illiterate black chauffeur, Hoke Coleburn, in the years between 1948 and 1973. A journey into old age helps to break down the bigotry that exists in Atlanta, Georgia.

The Baker's Wife (1978)

9 October–4 November 1989

Denise **Jill Martin**
Claude **George Raistrick**
Barnaby **Simon Clark**
Hortense **Myra Sands**
Therese **Tricia Deighton**
Antoine **Sidney Livingstone**
Casimir **Arthur Whybrow**
Pierre **Nicholas Lumley**
Doumergue **Edward Phillips**
Monsieur Martine **John Bennett**
M le Cure **Neil McCaul**
M le Marquis **James Villiers**
Simone **Liz Izen**
Inez **Vanessa Leagh Hicks**
Nicole **Janet Devenish**
Dominic **Drue Williams**
Phillipe **Rob Jarvis**
Aimable Castanier **Alun Armstrong**
Genevieve **Sharon Lee Hill**
Pompom, a cat **Trixie/Dixie**

Book **Joseph Stein**
Music and Lyrics **Stephen Schwartz** (based on the film *La Femme du Boulanger*)
Design **John Napier**
Lighting **David Hersey**

It was Trevor Nunn who laid the foundation stone of the Wolsey Theatre, and he promised Antony Tuckey that he would return to his home town to direct a production on the Wolsey stage. He fulfilled that promise in 1989 when he directed *The Baker's Wife* there prior to its move to the Phoenix.

The film, by Marcel Pagnol and Jean Giono, is one of the classics of the French cinema. Set in a small village in Provence in 1935, it is a simple tale of a middle-aged baker who arrives in the village with a young and attractive wife. She runs off with a young man, but later returns to her husband who once more begins to bake wonderful bread for the villagers. The strengths of Pagnol's writing and of the film are his essential humanity and sensitive observation of village life and custom. Joseph Stein and Stephen Schwartz embarked on their musical version of *The Baker's Wife* in 1977, but it suffered radical changes in America and the original production never reached New York. Nunn was intrigued by its history and asked the writers to exhume their work and allow him to collaborate with them in bringing it to the stage.

It begins well. Men are playing boule. The atmosphere of a village in which nothing ever changes is clearly evoked in an excellent opening song, *If It Wasn't For You*, sung by Denise, the wife of the café owner. As Denise, Jill Martin is one of the resounding successes of the show. The arrival of the new baker, his young wife and his 'fresh warm bread' stirs the village into action. It is human, light, gentle, leisurely. The

Costume **Andreane Neofitou**
Sound **Martin Levan**
Choreographer **David Toguri**
Musical Director **Gareth Valentine**
Director **Trevor Nunn**

problems arrive with the two young people at the heart of the musical, Genevieve and Dominic, for in writing and in performance they are neither of place nor period, and the songs that they share are quite dreadful.

Genevieve's desertion of her husband is the first thing to have happened in the village for 20 years, and it unites the quarrelling villagers. There are some catchy, tuneful melodies – including a glorious women's answer to the male domination of the village society – and some good pieces of characterisation, notably John Bennett as the teacher and James Villiers as the marquis, but with the weakness at the centre the show collapses, which is a pity.

One must emphasise that these comments are made on the evidence of a viewing at Ipswich, and it is likely that there could be some rewriting and restructuring when the show reaches London. It won't survive without them.

Breaking the Code followed *The Baker's Wife*, and Eastern Angles' production of *Waterland* was scheduled for late November. *Cider With Rosie* and *The Wizard of Oz* will take the Wolsey into the New Year.

This is a most attractive and thriving theatre. Its public relations and ambience are good; its standards are high.

KESWICK

Century Theatre

LAKESIDE, KESWICK, CUMBRIA CA12 5DJ
07687-72282

Artistic Director **Han Duijvendak**

The Century Theatre at Keswick is both a repertory and a touring theatre. Like most theatres, it has had its problems, not the least of which has been the lack of progress concerning the building of a new theatre in Keswick. As Nigel Illman, chairman of the council of management, stated in the splendidly presented annual report in March 1989, 'The link between Keswick and the company remains strong and the history of the Blue Box and its association with the town has given Century an image and identity which it is loath to lose. And yet this link with Keswick cannot survive much longer without a new theatre. There are few advantages to be gained from administering a touring company from the wilds of the Lake District in the middle of winter.'

It would be unfair and unwise to concentrate on these

negative aspects of Century Theatre. This is a wonderfully virile organisation. It is in the front rank of communicators in all aspects of its work. Box office receipts and fees from touring venues continue to increase, and artistic standards are jealously guarded. Productions continue to receive consistently high praise.

Cabaret (1966)

JOE MASTEROFF from the play by John Van Druten and stories by Christopher Isherwood

The Century Theatre entered the New Year with an exuberant and very popular production of *Cabaret*. It was the biggest box office success of the 1988–9 season.

Herr Schultz **John Ashby**
Ernst Ludwig **Tim Barron**
Frau Schneider **Joolia Cappleman**
Fraulein Kost **Nicola Esson**
Sally Bowles **Allison Harding**
Kit Kat Boys **Anthony Hunt and Michael Lunts**
Clifford Bradshaw **Wayne Morris**
Kit Cat Girls **Judith Sim and Julia Winwood**
Emcee **Kraig Thornber**

Music **John Kander**
Lyrics **Fred Ebb**

Design **Rodney Ford**
Lighting **Lawrence T Doyle**
Choreographer **Dennis Sayers**
Musical Director **Kate Edgar**
Director **Bob Carlton**

City Sugar (1975)

STEPHEN POLIAKOFF

One of the plays with which Stephen Poliakoff established his reputation, *City Sugar* is about a glib but desperate DJ, and it depicts the superficiality and emptiness of much modern living.

Leonard Brazil **John Ashton**
Rex **Michael Snelders**
Mick **Phil Bonney**
Nicola Davies **Annabelle Apsion**
Susan **Barbara Penny**
Big John **Geoffrey Burbidge**
Jane **Jenny Lynch**

Design **Rodney Ford**
Lighting **Chris Kempton**

Sound **Richard Cragg**
Director **Han Duijvendak**

They're Playing Our Song (1979)

NEIL SIMON

Sonia Walsk **Nicola Esson**
Vernon Gersch **John Wild**
Voices of Sonia Walsk **Caroline England, Alison Gunn and Sarah Michael**
Voices of Vernon Gersch **Barrie**

'Fast-moving, energetic and happy, creating a bond of sympathy between the characters and their audience', was how one critic described Han Duijvendak's production of Neil Simon's musical about a song-writer and his singer–song-writer wife who can neither live nor work with or without each other. *The Stage* found it delightful.

16. John Ashton as Len Brazil in City Sugar, *Century Theatre.*

17. John Wild and Nicola Essen, *a splendid partnership in* They're Playing Our Song, *at Keswick.*

Jamieson, Dominic Kemp and
Michael Wilcox

Design **Paul Lanham**

Lighting **Stephen Henbest**
Choreographer **Lorelei Lynn**
Music **Marvin Hamlisch**
Lyrics **Carole Bayer Sager**

Musical Director **Kate Edgar**
Director **Han Duijvendak**

Play It Again, Sam (1970)
WOODY ALLEN

Allan Felix **Barrie Jamieson**
Bogey **Dominic Kemp**
Dick Christie **Michael Wilcox**
Linda Christie **Nicola Esson**
Daydream Women **Sarah Michael**
Sharon Lake/Barbara **Alison Gunn**

Design **Kari Furre**
Costume **Annie Brown**
Lighting **Stephen Henbest**
Musical Director **Michael Wilcox**
Director **Han Duijvendak**

Having scored an immense hit with their opening show of the summer season, Century Theatre followed with another resounding success in the Woody Allen comedy of the film critic who has to summon the spectre of Humphrey Bogart to help him gain confidence in his sexual activities. Andrew Wilson felt that the production brought out 'the best in this particular play and provides superb entertainment'.

18. Barrie Jamieson, Dominic Kemp and Nicola Essen in Play It Again, Sam, *at Keswick.*

Arms and the Man (1894)

GEORGE BERNARD SHAW

Raina **Sarah Michael**
Catherine **Caroline England**
Louka **Nicola Esson**
Bluntschli **Dominic Kemp**
Russian Officer/Nicola **Barrie Jamieson**
Petkoff **John Wild**
Sergius **Michael Wilcox**

Design **Rodney Ford**
Lighting **Stephen Henbest**

The most thought provoking of Century's summer offering of three plays was their last. *Arms and the Man*, Shaw's gentle satire on soldiers, women and war. Century has a fine reputation for its work on Shaw, and *Arms and the Man* did not disappoint. Duijvendak's production realised that Shaw's pill is at its most palatable when his sparkle, wit and ability to entertain are allowed to flourish. 'Another great night's entertainment which completed the theatre's summer repertoire triad in great style.'

Director **Han Duijvendak**

LANCASTER

The Dukes

MOOR LANE, LANCASTER LA1 1QE
0524-66645

Artistic Director **Ian Forrest**

Othello (1604)

WILLIAM SHAKESPEARE

25 January–25 February 1989

Bianca **Joanna Bacon**
Cassio **Jon Glentoran**
Roderigo **John Griffin**
Iago **Michael Gunn**
Duke/Montano/Gentleman **Peter Hurle**
Othello **Wyllie Longmore**
Desdemona **Amanda Pointer**
Emilia **Ellen Sheean**
Brabantio/Lodovico **Stephen Tomlin**

This was the first time that *Othello* has been staged at The Dukes, and the first Shakespeare play that Ian Forrest has directed at the theatre. The production substituted England for Venice and set the play in Cyprus in the sixties. An hypnotic set of four white cubes was, for some, spoiled by the over-use of banal pop music of the sixties, but there were three outstanding performances from Ellen Sheean, Wyllie Longmore and Amanda Pointer.

Design **Paul Kondras**
Lighting **Mark Frisby**

Sound **Sue Yeo**
Director **Ian Forrest**

When I Was a Girl I Used to Scream and Shout (1984)

SHARMAN MacDONALD

15 March–15 April 1989

Vari **Barbara Watt**
Fiona **Fay Blockley**
Morag **Pam Buckle**
Ewan **Gary McLeod**

Design **Ashley Sharp**

Some good performances from an all-Scottish cast in Sharman MacDonald's reflections on past mishaps highlighted The Dukes's production. Barbara Watt gained special mention.

Lighting **Mark Frisby** Director **Simone Vause**
Sound **Sue Yeo**

Much Ado About Nothing (1599)

WILLIAM SHAKESPEARE

1 June–29 July 1989

Don John **Fergus McLarnon**
Dogberry **Ian Blower**
Hero **Jane Nash**
Beatrice **Buffy Davis**
Benedick **Terence Beesley**
Borachio **Chris Larner**
with **Angela Bain, Julian Bleach, Polly Highton, Reginald Jessup, Robert McCulley, Francis Middleditch and Ted Richards**

The Dukes's promenade season in Williamson Park began with a Georgian version of *Much Ado About Nothing*. As ever, this was a spectacularly beautiful setting although some saw the Edwardian splendour of the park as not entirely suitable for the post-Napoleonic-wars setting of the play. Fergus McLarnon and Ian Blower were singled out for their striking performances.

Design and Costume **Ashley Sharp** Director **Ian Forrest**
Music **Chris Larner**

The Wind in the Willows (1989)

CHRIS HAWES from the book by Kenneth Grahame

22 June–5 August 1989

Toad **Frank Middleditch**
Rat **Julian Bleach**
Mole **Ian Blower**
Badger **Ted Richards**
Kenneth Grahame **Reginald Jessup**
Alistair **Same Kaye/Isaac Allison**
with **Angela Bain, Terence**

Running in repertoire with *Much Ado About Nothing* was *Wind in the Willows*, the run of which was extended because more than 10,000 people had crowded in to see the two plays. It was estimated that by the end of the run some 20,000 people would have been to Williamson Park. *The Wind in the Willows* was ideally suited for its venue in what Robin Duke in *The Stage* described as a 'magical theatrical event'.

Beesley, Buffy Davis, Robert McCulley, Fergus McLarnon and Jane Nash

Director **Ian Forrest**

One for the Road (1976)

WILLY RUSSELL

23 August–16 September 1989

Dennis **Robert McCulley**
Jayne **Christine Mackie**
Pauline **Joanne Allen**
Roger **Colin Meredith**

Design **Ashley Sharp**
Lighting **Michael Hall**

The autumn season began with a popular production of Willy Russell's humorous examination of mid-life male crisis in suburbia. Christine Mackie was highly praised for her performance.

Sound **Sue Yeo**

Director **Ian Forrest**

The Country Wife (1675)

WILLIAM WYCHERLEY

27 September–21 October 1989

Mr Pinchwife **Gerard Bell**
Sir Jasper Fidget **Ian Blower**
Lady Fidget/Lucy **Francesca Ryan**
Alithea/Quack Doctor **Ruth Gemmell**
Sparkish **Julian Bleach**
Harcourt **Stefan Escreet**
Horner **Mark Spalding**
Margery **Alex Kingston**

The Country Wife gave great problems to Ian Forrest, not the least of which was an illness which forced Bev Willis to withdraw from the role of Pinchwife two days before the show was due to open.

An enterprising season continued with *'Tis Pity She's a Whore*, *Jack and the Beanstalk*, *The Price* and *Bring Down the Sun*, a new play by writer-in-residence Chris Hawes.

Design **Paul Kondras**

Director **Ian Forrest**

LEEDS

Leeds Playhouse

CALVERLEY STREET, LEEDS LS2 3AJ
0532-442111

Artistic Director **John Harrison and Jude Kelly**

The Little Foxes (1939)
LILLIAN HELLMAN

12 January–4 February 1989

Addie **Cynthia Powell**
Cal **Willie Payne**
Birdie Hubbard **Linda Gardner**
Oscar Hubbard **Terence Booth**
Leo Hubbard **Grahame Caylow**
Regina Giddens **Barbara Ewing**
William Marshall **Douglas W Iles**
Benjamin Hubbard **Bob Cartland**
Alexandra Giddens **Harriette Ashcroft**
Horace Giddens **Howard Southern**

The Hubbard family are aristocratic Southerners, but behind their veneer of gentility is a relentless rapacity which tramples all in its path. The most powerful and ruthless of the Hubbards is Regina, married to a banker; the part of Regina was played most memorably in the film version by Bette Davis. It is to the credit of Barbara Ewing that her performance was seen as 'icily ruthless' in a highly praised revival with an excellent cast.

Design **Lez Brotherston**   Director **Helena Kaut-Howson**
Lighting **Ian Gibson**
Music **Debra Salem**

The Shoemaker's Holiday (1599)
THOMAS DEKKER

9 February–4 March 1989

Simon Eyre **John Arthur**
Mrs Eyre **Linda Polan**
Hodge **Andy Readman**
Firk **Trevor Laird**
Lacy **Guy Scantlebury**
Rose **Ainslie Foster**
Earl of Lincoln **David Monico**
Sir Roger Otley **Seamus O'Neill**
with **Angela Bain, Terence Booth, Stephen Boswell, Robert Bowman, Alan Cowan, James Burke, Dan Maxwell and Sally Millest**

Jude Kelly, appointed artistic director of the new West Yorkshire Playhouse – the 'national theatre of the north', which is to open in March 1990 – began her career in Leeds with a production of *The Shoemaker's Holiday*. It is a joyful play about young love and about older love, too, as Simon Eyre, the shoemaker, rises to become Lord Mayor of London. A happy production in which John Arthur won very high praise for his Simon Eyre.

Design **Tim Reed**   Director **Jude Kelly**
Lighting **Ian Gibson**
Musical Director **Harvey Brough**

9 March–1 April 1989, the Leeds Playhouse presented Tom Stoppard's *Hapgood* (1988). Design was by Norman Coates and direction by John Harrison.

Captain Swing (1978)

PETER WHELAN

6–23 April 1989

Gemma Beech **Niamh Cusack**
Mathew Hardness **Rob Spendlove**
Michael O'Neil **Robert Bowman**
Jack Slipper **David Neilson**
Farquharson **Terence Booth**
Parson Aston **Alan Cowan**
Lady Cummings **Jeni Giffen**
Robert Whatley **Bernard Martin**
Corporal Moat **Ian Blower**
Lieutenant Tublin **Dan Maxwell**
John Povey **Grahame Caylow**
Ned **David Hatton**
Daniel **Richard Henders**
Sam **Christopher McHallem**
Tom **Timothy Morand**

Set in 1830, in a Sussex village, *Captain Swing*, 'a series of superbly varied stage pictures', tells of the unrest of the villagers as rents rise and they go short of food. A stranger suffering from severe burns arrives in their midst, and with farm labourers elsewhere burning hayricks and wrecking machinery, there is a cry for revolution. The play questions the place of violence in political action. It was first performed by the RSC in 1978, and the Leeds Playhouse received a special grant from the Arts Council to help stage this second production of a new play.

Innkeeper's Wife/Agnes **Debbie Norman**
Grannie Brindlay **Ann Rye**

Design **Robert Jones**
Lighting **Jenny Cane**
Musical Director **Roland Saggs**
Director **Jude Kelly**

A Month in the Country (1872)

IVAN TURGENEV in a version by John Harrison

4–27 May 1989

Arkadi Islayev **David Fleeshman**
Natalya **Karen Drury**
Belayev **Robert Bowman**
Rakitin **Paul Spence**
Kolya **Stuart Bates**
Anna Islayev **Ann Rye**
Lizaveta Bogdanov **Laura Cox**
Herr Schaff **Peter Hurle**
Vera Alexandrovna **Erika Spotswood**
Dr Shipgelsky **James Tomlinson**
Bolshintsov **Alan Partington**
Katya **Isobel Arnett**

John Harrison's own version of Turgenev's masterpiece about the arrival of a handsome young student on the country estate of a wealthy family was most enthusiastically received. The play was written in 1849, but censorship delayed its presentation until 1872. Harrison's version captured the social criticism that the author intended, and made the play more than light comedy. In performance and in the integrity of the production, the Leeds Playhouse version was not to be missed.

Matvei **Glyn Morrow**

Design **Simon Higlett**
Lighting **Ian Gibson**

Music **Glyn Morrow**
Director **John Harrison**

Habeas Corpus (1973)

ALAN BENNETT

1–24 June 1989

Alan Bennett's farce about a philandering doctor closed the Leeds Playhouse spring season. Jude Kelly's direction captured 'every ounce of fun' in the play.

Arthur Wickstead **James Tomlinson**
Muriel Wickstead **Patricia Leach**
Dennis Wickstead **Grahame Caylow**
Connie Wickstead **Laura Cox**
Mrs Swabb **Michael Bertenshaw**
Canon Throbbing **Alan Cowan**

Sir Percy Shorter **David Hatton**
Mr Purdue **Stephen Boswell**
Mr Shanks **Michael Cule**

Design **Robert Jones**
Lighting **Tim Thornally**
Director **Jude Kelly**

Mrs Klein (1988)

NICHOLAS WRIGHT

September 1989

Following the summer production of *The Sleeping Beauty*, the company began its last season in the old Playhouse with the first production outside London of Nicholas Wright's play about psychoanalyst Melanie Klein and her relationship with her daughter.

Mrs Klein **Linda Polan**
Melitta **Stephanie Turner**
Paula **Linda Gardner**

Design **Norman Coates**
Lighting **Tim Thornally**
Director **John Harrison**

Spoils of War (1987)

MICHAEL WELLER

October 1989

The first play at the Leeds Playhouse in 1989 which was not directed by either John Harrison or Jude Kelly, *Spoils of War* was first presented in New York. It looks at the effects of divorce on a child.

Most energies in Leeds are now centred on the big move to the new theatre.

Martin **Gary Parker**
Elise **Trudy Weiss**
Andrew **David Allister**
Penny **Catherine Furshpan**
Emma **Lolly Susi**
Lew **David Crean**

Design **Paul Fransworth**
Lighting **Tim Thornally**

Sound **Mic Pool**

Director **Tim Luscombe**

LEICESTER

Haymarket Theatre

BELGRAVE GATE, LEICESTER LE1 3YQ
0533-539797

Artistic Director **Peter Lichtenfels**

Kirti, Sona and Ba (1989)
JYOTI PATEL and JEZZ SIMONS

Studio 25 January–18 February 1989

Kirti **Shaheen Khan**
Sona **Meera Syall**
Mother Ba **Charubala Choksi**

Design **Rashshied Ali Din**
Director **David O'Shea and Jyoti Patel**

A new play by two Leicester playwrights and written in English and Gujarati, *Kirti, Sona and Ba* tells of a mother and sister awaiting the return to Leicester of Sona.

In January and February, the Studio Company toured their productions of *The Broken Heart*, *Drums in the Night* and *The Bells*.

Stepping Out (1987)
RICHARD HARRIS

2 February–4 March 1989

Mavis Turner **Josephine Blake** with **Joan Savage, Charlotte Avery, Hetty May Bailey, Helen Bennett, Tony Crean, Cate Fowler, Shelagh Lawrence-Davies, Clovissa Newcombe and Myra Sands**

Actor Tim Slavin made his directorial début with a lively production of Richard Harris's play about a class of tap-dancers and their personal problems.

Design **Michael Pavelka**   Director **Tim Slavin**

---

24 March–8 April 1989, *M. Butterfly* – transferred to the Shaftesbury Theatre, London, under which details will be found.

The Widowing of Mrs Holroyd (1913)

D H LAWRENCE

13 April–6 May 1989

Mrs Holroyd **Anna Carteret**
Blackmore **Kevin Whately**
Holroyd **Philip Whitchurch**
His Mother **Mary McLeod**
Holroyd Children **Molly Mackay and Jeremy Cotton**
with **Robert Aldous, Karen Lewis, Raymond Lewis, Susan Porrett and Martyn Whitby**

A most welcome revival of Lawrence's fine play set in the mining community which nourished his best work, John Dove's production was received tepidly by Quentin Clark in *The Stage*.

Design **Kenny Miller**
Director **John Dove**

Yes and No But (1989)

GRAHAM ALBOROUGH

Studio 19–29 April 1989

Elaine **Lucy Aston**
Eddie **Paul Brightwell**
Steve **Neal Swettenham**

Design **Anthony Lambel**
Lighting **Ian Moulds**
Sound **Paul Bull**

The first in a series of four new plays, *Yes and No But* is a comedy about three people living in the Home Counties, one of whom accidentally electrocutes 354 pigs. It examines the use and abuse of the written word, particularly in the gutter press, and it was most warmly received.

Costume **Beatrice Stein**
Director **David O'Shea**

Return to Dreams (1989)

DAVID DRANE

Studio 1–13 May 1989

Cryland **Stuart Linden**

Director **Christopher Hynes**

Pale Performer (1989)

DAVID DRANE

Studio 1–13 May 1989

Leonard Knights **George Innes**
Ormonde **Steven Beard**
Murk **Stuart Linden**

Design **Anthony Lambel**

The new plays' season continued with a double-bill by David Drane which centred on remembering past glories.

Costume **Beatrice Stein**

Director **Simon Usher**

Low People (1989)

DICK EDWARDS

Studio 15–27 May 1989

Ursula **Deborah Hurst**
Nadir **Denise Stephenson**
Leo **Michael Brogan**
Benthos **Jack Elliott**
Verity **Karen Ward/Sarah Brittain**

Design **Anthony Lambel**
Costume **Beatrice Stein**

A larger cast than the three scheduled for the first two plays presented a powerful allegory about good and bad faith. *Low People* is a political parable about a factory worker, living in abject poverty, who fights for compensation after an industrial accident.

Lighting **Sam Moon**
Sound **Paul Bull**

Director **David O'Shea**

A Doll's House (1879)

HENRIK IBSEN in a version by Nick Ward from a translation by Knut Grimstad

25 May–10 June 1989

Torvald Helmer **Daniel Massey**
Nora **Miranda Foster**
Dr Rank **T P McKenna**
Mrs Kristine Linde **Michelle Newell**
Nils Krogstad **Matthew Scurfield**
Anne Marie **Gabrielle Hamilton**

Design **Brian Vahey**
Lighting **Chris Ellis**

Ibsen's powerful drama of a woman's rights within marriage was given a most forceful adaptation at the Haymarket where Nick Ward's production was seen by Alex Renton in *The Independent* as 'severe and disturbing'. 'Where Ward shocks', Renton wrote, 'is in the overtones of the sexual underplay.' A highly acclaimed revival, with some excellent performances.

Sound **Paul Bull**
Choreographer **Lee Sprintall**

Music **Gavin Bryars**
Director **Nick Ward**

Looking at You (Revived) Again (1989)

GREGORY MOTTON

Studio 29 May–10 June 1989

Abe Driscoll **Tony Rohr**
Mrs James **Veronica Quilligan**
Peragrin's Daughter **Susannah Doyle**

Design **Anthony Lambel**
Lighting **Sam Moon**

The last play in the series of new works is about misaligned friendship and love. It is a lyrical piece exploring lost lives and the delusions of memory. The play was highly praised and ran later for a month at the Bush Theatre in London.

Music **Corin Buckeridge**   Director **Simon Usher**

Dames at Sea (1966)
GEORGE HAIMSOHN and ROBIN MILLER

14 July–26 August 1989

with **Bonnie Langford, Floyd Bevan, Nick Burge, Teddy Green, Melanie Rose, Joan Savage, Lee Sprintall and Mark White**

Design **Michael Pavelka**
Lighting **Chris Ellis**
Choreographer **Tim Flavin**
Music **Jim Wise**

One of the lesser-known musicals on a well-known theme, *Dames at Sea* tells of Ruby's arrival on Broadway where, within 24 hours, she is in love and in a show. The leading lady tries to steal her man, but the US navy saves her, and all ends happily. An exuberant production, with Bonnie Langford's enchanting dancing, proved highly popular with critics and public alike.

Musical Director **Charles Miller**   Director **Tim Flavin**

Hamlet (1602)
WILLIAM SHAKESPEARE

14 September–7 October 1989

Hamlet **Daniel Webb**
Claudius **Andrew Jarvis**
Ghost/Player King **David Gant**
Gertrude **Anne White**
Polonius **Richard Durden**
Laertes **Lloyd Owen**
Ophelia **Veronica Smart**
Horatio **Martin McKellan**
Rosencrantz/Osric **Michael Brazier**
Guildenstern/Reynaldo/Gravedigger **James Nesbitt**
Gravedigger/Player **Richard Strange**
Marcellus/Soldier/Player **Malcolm Jacobs**
Musician/Player **James T Ford**

Ever internationally minded, 'world theatre at the heart of the UK', the Haymarket Theatre engaged the Russian director Yuri Lyubimov to direct *Hamlet*. Following its opening at Leicester, the production toured Australia, Japan, Russia, Israel and Western Europe as well as playing, briefly, at The Old Vic. It received support from industry and toured with the blessing of the British Council. It must be one of the saddest events of the theatrical year that a production of this nature represented Great Britain abroad as well as the Haymarket Leicester, for the Haymarket is a dynamic theatre with a standard of work far superior to that seen in this version of *Hamlet*.

  It begins with what we presume is the dead King's funeral. The grave is ever present with us at the front of the stage. The enormous tapestry, specially woven, menaces the mourners and suggests that they have intimations of old Hamlet's ghost. Claudius's opening speech is accompanied by loud drumbeats

Player Queen **Elizabeth Rider**
Barnado/Soldier/Player **Joao de Sousa**
Player/Prompter **Sonia Forbes Adam**

Design **David Borowsky**
Lighting **Krystof Kozlowski**
Sound **Paul Bull**
Choreographer **Chiang Ching**
Music **Yuri Butsko and James T Ford**
Director **Yuri Lyubimov**

at the end of each line. This not only destroys the meaning of the speech, it also heralds a theme of the evening – that actors will have to battle against a cacophony of sound in order to make themselves heard.

Although Fortinbras, and much else, is cut, there is room for interpolations and the transposition of speeches. Laertes enters with a forward roll and squeezes his spots while Ophelia is saying something rather important at the other side of the stage. But, in Lyubimov's conception, the words are of secondary importance to a pyrotechnic display of lighting that would embarrass a melodrama and music that overpowers the actors. 'The time is out of joint' is spoken by Polonius and Claudius as well as by Hamlet, and 'To be or not to be' is said by a variety of characters. The famous soliloquy is split in half by another scene before Hamlet is finally left, almost alone, to deliver the end of it.

Claudius's prayer scene, battered by music, is extended to an interminable length, and Gertrude has to turn her eyes into her very soul while she is taking off her make-up with cold cream. This scene is divided by the interval. As Hamlet muses upon the skull of Yorick, a burst on the bagpipes drowns him. He dies without being sent by flights of angels to his heavenly rest, some words over a loudspeaker providing the epitaph as the tapestry again swirls across the stage – but then the actors have fought with it for most of the evening.

Some would dismiss any criticism of this self-indulgent travesty as merely the words of a purist unable to come to terms with expressionism and 'theatre'. But it is of no great moment for a professional director to create pretty pictures which often have little relevance to the text; there is far greater integrity in experimenting with one's own words than in trying to improve the words of others without seeking to illuminate.

The saddest thing of all is that beneath the clatter and the clutter is a potentially good, boisterous Hamlet from Daniel Webb and an equally promising Ophelia from Veronica Smart. For the rest, it should be silence.

Catastrophe (1982)

SAMUEL BECKETT

Studio 5–28 October 1989

The Protagonist **David Warrilow**
The Director **Tom Knight**
The Assistant **Christina Paul**

Krapp's Last Tape (1958)

SAMUEL BECKETT

Studio 5–28 October 1989

Krapp **David Warrilow**

Design **Jocelyn Herbert**
Lighting **Ben Ormerod**
Director **Antoni Libera**

Continuing with the season of major world drama, the Haymarket offered two Beckett plays directed by the Polish director Antoni Libera, who has a close working relationship with Beckett. Krapp is a 69-year-old writer who relives the past by using his recorded voice. *Catastrophe* is an allegory on the oppressed masses. The productions at Leicester were greeted with great respect and enthusiasm. They later had an international tour.

Fashion (1987)

DOUGLAS LUCIE

19 October–11 November 1989

Paul Cash **Paul Freeman**
Liz Scouler **Karen Lewis**
Robin Gingham **Paul J Medford**
Stuart Clarke **Norman Rodway**
Eric Bright **Robin Soans**
Howard Lampeter **Michael Culver**
Amanda Clarke **Gillian Eaton**
Dooley **Paul Higgins**
Gillian Huntley **Laura Davenport**

Another Haymarket production destined for a transfer to London, *Fashion* is a revival of the play first produced by the RSC which deals with the world of advertising and the way in which advertising is used by the current government to manipulate public opinion. Michael Attenborough directed a very strong cast.

Design **Michael Pavelka**   Director **Michael Attenborough**
Lighting **Bill Bray**

World premières of two Howard Barker plays, and Christmas and New Year productions of *Stig of the Dump* and *Cabaret*, formed the immediate plans for this exciting theatre, which was also to undergo some restructuring.

LIVERPOOL

Everyman Theatre

HOPE STREET, LIVERPOOL L1 9BH
051-709-4776

Artistic Director **John Doyle**

Slaughterhouse 5 (1989)

VINCE FOXALL and PADDY CUNNEEN from the novel by Kurt Vonnegut, Junior

18 May–17 June 1989

An adaptation of Kurt Vonnegut's novel, a science fiction approach to Dresden at the time of the bombing.

Paul Lazzarro **Barry Birch**
Montana Wildhack **Jemma Churchill**
Billy Pilgrim **Peter Darling**
Valencia Pilgrim **Linda Dobell**
Roland Weary **Andrew Hobday**
Elliott Rosewater **Paterson Joseph**
Wild Bob **Chris Mellor**

Kurt Vonnegut **Jeff Nuttall**
Mary O'Hare **Taiwo Paine**
Howard Campbell **Malcolm Scates**
Edgar Derby **Bev Willis**

Design **Paul Kondras**
Lighting **Mo Hemming**
Choreographer **Linda Dobell**
Director **Paddy Cunneen**

The Trojan Women (415 BC)

EURIPIDES translated by Philip Vellacott

5 October – 25 November 1989

Poseidon **Nicholas Monu**
Athene **Linda Dobell**
Hecabe **Clare Dow**
Talthybius **Stephen Earle**
Cassandra **Maria Gough**
Andromache **Karen Mann**
Menelaus **Johnson Willis**
Helen **Irma Inniss**
Astyanax **Oliver Gerg**

Design **Elizabeth Ascroft**
Lighting **Bernie Shaw**
Choreographer **Linda Dobell**

'A bold and uncompromising enterprise' was how this production of Euripides' anti-war play was heralded. It was the first presentation in John Doyle's schematic programme for the Everyman which will take the company up to next June and the presentation of plays by Gubaryev and Solzhenitsyn. *The Trojan Women* ran in repertoire with *Wild, Wild Women* (a musical version of *Lysistrata*), and *The Gods Are Not to Blame* (see Riverside Studios, London Fringe) was also presented.

Sleeping Beauty, *'Tis Pity She's a Whore* and *Love at a Loss* were to take the company into 1990.

Music **Catherine Jayes**   Director **John Doyle**

Liverpool Playhouse

WILLIAMSON SQUARE, LIVERPOOL L1 1EL

Artistic Director **Ian Kellgren**

Fear and Misery of the Third Reich (1939)

BERTOLT BRECHT

Studio 17 January–4 February 1989

with **Julie Bennett, Louise Duprey, Jon Huyton, Charlotte Metcalf, Mark Moraghan, Ayshe Owens, Jon Sotherton and Mark Roper**

The play was in repertory with, and played by the same cast, as the following series of short plays.

Fears and Miseries of the Third Term (1989)

with **Kay Adshead, Anne Caulfield, Trisha Cooke, Nick Darke, Noel Greig, Catherine Hayes, Terry Heaton, Debbie Horsfield, Charlotte Keatley, Frank McGuinness and Jim Morris**

Poems by **Adrian Henri**
Music and Lyrics **Patrick Dineen**
Design **Hannah Mayall**
Lighting **Matthew O'Connor**

The linking of Brecht's series of cameos on the political pressures on people in Germany in the 1930s with a series of plays and sketches which, by implication, allied Hitler and Thatcher caused the Tory councillors of Liverpool to suggest withdrawing funds from the theatre – thereby proving the point of the plays. In the event, most critics found the series of modern plays a little too bland to have any significant impact other than through their collective title.

Sound **Mark Armstrong**
Musical Director **Patrick Dineen**
Director **Kate Rowland**

Of Mice and Men (1937)

JOHN STEINBECK

1 February–4 March 1989

Georgie **Eamon Boland**
Lennie **Ian Burfield**
Candy **Barry J Gordon**
Boss **David Williams**

Steinbeck's famous tale of the companionship of a man of strength with a simple mind and his partner does not transfer easily to the stage, but under Julian Webber's direction it was a moving experience.

Curly **Sam Graham**
Curly's Wife **Lise-Ann McLaughlin**
Slim **James Earl Adair**
Carlson **Jeremy Pearce**
Whit **Michael Bottle**
Crooks **Lloyd Anderson**

Design **Gillian Daniell**
Lighting **Kim Nichols**
Director **Julian Webber**

Crimes of the Heart (1979)

BETH HENLEY

8 March–1 April 1989

Lenny Magrath **Serena Harragin**
Chick Boyle **Jacquetta May**
Doc Porter **John Graham Davies**
Meg Magrath **Kit Hollerbach**
Babe Botrelle **Matilda Ziegler**
Michael Higgs **Barnette Lloyd**

Beth Henley's prize-winning, witty play about three sisters who make their peace with a world that can't really cope with them.

Design **Eve Stewart**
Lighting **Johanna Town**

Sound **Andrew Waddington**
Director **Kate Rowland**

Shirley Valentine (1986)

WILLY RUSSELL

Shirley **Paula Wilcox**

Design **John Knowles**
Lighting **Ron Beattie**
Director **Richard Oliver**

This production was first mounted at the Thorndike Theatre, Leatherhead. The play had its première at the Everyman, Liverpool, in 1986.

Be Bop A Lula (1988)

BILL MORRISON with Spencer Leigh

Sharon Sheeley/Girls **Amelia Bullmore**
Brian Bennett **Paul Codman**
Larry Parnes/Bass Player **David Edge**
Georgie Fame/Julian X/Car Driver **Chris Garner**
Joe Brown **Paul Kissaun**
Billy Fury/Jack Good **Gary Mavers**
Eddie Cochran **Martin Glyn Murray**

Having been a great success when it first opened at the Playhouse in July 1988, the story of Eddie Cochran's 1960 tour returned to the theatre a year later.

Gene Vincent **Andrew Schofield**
Girl with Sax/Girl from Leeds **Samantha Shaw**
Hal Carter/Announcer/Interviewer **Michael Starke**

Design **Poppy Mitchell**
Lighting **Robert Longthorne**
Costume **Anne-Marie Allison**
Musical Director **Rick Juckes**
Director **Bill Morrison**

Dead of Night (1989)

PETER WHALLEY

Jack **Philip Madoc**
Maggie **Jackie Lye**
Dennis **Geoffrey Hughes**
Lynne **Sally Watts**

Design **Elroy Ashmore**
Lighting **Leslie Lyon**
Sound **Mark Armstrong**
Director **Ian Kellgren**

A new play by a Lancashire-born playwright. It tells of Jack, who has been cleared of a manslaughter charge, but, in fact, he has shot the man to prevent his wife leaving him. She takes her revenge.

19. *Jackie Lye and Philip Madoc in* Dead of Night *at the Liverpool Playhouse.*

The Shadow of a Gunman (1923)

SEAN O'CASEY

Donal Davoren **Killian McKenna**
Seumas Shields **Sean Cranitch**
Maguire/Tommy Owens **Graham Norton**
Mr Mulligan/Adolphus Grigson **Walter McMonagle**
Minnie Powell **Mary Ann O'Donoghue**
Julia Henderson **Nora Connolly**

The first play in O'Casey's great trilogy concerning the 'troubles' received a fine revival at the Liverpool Playhouse. There were plans to follow it with another political study, *Madame Mao*.

James Gallogher **Desmond Jordan**
Debby Grigson **Valerie Lilley**

Design **Russ Barson**

Lighting **Johanna Town**
Sound **Mark Armstrong**
Director **Eric Standidge**

LUDLOW

Ludlow Castle

CASTLE SQUARE, LUDLOW, SHROPSHIRE SY8 1AY
0584-5070

Julius Caesar (1599)

WILLIAM SHAKESPEARE

24 June–8 July 1989

Michael Napier Brown again directed the Ludlow Festival's Shakespeare contribution. It was the first production of *Julius Caesar* in what was the festival's 30th season. It was a respectful and faithful production with the central themes 'sharply focused'.

Flavius/Artemidorus/Octavius Caesar **Timothy Watson**
Marullus/Metellus Cimber/Messala **Kim Wall**
Cobbler/Lucilius/Decius Brutus **Derek Ware**
Carpenter/Servant/Cinna the Poet **Mark Carey**
Julius Caesar **John Franklyn-Robbins**
Calphurnia **Vilma Hollingbery**
Marcus Antonius **Paul Jones**
Soothsayer/Titinius **Simon Linnell**
Casca/Pindarus **Chris Matthews**

Marcus Brutus **Robert Grange**
Cassius **Gareth Armstrong**
Cicero/Lepidus/Dardanius **Fraser Reed**
Cinna/Volumnius **Bill Neville**
Lucius **Garth Napier Jones**
Trebonius/Strato **Michael Vivian**
Portia **Holly Wilson**

Servant/Young Cato **Gary Ross**

Design **Ray Lett**
Costume **Terry Brown**
Lighting **Kevin Roach**
Director **Michael Napier Brown**

MANCHESTER

Contact Theatre Company

OXFORD ROAD, MANCHESTER M15 6JA
061-274-4400

Artistic Director **Brigid Larmour**

Master Harold and the Boys (1982)

ATHOL FUGARD

2–25 February 1989

Hally **Simon Gregor**
with **Sydney Cale**

Design **Craig Hewitt**

Fugard's simple comment on apartheid is set in a café in Port Elizabeth. Master Harold, reacting to the news of his father's discharge from hospital, turns angrily on his two black friends and inalienably severs the contact with them which has

Director **James Macdonald**

nourished him through his childhood. 'Superb performances by all three actors', said Natalie Anglesey.

The Idiot (1988)

JOHN GINMAN from the novel by Fyodor Dostoevsky

6 April–6 May 1989

with **Karen Henhorn, Alex Kingston, Simon Molloy, Martin Reeve, Pam Scobie, Steve Swinscoe, James Vaughan and Jem Wall**

The story of Prince Myshkin, the innocent in a corrupt world, was 'stunningly' adapted for the stage in what was seen as 'a superb team effort'. 'Theatre at its very best', said *The Stage*.

Design **Ian MacNeil**   Director **John Ginman**

Fool for Love (1983)

SAM SHEPPARD

25 May–24 June 1989

with **Sam Dale, David Fielder, Malcolm Hebden and Noreen Kershaw**

Design **Kendra Ullyart**

The isolation of an American cowboy who lassoes bedposts instead of cows and who is entangled with a woman who believes he will 'erase' her.

Director **James Macdonald**

The Duchess of Malfi (1613)

JOHN WEBSTER

21 September–21 October 1989

Duchess of Malfi **Ellie Haddington**
Antonio **Wyllie Longmore**
Cardinal **James Quinn**
The Duke **Colin McFarlane**
Bosola **Scott Cherry**

Design **Kate Burnett**

A contemporary feel to the production was Anthony Clark's aim in one of his last works before moving to his post with the Birmingham Repertory Theatre.

Lighting **Chris Brockhouse**   Director **Anthony Clark**

Feminine Singular (1977–83)

DARIO FO and FRANCA RAME translated by Gillian Hanna and Ed Emery

26 October–25 November 1989

The Mother
The Rape
Coming Home

with **Susan-Jane Tanner**

Design **Kate Burnett**

Director **Ellie Haddington**

The Red Balloon (1989)

ANTHONY CLARK adapted from the book (and film) by Albert Lamorisse

8 December 1989–27 January 1990

with **Philip Aldridge, Amelia Bullmore/Louise Yates, Claude Close, Jane Cox, Andy Crook, Kieran Cunningham, Chris Garner, Jane Lancaster, Philip Ram and Rachel Spry**

Design **Kendra Ullyart**
Costume **Jacquie Davies**

Anthony Clark's farewell gift to Contact was his charming adaptation of *The Red Balloon* for the Christmas play. He was succeeded by Brigid Larmour, who was his associate in Manchester from 1985 to 1987. The first production planned for 1990 was a world première of *Meridian*.

Lighting **Chris Brockhouse**
Choreographer **Lorelei Lynn**
Music **Mark Vibrans**

Director **Anthony Clark**

Royal Exchange Theatre

ST ANN'S SQUARE, MANCHESTER M2 7DH
061-833-9833

Artistic Directors **Gregory Hersov, James Maxwell, Braham Murray, Casper Wrede**

Amongst Barbarians (1989)

MICHAEL WALL

9–25 February 1989

Bryan **Dominic Keating**
Ralph **Ronan Vibert**
Gaolers **Tariq Yunus, Zubie Dar** and **Anji Dar**
Lawyer **Sakuntala Ramanee**
George **Christopher Hancock**
Wendy **Avril Elgar**
Lilly **Kathy Burke**
Toni **Rosalind March**
Barman **Ricardo Sibelo**

The first production of the year at the Royal Exchange was the Mobil Prize-winning play, *Amongst Barbarians*. It is set in Malaysia where two young Englishmen await sentence for drug peddling. Their families fly out to join them, but they are of little support. It is a play with much humour, if a little uneven, and Michael Wall was credited with a great power of writing.

Design **David Millard**
Lighting **Vincent Herbert**

Sound **Alastair Golden**
Director **James Maxwell**

A Taste of Honey (1958)
SHELAGH DELANEY

2 March–1 April 1989

Jo **Caroline Milmoe**
Mother **Dinah Stabb**
Geoffrey **Graham Fellows**
Jimmy **Leo Wringer**
Peter **James Clyde**

Design **Michael Holt**
Costume **Sophie Doncaster**

Reset in Salford in the eighties with a band on stage, Ian Hastings's production of Shelagh Delaney's play about the lonely teenage girl who becomes pregnant and who is befriended by a homosexual enjoyed a two-month tour after playing at the Royal Exchange.

Lighting **Glyn Peregrine**
Sound **Philip Clifford**

Musical Director **Brendan P Healy**
Director **Ian Hastings**

In the Talking Day (1989)
DOLORES WALSHE

13 April–6 May 1989

Mia **Frances Tomelty**
Piet Schurmann **Terence Wilton**
Thulato Mdala **Norman Beaton**
Claus Schurmann **Wolfe Morris**
Paul Richardson **Philip Anthony**
Babo Schurmann **Jenny Quayle**
Jan Schurmann **Joseph Murray/Stuart Pickering**
Elijah **Joseph Mydell**

The world première of a prize-winning first play about a superior Afrikaaner family who are shaken by an unexpected event.

Samuel **Alex Tetteh-Lartey**
James **Andrew Francis**
Sipho **Wale Ojo**
Vos/Reunert **Peter Rutherford**

Design **Johann Engels**
Lighting **Robert Bryan**
Director **Braham Murray**

The Voysey Inheritance (1905)

HARLEY GRANVILLE BARKER

11 May–17 June 1989

Having been starved of work by Harley Granville Barker for far too long, the theatre public was warmed by two productions of *The Voysey Inheritance* by major companies within the space of a few weeks. This is indeed 'a play whose time has come'; by Gregory Hersov and the Royal Exchange, it was given an excellent, stylish production.

Mr Voysey **James Maxwell**
Peacey **Milton Johns**
Edward Voysey **Robert Glenister**
Major Booth Voysey **David Allister**
George Booth **Ralph Michael**
Denis Tregoning **Ian Driver**
Rev. Colpus **Bill Croasdale**
Alice Maitland **Laura Girling**
Honor Voysey **Ellie Haddington**
Beatrice Voysey **Helen Atkinson Wood**
Phoebe **Liz Lees**
Mrs Voysey **Anna Welsh**
Trenchard Voysey **Peter Harlowe**
Emily Voysey **Susan-Jane Tanner**
Hugh Voysey **John McAndrew**

Design **Michael Holt**
Costume **David Short**
Lighting **Michael Calf**
Sound **Tim McCormick**
Director **Gregory Hersov**

The Odd Couple (1965)

NEIL SIMON

22 June–5 August 1989

Ever-popular and perennially topical, *The Odd Couple* deals with separation, divorce and its consequences. It is a sizzlingly witty comedy, but much more. As stated by *The Daily Telegraph*, the Royal Exchange production was 'a complete triumph'.

Speed **Jack Chissick**
Murray **Edmund Kentle**
Roy **Andrew Francis**
Vinnie **Maurice Kaufmann**
Oscar Maddison **Derek Griffiths**
Felix Ungar **Sam Kelly**
Gwendolyn Pigeon **Elizabeth McKechnie**
Cecily Pigeon **Louise Pigeon**

Design **Johanna Bryant**
Lighting **Vincent Herbert**
Sound **Phil Clifford**

Director **Ronald Harwood**

The Parasol (1987)

FRANK DUNAI from the novel, *Three Years*, by Anton Chekhov

14 September–21 October 1989

Alexei Fyodorych Laptev **Simon Cadell**
Yulia Sergeyevna **Maggie O'Neill**
Dr Byelavin **Kevin Moore**

The lure of Moscow as the panacea for all ills for one from the country is at the heart of Dunai's adaptation. Yulia accepts Alexei's proposal believing that life in the capital will not only take her away from her father, but give her an exciting life. That

Grigory Nikolaich Panaurov **Geoffrey Beevers**
Fyodor Laptev **Kevin Elyot**
Pochatkin **Jeffrey Robert**
Fyodor Fyodorich Laptev **Peter Copley**
Polina Nikolaevna Rassudina **Jill Brassington**

proves not to be the case. The play was first performed in Scarborough and had an interesting and welcome revival at the Royal Exchange.

Pyotr **David Crellin**
Ivan Yartsev **Chris Hunter**

Design **Anthony Ward**

Lighting **Christopher Toulmin**
Sound **Frank Bradley**
Director **Tim Luscombe**

Winding the Ball (1989)

ALEX FINLAYSON

26 October–11 November 1989

with **Ian Bartholomew, Sydnee Blake, Gordon Case, Trevor Cooper, Lisa Eichhorn, Marcus Eyre, David Schofield, Ling Tai and Roberta Taylor**

Set in a small Appalachian town in the United States, Alex Finlayson's new play tells how the normal life of the town is disturbed by some extraordinary events.

Director **Gregory Hersov**

The Royal Exchange is blooming and prospering with good houses, increased sponsorship and grants, and an exciting and consistent standard of work. *The Glass Menagerie* and *She Stoops To Conquer* were scheduled to take the theatre into 1990 when the Royal Exchange will mount one of its biggest projects with Robert Lindsay in *The Count of Monte Cristo* at the Palace Theatre, Manchester.

MOLD

Theatr Clwyd

MOLD, CLWYD CH7 1YA
0352-55114

Artistic Director **Toby Robertson**

Treasure Island (1988)

JEREMY BROOKS adapted from the novel by Robert Louis Stevenson

2 December 1988–28 January 1989

Billy Bones/Tom/Gray **Paul Clayton**

Theatr Clwyd's Christmas–New Year show was a new musical

Jim Hawkins **Andrew Groves**
Mrs Hawkins **Genevieve Walsh**
Blind Pew/Israel Hands **Tim Pearce**
Anderson **Joe Fitzgerald**
Dick **Jared Harris**
Wilson **Nicholas Fry**
Morgan **Stephen Crane**
Johnson/Hunter **Anthony O'Driscoll**
Squire Trelawney **Edwin Richfield**
Dr Livesey **David Rose**
Redruth/George Merry/Joyce **Peter Armitage**

Long John Silver **Liam O'Callaghan**
Captain Smollett **Michael Walker**
Ben Gunn **Hugh Futcher**

Design **Colin Winslow**
Costume **Sarah-Jane McClelland**
Lighting **Pat Nelder**
Sound **Kevin Heyes**
Music **Donald Fraser**

Lyrics **Jeremy Brooks**
Musical Director **Martin Waddington**
Director **Roger Haines**

version of Stevenson's famous pirate yarn. The writers, Brooks and Fraser, had an earlier success with their version of *The Wind in the Willows*.

The Old Devils (1989)

ROBIN HAWDON from the novel by Kingsley Amis

17 February–1 April 1989

Alun Weaver **Philip Madoc**
Rhiannon Weaver **Meg Wynn Owen**
Malcolm Cellan-Davies **John Rowe**
Gwen Cellan-Davies **Ann Firbank**
Sophie Norris **Elizabeth Morgan**
Charlie Norris **David Lloyd Meredith**
Peter Thomas **John Sharp**
Muriel Thomas **Sheila Burrell**
Garth Pumphrey **Howell Evans**
Angharad Pumphrey **Patricia Kane**
Rosemary Weaver **Karen Gledhill**

A stage adaptation of Kingsley Amis's prize-winning novel was an inevitability, and it was equally inevitable that Theatr Clwyd should present the world première. The story of the novel is that Alun Weaver has made a reputation in England as a writer and television spouter about Wales. He returns home to South Wales, much to the apprehension of his friends. It is a difficult novel to adapt for the stage, but the production was applauded for its energy and ingenuity and for its humour.

William Thomas **Richard Clay-Jones**

Design **Sean Cavanagh**

Costume **Sarah-Jane McClelland**
Lighting **Kevin Sleep**
Director **Toby Robertson**

Getting Out (1977)

MARSHA NORMAN

21 April–13 May 1989

Arlene **Patti Love**
Arlie **Katerina Tana**
Bennie **Peter Barnes**
Guard/Ronnie **Martin McDougall**

A tremendous scoop for Theatr Clwyd, and a product of Toby Robertson's visit to America, *Getting Out* was first performed in the States 12 years ago. It had to wait until 1989, and Theatr Clwyd, for its British première. It is the story of Arlene, who arrives back in Louisville after years in an Alabama jail. It

Doctor/Principal/Psychiatrist/Ruby
Marlena Mackey
Mother **Elaine Ives-Cameron**
Carl/Warden **Greg Charles**

Design **John Jenkins**

examines the changes that have been brought about in her, and how they have been brought about. It received a meticulous and imaginative staging in Mold.

Lighting **Keith Hemming**
Sound **Kevin Heyes**

Director **Marina Caldarone**

The Birth of Merlin (1623)
WILLIAM SHAKESPEARE and WILLIAM ROWLEY

1 June–1 July 1989

Billy Rowley, a Clown **Roy Hudd**
Lord Donobert **John Crocker**
Cador **Andrew Groves**
Constantia/Lucina **Morag Nicholson**
Earl of Gloucester/Sir Nicodemus Nothing **David Gooderson**
Lord Edwyn **Bernard Wright**
Modestia **Polly Pleasence**
Toclio **Graham Hubbard**
Aurelius **Nick Sampson**
Artesia **Cheryl Pay**
Anselme/Gentleman **Ian Taylor**
Proximus **Philip Dunbar**
Joan Go-To-It/Sprite/Gentlewoman **Anna Karen**
Prince Uter **Guy Burgess**
General Edol/Achilles/Bishop **Tim Pearce**
Ostorius **Martin McKellan**
Devil/Vortigern **Bill Homewood**

Design **Alan Barrett**
Lighting **Jenny Cane**

The rise and rise of Theatr Clwyd seems unending, as yet another brilliant coup was to prove. One of the Shakespeare apocryphal plays, *The Birth of Merlin* may have some words by the bard, but this has never been proved. What was proved with the scintillating production at Mold – where the play opened the third festival – was that it can be great entertainment. Billy Rowley, a rollicking Roy Hudd, is sucked back into the past and provides a perpetual link and narration with his stand-up comedy act. The plot is sexually complicated, but the audience enjoys an anachronistic festive entertainment. Rapturously received.

Sound **Guy Colyer**
Music and Musical Director **Stuart Gordon and R J Stewart**
Director **Denise Coffey**

Branwen (1986)
TONY CONRAN

22 June–1 July 1989

Branwen **Amanda Wright**
Manawydan **Eilian Wyn**
Efnisien **Ian Puleston-Davies**
Nisien **Kieran McCrystal**
Matholwch **Dorien Thomas**
Fergus **Nick Dowsett**

The Made in Wales Theatre Company gave Theatr Clwyd another première with this revolutionary tragedy. Taken from the *Mabinogion*, it tells how Branwen is given to the King of Ireland in marriage, how her half-brother Efnisien is outraged and of the eventual disaster and destruction of two nations. This was seen as a most courageous presentation.

The Cadi **Lynn Hunter**
Girl **Rakie Ayola**

Design **Rona Lee**
Lighting **Keith Hemming**
Music **Philip Thomas**

Choreographer **Nick Dowsett**
Musical Director **Matthew Bailey**
Director **Gilly Adams**

The immediate plans for this vital theatre are Toby Robertson's production of *Othello*, Schnitzler's *Anatol in Love* and the Christmas–New Year presentation of *Peter Pan*.

NEWCASTLE UPON TYNE

Northern Stage Company
(Formerly Tyne Theatre Company)

67a WESTGATE ROAD, NEWCASTLE UPON TYNE NE1 1SG
091-232-3366

Artistic Director **Andrew McKinnon**

The Wizard of Oz (1987)
L FRANK BAUM

Tyne Theatre 7 December 1988–21 January 1989

A production in conjunction with the Theatre Royal, Plymouth, *The Wizard of Oz* proved to be a most popular and highly successful Christmas–New Year show. It filled the main house, while the production in the Gulbenkian Studio Theatre proved an equally popular show among the very young.

Dorothy **Jessica Martin**
Aunt Em/Glinda **Cristina Avery**
Hickory/Tinman **Geoffrey Davies**
Shem/Scarecrow **Grant Baynham**
Uncle Henry/Lord Growlie **Patrick Moore**
Zeke/Lion **Michael Sharvell-Martin**
Elvira Gulch/Wicked Witch of the West **Margaret Ashcroft**
Mayor/General **Andy Herrity**
Barristers/Generals **Tony Allison and Jonathan Craige**
Coroner/Monkey **Ian Poitier**
Farmer/Monkey **Keith Chapman**
President of the Peppermint League **Gioia Izquierdo**

Leader of the Lollipop Guild **Susan Kenny**
Private **Henry Grahame-Smith**
Lady **Antoinetta Evans**
Gloria **Ruby-Marie Hutchinson**
Wizard of Oz **Alan Hockey**
Toto **Toto**
Munchkins, Jitterbugs etc. **Pupils of the Reavley Theatre School, trained by Sandra Reavley**

Design **Philip James Walker**
Lighting **Durham Marenghi**
Sound **Mic Pool**
Choreographer **Carole Todd**
Music and Lyrics **Harold Arlen and E Y Harburg, from the MGM motion picture**
Musical Director **Peter Aylin**
Director **Andrew McKinnon**

Fishy Tales (1988)

CHRIS SPEYER

Gulbenkian Studio 14 December 1988–14 January 1989

Plodge **Eddie Nestor**
Professor Snorkle **Fiona MacPherson**
Herman **Ivan Sears**
The Sea Serpent **Charlie Hardwick**

Design **Helen Skillicorn**
Lighting **Richard Orr**
Music **Ivan Dears**

Director **Chris Bostock**

Educating Rita (1979)

WILLY RUSSELL

8 February–4 March 1989

Frank **Julian Glover**
Rita **Helen Lederer**

Design **David Cockayne**
Lighting **Benny Ball**
Director **Andrew McKinnon**

Willy Russell's tale of the hairdresser who awakens to life through literature, the Open University and her contact with Frank, her alcoholic tutor, has become a hardy perennial. It is a far better play than it is a film – the expansiveness and outside scenes took away the necessary intimacy between Frank and Rita. The problem of each new production is to offer something fresh. In this respect, in Newcastle, Helen Lederer – an ebullient, lively actress – had the talent to make the part her own; and Julian Glover complemented her with a balanced performance.

20. *Julian Glover as Frank and Helen Lederer as Rita in the Northern Stage Company's Educating Rita.*

The American Clock (1980)

ARTHUR MILLER

15 March–1 April 1989

Arthur Miller's father was a clothing manufacturer hit hard by the Depression. *The American Clock* traces the years up to the Wall Street crash in 1929 and the Depression that followed, measuring its effect upon the lives of ordinary American people. The play was a failure in the United States, but it was reclaimed in Great Britain – as was Miller himself – and it is of tremendous credit to the Northern Stage Company that they had the courage and vision to mount *The American Clock*. It ranges widely, from 1929 to beyond 1936, from Brooklyn to Mississippi, and uses 25 pieces of music from Schumann to 'Brother, Can You Spare a Dime?'

Arthur Robinson **Andrew Normington**
Clarence/Louis Banks/Isaac **Chris Tajah**
Moe Baum **Jake D'Arcy**
Rose **Maxine Howe**
Lee Baum **James Telfer**
Grandpa/Kapush **Peter Laird**
Fanny Margolies **Vanessa Rosenthal**
Sidney **Max Burrows**
Lucille/Mrs Taylor/Isabel/Grace **Anne Orwin**
Joey **Billy Fellows**
Frank/Arthur Clayton/Mr Graham/Rudy **Anthony Corriette**
Dr Rosman/Doris Gross **Rowan Stuart**
Broadway Tony/Henry Taylor/Ryan **Sammy Johnson**
Jesse Livermore/Theodore K Quinn/Dugan/Stanislaus **Richard Rees**
William Durant/Sheriff/Bush **Finetime Fontayne**
Diana Morgan/Edie **Teddie Thompson**
Miss Fowler/Irene **Delmozene Morris**

Ralph/Toland **Malcolm McKee**

Design **Ken Harrison**
Lighting **Benny Ball**
Sound **Mic Pool**
Director **Andrew McKinnon**

The Importance of Being Earnest (1895)

OSCAR WILDE

19 April–13 May 1989

John Worthing, JP **Gary McDonald**
Algernon Moncrieff **Ben Thomas**
Lady Bracknell **Mona Hammond**
Gwendolen Fairfax **Juanita Waterman**
Cecily Cardew **Jeohna Williams**
Miss Prism **Leonie Forbes**
Rev. Canon Chasuble **Oscar James**
Lane **Christopher Tajah**
Merriman **Andrew Goth**

Design **Ellen Cairns**

Produced in conjunction with Talawa Theatre Company, *The Importance of Being Earnest* featured an all-black cast and provided one of the great theatrical debating points of the year. The play has always been cited as the one least appropriate to black actors, so that Talawa's choice was something of a defiant one – it is a good play and they are a talented company. The production concentrated on giving serious attention to character and the social setting of those characters. *City Limits* saw it as 'easily the best of the current crop of Wilde revivals'.

Lighting **Richard Moffat**
Sound **Mic Pool**

Music **Samuel Coleridge Taylor**
Director **Yvonne Brewster**

21. The Talawa Theatre Company's The Importance of Being Earnest – Gary McDonald as Jack and Juanita Waterman as Gwendolen.

On 6 September, the company broke its permanent link with the Tyne Theatre and took on the role of the major professional producing theatre company for Newcastle and the northern region. It was renamed the Northern Stage Company. Andrew McKinnon stated, 'Our aim is to establish a company which can maximise the amount of resources to be used for the production of shows; and minimise the amount that is eaten up in the overhead expenses of running and manning theatres.'

The first two projects, *Good* and *Beehive*, were scheduled for the Newcastle Playhouse, while *Out of the Blue* was to be produced in the Gulbenkian Studio.

NORTHAMPTON The Royal Theatre

GUILDHALL ROAD, NORTHAMPTON NN1 1EA
0604-32533/24811

Artistic Director **Michael Napier Brown**

On Golden Pond
ERNEST THOMPSON

2–25 February 1989

Memorable as a film with Katherine Hepburn and Henry and

Norman Thayer **David Neal**
Ethel Thayer **Dilys Hamlett**
Chelsea **Brenda Cavendish**
Bill Ray **Graham James**
Billy Ray **James Wingerath**

Design **Annette Sumption**

Jane Fonda, *On Golden Pond* moves easily to the stage with its gentle look at an elderly couple and family relationships. The Northampton production preluded a national tour.

Lighting **Paul Martin**

Director **Gareth Armstrong**

Noises Off (1982)

MICHAEL FRAYN

3 March–1 April 1989

Dotty Otley **Jacqueline Morgan**
Lloyd Dallas **Chris Matthews**
Garry Lejeune **Kim Wall**
Brooke Ashton **Mairéad Carty**
Poppy Norton-Taylor **Kate Napier Brown**
Frederick Fellowes **Graham James**
Belinda Blair **Holly Wilson**
Tim Allgood **Peter Merrill**

A bubbling production of Frayn's comedy about a touring theatre company and the trials and tribulations of life backstage. The second act is one of the funniest creations in the British theatre. *Noises Off* proved to be a fine climax to the Royal Theatre's 1988–9 winter programme.

Selsdon Mowbray **David Neal**

Design **Ray Lett**

Lighting **Jacqui Leigh**
Director **Michael Napier Brown**

A Tale of Two Cities (1989)

DAVID HORLOCK from the novel by Charles Dickens

6–29 April 1989

Sydney Carton **Kim Wall**
Jarvis Lorry **Chris Matthews**
Coachman/Mr Stryver/Marquis St Evremonde/Fourth Jacques/Officer/Sergeant **Simon Linnell**
Guard/Mr Miggs/Gabelle/Roadmender/John Barsad **Fraser Reed**
Jerry Cruncher/Attorney General/Gaspard/First Jacques/Gaoler/Woodcutter **Bill Neville**
Lucie Manette **Mairéad Carty**
Miss Pross **Jacqueline Morgan**
Ernest Defarge **Paul Tomany**
Therese Defarge **Holly Wilson**

The Royal Theatre's contribution to the bicentennial celebrations of the French Revolution, this adaptation of *A Tale of Two Cities*, according to Caroline Morris in *The Stage*, assumed too much of its audience. However, she felt that the theatre must be congratulated yet again on the brilliant set and lighting: 'Designer Ray Lett continues to create a stream of imaginative and workable sets for the most demanding of productions, this being no exception.'

Dr Alexander Manette **David Neal**
Charles Darnay **William Hayes**
Judge/Second Jacques/President **Lionel Hamilton**
Third Jacques/Seamstress **Fiona Jameson**

Little Lucie **Charlotte Walker**

Design **Ray Lett**
Lighting **Jacqui Leigh**
Sound **Paul Martin**
Director **Michael Napier Brown**

Long Day's Journey Into Night (1940)

EUGENE O'NEILL

4–20 May 1989

James Tyrone **Michael Napier Brown**
Mary Cavan Tyrone **Diana Fairfax**
James Tyrone, Jnr **Kim Wall**
Edmund Tyrone **Bill Neville**
Cathleen **Mairéad Carty**

Design **Ray Lett**
Lighting **Paul Martin**
Director **Mark Clements**

Long Day's Journey Into Night was not seen on the stage until 1956, three years after O'Neill's death. It is an autobiographical study, a day in the life of the Tyrone (O'Neill) family. James, the father, is a miser, hoarding property and living on past dreams as an actor. His wife is morphine addicted, and his two sons are Jamie, an extrovert drinker, and Edmund (Eugene), a young, tubercular artist. It is a mighty, challenging play that has attracted some of the greatest actors, including, memorably, Laurence Olivier and Constance Cummings at the National Theatre at The Old Vic in 1971. In electing to perform the play at the Royal Theatre, Michael Napier Brown set himself one of the most dangerous and courageous tasks by a regional theatre for many years, but to live with danger is the true excitement of the theatre. *The Guardian* said of him that, as James Tyrone, he 'captures perfectly that testy Irishness that doesn't need the brogue to bring it out, and has a way of looking hopelessly defeated whilst still carrying himself as a matinée idol'. Diana Fairfax showed 'profound insight into the role of Mary', and Kim Wall and Bill Neville were equally praised in a production which, if overlong, had 'passion, poetry, anguish and despair'.

Rock-a-Bye Sailor (1962)

PHILIP KING and FALKLAND L CARY

25 May–17 June 1989

Edie Hornett **Deddie Davies**
Emma Hornett **Mollie Sugden**
Henry Hornett **William Moore**
Mrs Florrie Lack **Genevieve Walsh**
Albert Tufnell, AB **Kim Wall**
Shirley Tufnell **Mairéad Carty**
Daphne Bligh **Dawn Bowden**
Carnosutie Bligh, AB **John Ogilvie**
Robin Stebbington **Anthony Howes**

Design **Alec Davis**

Michael Napier Brown is not only a brave artistic director, he is also a realist, and the O'Neill epic was followed by the popular sequel to *Sailor Beware*. The first play dealt with the wedding; the second deals with the christening. Mollie Sugden played the interfering mother-in-law, the role created by Peggy Mount. In conjunction with Newpalm Productions, *Rock-a-Bye Sailor* played for the summer season in Eastbourne.

Costume **Judith King**
Lighting **Paul Martin**
Sound **Claire Allison**

Director **Mark Clements**

The Ragged Child (1987)

7–26 August 1989

Lord Shaftesbury **David King**
Judge/George Lloyd/Lord Ganlian/Drunk **Matthew Davies**
Joe Cooper **Frazer Corbyn**
Annie **Alexandria Rowbotham**
Sir Giles Merridew/Policemen **Ivan Miller**
Clerk **Nicholas Winston**
Policemen/Rat Fight Man **Mark Jones**
Crossing Sweeper **Paul Carpenter**
Leary **Ross Newman**
Officer/Lanigan/Drunk **Kevin Tomlinson**
The Patterer/Lord Flitterby **Ian Gardner**
Alice/Drunk **Samantha Jane**
Aggy **Georgina Pearson**
Syd **Michael Underwood**
Perkins/Flunky **Matthew Clapton**
Mrs Crimple **Becky McCutcheon**
Molly/Maid **Tamsin Suter**
Mrs O'Lafferty **Claire Lewins**

Conceived originally by the National Youth Music Theatre, *The Ragged Child* is set in 1849 and tells of the struggle for survival of Joe Cooper and his sick sister Annie. In the background is the reforming zeal of Lord Shaftesbury. More than 250 children were auditioned for parts in the musical, and 38 were in the cast.

Mary/Gang Member **Amy Brownridge**
Ethel **Fiona Cuff**
Doris/Mrs Underby Pugh **Alison Pettitt**
Sam **Steven Kendall**
Polly/Gang Member **Joanne Tonsley**
Mrs Ingleby **Kirsty Wilcox**
Mrs Sterncastle **Christine Adams**
Lady Ursula Epp **Susila Sivapragasam**
Lady Grangemouth **Melanie Saunders**
Maid **Kerry Bray**
Flunky **James Whatton**

Girl/Drunk **Pippa Giles**
Pie-Lane Boy **Paul Lyon**
Girl **Michelle Hofford**
Drunk **Anouska Burrage**

Book and Lyrics **Jeremy James Taylor and Frank Whately**
Music **David Nield**
Design **Christopher Richardson and Ray Lett**
Lighting **Keith Upton**
Sound **Paul Martin**
Choreographer **Dollie Henry**
Musical Director **David Roper**
Director **Michael Napier Brown**

Rosie Blitz (1989)

RICHARD PINNER

Touring production

Onkel Willie **Anthony Murray**
Mrs Dandridge/Moma Walensk **Janice McKenzie**
ARP Warden/Victor **Greg Greenidge**
Mitzy/Ivy **Karyn Rawles**
Rosie Blitz **Lizi Hann**

A play with music which provided entertainment and instruction for all the family and which centred upon life during the Blitz.

Design **Alec Davis**
Music **Andy Dodge**
Musical Director **Kate Somerby**

Director **Gavin Stride**

Jane Eyre (1989)

LIONEL HAMILTON from the novel by Charlotte Brontë

1–23 September 1989

Mrs Fairfax **Margaret Ashcroft**
Grace Poole **Sarah Whitlock**
John **Fraser Reed**
Jane Eyre **Charlotte Harvey**
Adele Varens **Sarah Henderson Harding**
Edward Rochester **Richard Warwick**
Bertha/Hannah **Cynthia Cherry**
Richard Mason/Rev. St John Rivers **Simon Linnell**

Rev. Wood **Malcolm Farquhar**
Mr Briggs **Gary Ross**
Diana Rivers **Vivienne Glance**

Design **Ray Lett**
Lighting **Keith Upton**
Director **Michael Napier Brown**

Sponsored by the newly formed Friends of the Royal who raise money on behalf of the theatre, *Jane Eyre*, although showing some deviations from Charlotte Brontë's tale, was a huge success and provided yet another national tour for the Northampton Repertory Players. *The Stage* described it as 'enthralling, totally compelling' and felt that 'Michael Napier Brown has certainly excelled himself with this production'.

The Gambler (1987)

EDWARD CANFOR-DUMAS and SIMON LINNELL from the novel by Fyodor Dostoevsky

14 and 21 September 1989

with **Simon Linnell**

Director **Robert Kitson**

A late-night extra which relates how Alexei Ivanovich has come to be alone and desperate in a garret in Homburg.

The Long and the Short and the Tall (1961)

WILLIS HALL

28 September–14 October 1989

Sgt Mitchem **Sebastian Abineri**
Colonel Johnstone **Michael Brogan**
L/Cpl Macleish **Richard Hainsworth**
Pte Whitaker **Alan Gilchrist**
Pte Evans **Jon Atkins**
Pte Bamforth **Joe McGann**
Pte Smith **David Boyce**
Japanese Soldier **Julian Lyon**

Design **Ray Lett**

Lighting **Keith Upton**

Director **Chris Hayes**

Set in the Malayan jungle in 1942, Willis Hall's famous play, a long-established examination text, tells of the friction that occurs between a group of British soldiers when they capture a young Japanese soldier. The play has tension and humour although it is beginning to age a little. In association with North Bank Productions, this was another play from Northampton destined for a national tour.

Hello and Goodbye (1965)
ATHOL FUGARD

Studio 18–28 October 1989

Johnny **Kevin Dyer**
Hester **Marian McLoughlin**

Design **Alec Davis**
Lighting and Sound **Claire Allison**

A most welcome production of Fugard's moving and compelling play about poverty among white South Africans, and the plight of the nation.

Director **Gavin Stride**

When I Was a Girl I Used to Scream and Shout (1984)
SHARMAN MacDONALD

19 October–11 November 1989

Morag **Jill Graham**
Fiona **Susie Baxter**
Vari **Sunny Ormonde**
Ewan **John Ogilvie**

Design **Annette Sumption**
Lighting **Keith Upton**

One of the most popular revivals of 1989, Sharman MacDonald's play has come many miles since the Bush Theatre in 1984. It is a delicate plant, and the recollections of a rather embittered woman about her teenage errors and her family relationships need careful handling.

Director **Sue Wilson**

Veronica's Room (1973)
IRA LEVIN

16 November–9 December 1989

The Woman **Jill Graham**
The Man **Chris Matthews**
The Girl **Kate Napier Brown**
The Young Man **John Ogilvie**

Design **Carol Stevenson**

A suspense drama in which a young girl is trapped in a terrifying situation, Ira Levin's play is a mixture of wit, horror, fantasy, reality and mystery.

Lighting **Keith Upton**   Director **Michael Napier Brown**

Mother Goose (1989)

VILMA HOLLINGBERY

18 December 1989–3 February 1990

Mother Goose **Martin Friend**
Muffin **Richard Cheshire**
Squire Suet **Chris Matthews**
Twinkle **Kate Napier Brown**
Whippet **Mark Carey**
Whoppet **John Ogilvie**
Eider Down **Alexa Povah**
Reynardo Fox **Glynn Sweet**
Colin **Sian Howard**
Priscilla the Goose **Claudia Bryan**

The Royal Theatre was one of the few places to offer a traditional pantomime for Christmas. Mother Goose has two sons, Colin and Muffin, and all her geese have been eaten by the wicked fox. There is the goose that lays the golden eggs and the wicked squire, and Colin is in love with the squire's daughter Twinkle – all the ingredients for a popular holiday entertainment.

Design **Ray Lett**   Director **Michael Napier Brown**
Musical Director **David Roper**

For 1990, this dynamic theatre has scheduled *Intimate Exchanges*, *Murderer*, *Teechers*, *Crystal Clear*, *Is This the Day?* and *The Way of the World*.

NOTTINGHAM

Nottingham Playhouse

WELLINGTON CIRCUS, NOTTINGHAM NG1 5AF
0602-419419

13 April–6 May 1989, the Playhouse offered J B Priestley's *An Inspector Calls* (1945).

Oliver! (1960)

LIONEL BART musical version of the novel, *Oliver Twist*, by Charles Dickens

18 May–10 June 1989

Oliver **Christian Doherty**
Fagin **Kenneth Alan Taylor**
Nancy **Susie McKenna**
Artful Dodger **Daimon Nash**
Mr Bumble **Philip Herbert**
Mrs Corney **Myra Sands**
Vendors **Sophia Winter, Jill Naldor** and Peter St James

An enthusiastically received revival of Lionel Bart's musical, the Nottingham production had an 'appealingly vulnerable Oliver', 'a formidable Fagin' and a Nancy who lit up the stage whenever she was on. A lively new production.

Design **Robert Jones**   Costume **Karen Bartlett**
Choreographer **Francesca Whitburn**   Musical Director **Tom Wakely**
                                       Director **Richard Frost**

Romeo and Juliet (1596)
WILLIAM SHAKESPEARE

15 June–8 July 1989

Chorus/Prince Escalus **Robert Aldous**
Sampson/Watchman **Martin Marquez**
Gregory/Watchman **Ian Soundy**
Abraham/Friar John/Guest **Adam Magnani**
Benvolio **Kevin McGowan**
Tybalt **Doug Smith**
Chief Officer/Cousin Capulet/Apothecary **Robert Kingswell**
Capulet **Philip Anthony**
Lady Capulet **Francesca Whitburn**
Montague **Brian Tully**

A thoughtful and fast-moving production of the tragic love story was the general verdict on Caroline Smith's *Romeo and Juliet*. The pace marred the performances of one or two actors, but there was much that was admired.

Lady Montague/Guest **Anne Pearson**
Romeo **John Dougall**
Paris **Richard Ryan**
Peter **Michael Kirk**
Nurse **Judith Barker**
Juliet **Jane Arden**
Mercutio **Kieron Jecchinis**
Friar Lawrence **Freddie Lees**

Balthasar **Matthew Warman**
Design **Karen Bartlett**
Lighting **Jason Taylor**
Sound **Mark Thompson**
Choreographer **Francesca Whitburn**
Director **Caroline Smith**

13 July–5 August 1989, Agatha Christie's *Spider's Web* (1954) was performed. It was followed a few weeks later, 7–30 September 1989, by Richard Harris's *Stepping Out* (1987).

Salt of the Earth (1988)
JOHN GODBER

5–28 October 1989

May Parker **Judith Barker**
Annie **Elizabeth Mickery**
Harry **Cliff Howells**
Paul **Paul Wyett**
Paul's Friend **Paul Oldham**
Girl Friend **Jessica Taylor**

Design **Robert Jones**
Lighting **Jason Taylor**

John Godber tells a tale of the Yorkshire coalfields from 1947 to the present day through the eyes of one community and their struggles. Godber's own experiences are seen most clearly in Paul, son of May and Harry, who escapes the pit when he goes to university but is inevitably distanced from the society that nourished him. A highly acclaimed production.

Sound **Philip Herring**

Director **Kenneth Alan Taylor**

The Godber play was followed by Arthur Miller's version of *An Enemy of the People*, *A Taste of Honey*, *Knife Edge* and *Aladdin*.

PERTH

Perth Theatre

HIGH STREET, PERTH, SCOTLAND PH1 5UW
0738-21031

Artistic Director **Joan Knight**

Gaslight (1938)
PATRICK HAMILTON

27 January–11 February 1989

Mr Manningham **Alec Heggie**
Mrs Manningham **Ann Scott-Jones**
Sergeant Rough **John Grieve**

Design **Trevor Coe**
Lighting **Simon Sewell**
Director **Joan Knight**

Gaslight has etched its way into British theatre as a perennial favourite, and few could have expected such success for the play when it was first performed more than 50 years ago. It is a straightforward mystery of a wife who is being driven insane by the noises she hears above her, by the constant loss of objects and by her husband's absences and cruelty. He is searching for something from his past. This was Joan Knight's last production before leaving for America to direct in Maine as part of a reciprocal agreement which had brought George Vafiadis to Perth in 1988 to direct *The Gin Game*.

Intimate Exchanges (1984)
ALAN AYCKBOURN

Studio 26 January–11 February 1989

A Garden Fete

Toby/Celia/Sylvie/Lionel/Joe **Helena Gillies, Kenneth Glenaan and Gordon Munro**

Design and Costume **Catherine Stewart and Sallie Wilcox**
Lighting **Fiona Smith**

Ayckbourn's delightful study of a prep school headmaster, his wife, their enthusiastic gardener and their enigmatic domestic help. It is one of 16 plays which comprise *Intimate Exchanges* and the lighting of a cigarette determines which way the action will flow.

Director **Liz Carruthers**

Relatively Speaking (1967)

ALAN AYCKBOURN

17 February–4 March 1989

with **Roger Kemp, Janet Michael, Liam Brennan and Sara Markland**

Design **Helen Wilkinson**
Lighting **Simon Sewell**
Director **Christopher Denys**

A directorial début at the Perth Theatre for Christopher Denys, the principal of the Bristol Old Vic Theatre School. One of Ayckbourn's earliest plays, *Relatively Speaking* is also one of his funniest, revolving around a man who mistakes his girlfriend's lover and the lover's wife for her parents.

Brighton Beach Memoirs (1983)

NEIL SIMON

10–25 March 1989

Eugene **Kenneth Glenaan**
Jack **Jimmy Logan**
Kate **Ann Scott-Jones**
Blanche **Jane Bolton**
Stanley **Liam Brennan**
Nora **Sara Markland**
Laurie **Helena Gillies**

The Scottish première of Neil Simon's semi-autobiographical play inspired an 'absolutely brilliant production at Perth'. Comedian Jimmy Logan, returning to the Perth Theatre after an absence of eight years, 'beautifully under-stated' the caring father of the Jerome family, while Kenneth Glenaan played Eugene with 'impish fullness'.

Design **Brian Currah**   Director **Clive Perry**

Golden Girls (1984)

LOUISE PAGE

31 March–15 April 1989

Marketing Boss **Jane Bolton**
Father **Roger Kemp**
Coach **John Buick**
Team Doctor **Ann Scott-Jones**
Athletes **Rachel Ogilvy, Shelaagh Ferrell, Cora Tucker, Sara Markland and Sandra Yaw**
Man Friend **Liam Brennan**
Journalist **Kenneth Glenaan**
with **Gordon Neish and Helena Gillies**

Louise Page's play tells of the pressures on the British Women's 100 Metre Relay Team as they prepare for the Olympics. It touches on drugs, sexism, exploitation, sponsorship and parental interference, and there is even a hint of racism. Liz Carruthers and designer Nigel Hook handled a difficult task well.

Design **Nigel Hook**   Director **Liz Carruthers**
Lighting **Simon Sewell**

Just a Verse and Chorus (1987)

ROY HUDD a musical celebration based on the songs of R P Weston and Bert Lee

26 April–13 May 1989

R P Weston and Bert Lee wrote songs for people such as Gracie Fields, Jack Buchanan and The Crazy Gang. Many of their songs – for example, 'When Father Papered the Parlour' and 'Hello, Hello, Who's Your Lady Friend?' – have been absorbed into folklore. *Just a Verse and Chorus* is a celebration of their work. It was affectionately presented in Perth and enthusiastically received by the audience.

with **Johnny Beattie, Jackie Farrell, David Barclay, Jean Reeve, Melvyn Whitfield and Yvonne Sadler**

Design **Janet Scarfe**
Lighting **Simon Sewell**
Choreographer **Anthony Ellis**
Musical Director **John Scrimger**
Director **Liz Carruthers, Anthony Ellis and John Scrimger**

Sweeney Todd (1979)

22 August–9 September 1989

The Perth Theatre's autumn season marked Joan Knight's 21st anniversary as artistic director of the company. This celebratory season began with a courageous production of one of Sondheim's most difficult musicals. It proved to be a resounding success. Realising the work was closer to opera

Sweeney Todd **Donald Maxwell**
Mrs Lovett **Vivienne Ross**
Johanna **Gail Mortley**
Judge Turpin **Stephen Hanley**
The Beadle **John Robertson**
Anthony **Richard Shilling**
Tobias **Terry John-Wood**
Pirelli **Gareth Lloyd**
Beggar Woman **Susannah Bray**
with **Nick Sadler, Chris Melville, Rachel Spry, Susan Cochrane, Moyra Paterson, Simon Brotherhood, Jeremy Jacka, Paul Herriott, John Brackenridge and Robert McWhir**

Music and Lyrics **Stephen Sondheim**
Book **Hugh Wheeler**
Design **Nigel Hook**
Lighting **Simon Sewell**

22. *An exuberant* Sweeney Todd, *Sondheim's musical, at Perth. Donald Maxwell as Todd, Vivienne Ross as Mrs Lovett.*

Sound **Geoff Minto**
Choreographer **Anthony Ellis**
Musical Director **John Scrimger**
Director **Clive Perry**

than the conventional musical, Clive Perry cast opera singer Donald Maxwell in the title role. Graham Fulton wrote, 'It is somewhat remarkable that Perth Theatre has the capability and imagination to mount such a production. It is a triumph.'

A Man for all Seasons (1960)

ROBERT BOLT

22 September–7 October 1989

Sir Thomas More **Alec Heggie**
The Common Man **John Grieve**
Henry VIII **William Pool**
Duke of Norfolk **James Cairncross**
Rich **James Telfer**
Thomas Cromwell **Roger Kemp**
Lady More **Janet Michael**
Meg **Lesley Moore**
with **John Buick, Roy Hanlon, Clare Richards, John Shedden, Edward Jordan and Graham MacGregor**

Design **Helen Wilkinson**

Joan Knight selected Robert Bolt's play about the conflict between Sir Thomas More and Henry VIII to mark her 21st anniversary at Perth Theatre. It was the first time that the play had been staged in Perth. Bolt uses the More story to clarify the general principles of integrity and honesty against the forces of political oppression. If the play has less force now than when the author was being imprisoned for his CND beliefs and activities, it is still a powerful piece of work. In an uneven production, John Grieve and Janet Michael were seen as outstanding, while the lovely Lesley Moore 'captured youth and enthusiasm as the daughter with a clear vision'.

Lighting **Simon Sewell**   Director **Joan Knight**

The Admirable Crichton (1902)

J M BARRIE

13–28 October 1989

Crichton **James Telfer**
Lord Loman **Martyn James**
Eliza **Maureen Carr**
Lady Agatha **Beth Tuckey**
Lady Catherine Lasenby **Rachel Spry**
Rev. John Treherne **Frank Stirling**
Lady Mary **Becky Baxter**

A welcome revival of Barrie's comedy of role reversals in Edwardian society. If Barrie is less fashionable than he once was, his plays still have charm.

Lady Brocklehurst **Janet Michael** with **Simon Egerton, Graham MacGregor and Edward Jordan**

Design **Ken Harrison**
Director **Clive Perry**

Breaking the Silence (1984)

STEPHEN POLIAKOFF

3–18 November 1989

with **Alec Heggie, Lesley Moore, Martyn James, John Buick, Edward Jordan, Graham MacGregor and Anne Kidd**

Design **Janet Scarfe**
Lighting **Simon Sewell**
Director **Joan Knight**

A great success when it was first performed by the RSC, *Breaking the Silence* concerns the Pesiakoff family who lived for four years in a railway carriage in the turbulent years of the early 1920s in Russia. The leader of the family (Poliakoff's grandfather) is a scientist–inventor who, in the railway carriage, creates the first talking pictures. It is a truthful, humorous, human and moving play.

23. *Alec Heggie and Lesley Moore in Poliakoff's* Breaking the Silence *at Perth.*

The final production for the autumn season was to be *The Chippit Chantie*, followed by *Mother Goose*. The spring programme for 1990 included *The Cat and the Canary*, *Me and Morag*, *Making History*, *Born Yesterday* and *A Chorus of Disapproval*.

PETERBOROUGH

Key Theatre

EMBANKMENT ROAD, PETERBOROUGH
0733-52439

The Key Theatre houses touring companies and really has no place in this section, but the theatre issues an excellent monthly newspaper giving full details of plays and performers. Details of most of the plays listed below will be found elsewhere in this annual.

Jesus Christ Superstar
24 January–4 February 1989

The Business of Murder
20–5 February 1989

An Ideal Husband
27 February–4 March 1989

And Then There Were None
20–5 March 1989

The Forsyte Saga
27 March–1 April 1989

Dangerous Obsession
24–9 April 1989

How the Other Half Loves
9–13 May 1989

Wuthering Heights
29 May–3 June 1989

Hobson's Choice
5–10 June 1989

Last of the Red Hot Lovers
12–17 June 1989

The Tart and the Vicar's Wife
3–8 July 1989

No Sex Please We're British
10–15 July 1989

Not With a Bang
17–22 July 1989

Hair
24–9 July 1989

Situation Comedy
31 July–5 August 1989

Macbeth
21–6 August 1989

Bell, Book and Candle
28 August–2 September 1989

Shirley Valentine
11–16 September 1989

The Old Country
18–23 September 1989

Jane Eyre
4–9 December 1989

PITLOCHRY

Pitlochry Festival Theatre

PERTHSHIRE PH16 5DR
0796-2680

Artistic Director **Clive Perry**

5 May–7 October 1989, plays run in repertory. The date on which each play joined the repertory is shown.

Lady Windermere's Fan (1892)
OSCAR WILDE

5 May 1989

Lady Windermere **Barbara Darnley**
Parker **Michael Cunningham**
Lord Darlington **Nicholas Hutchison**
Lord Windermere **Mark Wynter**
Duchess of Berwick **Elspeth Macnaughton**
Lady Agatha Carlisle **Sara Stewart**
Mr Dumby **Frank Stirling**
Mrs Cowper-Cowper **Lyndsay Maples**
Lady Stutfield **Sally Cassin**
Sir James Royston **Gerard Ahearn**
Guy Barclay/Footman **Darren Machin**
Mr Rufford **Paul Putner**

Mr Hopper **Colin Wyatt**
Lady Jedburgh **Linda Macintosh**
Miss Graham **Greer Haskell**
Lord Augustus Lorton **Leon Sinden**
Arthur Bowden/Footman **Owen Hopkins**
Mrs Arthur Bowden/Rosalie **Virginia Walshaw**

Mr Cecil Graham **Simon Egerton**
Lady Plymdale **Anna Chancellor**
Mrs Erlynne **Miranda Kingsley**

Design **Trevor Coe**
Costume **Helen Wilkinson**
Lighting **Richard Moffatt**
Director **Clive Perry**

The Festival opened with a production which captured 'all the splendour and elegance of the theatre in the hills'. Wilde's social drama was beautifully set and played. It tells of Lady Windermere's suspicions of her husband and Mrs Erlynne, but it is the mysterious Mrs Erlynne who later saves Lady Windermere from an indiscretion and, in doing so, ruins her own reputation.

Private Lives (1930)
NOEL COWARD

10 May 1989

Sibyl Chase **Barbara Darnley**
Elyot Chase **Mark Wynter**
Victor Prynne **Nicholas Hutchison**
Amanda Prynne **Miranda Kingsley**
Louise **Greer Haskell**

Among the most delightful of Coward's comedies, famed for its witty lines and potent, cheap music, *Private Lives*' tale of the divorced couple who become reunited when they meet on their honeymoons with their new partners has lost little of its charm. It was an appropriate choice for the Festival, for it was in Scotland that the play had its première 60 years ago.

Design **Trevor Coe**
Costume **Helen Wilkinson**
Lighting **Richard Moffatt**
Director **Clive Perry**

24. *Mark Wynter and Miranda Kingsley in Noel Coward's* Private Lives *at the Pitlochry Festival.*

Witness for the Prosecution (1953)
AGATHA CHRISTIE

17 May 1989

One of the least produced of Agatha Christie plays because it needs such a large cast, *Witness for the Prosecution* is, nevertheless, one of the thriller writer's best pieces of theatre. Joan Knight's production put the audience in the place of the jury at the trial of a young man accused of murdering a spinster for her money. In atmosphere and performance, it was a production that was very well received.

Greta **Greer Haskell**
Carter/Barrister **Michael Cunningham**
Mr Mayhew **Martin Heller**
Leonard Vole **Nicholas Hutchison**
Sir Wilfred Robarts, QC **Martyn James**
Inspector Hearne **Simon Egerton**
Detective/Policeman **Owen Hopkins**
Romaine **Ann Scott-Jones**
Clerk of the Court **Frank Stirling**
Mr Justice Wainwright **Leon Sinden**
Miss Myers, QC **Miranda Kingsley**
Solicitor **Graeme Dewar**

Stenographer **Anna Chancellor**
Warder **Paul Putner**
Clerk **Darren Machin**
Barristers **Lyndsay Maples, Sally Cassin and Lynda McQueen**
Dr Wyatt **Colin Wyatt**
Janet MacKenzie **Elspeth Macnaughton**

Miss Clegg **Linda Macintosh**
The Other Woman **Sara Stewart**

Design and Costume **Janet Scarfe**
Lighting **Richard Moffatt**
Director **Joan Knight**

While the Sun Shines (1943)

TERENCE RATTIGAN

24 May 1989

Horton **Martin Heller**
Earl of Harpenden **Nicholas Hutchison**
Lt Mulvaney **Mark Wynter**
Lady Elizabeth Randall **Barbara Darnley**
Duke of Ayr and Stirling **Martyn James**
Lt Colbert **Frank Stirling**
Mabel Crum **Sara Stewart**

Design **Trevor Coe**

Once the most popular of playwrights, Rattigan is only now beginning to emerge from the eclipse that he suffered with the advent of harsh realism in the theatre. This means that a production of *While the Sun Shines* has become something of a rarity. The play itself, set in wartime London, is a gentle confusion of love interests between nationalities with Lady Elizabeth Randall the focus of all attention. Rattigan's strength was his theatrical craftsmanship, and Joan Knight's production, with well-judged performances, did him justice.

Costume **Helen Wilkinson**
Lighting **Richard Moffatt**
Director **Joan Knight**

Dear Brutus (1917)

J M BARRIE

28 June 1989

Mrs Purdie **Anna Chancellor**
Mrs Coade **Elspeth Macnaughton**
Mrs Dearth **Ann Scott-Jones**
Joanna Trout **Barbara Darnley**
Lady Caroline Laney **Sara Stewart**
Matey **Simon Egerton**
Lob **Michael Cunningham**
Mr Coade **Leon Sinden**
Mr Purdie **Frank Stirling**
Mr Dearth **Mark Wynter**
Margaret **Greer Haskell**

Design and Costume **Janet Scarfe**
Lighting **Richard Moffatt**
Director **Bill Pryde**

An ill-assorted group of people are guests of the mysterious Lob on Midsummer's Eve. The group includes a failed artist, an embittered wife and an adulterer. Lob leads them into a

25. Michael Cunningham as Lob in Dear Brutus at the Pitlochry Festival.

magic wood where life seems to offer a second chance. This fantasy seemed well suited to the idyllic Pitlochry and, as Graham Fulton wrote, the piece was given 'a delightful revival with a lightness of touch' that ensured its success. In production, design and acting, *Dear Brutus* was a triumph.

Sly Fox (1976)

LARRY GELBART adapted from Ben Jonson's *Volpone*

2 August 1989

The last play to join the repertoire at the Festival was Larry Gelbart's version of *Volpone*. Gelbart, author of *A Funny Thing Happened On The Way To The Forum*, sets his adaptation in San Francisco after the Gold Rush, but the degrees of rapacity are the same.

Simon Able **Nicholas Hutchison**
Servants **Greer Haskell and Linda Macintosh**
Foxwell J Sly **Martyn James**
Lawyer Craven **Martin Heller**
Jethro Crouch **Michael Cunningham**
Abner Truckle **Simon Egerton**
Miss Fancy **Miranda Kingsley**
Mrs Truckle **Sara Stewart**
Servant/Policeman **Paul Putner**
Captain Crouch **Mark Wynter**
Chief of Police **Colin Wyatt**

Policeman **Darren Machin**
Policeman/Bailiff **Owen Hopkins**
Clerk **Gerard Ahearn**
Judge **Frank Stirling**
with **Sally Cassin, Anna Chancellor, Lyndsay Maples and Virginia Walshaw**

Design **Trevor Coe**
Costume **Annie Gosney**
Lighting **Richard Moffatt**
Director **Clive Perry**

The Pitlochry Festival of 1989, helped by fine weather, was one of the most successful in the history of the event. In 1990, Pitlochry celebrates its 40th Anniversary Season. The programme announced is *Arsenic and Old Lace, Sailor Beware, Separate Tables, The Circle, Who's Afraid of Virginia Woolf?* and *The Cherry Orchard*.

PLYMOUTH

Theatre Royal

ROYAL PARADE, PLYMOUTH PL1 2TR
0752-669595

Artistic Director **Roger Redfarn**

Up On the Roof (1987)

SIMON MOORE and JANE PROWSE

Drum Theatre 11–21 January 1989

Angela **Edwina Lawrie**
Scott **Steve McGann**
Tim **Conrad Nelson**
Bryony **Arabella Weir**
Keith **James Nesbitt**

Director **Jane Prowse**

A musical which was nominated for three awards when it moved to the West End after its Plymouth première in 1987, *Up On the Roof* is about five young students who compare their lives when they meet up ten years on. Roger Malone felt that the new production, which later had a national tour, was a stronger contender for honours than the first.

Fiddler on the Roof (1965)

JOSEPH STEIN based on stories by Sholem Aleichem

13 February–18 March 1989

Teyve **Tony Selby**
Golde **Elaine Loudon**
Tzeitel **Belinda Cryer**
Hodel **Karen Broughton**
Chava **Julia Howson**
Shprintze **Leanne Rogers**
Bielke **Simone White**
Yente **Pat Keen**
Motel **Jonny Myers**
Perchik **Simon Hayden**
Lazar Wolf **Marcus Eyre**
Mordcha **Graham Howes/Robin Lloyd**
Mendel **Clive Marlow**
Avram **Tim Willis**
Nachum **Halcro Johnston**
Grandma Tzeitel/Anya **Anita Marquez**
Fruma-Sarah/Berilla **Karen Davies**

The story of a Jewish community in pre-socialist Russia provided the basis for one of the most successful musicals in theatre history. It was no surprise that, following his recent successes and London transfers, Roger Redfarn should turn to it. The result was a production consistent in style and mood.

Constable **Trevor Danby**
Fyedka **Tom Roberts**
Shandel **Clare Welch**
The Fiddler **Tim Flannigan**
Schmeril **Jason di Mascio**
Yitzuk **Trevor Wood**
Duvidel **Stephen Rouse**
Label **Derek Richards**
Hershel **Karl Lines**
Mischa **Medwyn Williams**
Shloime **Shahar Kazaea**
Yakov **Darren Woods**
Fredel **Brenda Longman**
Mirala **Anne Grayson**

Sima **Nicola Dewdney**
Rivka **Ellen Jackson**
Yussel **Richard Ratcliffe**
Vladimir **Michael Garrick**
Sasha **Hugh Rathbone**
Moishe **Chaz Lawrence**
Chaim **Austin Griffiths**

Design **Boris Aronson**
Lighting **Jenny Cane**
Music **Jerry Brock**
Lyrics **Sheldon Harnick**
Director **Roger Redfarn**

Rat in the Skull (1984)

RON HUTCHINSON

Drum Theatre 22 February–4 March 1989

Director **Wyn Jones**

Entertaining Mr Sloane (1964)

JOE ORTON

Drum Theatre 8–25 March 1989

Ed **Ian Stirling**
Kath **Helen Cotterill**
Sloane **Roger Moss**
Kemp **John Biggerstaff**

Director **Roger Redfarn**

Sloane is an attractive young murderer who thinks he has captivated Kath and her brother into giving him a comfortable life, only to find that he is trapped into becoming a sexual toy. The first of Orton's plays to be staged, and in many ways the most accomplished, *Entertaining Mr Sloane* was given a lively production at the Drum, with Helen Cotterill 'exquisitely rampant in her transparent desire'.

20 March–1 April 1989, the Theatre Royal presented Tim Rice and Andrew Lloyd Webber's *Joseph and The Amazing Technicolor Dreamcoat* (1973).

Animal Island (1989)

MIKE POTTERTON

Drum Theatre 5–15 April 1989

with **Simon Browne and Ray Brandon**

A new play for children.

The King's General (1989)

JUDITH COOK from the novel by Daphne du Maurier

20 April–6 May 1989

Honor Harris as a child **Zena Birch**
Honor Harris **Juliet Grassby**
Robin Harris **Giles Watling**

It was appropriate to stage the world première of Judith Cook's play based on Daphne du Maurier's novel at Plymouth, for it is a story of the Civil War and how it affected Devon and

Kit Harris/John **Bruce Barnden**
Jo Harris/William Sawle/Ambrose Manaton/Workman **Jonathan Howell**
Mary Rashleigh **Janis Winters**
Bridget Harris/Joan/Lady **Stephi Hemelryk**
Mrs Harris/Temperance Sawle **Clare Welch**
Matty **Pat Keen**
Sir Richard Grenville **Graham Pountney**
Gartred **Meg Davies**
Sir Bevil/Prince of Wales/William Rashleigh/Officer **Alan Penn**
Dick Grenville **Stephen Wilson**
Joe Grenville **Matthew Davey**

Cornwall. It was a massive undertaking with 20 scenes and several battles, and as a play and a spectacle it was a tremendous success. The core of the story is the love affair between Grenville and Honor Harris, who becomes a chair-bound cripple because of the wiles of Grenville's sister Gartred. The play opened the day after Daphne du Maurier died at the age of 82.

Betty/Lady/Alice/Mrs Rashleigh **Vivien Keene**
Jonathan Rashleigh/Mayor of Plymouth/Pender **Robin Lloyd**
Sir Peter Courtenay/Edward Champemowne/Architect **John Baxter**
Lord Robartes/Officer/Duke of Buckingham **Marcus Eyre**

Officer/Servant **Paul Kynman**
Trooper/Servant **Niall Refoy**
Soldiers **Clay Knight and Christopher Williams**

Design **Terry Parsons**
Lighting **Jenny Cane**
Director **Roger Redfarn**

How the Other Half Loves (1969)
ALAN AYCKBOURN

Drum Theatre 26 April–13 May 1989

William Featherstone **Angus Barnett**
Mary Featherstone **Kate Dunn**
Frank Foster **Phillip Manikum**
Fiona Foster **April Walker**
Bob Phillips **Mark Buffery**
Teresa Phillips **Cate Fowler**

An enterprising directorial début at the Drum for Chris Harris was successful enough to warrant an extra performance by public demand. *How the Other Half Loves* is one of Ayckbourn's most dazzling technical creations as well as one of his most sharply comic looks at class, sex and marriage. It was well served at Plymouth by a good cast.

Director **Chris Harris**

When I Was a Girl I Used to Scream and Shout (1984)
SHARMAN MacDONALD

Drum Theatre 31 May–17 June 1989

with **Jilly Bond, Stella Tanner, Angela Catherall and Richard Good**

Sexual misadventures and misconceptions and the mother–daughter relationship were in evidence in Plymouth, as they were in several other theatres in the country in 1989.

Director **Amanda Knott**

Wodehouse on Broadway (1989)
TONY STAVEACRE

22 June–1 July 1989

P G Wodehouse **Peter Woodward**
Guy Bolton **Tony Slattery**
Jerome Kern **Gary Yershon**
with **Charlotte Avery, Nicolas Colicos, Michael Crossman, Nicola Dewdney, Brad Graham, Julia Hampson, Margaret Houston and Kelly Hunter**

Design **Keith Cheetham**
Costume **Ian Adley**
Lighting **Tim Mitchell**
Choreographer **Brad Graham**
Musical Director **Gary Yershon**
Director **Keith Cheetham**

South Pacific returned to Plymouth for a fortnight after its successful year in London. It was followed by another Plymouth coup, *Wodehouse on Broadway*, presented in association with BBC Television, which filmed the show at the Theatre Royal for later transmission on BBC 2. It is the story of Wodehouse from 1916 to 1926 when he earned his living as a lyric writer for Broadway shows, mostly in partnership with Jerome Kern. Peter Woodward was particularly praised for his portrayal of Wodehouse in a hard-working and often engaging production.

Another musical played at the Theatre Royal after its success in London when David Merrick's *Forty-Second Street* ran from 1 August to 9 September.

The Art of Success (1986)
NICK DEAR

Drum Theatre 25 August–16 September 1989

Sarah Sprackling **Denise Black**
William Hogarth **Garry Cooper**
Hogarth's Wife **Claire Hirsch**
Robert Walpole **Robin Hooper**
with **Tina Jones, Di Langford, Reena Vetz and James Walker**
Harry Fielding **Andrew Woodall**

Design **Simon Vincenzi**

Nick Dear's prize-winning play about Hogarth, opportunism and lust played for a fortnight at the Drum before representing British theatre in a festival in Holland and moving to London in November. Garry Cooper played Hogarth in 'a commanding manner', and Denise Black captured 'the venomous spirit of the country girl turned killer'.

Lighting **David Lawrence**
Choreographer **Yolande Snaith**
Director **Pip Broughton**

Shadowlands (1989)
WILLIAM NICHOLSON

5–14 October 1989

C S Lewis **Nigel Hawthorne**
Joy Davidman **Jane Lapotaire**

Having previewed *Buddy* before it went to London, the Theatre Royal offered its audiences the world première of

26. Nigel Hawthorne and Jane Lapotaire, stars of Shadowlands *in Plymouth.*

Warnie **Geoffrey Toone**

Design **Mark Thompson**
Director **Elijah Moshinsky**

Shadowlands, which was later to move to the Queen's Theatre, London.

Shadowlands began life as a prize-winning television play, and author William Nicholson was persuaded to adapt it for the stage. It is based on the true love story of C S Lewis and an American divorcee with one child. Their marriage is brief, ended by her tragic early death. This causes Lewis to reassess his beliefs, in God and much else. It is essentially an intellectual play, and the general feeling was that it had never transferred comfortably from the small screen.

An Inspector Calls (1945)
J B PRIESTLEY

8–18 November 1989

Inspector Goole **Ronnie Stevens**
Arthur Birling **Paul Williamson**
Eric Birling **Stifyn Parri**
Edna **Allison Rowe**
Sybil Birling **Dilys Hamlett**
Sheila Birling **Jane Leonard**

Priestley's socialist morality play seems as pointed today, perhaps even more so, than when it was first performed more than 40 years ago.

Gerald Croft **James Mansfield**   Director **Roger Redfarn**

A Day in the Death of Joe Egg (1967)
PETER NICHOLS

Drum Theatre 11–28 October 1989

Bri **Anthony Allen**
Sheila **Lesley Nicol**

Nichols's first stage play and still one which is both humorous and deeply moving. The spastic daughter of Bri and Sheila

Pam **Charlotte Willis**
Freddie **Ian Barritt**
Mother **Rosalind Boxall**
Joe **Colette Gleeson**

Design **Philip Walker**

Joe, was played by Colette Gleeson, who was making her professional début. Roger Redfarn's production was most warmly received.

Director **Roger Redfarn**

Trafford Tanzi (1978)
CLAIRE LUCKHAM

Drum Theatre 2–18 November 1989

Trafford Tanzi **Mandy Lassalles**
Mother **Di Botcher**
Dad **Steve Ashton**
The Referee **Dean Harris**
Platinum Sue **Jacqueline King**
Dean Rebel **Howard Anthony**

Costume **Bill Butler**

A splendidly entertaining play which started life in northern clubs, *Trafford Tanzi* uses the metaphor of wrestling to speak of women's liberation. It is a demanding, physical play which excitingly engages the audience.

Lighting **Nick Richings**   Director **Amanda Knott**

27. The cast of Plymouth Theatre Royal's Sleeping Beauty.

The Sleeping Beauty (1989)
ROY HUDD

18 December 1989–3 February 1990

Evil Evadne **Hinge and Heavenly Hilda Brackett**
Nurse Trot **Jeffrey Holland**
Lord Chamberlain **Bernard Bresslaw**
The Prince **Bobby Crush**
Muddles **Peter Goodwright**
The Sleeping Beauty **Gemma Page**

A new pantomime in the traditional manner by Roy Hudd brought the year to a close at the Theatre Royal. Roger Redfarn assembled a sparkling cast for his Christmas show.

Design **Terry Parsons**
Lighting **Jenny Cane**
Choreographer **Stephanie Carter**
Musical Director **David Steadman**
Director **Roger Redfarn**

SCARBOROUGH

Stephen Joseph Theatre

VALLEY BRIDGE PARADE, SCARBOROUGH YO11 2PL
0723-370541

Artistic Directors **Alan Ayckbourn and Robin Herford**

The Revengers' Comedies (1989)
ALAN AYCKBOURN

June 1989

Henry Bell **Jon Strickland**
Karen Knightly **Christine Kavanagh**
Lorry Driver/Bruce Tick/Fireman/Motor Cyclist **Jeff Shankley**
Winnie/Mrs Bulley **Doreen Andrew**
Norma/Tracey Willingforth **Claire Skinner**
Oliver **Adam Godley**
Lady Ganton/Veronica Webb **Ursula Jones**
Col. Marcus Lipscott **Donald Douglas**
Percy Cutting **Martin Sadler**
Councillor Daphne Teale/Hilary Tick **Alwyne Taylor**

A two-part five-hour play – or two plays – celebrated Ayckbourn's 50th birthday. A man and a woman meet on Albert Bridge as they are about to commit suicide. They decide instead on helping each other to be revenged on those who have brought them to this state. Some wonderfully witty black comedy, superbly acted – but likely to be trimmed before reaching London was the general verdict.

Anthony Staxton-Billing/Eugene Chase **Rupert Vansittart**
Imogen Staxton-Billing **Elizabeth Bell**
Lydia Lucas **Frances Jeater**
Graham Seeds/Jeremy Pride **Frank Lazarus**

Design **Roger Glossop**
Costume **Liz Da Costa**
Lighting **Mick Hughes**
Director **Alan Ayckbourn**

June Moon (1929)

GEORGE S KAUFMAN and RING LARDNER

July 1989

Fred **Adam Godley**
Edna **Claire Skinner**
Paul **Jeff Shankley**
Lucille **Alwyne Taylor**
Eileen **Christine Kavanagh**
Maxie **Frank Lazarus**
Benny **Jon Strickland**
Mr Hart **Donald Douglas**
Goldie **Frances Jeater**

Receiving its British première 60 years after its Broadway staging, *June Moon*, as its title suggests, is a satire on Tin Pan Alley. Charles Osborne saw this as an 'inventive production' with a 'talented and engaging cast'.

Miss Rixey **Melissa Greenwood**
Window Cleaner **Martin Sadler**

Design **Michael Holt**

Lighting **Jackie Staines**
Musical Director **John Pattison**
Director **Alan Strachan**

Wolf At The Door (1882)

HENRY BECQUE translated by David Walker, adapted by Alan Ayckbourn

27 September–21 October 1989

M Vigneron **James Tomlinson**
Mme Vigneron **Elizabeth Bell**
Judith **Jennifer Wiltsie**
Marie **Robin McCaffrey**
Blanche **Claire Skinner**
Gaston **Ian Dunn**
Auguste **Daniel Collings**
Rosalie **Doreen Andrew**
Mme de Saint-Genis **Alison Skilbeck**
Merckens **Sean Chapman**
Teissier **Bernard Hepton**
Bourdon **Jon Strickland**
Lenormand **Robin Newman**
George de Saint-Genis **Dean Daley**

A play and an author which are both virtually unknown entered the Scarborough season. *Les Corbeaux* shows a prosperous family about to celebrate the wedding of their youngest daughter. The sudden death of the father changes all as wolves gather for their pickings from the estate. It is a funny, but disturbing, play showing what 'high capitalism does to the weak'. This was a universally welcomed discovery and production, and one hopes that it is made available to a wider audience.

Gen. Fromentin/Lefort **Robin Bowerman**
Dupuis **Bill Moody**

Design **Michael Holt**

Lighting **Francis Stevenson**
Music **John Pattison**
Director **Alan Ayckbourn**

SHEFFIELD

Crucible Theatre

NORFOLK STREET, SHEFFIELD S1 1DA
0742-769922

Artistic Director **Clare Venables**

Blues for Mr Charlie (1964)

JAMES BALDWIN

26 January–18 February 1989

Meridian Henry **Burt Caesar**
Thomasina **Jade Nanton**
Juanita **Morel Bernard**
Lorenzo **Richard Sharp**
Pete **Michael Buffong**
Mother Henry **Maria Warner**
Lyle Britten **Christopher Fairbank**
Jo Britten **Ellie Haddington**
Parnell James **Paul Whitworth**
Richard **Ray Shell**
Papa D **Ruddy L Davis**
Hazel **Patricia Bradlaw**
Lillian **Antoinette van Belle**
Ellis **Mark White**

James Baldwin based his play on a true event, the acquittal by a white jury of two white men who had murdered a black man from Chicago in 1955. Meridian Henry is a black minister who wrestles with his faith as he sees the injustice surrounding his son's murder, and Parnell James is the white liberal journalist who tries to straddle both communities. Like all of Baldwin's writing, it is, at times, painfully raw in its passion. It was given a most welcome and worthy revival at the Crucible.

Rev. Phelps **Brian Panton**
Townspeople **Geoffrey Hazell, Nigel Lang, Brenda O'Connor, Michael Poyser, Flora Bandele and Trevor Jones**

Design **Michael Vale**
Lighting **Rory Dempster**
Sound **Trevor Dunford**
Music **John Tams**
Director **Clarke Peters**

William Tell (1804)

FRIEDRICH VON SCHILLER adapted by Stephen Lowe

3–25 March 1989

Stauffenburg **Michael Irving**
Baumgarten **David Becalick**
Jenni **James Mansfield**
Kuoini **Martyn Ellis**
William Tell **Neil Morrissey**
Ruodi **Tim Wallers**
Gertrude **Tamara Ustinov**
Bertha **Antoinette van Belle**
Melchtal **James McKenna**
Furst **Andrew Wickes**
Attinghausen **Frank Harling**
Rudenz **Simon Roberts**

One cannot imagine a braver start to the year than to follow Baldwin with Schiller's retelling of the William Tell legend, a piece rarely seen in England. The story of a struggle for liberty is clearly told, and there is a wonderfully dramatic climax. The vigour and pace of Clare Venables's production were highly praised.

Rosselman **Richard Grayson**
Reding/Rudolph **Tim Swinton**
Ulrich/Leuthold **Martin Troakes**
Walter **Nigel Marsh**
Hedwig **Buffy Davis**

Freisshardt/Duke John **Mark Womack**
Gessler **Peter Kelly**
Girl **Tanya Jones**
Wilhelm **Giles Carre**

Dietelm **Richard Dixon**
Girl **Katie Powell**
with **Martin Holmshaw, Roy King, David Ridley, Jason Morrell, Paul Tyree, Peter Bramley, Vicky Johnson, Andrew Shepherd,** David Woodward, Martin Bedford, Peter Goodley, Peter George, John Pitts and Carmel O'Neill

Design **Tim Reed**

Lighting **Davy Cunningham**
Music **Orlando Gough**
Sound **Trevor Dunford**
Director **Clare Venables**

She Stoops To Conquer (1773)
OLIVER GOLDSMITH

25 May–17 June 1989

This simple, human and delightful comedy never fails to amuse, but it can become a little tired through familiarity. This was not the case with Paul Whitworth's production at the Crucible, which Michael Schmidt in *The Daily Telegraph* described as 'the funniest and most faithful I have seen, a triumph of design, direction and performance'. It was Whitworth's directorial début at Sheffield.

Mrs Hardcastle **Janet Henfrey**
Mr Hardcastle **George Raistrick**
Tony Lumpkin **Geoffrey Church**
Kate Hardcastle **Caroline Holdaway**
Constance Neville **Mary Askham**
Marlow **Ian Fitzgibbon**
Hastings **Richard Clifford**
Stingo/Sir Charles Marlow **Lionel Taylor**
Diggory/Slang **James Thackeray**
Roger/Muggins **Harry van Gorkum**
Pimple **Kate Wood**
Cripplegate/Tom Twist **Roderick Skeaping**
Little Aminadab/Servant **Keith Thompson**
Jeremy **Stephen Fulton**

Design **Tim Reed**

Lighting **Hugh Vanstone**
Sound **Trevor Dunford**
Musical Director **Roderick Skeaping**
Director **Paul Whitworth**

The Northern Mystery Plays
adapted by JOHN TAMS

23 June–15 July 1989

Eve **Jan Alphonse**
Adam/King **Ian Aspinall**
Mak **Ray Ashcroft**
Lucifer/King **Paul Brightwell**
God/Shepherd **Kevin Costello**
Mrs Noah/Gill **Jeannie Crother**
Gabriel **Joe Dixon**
Noah/Herod **Russell Dixon**
Abel/Shepherd **Kulvinder Ghir**
Cain/Herod's Son **Paul Slack**
Chancellor/King **David Sterne**

A spectacular adaptation of the medieval mysteries which centred the Creation in Sheffield and had angels wearing hard hats. Bruno Santini's ingenious set, appropriately, offered plenty of steel. There were few who could resist this vigorous and entertaining version. The Crucible's press office billed it as 'Murder, Floods and Unexpected Pregnancy...'. Clare Jenkins in *The Stage* was adamant that in Tams's adaptation, 'the simple yet stirring spirit of the original pours through, to be placed firmly in our broader folk tradition'. A triumphant end to the first part of the year at the Crucible.

Joseph **Dean Sullivan**
Knight **Andrew Tansey**
Shepherd **Dave Warburton**
Mary **Kate Wood**

Design **Bruno Santini**
Lighting **David Lawrence**
Sound **Trevor Dunford**
Choreographer **Mick Peat and**

Harry Pitts
Musical Director **Barry Coope**
Director **Mike Kay and John Tams**

A Tale of Two Cities (1989)

ANDREW WICKES from the novel by Charles Dickens

28 September–21 October 1989

Jarvis Lorry **Richard Mayes**
Dr Alexander Manette **Peter Laird**
Lucie Manette **Ella Knight**
Miss Pross **Patricia Heneghan**
Lucie's Daughter **Clare Wormald**
Attorney General/Gabelle/
Woodsawer **Christopher Birch**
Mr Stryver/Gaspard **Laurence Kennedy**
Sydney Carton **Michael Mueller**
Jerry Cruncher **John Dallmore**
Mrs Cruncher/The Vengeance **Barbara Watt**
Young Jerry **Jonathan Cook**
John Barsad **Richard Freeman**
Marquis St Evremonde/President of Tribunal **Robert Gladwell/Andrew Wickes**
Ernest Defarge **Gregory Cox**
Mme Defarge **Sharon Bower**
Gaspard's Son **Scott Noble**
Lucile Cadoux **Joella Cooper**

Having been part hosts of the Sheffield International Festival for Children and of the Festival of Local Theatre, and having staged touring productions of *Joseph and the Amazing Technicolor Dreamcoat* and *Shirley Valentine*, the Crucible Theatre began its new season with an adaptation of Dickens's novel about the French Revolution. Wickes's version was written especially for the thrust stage. It was another most ambitious production, full of trolleys and traps, and it made a highly entertaining and spectacular start to the new season.

Design **Tim Reed**
Lighting **Davy Cunningham**
Music **Simon Joly**
Sound **John Leonard**
Director **Andrew Wickes**

Seven Lears (1989)

HOWARD BARKER

Studio 13–28 October 1989

Lear **Nicholas Le Prevost**
Clarissa **Jemma Redgrave**
and others

Design **Dermott Hayes**
Lighting **Ace McCarron**
Sound and Music **Matthew Scott**
Director **Kenny Ireland**

The Wrestling School is devoted to interpreting the works of Howard Barker, and this production was mounted by the Crucible in conjunction with the Haymarket, Leicester, where it played in November. Barker's new play is an exploration of corruption and collusion in politics. His Lear is pre Shakespearean. He kills those who cross him and marries Clarissa, the daughter of his mistress.

The Crucible's adventurous programme continues with *Design for Living*, *Leonce and Lena*, *Babes in the Wood*, *Britannicus*, *The Boys from Syracuse* and *Born Yesterday*.
This is a theatre that is very much alive.

SONNING

The Mill at Sonning

THE MILL, SONNING EYE, READING RG4 0TW
0734-698000

Artistic Director **Sally Hughes**

Round and Round The Garden (1973)

ALAN AYCKBOURN

21 February–1 April 1989

Annie **Anne Atkins**
Norman **Tim Hardy**
Tom **Steven Harrold**
Ruth **Sue Holderness**
Sarah **Joanna Wake**
Reg **Barry Woolgar**

Following the success enjoyed with the other two parts of the *Norman Conquests*, the Mill completed the trilogy with Anna Barry directing a very strong cast in *Round and Round The Garden*.

Design **Matthew Beacham**
Lighting **Roz Nash**

Director **Anna Barry**

Shock

BRIAN CLEMENS

4 April–6 May 1989

Peter **Stephen Flynn**
Jenny **Sally Hughes**
Ann **Mary Maude**
Andy **Danny McGrath**
Terry **Graham Weston**
Steve **Hugo Morley**
Maggie **Brenda Packham**

The Mill had premièred a Brian Clemens play in 1988, and it revived his thriller, *Shock*, in 1989. Artistic director Sally Hughes took one of the leading roles.

Design **John Elvery**
Lighting **David Hancock**

Director **Ian Lindsay**

My Dearest Ivor (1989)

ANNIE HILL and MAURICE LEANARD

9 May–10 June 1989

Ivor Novello **Vince Hill**

Director **Ted Craig**

The world première of a work celebrating the life and music of Ivor Novello.
      This was followed by *The Odd Couple*, *A Boston Story* and

Anybody for Murder? Unfortunately, we know little else of this beautiful theatre's plans.

WATFORD

Palace Theatre

CLARENDON ROAD, WATFORD WD1 1JZ
0923-225671

Artistic Director **Lou Stein**

The Patchwork Girl of Oz (1988)

ADRIAN MITCHELL from the novel by L Frank Baum

16 December 1988–14 January 1989

The Tin Woodman/MMM/Prime Minister/Soldier **Paul Keown**
Princess Ozma of Oz/Nightingale **Margaret Houston**
The Scarecrow **Simon Butteriss**
Ojo the Unlucky **Clare Grogan**
Unc Nunkie/Prince of the Mangaboos **David Shaw-Parker**
Dr Pipt/Man/Yoop **Richard Syms**
Scraps **Carla Mendonça**
Bo Cloako/Bo Croako/Bo Blokeo/Dodo/Bo Joko/Bo Crocko/ Bo Hoko **John Conroy**

Enterprisingly, the Palace Theatre commissioned a new Christmas show, and Adrian Mitchell and composer Andy Roberts turned to one of the last of the Baum stories which were spawned by the success of *The Wizard of Oz*. *The Patchwork Girl of Oz* was published in 1913 and revolves around Scraps and her adventures. A splendid addition to theatre for all ages.

Gardener/Tollydiggle **Lesley Nicol**
The Woozy/Canary **Ben Thomas**

Design **Martin Sutherland**
Lighting **Davy Cunningham**

Choreographer **Pat Garrett**
Music **Andy Roberts**
Musical Director **Stewart Mackintosh**
Director **Lou Stein**

The History of Tom Jones (1989)

ANDREW WICKES from the novel by Henry Fielding

26 January–18 February 1989

Tom Jones **Rupert Graves**
Sophia/Lawyer Dowling etc. **Jan Ravens**
Mr Allworthy/Aunt Western/Fitzpatrick etc. **Hugh Ross**
Squire Western/Black George/Upton Landlady etc. **James Saxon**
Bliful/Mrs Fitzpatrick/Gregory etc. **William Relton**

The greatest wonder of Andrew Wickes's adaptation of Fielding's great picaresque novel was that six performers between them coped with more than 50 characters and a plethora of exits and entrances. Rupert Graves was most warmly applauded for having captured the character of Tom Jones so completely, but there was high praise for all for their stamina and versatility.

Lady Bellaston/Jenny Jones/Honour etc. **Alison Skilbeck**

Mr Partridge/Thwackum/Fellamar
etc. **David Killick**

Design **Ultz**
Lighting **Rick Fisher**
Sound **John Leonard**

Songs **Jeremy Sands**
Director **Matthew Francis**

Diplomatic Wives (1989)
LOUISE PAGE

2–25 March 1989

Christine **Charlotte Cornwell**
John **Will Knightley**
Libby **Anna Carteret**

Design **Martin Sutherland**
Lighting **Rory Dempster**
Sound **Peter Key**
Director **Lou Stein**

The world première of a play by the author of *Golden Girls* and *Salonika* was one of the main events of the year. Louise Page's new play deals with the conflicts between career and marriage, between private and public life. John has not advanced as far in the diplomatic service as had once seemed possible. His wife, Christine, is a working-class girl who sacrificed her own career in the Foreign Office for her husband, but is now offered a posting to Tunisia. The conflict is sharpened by the arrival of their ex-history tutor, Libby. It was welcomed as a civilised and intelligent play.

Awake and Sing! (1935)
CLIFFORD ODETS

30 March–22 April 1989

Ralph **Michael Grandage**
Myron **Martin Friend**
Hennie **Elaine R Smith**
Jacob **Cyril Shaps**
Bessie **Doreen Mantle**
Schlosser **Richard Henry**
Moe **Michael J Jackson**
Uncle Morty **Matt Zimmerman**
Sam **Mark Coleman**

Design **Martin Johns**
Lighting **Leonard Tucker**
Director **Lou Stein**

Watford maintained its high profile with a most interesting revival of the play which established Clifford Odets as a critical and commercial success. The play is set in 1935 and depicts the struggles of a Jewish family in the Bronx who are trying to survive the Depression. This was greeted as an 'impeccable production'. Bessie is the mother of the family, 'so brilliantly played by Doreen Mantle', who forces her pregnant daughter Hennie into a loveless marriage for financial reasons. The strength of Odets is that he can find humour in a bleakly pessimistic landscape, and the strength of this production was that it did such justice to his work with a string of fine performances. Indeed, Charles Osborne in *The Daily Telegraph* wrote of grandfather Jacob, who worships Karl Marx and Caruso, 'it would be hard to better the performance of Cyril Shaps'. As Hennie, Elaine R Smith (who has won fame in 'Neighbours' as Daphne) had an accent that was uneven, but she was crisp, matter of fact and smouldered enticingly. This was a brave, necessary and totally worthy revival of a too-much neglected playwright.

Two For the Seesaw (1958)

WILLIAM GIBSON

27 April–20 May 1989

Jerry Ryan **Bruce Montague**
Gittel Mosca **Judy Buxton**

Design **Terry Parsons**
Lighting **Paul Pyant**
Director **Christopher G Sandford**

A revival of William Gibson's gentle, witty and moving observation of a passing love affair between two people in New York. He is a lawyer from Omaha dominated by his wife; she is an insecure second-rate dancer. For a while they fulfil a need in each other before they go their separate ways, happier and enriched by the experience. It was performed and staged in such a way at Watford as to make it 'special and timeless'.

28. *Bruce Montague and Judy Buxton in* Two For the Seesaw *at Watford.*

Candle-Light (1929)

P G WODEHOUSE based on the play by Siegfried Geyer

7–30 September 1989

Josef **Aden Gillett**
Prince Rudolph **Philip Bird**
Chauffeur/Waiter/Baron von Rischenheim **Arthur Bostrom**
Marie **Serena Evans**
Liserl/Baroness von Rischenheim **Helen Atkinson Wood**

Wodehouse's farce was performed on Broadway in 1929 with Leslie Howard and Gertrude Lawrence in the leading roles, but until Lou Stein presented it at the Palace Theatre, Watford, it had never been seen in England. The play has a Ruritanian setting and concerns a prince's valet who poses as the Prince when his master is out for the evening and, in his superior role, attempts to seduce a girl to whom he has spoken on a crossed

29. An exciting discovery – Philip Bird and Aden Gillett in P G Wodehouse's Candle-Light *at Watford.*

Design **Norman Coates**
Lighting **Leonard Tucker**
Musical Director **Paul Maguire**
Director **Lou Stein**

John **Simon Slater**

telephone line. The Prince returns and sustains the charade by accepting the role of his own servant. The point now is whether the girl will fall for the servant/master or the master/servant. Serena Evans, fresh from her triumph in *Henceforward*, won more critical acclaim for her performance as the sexually mischievous heroine. Indeed, the whole production was most warmly received and Lou Stein and the Palace were most warmly congratulated for their coup.

Roll on Friday (1974)
ROGER HALL

5–28 October 1989

Roger Hall won the Comedy of the Year award for *Middle Aged*

Jim **Brian Murphy**
Hugh **Paul Kelly**
Beryl **Annette Badland**
Michael **Phil Willmott**
Boss **George Waring**
Wally **Dave Atkins**

Design **Kate Robertson**

Spread, but *Roll on Friday*, which preceded it by five years, was less enthusiastically received when seen at Watford. It is set in the stores department of a government office in Wellington, New Zealand. It concerns a day in the life of the six people who work there on which they run out of forms and the boss, worried about his retirement, drops a bombshell.

Lighting **Mark Pritchard**   Director **Peter Duguid**

A Raisin in the Sun and *Cinderella* were to take the theatre into 1990 when, no doubt, Lou Stein will have more surprises and discoveries in store.

WESTCLIFF-ON-SEA

Palace Theatre Centre

430 LONDON ROAD, WESTCLIFF-ON-SEA, ESSEX SS0 9LA
0702-342564

Artistic Director **Christopher Dunham**

The Unexpected Guest (1958)

AGATHA CHRISTIE

19 January–4 February 1989

Laura Warwick **Liz Payne**
Michael Starkwedder **David Beckett**
Miss Bennett **Lynne Christie**
Jan Warwick **Jason Hall**
Mrs Warwick **Margaret Wedlake**
Henry Angell **Brian Tully**
Sgt Cadwallader **Peter Quilter**
Inspector Thomas **Tony Jackson**
Julian Farrar **Andrew Powrie**

Following the record-breaking box office success of their Christmas production, *The Lion, The Witch and The Wardrobe*, the Palace Theatre, like so many other regional theatres, opened the New Year with an Agatha Christie play. A highly entertaining and competent production of *The Unexpected Guest* proved to be another box office success.

Design **Richard Baker**   Lighting **Peter Edwards**
Costume **Alison Williams**   Director **Christopher Dunham**

Orphans (1985)

LYLE KESSLER

Dixon Studio 6–25 February 1989

Treat **Christopher Wright**
Phillip **Malcolm Hassall**

Winner of the Rose Bruford Trust, Graham Watts followed his successes at the Almeida Theatre in 1988 with a most

30. Christopher Wright as Treat towers over Malcolm Hassall as Phillip in *Orphans at Westcliff*.

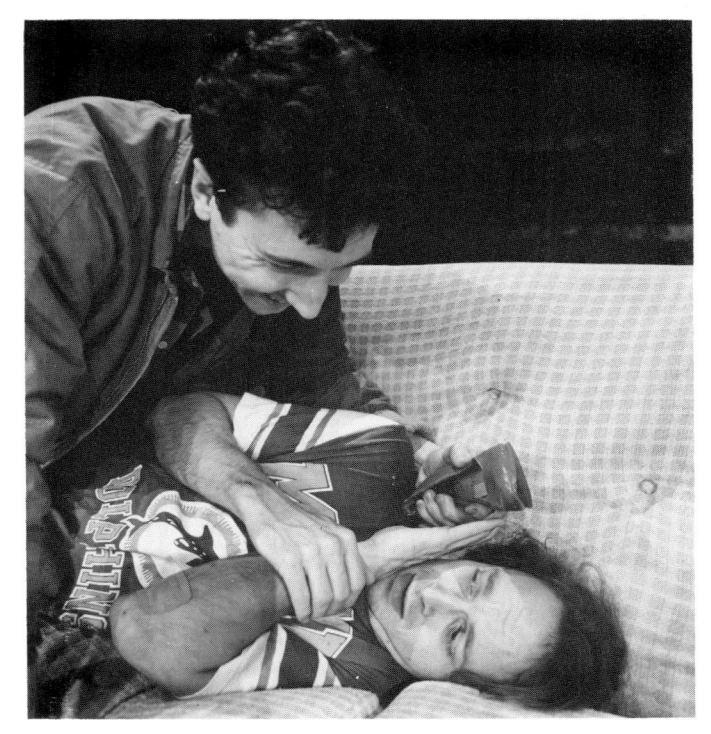

Harold **Eric Mason**

Design **Richard Baker**
Costume **Alison Williams**
Lighting **Peter Edwards**
Director **Graham Watts**

sympathetic and well-judged production of *Orphans* in the Dixon Studio. Lyle Kessler's play was first produced by the Steppenwolf Theatre Company in Chicago and New York in 1985 and reached London a year later. It tells the story of two brothers, Treat and Phillip, who live alone in an old row house in north Philadelphia. Phillip, believed to be illiterate and confined to the house, is looked after by Treat who lives a life of petty robbery in order to keep them. He brings home Harold, an older man, whom he has met in a bar and intends to ransom, but Harold proves to be a big-time racketeer, and he turns the tables on the small-time crook. He revolutionises the lives of both of the boys, and the dependence of the three upon one another is both moving and amusing. The language is often violent, but there are moments of silent tenderness, and in the hands of three gifted actors and a most promising young director, *Orphans* emerges as a play of quality, depicting man's need for man. Christopher Wright catches the restless, seething violence of Treat with an accuracy which underlines the innocence beneath the menace. Malcolm Hassall is a deeply sensitive, inquisitive Phillip, his eagerness to learn and to move outside shackled by his fear of his brother and of the unknown. The survival of Treat and Phillip is their need for each other, and Wright and Hassall convey this with an understanding that never resorts to sentimentality. Eric Mason as the intruder and the life-giver offers them a parental authority and a glimpse of love that they have never known, and again the performance is beautifully judged, shrouded by an air of worldly wisdom and of a life outside the brothers' flat. *Orphans* at the Dixon Studio provided an early gem for 1989.

Stepping Out (1987)
RICHARD HARRIS

9–25 February 1989

Mavis **Nadine Hanwell**
Mrs Fraser **Andrea Turner**
Lynne **Susan Howlett**
Dorothy **Lynne Christie**
Maxine **Maria Kelly**
Andy **Liz Payne**
Geoffrey **Tony Jackson**
Sylvia **Helen Watson**
Rose **Cleo Sylvestre**
Vera **Helen Fraser**

Design **Anne Karine Skatun**
Costume **Alison Williams**
Lighting **Peter Edwards**
Choreographer **Pamela Freedman**
Director **Christopher Dunham**

Stepping Out is not only an immensely popular and amusing play, it is also a very good one with quiet and sympathetic observations of the human condition. Christopher Dunham's exuberant production revealed all the play's strengths and hid its weaknesses. The play revolves around a motley crew of ladies, and one man, who attend a weekly tap-dancing class which is run by Mavis, intelligently played by Nadine Hanwell, who is passionate about the achievements with her class but has the haunted look of a woman whose private life is not easy. Helen Watson as the busty Sylvia captured the comic, sexual zest of the character without ever over-playing while Helen Fraser's Vera was all fussiness and skips and hops. Cleo Sylvestre as the cheerful coloured girl and Tony Jackson, the solitary man, were equally impressive in a generally strong cast. A lively production which reached a spectacular climax.

An Inspector Calls (1945)
J B PRIESTLEY

2–18 March 1989

Arthur Birling **Eric Mason**
Gerald Croft **Christopher Wright**
Sybil Birling **Margaret Wedlake**
Sheila Birling **Pia Henderson**
Edna **Susan Howlett**
Eric Birling **Malcolm Hassall**
Inspector Goole **Brian Tully**

Design **Anne Karine Skatun**

Following his successful studio production of *Orphans*, Graham Watts offered a vigorously fresh production of Priestley's socialist fable, *An Inspector Calls*, in the main house. Aided by an intelligently attractive set and a consistently good cast, Watts portrayed the play as part of Priestley's time theory, freezing the action at the beginning and ending of each scene. Brian Tully was chillingly sinister and enigmatic as the inspector who disturbs the complacency and self-satisfaction of the wealthy Birling family with the news

31. Brian Tully as Inspector Goole confronts Margaret Wedlake as Mrs Birling in An Inspector Calls *at the Palace Theatre, Westcliff.*

Costume **Alison Williams**
Lighting **Peter Edwards**
Director **Graham Watts**

that a girl has committed suicide because of the state of misery to which she has been reduced. Confronting each of the family individually, he brings them to see the part that each of them has had in bringing unhappiness to another before disappearing as mysteriously as he arrived. Priestley sees hope in youth, and Pia Henderson gave a fine performance as the daughter of the house who moves from the self-assurance given by wealth and position to a genuine social concern.

Fit To Bust (1989)

JONATHAN IZARD and CHRISTOPHER LILLICRAP

30 March–15 April 1989

Richard Proctor **John Kearns**
Chester Williams **Susie Lee-Hayward**
Wendy Williams **Anna Nicholas**
Kay Elliman **Susan Howlett**
Helga Helgasson **Lynda Craig**
Randy Goldblum **Phil Croft**

Design **Richard Baker**
Costume **Glynis Banyard**
Lighting **Peter Edwards**
Director **Mike Fields**

A production which chose the Palace Theatre as the starting-point for a proposed national tour, *Fit To Bust* tells of a man who goes to a health farm in order to reinvigorate himself. He is a plastic surgeon specialising in women's anatomy. The title of the 'comedy' tells all. Hugh Homan in *The Stage* described it as a 'slow, laboured farce', and there were those who thought that he was being generous with that description. The cast deserved better meat than this play offered, and one is particularly sorry for Susan Howlett, a young actress of charm, vitality and much promise.

When I Was a Girl I Used to Scream and Shout (1984)

SHARMAN MacDONALD

20 April–6 May 1989

Morag **Lynne Christie**
Fiona **Lorraine Ashbourne**
Vari **Beth Tuckey**
Ewan **William Steel**

Design **Anne Karine Skatun**
Costume **Alison Williams**
Lighting **Peter Edwards**
Director **Christopher Dunham**

It is five years since Sharman MacDonald's play was first staged at the Bush Theatre; and Edinburgh, London and most of the country have seen it since then. It is a tender, affectionate, moving and very funny exploration of the adolescent's interest in sexual matters. Sadly, the Palace Theatre production was almost humourless, and the result was an aggressively, at times offensively, sexual attack on the audience with no glimmer of light. The tone of the production was mirrored in the bleak set. Fiona's plea to God was closer to Horvath than to Sharman MacDonald, and only Beth Tuckey emerged from the production with much credit.

Company (1970)

18 May–10 June 1989

Robert **Leo Andrew**
Sarah **Liza Sadovy**
Harry **Oliver Haden**
Susan **Lesley Moore**
Peter **Tom Griffin**
Jenny **Carole Brooke**
David **Philip Wrigley**
Amy **Anne Smith**
Paul **James Telfer**
Joanne **Clare Rimmer**
Larry **Johnathan Courage**
Marta **Beth Tuckey**
April **Suzanne Rigden**
Kathy **Karen Henson**

Music and Lyrics
Stephen Sondheim
Book **George Furth**

Company was first staged in New York, where it is set, in 1970 and ran for 706 performances. It is the story of Bobby, a bachelor in his middle 30s, who decides to remain single when he views the marriages and relationships of the couples who are his friends. If it takes a somewhat cynical look at marriage, it concedes the need we all have for company. It is a lively and

32. Company, *Sondheim's musical at Westcliff, with Leo Andrew, Carole Brooke and Philip Wrigley.*

Musical Director **James Simpson**
Design **Richard Baker**
Costume **Glynis Banyard**
Lighting **Peter Edwards**
Choreographer **Gail Gordon**
Director **Christopher Dunham**

witty show, full of good numbers, superior in every way to *Follies*; and Christopher Dunham's revival at the Palace Theatre, Westcliff, was as exhilarating as it was welcome. If the lighting was at times a little dim and uncertain, the acting and singing were of a consistently high standard. As Bobby, Leo Andrew showed verve and intelligence, meeting the questioning demands of the character. Liza Sadovy was gloriously funny as the slimming, karate-keen Sarah, and Anne Smith was vitally amusing and neurotic as Amy who is 'not getting married to-day'. Indeed, this was a strong company in every respect in a production which never flagged and which showed a keen awareness of the more serious arguments that the musical forwards.

The Man Who Lost America (1989)

MICHAEL BURRELL

Dixon Studio 6–8 July 1989

The Officer **Michael Burrell**
The Ranker **Nicholas Moore**
Voice of the Intruder **Clive Swift**

Design **Peter Froste**
Costume **Ann Masters**
Sound **Philip Isom**
Director **Philip Grout**

The Man Who Lost America had its world première at the Palace Theatre, Westcliff, prior to going to Canada for the Montreal festival. The scene is a cowshed near Saratoga in November 1777, where General Burgoyne has sought a moment's calm in an effort to reflect upon life following his defeat in the battle that finally cost England the American colonies. He discovers a soldier who has deserted, momentarily at least, and he uses the soldier as his audience. Michael Burrell has conceived Burgoyne as a man of artistic sensitivity who is highly intelligent, realistic and humane. He considers the rewards of defeat and victory and the thin line between them, and all is delivered with a gentle irony in a voice that is both engaging and compelling. Michael Burrell has created and plays a character of great charm. The language of the play is a delight, and it deserves a wide and appreciative audience. Nicholas Moore makes a highly competent début as the soldier.

With the theatre filled by touring companies for the summer season, Christopher Dunham took the opportunity to announce his autumn and winter programme. Once again the theatre offered a varied and exciting blend. *Brighton Beach Memoirs*, *Master Harold and the Boys*, *Equus*, *Absurd Person Singular* and *Wind in the Willows* formed the programme until Christmas 1989, with *Towards Zero* filling the usual Agatha

Christie spot in January. Moreover, Christopher Dunham was able to announce that the programme was to be sponsored for the first time by The Royals Shopping Centre, the new development in Southend High Street. This is a major achievement by this virile theatre and could help towards maintaining its high standards against the inevitable vagaries of the Eastern Arts Council.

33. Eugene (Gary Whitaker) in man-to-man talk with Stanley (Duncan Law) in Brighton Beach Memoirs *at Westcliff.*

Brighton Beach Memoirs (1983)

NEIL SIMON

7–30 September 1989

Eugene **Gary Whitaker**
Blanche **Shenagh Govan**
Kate **Sally Sanders**
Laurie **Vicky Blake**
Nora **Jan Ruppe**
Stanley **Duncan Law**
Jack **Eric Mason**

The autumn season opened with a sensitive production of Neil Simon's semi-autobiographical play. The action revolves around and the story is told by Eugene, a 15-year-old Simon who is discovering life, girls and writing. Kate, the mother, says 'The world doesn't survive without families', and it is the family group, a Jewish family living in the Brighton Beach section of Brooklyn at the outbreak of the Second World War, which gives the play its special warmth. Jack, played with

Design **Richard Baker**
Costume **Glynis Banyard**
Lighting **Peter Edwards**
Director **Christopher Dunham**

strength and understanding by Eric Mason, struggles to support his wife, two sons, widowed sister-in-law and her two daughters. There are frictions and misunderstandings, but there is much humour, and Christopher Dunham's production does justice to all aspects of the play, save perhaps the ultimate worry as to how they will cope when refugee relatives arrive from Europe. This worry is soon thrown off in the joy that they are safe.

The production is intelligent and exact in its portrayal of the family group, and it is evocative of the period, suggesting always a sense of things past warmly remembered. The design reflected this understanding and sensitivity as it should.

Gary Whitaker was bubblingly questioning in the central role, and it was a cast without a weak link – although one was slightly disturbed by the diversity and inconsistency of accents.

Equus (1973)

PETER SHAFFER

5–21 October 1989

Martin Dysart **Richard Frost**
Alan Strang **Adam Warren**
Frank Strang **Eric Mason**
Dora Strang **Sally Sanders**
Hesther Salomon/Horse **Shenagh Govan**
Jill Mason **Jan Ruppe**
Harry Dalton/Horse **Bill Cashmore**
Young Horseman/Horse **Duncan Law**
Nurse/Horse **Oona Beeson**
Horse **Grant Masters**

Design **Richard Baker**

For those who know it, *Equus* is becoming something of a tired play; yet it still grips those who are coming to it for the first time. Sonia Fraser's production was best when it trusted the play; worst, as at the end of the first act, when it panicked into flashing lights, whirling stage and agitated movement. Certainly the performances could not be faulted. Richard Frost was an intelligently troubled and wearied Dysart; and there were good cameos from Sally Sanders and Shenagh Govan. But there was an aridity about the set which seemed to thread its way through the play.

Costume **Glynis Banyard**
Lighting **Peter Edwards**
Choreographer **Oona Beeson**

Director **Sonia Fraser**

Master Harold and the Boys (1982)

ATHOL FUGARD

Dixon Studio 9–28 October 1989

Willie **Andrew Francis**
Sam **Ben Ellison**

Master Harold and the Boys is now being absorbed into the listings of theatres all over Great Britain, but it could have few

Hally **Gary Whitaker**

Design **Richard Baker**
Costume **Alison Williams**
Lighting **Peter Edwards**
Choreographer **Pamela Freedman**
Director **Christopher Dunham**

better productions than the one that it had at Westcliff. The scene is a simple one – a tea room in Port Elizabeth where two black men, Willie and Sam, work and where the owners' son, Harold, calls in after school to chat, have his tea and do his homework. Hally's father is crippled and in hospital. He is also a drunkard. The news that he is to be discharged prompts an explosion of anger in Hally who treats Sam – the black man who, in effect, has replaced his father in his affections – with the contempt that one associates with upholders of apartheid. The strength of Christopher Dunham's production is that even in the first part of the play when Sam and Hally exchange ideas, when they talk of their friendship, their past and the making of a kite, one is mindful of the demarcation that exists between black and white in the world outside the tea shop. Hally is fascinated by Sam's world, the story of the dancing championships and much else, and his love and respect for the man are apparent. This is what makes the final break all the more agonising. Hally has said things a man should never say, and in doing so he destroys the one thing of value in his life. The conditions outside the tea shop, of which sensitive direction has made us aware, make the break irreversible. Ben Ellison is a splendid Sam, a man of intelligence, dignity, forbearing and compassion. Gary Whitaker captures the disaster of Hally with a terrible poignancy. He is like a boy going down hill on a bike with no brakes. Andrew Francis as Willie is measured to the right quantities of enthusiasm and apprehension. Richard Baker set the play well, in a tea room that was realistic, suggestive of a world beyond and never cluttered. Chris Dunham fuses the whole into a deeply moving and probing experience.

Absurd Person Singular (1972)
ALAN AYCKBOURN

2–18 November 1989

Sidney **Simeon Andrews**
Jane **Christine Absalom**
Ronald **John Pennington**
Marion **Charmian May**
Geoffrey **Bill Cashmore**
Eva **Shenagh Govan**

Design **Julie Godfrey**
Lighting **Peter Edwards**
Costume **Glynis Banyard**

Confronted with another Ayckbourn revival, one is apt, now and again, to wonder whether one has not had a surfeit of the author's comments on middle-class marriage; but then one is presented with a production that is fresh and vital and brings out both the humour and the darkness of Ayckbourn's comedy. Such was the Palace Theatre production. *Absurd Person Singular* is the story of three couples over a period of three Christmases. In the first scene Sidney and Jane are nervously entertaining as he wants to borrow money from bank manager Ronald. In the second, Eva is trying to commit suicide while all

Director **Christopher Dunham**

around her people insensitive to her predicament are cleaning the kitchen, mending the sink and fixing the lights. In the final scene, roles have been reversed. Eva is now on top of Geoffrey, once a philanderer, now a failed architect. Ronald's wife has become submerged by alcohol. Sidney now has the wealth and the power, and all must dance to his tune. Indeed, the curtain falls with him as puppet master ordering all to dance. It is a chilling finale. The strength of Christopher Dunham's production is that, while it allows you to laugh heartily, it never allows you to lose sight of the human agony that is just below the surface.

Simeon Andrews was a totally credible upwardly mobile developer. Christine Absalom was marvellously funny as Jane, ever dusting and polishing; and Charmian May, clear cut in class, moved from a delight in a drink to alcoholism with silky smoothness. Shenagh Govan, silent in the second act as she tries unsuccessfully to end her life, captured the desolation and ultimate strength of Eva with frightening clarity.

This was the Palace Theatre's last production before the Christmas offering of *Wind in the Willows*. It is a theatre which never fails to delight and to challenge as it walks that perpetual tightrope between the Eastern Arts Association and the public. It satisfies the needs of both without ever losing sight of quality and integrity.

WINDSOR

Theatre Royal

THAMES STREET, WINDSOR, BERKSHIRE SL4 1PS
0753-853888

Artistic Director **Mark Piper**

Taking Steps (1980)
ALAN AYCKBOURN

24 January–11 February 1989

Elizabeth **Angela Scoular**
Mark **Alister Cameron**
Tristram **David Janson**
Roland **Simon Merrick**
Leslie **Jeffrey Robert**
Kitty **Rosie Timpson**

The Theatre Royal maintained the pace of entertainment after the pantomime, *Dick Whittington*, with an enjoyable production of *Taking Steps*. It is a play of comic confusions and ultimate reconciliation.

Design **Julian Saxton**   Director **John David**
Lighting **Matthew Evered**

The Chalk Garden (1955)

ENID BAGNOLD

14 February–11 March 1989

Miss Madrigal **Eleanor Bron**
Maitland **David Swift**
A Little Lady **Marina McConnell**
A Grander Lady **Elisabeth Choice**
Laurel **Helena Bonham Carter**
Mrs St Maugham **Dulcie Gray**
Nurse **Katie Evans**
Olivia **Diana Marchment**
The Judge **Michael Denison**

Mark Piper revived one of the great favourites of the fifties, Enid Bagnold's *The Chalk Garden*. It revolves around Mrs St Maugham, who lives for her garden, and her rather difficult granddaughter. She engages a companion for the girl, but a judge reveals that the companion is a convicted murderess. It is a play that demands an all-star cast, which it had at the Haymarket in 1955 and at Windsor in 1989.

Design **Alexander McPherson**   Director **Mark Piper**
Lighting **Matthew Evered**

The Bread-Winner (1930)

W SOMERSET MAUGHAM

14 March–8 April 1989

Charles Battle **George Cole**
Margery **Ciaran Madden**
Judy **Lois Harvey**
Patrick **Lucien Taylor**
Alfred Granger **Gary Waldhorn**
Dorothy **Penny Morrell**
Diana **Sally Cookson**
Timothy **Samuel West**

The last comedy that Somerset Maugham wrote for the stage is of great interest but is now rarely performed. In the original production in 1930, Ronald Squire and Marie Lohr played the broker and his wife, with Jack Hawkins and Peggy Ashcroft as their children.

Design **Alexander McPherson**   Lighting **Matthew Evered**
Costume **Tom Rand**   Director **Kevin Billington**

Inside Job

BRIAN CLEMENS

12–29 April 1989

Suzy **Prunella Gee**
Larry **Robin Sachs**
Alex **Gareth Thomas**

Design **Julian Saxton**
Lighting **Matthew Evered**

A thriller in one set for three characters was the task that Brian Clemens set himself in *Inside Job*. Clemens has a string of television successes from 'The Avengers' to 'The Professionals'.

Director **Mark Piper**

Move Over Mrs Markham

RAY COONEY and JOHN CHAPMAN

2–20 May 1989

Deceptions, hopeful lovers, fur coats and a flat are the main ingredients of this tasteless but highly popular farce.

Joanna Markham **Maggie Henderson**
Alistair Spenlow **Liam Kennedy**
Sylvie **Lisa Bloor**
Linda Lodge **Bridget McConnel**
Philip Markham **Royce Mills**
Henry Lodge **Anthony Verner**
Walter Pangbourne **Robert Mill**
Olive Harriet Smythe **Zara Nutley**
Miss Wilkinson **Jo Rideout**

Design **Alexander McPherson**
Lighting **Matthew Evered**
Director **Joan Riley**

Habeas Corpus (1973)

ALAN BENNETT

23 May–10 June 1989

The theme of comedy continued at Windsor with Alan Bennett's farce about a philandering middle-aged general practitioner and a rather eccentric assortment of people.

Arthur Wicksteed **Peter Cartwright**
Muriel Wicksteed **Alexandra Dane**
Dennis Wicksteed **Gordon Lovitt**
Constance Wicksteed **Miranda Bell**
Mrs Swabb **Elisabeth Wade**
Canon Throbbing **Richard Denning**
Lady Rumpers **Pamela Buchner**
Felicity Rumpers **Janine Wood**
Mr Shanks **Davyd Harries**
Sir Percy Shorter **Alan Hay**
Mr Purdue **Duncan Brown**

Design **Julian Saxton**
Lighting **Matthew Evered**
Choreographer **Hazel Gee**
Director **Mark Piper**

Ten Times Table (1977)

ALAN AYCKBOURN

13 June–1 July 1989

The second Ayckbourn play of the year at Windsor, *Ten Times Table* first examines our passion for committees and the resultant dissensions and then concludes with the chaos that takes place at the festival which the committee has been arranging.

Ray **Robin Bowerman**
Donald **Roger Kemp**
Helen **Marcia Warren**
Sophie **Charlotte Attenborough**
Eric **Dominic Letts**
Audrey **Elizabeth Kelly**
Lawrence **John Arthur**
Tim **Michael Burrell**
Philippa **Lorraine Brunning**
Max Kirkov **Jonathan Brown**

Design **Julian Saxton**
Lighting **Matthew Evered**
Director **Robin Herford**

Up and Running (1989)

ERIC CHAPPELL

4–29 July 1989

Higgs **Tony Caunter**
Rt Hon. Philip Conway, MP **Keith Barron**
Vicky **Susie Blake**
Lorna Fiske **Bridget McConnel**
George Reynolds, MP **Philip Madoc**
Lionel Berryman, MP **Peter Cellier**
Rt Hon. John Henderson, MP

A new play which takes a cynical look at the world of politics, *Up and Running* concerns an aspirant to the highest office who strives not to become compromised by the presence of a lady in his hotel bedroom.

Angus Mackay

Design **Alexander McPherson**

Lighting **Matthew Evered**
Director **Mark Piper**

31 July–19 August 1989, *Towards Zero* (see touring companies, Churchill Theatre).

Lend Me a Tenor

KEN LUDWIG

22 August–9 September 1989

Max **Ian Sharrock**
Maggie **Erika Hoffman**
Saunders **John Barron**
Bellhop **Gordon Kane**
Tito **Emile Belcourt**
Maria **Susannah Morley**
Diana **Karen Tarleton**
Julia **Eira Griffiths**

Design **Alexander McPherson**
Lighting **Matthew Evered**

Set in Cleveland, Ohio, in 1934, *Lend Me a Tenor* concerns a gala performance of Verdi's *Otello*, the apparent death of the star, Tito, and the emergence of his understudy, Max. The star turns out to be well, and chaos – threaded with his and the understudy's various ladies – ensues. Eric Braun in *The Stage* was delighted by the production, which he called 'teamwork at its most *fortissimo*'. Incredibly, Ian Sharrock, highly praised for his performance, was making his stage début after nine years in 'Emmerdale Farm' on television.

Musical Director **Rod Argent**   Director **Stephen Barry**

The Importance of Being Earnest (1895)

OSCAR WILDE

12 September–7 October 1989

Lane **Brendan Barry**
Algernon Moncrieff **David Yelland**
John Worthing, JP **Bruce Bould**

The sixth production of Wilde's masterly comedy to be staged at Windsor in the past 50 years, Robert Chetwyn's production boasted a very fine cast.

Lady Bracknell
Eleanor Summerfield
Hon. Gwendolen Fairfax **Sabina Franklyn**

Cecily Cardew **Lucy Aston**
Miss Prism **Dilys Laye**
Rev. Canon Chasuble **James Bree**
Merriman **Charles Rea**

Design **Alexander McPherson**
Lighting **Matthew Evered**
Director **Robert Chetwyn**

---

10 October–4 November 1989, *Shirley Valentine* (touring production, see Liverpool Playhouse).

The Reluctant Debutante (1955)
WILLIAM DOUGLAS HOME

14 November–9 December 1989

Jimmy Broadbent **Frank Thornton**
Sheila Broadbent **Barbara Murray**
Jane **Sally Geoghegan**
Mabel Crosswaite **Jill Melford**
Clarissa **Laura Brattan**
David Bulloch **Tom Melly**
David Hoylake-Johnson **Ben Stevens**
Mrs Edgar **Beryl Evans**

Another splendid cast was assembled for this welcome revival of Home's gentle comedy about the prejudices and whims of the upper middle class. It was followed by the pantomime, *Jack and the Beanstalk* and, early in 1990, by the touring production of *Dangerous Obsession*.

Design **Terry Parsons**
Lighting **Matthew Evered**

Director **Hugh Goldie**

YORK

Theatre Royal

ST LEONARD'S PLACE, YORK YO1 2HD
0904-623568

Artistic Director **Derek Nicholls**

The season at York began with *The Royal Baccarat Scandal*, 6–18 February, which transferred to the Haymarket Theatre, London, under which details will be found. The Nottingham Playhouse production of *The Hobbit* was followed by the touring production of *And Then There Were None*.

From 23 March to 15 April 1989, the production of *The Fifteen Streets*, which began life in Coventry and was seen at The Playhouse Theatre, London, in 1988, was staged.

Death of a Salesman (1949)

ARTHUR MILLER

18 May–3 June 1989

Willy Loman **Fred Pearson**
Linda **Yvonne Bryceland**
Biff **Michael Packer**
Happy **John Cagan**
with **Tom Bowles, Frankie Cosgrave, Michael Poole and**

A strong production of Miller's powerful drama with a consistently good cast and special music by Stephen Warbeck.

Richard Conway

Design **Michael Taylor**

Lighting **Michael Thomas**
Director **Terry Johnson**

One Big Blow (1981)

JOHN BURROWS

13–17 June 1989

with **Finetime Fontayne, Andy Hockley, John Middleton, Malcolm Raeburn, Tony Turner and Gordon Duffy**

Music **Rick Lloyd**
Director **Martin Jameson**

'A brilliant illusion of raw pit humour about the life of the modern miner and his love of the sound of brass' was how Bill Anderson described this touring show. It said much about the sacrifices of the miner and told its story swiftly as six actors played many roles and used mime and music to great advantage.

She Stoops to Conquer (1773)

OLIVER GOLDSMITH

3 July–12 August 1989

Mr Hardcastle **Jack Smethurst**
Mrs Hardcastle **Jean Fergusson**
Tony Lumpkin **Martin Barrass**
Kate Hardcastle **Lucy Jenkins**
Constance Neville **Georgia Mitchell**
Diggory/Bear Master **Tony Turner**
Roger/Master Muggins **Royce Ullah**
Pimple **Janette Schofield**
Charles Marlow **Jonathan Donne**
George Hastings **Jim Findley**
Jeremy **Royce Ullah**

Derek Nicholls's first production as artistic director of the Theatre Royal provided an 'illuminating introduction' to his approach. His interpretation was light and charming. He ignored what some see as the darker sides of Goldsmith's comedy of courtship and marriage, but the production was very well received.

Sir Charles Marlow/Landlord
Bernard Martin

Design **Robert Jones**
Costume **Ian McNeil**

Lighting **Mick Thomas**
Music **Stephen Warbeck**
Director **Derek Nicholls**

The Railway Children (1988)

DAVE SIMPSON from the novel by E E Nesbit

17 August–16 September 1989

Perks **Geoffrey Wilkinson**
John **Martin Harman**
Mother **Tamara Hinchco**
Peter **Paul Russell**
Phyllis **Sally Noden**
Roberta **Sarah Burghard**
Mr Szczepansky **Royce Ullah**
Gentleman **Sidney Malin**
Dr Forest **Hayward Morse**

Design **Simon Higlett**

Derek Nicholls had produced this children's classic at Birmingham in 1988 and restaged it at the Theatre Royal, York, as a prelude to a national tour. It was rapturously received – 'a spiffing treat for all ages'. A huge steam train was part of an imaginative design, the performances were universally praised and Bill Anderson felt that the production was 'a shining example to theatres who normally sit and suffer out the lean and silly late summer months'.

Lighting **Chris Parry**   Director **Derek Nicholls**

The programme scheduled to follow *The Railway Children* was *Stepping Out, An Inspector Calls, A Taste of Honey* and *Aladdin*.

SECTION SIX

The Touring Companies

The work of some touring companies appears under Outer London, Fringe and Theatre Clubs (Section Four)

1. Another vital theatrical experience from Cheek By Jowl. Patrick Toomey and Catherine White at the rear; Phil McKee, Lawrence Evans and Lucy Tregear at the front; in Declan Donnellan's *Lady Betty*.

Cambridge Theatre Company

8 MARKET PASSAGE, CAMBRIDGE CB2 3PF
0223-357134

Artistic Director **Robin Midgley**

The Way of the World (1700)
WILLIAM CONGREVE

Fainall **Michael Hadley**
Mirabell **Glyn Grain**
Witwoud **Ian Gelder**
Petulant **Kevin Elyot**
Sir Wilfull Witwoud **Peter Gordon**
Waitwell **Richard Errington**
Servants **Paul Corrigan**
Lady Wishfort **Eleanor Summerfield**
Mrs Millamant **Susan Brown**
Mrs Marwood **Amanda Boxer**
Mrs Fainall **Isabelle Amyes**
Foible **Jane Galloway**
Mincing **Angela Curran**

Design **Poppy Mitchell**

Bill Pryde ended his reign as artistic director of the Cambridge Theatre Company with productions of *The Way of the World* and *The Late Christopher Bean*. The choice of the greatest of Restoration comedies as one of his farewell productions was most appropriate. A complicated plot of love and subterfuge revolves around Mirabell's efforts to marry Millamant and the barriers put in his way by Lady Wishfort, who would like him for herself. The production was generally received with enthusiasm. Eleanor Summerfield's Lady Wishfort was seen by Peter Kemp in *The Independent* as having 'all the cruel comedy of the superannuated belle', while Angela Curran and Jane Galloway were highly praised for their hilarious contributions as the maids, Foible and Mincing.

Lighting **Mick Hughes**
Choreographer **Sue Lefton**
Music **Max Early**
Director **Bill Pryde**

The Late Christopher Bean (1933)
EMLYN WILLIAMS

Dr Haggett **Jerome Willis**
Mrs Haggett **Andree Evans**
Susan Haggett **Susannah Doyle**
Ada Haggett **Joanna Myers**
Gwenny **Rhoda Lewis**
Tallant **Desmond McNamara**
Bruce McRae **Colin Gurley**
Rosen **Jim McManus**
Davenport **Alec Linstead**

Design **Tanya McCallin**
Lighting **Leonard Tucker**
Director **Bill Pryde**

Bill Pryde's farewell production for the CTC was a revival of an Emlyn Williams play which was itself a reworking of Sidney Howard's translation of Fauchois's *Prenez Garde à la Peinture*. Gwenny is the Welsh maid who is leaving the service of Dr Haggett and his family after 15 years. She loved and cared for an alcoholic painter, Christopher Bean, who died of tuberculosis ten years before the play begins. Bean was unrecognised in his lifetime, but his work has now become desirable and Gwenny has possession of many of his canvases. It is this fact which provides the basis of this comedy with dark undertones. Edith Evans had much success in the original although the play was never seen in the West End.

How the Other Half Loves (1969)
ALAN AYCKBOURN

Frank Foster **Peter Bayliss**
Fiona Foster **Marilyn Cutts**
Mary Featherstone **Vicky Ogden**
William Featherstone **Bob Hewis**
Teressa Phillips **Jane Griffiths**
Bob Phillips **Colin Gourley**

Design **Clive Lavagna**
Lighting **Richard Moffatt**
Director **Robin Midgley**

New director of the Cambridge Theatre Company, Robin Midgley, returned to the play he directed when it first came to London in 1970, *How the Other Half Loves*. Ayckbourn's play, which had a successful revival in the West End in 1988, tells of a timorous couple who are seen dining simultaneously in two different households on successive evenings. It is a comedy about class, deception, marital discord and much else.

2. Peter Bayliss as Frank and Marilyn Cutts as Fiona in How the Other Half Loves, *directed for the Cambridge Theatre Company by their new artistic director Robin Midgley.*

The Cambridge Theatre Company also mounted a production of Tennessee Williams's *The Glass Menagerie*. Unfortunately, active and successful as the company is on stage, their press relations department is less active and less successful in giving information off it.

Takeaway (1989)

Devised by **Denni Sayers**
Choreographer **Denni Sayers**
Music and Lyrics **Christopher Benstead**

Using more than 50 local children, Cambridge Theatre Company presented this 'tropical topical musical'. It told of a tribe living in an equatorial rain forest who are driven from their land by a big business concern that wants to use the area

Design **Margaret Woznica**
Lighting **Simon Bayliss**

to graze cattle which will later become beefburgers. It is a green play concerned with the devastation of the earth for quick profit.

Petula Clark, Dave Willetts, Clive Carter, Jane Arden, Joanne Campbell, Lewis Rae and Michael Seraphim toured in *Someone Like You* throughout October and November, and it was anticipated that the musical would later move into the West End. With music by Petula Clark, lyrics by Dee Shipman and book by Fay Weldon, *Someone Like You* tells of an Englishwoman who arrives at a military hospital at the end of the American Civil War in search of her husband. The show is directed by Robin Midgley, designed by Tim Goodchild, lit by Robert Bryan and choreographed by Denni Sayers.

Cavalcade Theatre Company

57 PELHAM ROAD, LONDON SW19 1NW
01-540-3513

Artistic Director **Carol Crowther**

The Adventures of Brer Rabbit (1989)

Uncle Remus **Roger Kain**
Brer Rabbit **Kim Joyce**
Brer Fox **Gavin Conrad**
Brer Dog/Brer Turtle **Geoffrey Howse**
Brer Bear **Richard Ruck**
Sister Mouse **Katherine Webb**
Brer Frog **Mark Lemon**

Music **Michael-Ward Allen**

A lively and likeable musical adaption of Joel Chandler Harris's moral tales, *Brer Rabbit* toured extensively. The noted clown Kim Joyce, an actor of rich experience, played Brer Rabbit and directed the show. He was supported by a good cast which included, among others, the highly talented Katherine Webb.

Book and Lyrics **Carol Crowther**
Based on the stories of **Joel Chandler Harris**

Musical Director **Paul Nicholson**
Choreographer **Kim Joyce**
Director **Kim Joyce**

3. Cavalcade Theatre's production of The Adventures of Brer Rabbit. *Geoffrey Howse (Brer Turtle) and Gavin Conrad (Brer Fox) offer advice to Kim Joyce (Brer Rabbit).*

4. Lorinda King as Alice and Geoffrey Howse as the Duchess in Cavalcade's *Alice in Wonderland.*

Alice in Wonderland (1978)

CAROL CROWTHER adapted from the novel by Lewis Carroll

Alice **Lorinda King**
The White Rabbit **Graham Ashe**
Canon Duckworth/The Caterpillar/The Mad Hatter/The Mock Turtle **John Catteli**
Lorina, Alice's sister/The Cook/The Queen of Hearts **Karen Hodson**
Lewis Carroll/The Frog Footman/The March Hare/The King of Hearts **David Howe**
The Duchess/The Dormouse/The Gryphon **Geoffrey Howse**
The Fish Footman/The Executioner/The Knave of Hearts **Tony McManus**

Musical Director **Paul Nicholson**
Choreographer **Kim Joyce**
Director **Kim Joyce**

A musical version of Lewis Carroll's children's classic, Cavalcade's production tells the story with songs, dances and much audience participation. First presented in 1978, it was revived for the Lewis Carroll Centenary in 1982 and again in 1989. Lorinda King, fresh from three years in the *Rocky Horror Show*, and theatrical all-rounder Graham Ashe are at the centre of a hard-working cast in a production described in the press as 'sheer delight'.

Both *The Adventures of Brer Rabbit*, a delightful and exciting show, and *Alice in Wonderland* are booked for touring Britain well into 1990. Cavalcade are also touring *Joey the Clown*, the adventures of Harlequin and Columbine as they try to escape the clutches of Old Pantaloon. This was first produced at the Edinburgh Festival in 1978 to mark the bicentenary of the birth of Joey Grimaldi, and it is a lively homage to a significant and charming piece of theatrical history.

In similar vein is *Pantomania* – with actor/director Kim Joyce at the centre of a cast of four – in that it celebrates British Pantomime.

Here Come The Clowns has played in more than 200 theatres in Great Britain and abroad. Four clowns demonstrate the whole range of clowning in a variety of programmes.

The Owl and the Pussycat, a new musical version of Edward Lear's poem, is in preparation to add to Cavalcade's productions at the end of 1989. It is adapted by Carol Crowther and has songs which evoke the Edwardian era.

> # Cheek By Jowl

ALFORD HOUSE, AVELINE STREET, LONDON SE11 5DQ
01-793-0153

Artistic Directors **Declan Donnellan and Nick Ormerod**

The Doctor of Honour (1635)
PEDRO CALDERON DE LA BARCA translated by Roy Campbell

Don Pedro **William Hope**
Don Henry **Neil Pearson**
Don Gutierre Alfonso Solis **Nigel Terry**
Don Arias/Ludovico **Kilian McKenna**
Don Diego **Ben Onwukwe**
Dona Mencia de Acuna **Michelle Fairley**
Dona Leonor **Claire Benedict**
Coquin **Mark Williams**
Jacinta **Sue Devaney**

Design **Julian McGowan**
Lighting **Rick Fisher**
Musical Director **Stephen Warbeck**
Director **Lindsay Posner**

As we have come to expect over the past eight years, Cheek By Jowl have taken a little known and little produced play from the past, dusted it down and presented it with a vigour and a freshness that continues to excite and amaze. Calderon's plays have never been particularly popular in England, for, as in *The Doctor of Honour*, he offers a morality which is not to our taste.

5. *Nigel Terry as Gutierre, arrogant and absurd detachment, and...*

6. ... *Michelle Fairley as Mencia, doomed beauty, 'an actress with fire in her eyes', in Lindsay Posner's chilling production of* The Doctor of Honour.

When her great love, Prince Henry, left Spain, Mencia married Gutierre in order to avoid entering a convent. Gutierre had been betrothed to Leonor, but he simply casts her aside. Prince Henry returns and rediscovers Mencia. He presses her, but Mencia remains faithful to her husband. It does her little good, for Gutierre, suspecting his wife of adultery, employs a bloodletter to drain her blood from her and so kill her. When the truth is revealed, the punishment inflicted upon Gutierre by the King is that he should marry Leonor, the girl he once jilted, and so make amends. Calderon does not condone the judgement. The play is a critique of the Spanish code of honour.

This is the first Cheek By Jowl production not directed and designed by the founders of the company, but Lindsay Posner has maintained the style which has deservedly won acclaim and popularity. A chess-board floor and a pile of tiles provide the setting, and the company of nine sits in stately order at the rear, taking the floor with urgency when required. As ever in a Cheek By Jowl production, the ensemble playing is impeccable

Cold lighting and luminous shadows emphasise that love and honour are passions of the spirit, and all is grandeur and dignity. Michelle Fairley has a doomed beauty in her portrayal of Mencia. She is an actress with fire in her eyes, and this is a performance of intelligence, passion and sensitivity. Nigel Terry's Gutierre has the right air of arrogant and absurd detachment, while Claire Benedict's Leonor is beautifully controlled, exquisitely spoken and admirably poised. Mark Williams is an engaging clown, but the dominant strength of the production is its clarity, its tone and its freshness. 'All Troy is burning here' – and we smoulder with it in one of the finest offerings of the year.

The True Story of Lady Betty (1989)
DECLAN DONNELLAN

Betty **Sally Dexter**
John/Oliver/Captain Mills **Tim McMullan**
Father Molloy/Michael Flynn **Gerard O'Hare**
Sarah/Morning **Lucy Tregear**
Night/Bridie O'Byrne **Catherine White**
Silence/George/Rev. Blakeney **Lawrence Evans**
Cold/Liamog Hanrahan **Phil McKee**
O'Leary/Liam Hanrahan **Ray McBride**
Mrs Mills/Peggy Hanrahan **Charlotte Medcalf**
Dunne/Christie O'Flaherty **Patrick Toomey**

Design **Nick Ormerod**
Lighting **Ben Ormerod**
Music **Paddy Cunneen**
Director **Declan Donnellan**

Economy of style, inventiveness, simplicity and clarity are the characteristics of any Cheek By Jowl production and, in their second touring piece of 1989, these qualities were brought to bear upon an original piece by Declan Donnellan. He has taken as his theme the life of Lady Betty, who was probably the executioner at Roscommon Gaol from 1780 to 1810.

Seduced by her master when in service, Betty gives her child away. She is driven into solitude and near starvation, and her only comfort is the night, which promises her silence, cold and a knock at the door. The knock at the door arrives in the form of her son who, now a gentleman, is inquisitive about the identity and whereabouts of his real mother even though 'romantic speculations about the peasantry are no longer in fashion'. Betty murders him for his money and his food, and dawn brings with it three gifts – gold, blood and the letter which reveals the identity of the murdered man. Betty is taken to Roscommon to be hanged alongside Flynn, an Irish patriot, but the hangman absconds for fear of what will be done to him if he hangs Flynn. Betty volunteers to do the job and earns a reprieve for doing it. She lives ever after in the safety of the prison and rules over the area with cruelty and a vigorous use of the hangman's rope.

Sally Dexter is a vital, disturbing Betty, the victim of a past which destroys all. Inevitably, there is some wonderful ensemble playing by a cast who must sing, dance, leap and play without respite. Nick Ormerod's simple set of groups of poles is put to a number of ingenious uses: now the prison cell; now the castle walls; now symbolic of the three crosses, with Betty, momentarily, a Christ figure. The music is haunting and

7. Lady Betty (Sally Dexter) and Michael Flynn (Gerard O'Hare) prepare to die in Declan Donnellan's Lady Betty.

melodious; the dancing urgent and compelling. The delightful O'Leary interrupts the action to distance us in Brechtian manner and to give us respite from the gloom and politics, but they are never far away in this thought-provoking and virile piece of theatre.

Churchill Theatre, Bromley

CHURCHILL THEATRE, HIGH STREET, BROMLEY, KENT
BR1 1HA
01-460-1401
with
GRANGEWOOD PRODUCTIONS LTD, 20 RUPERT STREET, LONDON W1V 7FN
01-437-0127

8. Glynn Edwards and Marius Goring in the Churchill Theatre/Grangewood touring production of Towards Zero.

Towards Zero (1956)
GERALD VERNER and AGATHA CHRISTIE from the novel by Agatha Christie

Thomas Royde **Eric Carte**
Kay Strange **Miranda Baker**
Mary Aldin **Liz Edmiston**
Mathew Treves **Marius Goring**
Nevile Strange **Michael Cashman**
Lady Tressilian **Betty Benfield**
Audrey Strange **Gay Hamilton**
Ted Latimer **Anthony Laurie**
Superintendent Battle **Glynn Edwards**
Inspector Leach **Alan Palmer**
PC Benson **Richard Tyrell**

Design **Tim Goodchild**
Lighting **Jenny Cane**
Director **Christopher Renshaw**

A rich and lonely widow, Lady Tressilian, lives in the isolated Gull's Point with her downtrodden housekeeper. A strange assortment of guests gather at the house, including Lady Tressilian's ward and heir, Nevile Strange, his rather blousy second wife, Kay, and his first wife, Audrey. Such a setting and such a gathering is ripe for the murders which follow.

A star-studded cast including television celebrities and the veteran Marius Goring premièred the production at the Churchill Theatre in March, after which it went on an extensive national tour.

The production was well received by the press, who acknowledged Christopher Renshaw's considerable control over the action and the company's achievement in making 'the most of the devious mind of the author to keep the audience gasping for that final shock'.

9. Miranda Baker as Kay and Michael Cashman as her husband Nevile in Agatha Christie's Towards Zero.

Beyond Reasonable Doubt (1987)
JEFFREY ARCHER

Court Usher **John Walters**
Clerk of the Court **Robin Lloyd**
Stenographer **Valerie Newbold**
Mr Justice Tredwell **Michael Bevis**
Anthony Blair-Booth, QC **Edward de Souza**
Det. Chief Insp. Travers **Peter Hurle**
Sir David Metcalfe, QC **Frank Finlay**
Prison Officer **Daniel Finlay**
Mrs Rogers **Angela Ellis**
Dr Weeden **Robert Mill**
Lionel Hamilton **Robert James**
Mr Cole **Richard Sockett**

Following its great success in London at the Queen's Theatre, *Beyond Reasonable Doubt* began a national tour at the Churchill Theatre at the beginning of August. On this occasion, the Churchill Theatre joined with Lee Menzies to mount the production. Wendy Craig and Frank Finlay, who were in the original production at the Queen's, returned to head a strong cast, and the play proved as popular on tour as it had done in the West End.

Robert Pierson **Edward Arthur**
Lady Metcalfe **Wendy Craig**

Design **Tim Goodchild**
Lighting **Jenny Cane**
Director **David Gilmore**

Compass Theatre Limited

13 SHORTS GARDENS, LONDON WC2H 9AT
01-379-7501

Artistic Director **Sir Anthony Quayle** (died October 1989)
Tim Pigott-Smith

The Royal Hunt of the Sun (1964)
PETER SHAFFER

Martin Ruiz **Trevor Martin**
Martin as a boy **Matthew Sim**
Francisco Pizarro **Denis Quilley**
Hernando De Soto **Kenneth Gilbert**
Fray Vicente Valverde **Timothy Kightley**
Fray Marcos De Nizza **Rufus Sewell**
Diego De Trujillo **Colum Convey**
Salinas **Michael Mawby**
Rodas **Malcolm Kaye**
Vasca **Roy Heather**
Domingo **Liam Clarke**
Juan Chavez **Philip Barnes**
Pedro Chavez **James Lailey**
Blas **Michael Dray**
Felipillo **Rob Dixon**
Pedro De Candia **Robert Clare**
Miguel Estete **Tim Stern**
Atahuallpa **Jack Klaff**
Villac Umu **Andrew Baker**
Challcuchima **Andrew Hilton**
Manco **Paul Gunn**
Headman **Martin Bax**
Chieftain **Martin Marquez**
Inti Coussi **Nicola Burnett Smith**
Oello **Tessa Dickinson**
Indians **Dominic Hingorani, Benedict Martin, Jonathan Robinson and Debbie Rogers**

Design **Paul Hernon**
Lighting **Stephen Wentworth**
Choreographer **Stuart Hopps**
Music **Simon Franglen**
Director **Tim Pigott-Smith**

A bare, black sloping stage is suddenly illuminated at the entrance of Pizarro, who is about to set out on his conquest of Peru. Denis Quilley's Pizarro has the rugged looks of Michelangelo. He is the social outcast ever seeking to be accepted, but ever rejected. He finds his succour in soldiering, conquest and the search for gold, but he is an essentially lonely man, and Quilley captures his defiant independence and moral uncertainty with intelligence and a rugged sensitivity. It makes the meeting and friendship with Atahuallpa inevitable and credible. Atahuallpa's stillness, dignity, strength and inner certainty complement Pizarro just as Jack Klaff's performance as the Sovereign Inca gives roundness and finality to Quilley's interpretation. It is logical that both men should be destroyed and, in a sense, dishonoured, for they had need of each other.

Pizarro's soldiers and the Christian Church bring greed, hunger, defilement and death to the Incas. They have lived in a tranquil state of social equality, but the weakness of their society is that it is without pain, a society in which tomorrow will always be like today.

Peter Shaffer's play is a quarter of a century old, and it has weathered well. Tim Pigott-Smith's impressive directorial début captures the ritualistic elements of the play, and he emphasises them with engaging patterns of sound and light. He is well served by a strong cast. In the principal roles, Denis Quilley and Jack Klaff give towering performances, but they are admirably supported, particularly by Trevor Martin and Matthew Sim as Martin Ruiz man and boy. One has watched Matthew Sim since his earliest days on the stage, and he has now matured into an actor of presence and great strength of purpose.

Compass Theatre was formed 15 years ago by Sir Anthony Quayle, who died in October. He fought to establish a company of quality which would bring plays of importance to a wider audience throughout the country. He engaged Tim Pigott-

Smith as his co-director at the beginning of 1989, and he will have died content in the knowledge that the company for which he did so much and gave so much of his life is now in excellent hands.

10. Denis Quilley as Pizarro and Jack Klaff as Atahuallpa in Tim Pigott-Smith's intelligent production of The Royal Hunt of the Sun. Towering performances for Compass Theatre.

Eastern Angles Theatre Company

SIR JOHN MILLS THEATRE, GATACRE ROAD, IPSWICH
IP1 2LQ
0473-211498

Director of Productions **Ivan Cutting**

John Barleycorn (1988)
IVAN CUTTING

with **Mike Gallant, Antonia Neame and Don Williams**
Musician **Adrian May**

Researched and written by Ivan Cutting and the company from documentary sources, *John Barleycorn* is an energetic and entertaining portrayal of 'barley and beer' over 500 years of traditional malting and brewing. The play takes us to the

Design **Julia Last**
Lighting **Roger Weaver**
Music and Musical Director **Pat Whymark**
Director **Ivan Cutting**

present day and the boardroom plots and deals which threaten the tradition. The tour began in Eye in September 1988, and ended in Norwich in January 1989.

Moll Flanders (1988)
IVAN CUTTING from the novel by Daniel Defoe

Robin/Captain/Gent **Mike Gallant**
Mary Godson (Moll Flanders) **Antonia Neame**
Mother/Nurse/Mother Midnight **Perry Mellor**
Daniel Defoe/Linen Draper/Banker **Giles Phibbs**
Daughter/Friend/Northcountrywoman **Beccy Booth**
Older Brother/Jemmy **Don Williams**
Musician **Chris Wood**

Design **Alison Ashton**
Lighting **Roger Weaver**
Musical Director **Pat Whymark**
Director **Ivan Cutting**

The indefatigable Ivan Cutting adapted Defoe's bawdy romp through England in the early 18th century and toured it through Eastern England until the middle of March. An entertaining and energetic production, it was a fine achievement by a small cast.

11. *Eastern Angles romping through* Moll Flanders.

Waterland (1989)
RICHARD HOGGER from the novel by Graham Swift

Tom Crick **Mark Bannister**
Price/Henry Crick/Thomas Atkinson **Richard Cant**
Dick Crick/Lewis/Ernest Richard Atkinson/Joe Shulberg **Neil Caple**
Sarah Atkinson/Barmaid/Helen Atkinson/Martha Clay **Carlene Reed**

Even by the standards of Eastern Angles this was a highly successful venture. Graham Swift's award-winning novel revolving around a family saga and adolescent love in the Fens was most movingly and grippingly adapted for the stage. The most apt praise came from those who, having seen the Eastern Angles' production, were moved to say 'It makes me want to read the novel.'

Mary Metcalf **Paula Stockbridge**

Design **Jane Green**
Music and Musical Director **Pat Whymark**
Lighting **Roger Weaver**
Director **Hettie Macdonald**

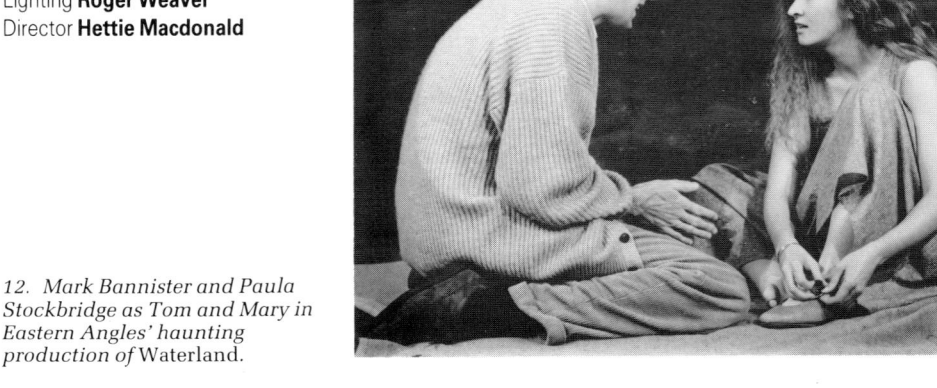

12. Mark Bannister and Paula Stockbridge as Tom and Mary in Eastern Angles' haunting production of Waterland.

Shout (1989)
IVAN CUTTING

with **Ian Ashpitel, Carolyn Pooley and Don Williams**
Musician **Jon Goddard**

Design **Alison Ashton**
Music and Musical Director **Pat Whymark**
Director **Ivan Cutting**

Using the formula that had been used for *John Barleycorn*, Ivan Cutting and his company again turned to documentary sources for their basis of *Shout*. In 1861 at the great Tooley Street fire, a wall collapsed and buried Jimmy Braidwood. One hundred and eight years later, two friends crawl through thick smoke into a burning block of flats. These two events are linked in *Shout* through words and music which celebrate the work and courage of the nation's firemen. *Shout* was first presented at Harlow Fire Station in October 1989 and toured until February 1990, often playing at fire stations as well as village halls schools and theatres.

Eastern Angles' Christmas–New Year production was scheduled for the Sir John Mills Theatre itself and was to be *Mr Pickwick Goes to Town*.

Hull Truck Company

SPRING STREET THEATRE, SPRING STREET, HULL
HU2 8RW
0482-224800

Artistic Director **John Godber**

Gargling With Jelly (1989)
BRIAN PATTEN

Liverpool poet Brian Patten's own adaption of his children's book provided Hull Truck Company with their family touring production for the early part of 1989. The production was designed by Liz Ascroft. She joined Hull Truck from the Theatre Royal, Plymouth, and had also worked extensively for the Orchard Theatre.

13. Stephen Crane, Andrea Thompson, Maureen Howells (lobster-topped) and Nicholas Lane in Gargling With Jelly *by the Hull Truck Company.*

Jimmy **Nicholas Lane**
Mam **Maureen Howells**
Dad **Stephen Crane**
Dr Sensible **Andrea Thompson**

Design **Liz Ascroft**
Lighting **Eamonn Hunt**
Costume **Chris Lee**
Music **Steve Pinnock**

Director **Robert Sian**

September in the Rain (1988)
JOHN GODBER

Jack **Andrew Dunn**
Liz **Adrina Carroll**

Design **Phil Swift**
Lighting **Eamonn Hunt**
Director **Neil Sissons and Jane Thornton**

Originally performed at the Edinburgh Festival in 1988 and seen also at the Waterman's Arts Centre in Brentford, Godber's play based on the life of his grandparents toured Yorkshire and Lincolnshire in February and March 1989.

Northern Lights (1989)
FREDERICK HARRISON

Jenny **Hannah K Andrews**
Peter Pearson **Tom Hutchinson**
Deb **Shirley A Jenkins**
Tracey **Alice Martin**
Embassy Official **Tom Hutchinson**

Design **Robert Cheesmond and Polly Dolman**
Lighting **Eamonn Hunt**
Director **Robert Sian**

Northern Lights had its première at the Spring Street Theatre in April 1989, prior to a national tour. Jenny, Deb and Tracey are forced by unemployment to leave their native Hull and to go to Iceland for six months. There they are to fillet worms from cod. They are greeted with hostility from the locals and resort to the bottle and repelling the advances of the foreman. Following the highly successful tour of *September in the Rain*, Frederick Harrison's play was seen as something of a disappointment and below the usual Hull Truck standard.

Twelfth Night (1602)
WILLIAM SHAKESPEARE

Olivia **Adrina Carroll**
Orsino/Officer **Andrew Dunn**
Malvolio **William Ilkley**
Sir Toby Belch **Nick Kemp**
Feste **Paul Rider**
Sir Andrew Aguecheek **Martin Ronan**

Hull Truck's modern dress touring production of *Twelfth Night* had a mixed reception. Khalid Omer Javed in *What's On* found it 'busy, funny, animated, ambitious and thoroughly entertaining', faithful to the 'intrinsic farcicality of the piece' but others were far less kind. Godber set his Illyria in present-day Oxbridge, and Orsino appears in whites with a cricket bat in his hand. The majority found the production

14. Alice Martin and Hannah K Andrews at variance in Iceland in Hull Truck's Northern Lights.

Viola **Meriel Scholfield**
Antonio/Captain/Valentine **Richard Stone**
Fabian/Curio **Steve Weston**
Sebastian **Tom Whitehouse**
Maria **Deborah Winckles**

heavy and a violation of the subtleties of the play, insensitive to the darker shadows which anticipate the great tragedies.

Design **Robert Cheesmond**
Lighting **Eamonn Hunt**
Music **Richard Stone and Steve Pinnock**
Director **John Godber**

Playing Away (1989)
DAVID LLEWELLYN

Gus Davidson **Gareth Tudor Price**
Sally Davidson **Julie Gibbs**
Nick Trueman **Charlie Dickinson**
Bridget Trueman **Siobhan Nicholas**

Design **Liz Ascroft**
Lighting **Eamonn Hunt**
Director **John Godber**

Although he is the author of several plays which have had considerable success on the fringe, David Llewellyn asserts that *Playing Away* is the first he has written from his own experience, that of meeting his own 'evil double' whilst on holiday in 1987. It is an amusing account of what happens 'when two over-educated English families lose everything – almost – on the Italian Riviera'.

15. Siobhan Nicholas and Julie Gibbs on the beach on the Italian Riviera in Hull Truck's Playing Away.

Teechers (1987)
JOHN GODBER

Salty **John Biggins**
Gail **Barbara Durkin**
Hobby **Shaaron Jackson**

Design **Liz Ascroft**
Lighting **Eamonn Hunt**
Costume **Chris Lee**
Music **Steve Pinnock**
Director **Robert Sian**

Recast and redirected after its London success, *Teechers* remains one of the most enjoyable and compulsive evenings in the theatre. Two actresses and an actor play the parts of the children and the staff of two schools, and they give a vivid, witty, amusing and highly entertaining picture of the state of secondary education in England. The sadness is that few people, and certainly none of the government, are willing to admit how accurate the picture is. We enthused over this play last year, and that enthusiasm has not diminished.

16. Shaaron Jackson, John Biggins and Barbara Durkin in the touring production of John Godber's gloriously entertaining and thought-provoking Teechers.

Bouncers (1985)
JOHN GODBER

Lucky Eric **Seamus O'Neill**
Judd **Robert Angell**
Ralph **Michael Callaghan**
Les **Andrew Grainger**

Lighting **Max Allatt**
Music **Steve Pinnock**
Director **Robert Sian**

Revived for its annual slot at the Edinburgh Festival and brought back to the Spring Street Theatre for the Christmas–New Year period, *Bouncers* continues to amaze and delight. Four men portray all the characters and all the events in a Saturday night out. They are the boys getting ready, boozing and wenching; the girls washing their hair and preparing for the encounters with the opposite sex; the bouncers organising and commentating; and the projector and participants in a blue movie. It is thrilling theatre, pertinent social comment and marvellous entertainment. If the Hull Truck Company had done nothing else but this, their place in theatre history would still be secure.

Catwalk (1989)
JANE THORNTON

Tom **David Allman**
Reg/Graham **Steven Alvey**
Kelly/Elsie **Julie Riley**
Lisa **Tatiana Strauss**

Jane Thornton's new play opened at the Spring Street Theatre in August prior to a national tour. As the title suggests, the play deals with the fashion world, and is a 'combination of chaos, glamour, jealousy and ambition'.

Design and Costume **Ruari Murchison**

Lighting **Eamonn Hunt**
Director **John Godber**

As well as *Bouncers*, John Godber's adaption of *A Christmas Carol* was offered at the Spring Street Theatre for the Christmas–New Year period. The Hull Truck Company has now entered its 19th year, and 1989 saw the company present seven shows at the Edinburgh Festival and tour four plays nationally. There seems no end to Hull Truck's energy, enterprise and success. It has never lost sight of its aim of bringing theatre to as many people as possible, not only through putting on its productions at village halls and community centres, but also in the work that it does within the community itself. As Barry Nettleton, administrator of the Hull Truck Theatre Company, has written, one remains bewildered as to why Hull Truck and other companies have to fight 'very hard for relatively small sums of public money in the form of grants' and why those in government fail to 'realise

17. Steven Alvey, David Allman and Tatiana Strauss in Jane Thornton's new play, Catwalk, *a look at the fashion world.*

the economic and cultural significance of the Arts in a balanced society'.

Newpalm Productions

26 CAVENDISH AVENUE, FINCHLEY, LONDON N3
01-349-0802

Gypsy (1959)

Uncle Jocko/Rich Man/Mr Kringelein/Theatre Manager **Peter Durkin**
Georgie/Mr Weber/Pop/Mr Goldstone/Pastey **Peter Schofield**

Newpalm's great touring success, in conjunction with Mark Furness, was their production of the popular musical *Gypsy* with Ruth Madoc in the title role. It is based on the mother-dominated life of striptease artist Gypsy Rose Lee, one of the last survivors of the American burlesque show.

Baby June **Nicola Stapleton/Lousinda Spencer/Rebecca Spencer/Julie Williams**
Baby Louise **Jane Horn/Jennifer Williams/Claire Russell/Amanda Armellino**
Rose **Ruth Madoc**
Herbie **John Bardon**
June **Susannah Jupp**
Louise **Catherine Terry**
Yonkers **Graeme Metcalfe**
LA/Bourgeron-Cochon **Graham**

MacDuff
Tulsa **Richard Cuerden**
Angie **Adam le Clair**
Miss Cratchitt/Phyllis/Mazeppa **Deborah Steel**
Agnes **Melanie Lewis**
Marjorie May/Renee **Samantha Warden**
Geraldine/Electra **Sally Taylor**
Tessie Tura **Amanda Prior**

Book **Arthur Laurents**

Music **Jule Styne**
Lyrics **Stephen Sondheim** based on the memoirs of Gypsy Rose Lee
Design **Richard Bullwinkle**
Costume **Jessica Bowles**
Choreographer **Stephanie Carter**
Orchestrations **Chris Walker**
Musical Director **Jae Alexander**
Director **Michael Winter**

My Wife Whatsername (1988)
CHRISTOPHER LILLICRAP and JONATHAN IZARD

Nigel Brotherton **Tim Raynham**
Zoe Speeking **Erika Hoffman**
Atash el Fasar **Shireen Shah**
Geoffrey Speeking **Windsor Davies**
Ahmed Ben Giza **Sumar Khan**
Rosemary Speeking **Andrée Melly**

A farce which came to rest at Devonshire Park Theatre, Eastbourne, for the month of July. The presence of television personality Windsor Davies and veteran actress Andrée Melly assured the play of good audiences.

Design **Geoffrey Scott**

Director **Jimmy Thompson**

Black Coffee (1930)
AGATHA CHRISTIE

Mrs Treadwell **Betty Cardino**
Lucia Amory **Lavinia Doran**
Caroline Amory **Mary Elliot-Nelson**
Richard Amory **Malcolm Tomlinson**

Barbara Amory **Louise Becket**
Edward Raynor **Jonathan Shard**
Dr Carelli **Chris Barnden**
Sir Claud Amory **Oliver Bradshaw**
Hercule Poirot **Denis Huett**

Capt. Arthur Hastings **Niall Lucas**
Inspector Japp **Lionel Chilcott**

Director **Lionel Chilcott**

Murder with Love
FRANCIS DURBRIDGE

Larry Campbell **Niall Lucas**
Jo Mitchell **Mary Elliot-Nelson**
Mrs Bedford **Betty Cardino**
Ernest Foster **Denis Huett**

David Ryder **Malcolm Tomlinson**
George Rudd **Ray Franklin**
Roy Campbell **Chris Barnden**
Clare Norman **Lavinia Doran**

Cleaver **Oliver Bradshaw**

Director **Lionel Chilcott**

Murder on the Nile (1945)
AGATHA CHRISTIE

Steward **David Wayne-Ralph**
Miss Ffoliot-Ffoulkes **Mary Mitchell**
Christina Grant **Katie Evans**
Smith **Mark Perry**
Louise **Caroline St John**

Dr Bressner **Peter O'Dwyer**
Kay Mostyn **Helen Kay**
Simon Mostyn **Kenneth Lodge**
Canon Pennyfeather **Gilbert Vernon**

Jacqueline de Severac **Jacqueline Davis**
McNaught **David Horne**

Director **David Horne**

Dangerous Corner (1932)
J B PRIESTLEY

Freda Caplan **Katie Evans**
Miss Mockridge **Mary Mitchell**
Betty Whitehouse **Jacqueline Davis**
Olwen Peel **Daphne Palmer**
Charles Stanton **Peter O'Dwyer**
Gordon Whitehouse **Mark Perry**
Robert Caplan **Kenneth Lodge**

Director **David Horne**

Newpalm Productions made an interesting contribution to the work of the touring companies in 1989 when they set four thrillers on the road. *Black Coffee* and *Murder with Love* were played by one company, and *Murder on the Nile* and *Dangerous Corner* by another. The companies switched venues so that one theatre could be served for a four- or eight-week period.

Black Coffee, set in the 1920s, features Hercule Poirot, who is involved with spies, secret formulas and mysterious poisons as well as the inevitable murder.

Two murders and suspicion of everyone is the basis of *Murder with Love*. In *Murder on the Nile*, set in the early part of the century, a newly-wed, Simon Mostyn, is on his honeymoon on a steamer on the Nile, only to find that the woman he has jilted is another of the passengers. Passion, murder and suspicion abound.

The most mature of the four plays, which were most competently performed, is *Dangerous Corner*. This is the first of Priestley's time plays, in which the characters presented have the opportunity not to turn that dangerous corner that would lead to disaster.

Orchard Theatre

108 NEWPORT ROAD, BARNSTAPLE, DEVON EX32 9BA
0271-73356

Artistic Director **Bill Buffery**

The Woman in Black (1987)
STEPHEN MALLATRATT from the novel by Susan Hill

Arthur Kipps **Graham Colclough**
The Actor **Andrew Wincott**

Design **Liz Ascroft**
Director **Nigel Bryant**

The Woman in Black, a ghost story about a man who seeks to re-create an experience and conjures up more than he expected, was first seen at the Stephen Joseph Theatre, Scarborough. It played in three theatres in London in 1989 prior to a national tour. The Orchard Theatre production anticipated the London production and toured the West Country in the second half of 1988.

The Lie of the Land (1988)
JANE BEESON

Gemma **Victoria Carling**
Henry **Stephen Tomlin**
Ken/Williams **David Whatley**
Joe/Ed **Paul Rainbow**
Cleo **Krissy Wilson**
Ally **Aletta Lawson**
Matt **Robert Hodges**

Design **Liz Ascroft**
Director **Nigel Bryant**

A production which received sponsorship from the Prudential Corporation – who have been supporting the Orchard Theatre since 1984, *The Lie of the Land* had its first performance at the Brewhouse Theatre, Taunton, in August 1988, and toured the West Country in the two months thereafter. Written by a farmer who has had considerable success with a television serial and with *The Cuckoo*, an earlier play, *The Lie of the Land* deals essentially with West Country issues. It is a moving and amusing story about the pressures on a modern farming couple and presents a vision of what lies ahead for the rural South West.

Macbeth (1606)
WILLIAM SHAKESPEARE

Banquo **David Bateson**
Ross **Stephen Chance**
Duncan/Porter **Graham Colclough**
Lennox **Richard Copestake**

The Orchard Theatre finished 1988 with a production of *Macbeth* which opened at the Northcott Theatre in Exeter in late September. It was a vigorous production of Shakespeare's tragedy and was both well received and well supported.

Macbeth **Michael Jenner**
Lady Macduff **Anna Keene**
Macduff **Martin Marquez**

Lady Macbeth **Pat Rossiter**
Malcolm **David Stevens**
Fleance/Macduff's son **Troy Webb**

Design **Liz Ascroft**
Director **Nigel Bryant**

The Pied Piper (1988)
DAVID WOOD and **DAVE** and **TONI ARTHUR** based on the traditional tale and Robert Browning's poem

The Mayor **Geoffrey Andrews**
The Tradesman **Richard Dean**
The Policeman **Simon Egerton**
The Vicar **Simon Fielder**
The Lame Child **Suzanne Gabriel**
The Pied Piper **Peter Leafe**
The Mother **Gill Nathanson**
The Lollipop Lady **Krissy Wilson**

Design **Anne Curry**
Choreographer **Sue Harris**
Musical Director **Alan Ellis**

This was Nigel Bryant's last production for the Orchard Theatre before he left his post as artistic director to take up an appointment with the BBC in Birmingham. He has made an outstanding contribution to theatre in the West Country, broadening the scope of the Orchard's work and helping to treble the audiences. *The Pied Piper* was the Christmas–New Year production and relied upon children from Yeovil, Exeter, Bideford, Plymouth, Frome and Falmouth to complete the cast as the children of Hamelin in the various centres in which it played.

Director **Nigel Bryant**

Cold Comfort Farm (1989)
SALLY HEDGES adapted from the novel by Stella Gibbons

Sneller the Butler/Amos Starkadder/Earl Neck **John Surman**
Mary Smiling/Judith Starkadder/Mrs Beetle **Molly Savile**
Flora Poste **Jilly Bond**
Aunt Ada Doom **Beryl King**
Reuben Starkadder/Richard Hawk-Monitor **Charles Bartholomew**
Adam Lambsbreath/Urk **Paul Sharples**
Seth Starkadder/Herr Doktor Adolph Mudel **Richard Worthy**
Elfine Starkadder/Meriam Beetle **Henrietta Voigts**

Cold Comfort Farm had its début at the Plymouth Theatre Royal on 1 February 1989. The play was directed by Amanda Knott, who is an associate director of the Theatre Royal. *Cold Comfort Farm*, Stella Gibbons's famous satire on the earthy type of novel that was popular in the 1930s, tells of the arrival of Flora Poste at the farm where many of her relatives live. It is 'crouched on a bleak hill-side' and 'fanged with flints', and there is always something nasty in the wood-shed. The novel was adapted for the stage by Sally Hedges, whose *Far From the Madding Crowd* has also been performed by the Orchard Theatre company and whose *Tess of the d'Urbervilles* was produced by both the Orchard and the RSC at The Swan.

Design **Tim Gosling**
Music **John Kirkpatrick**

Musical Direction **Mia Soteriou**
Director **Amanda Knott**

18. Jilly Bond as Flora Poste, well-educated and unsuspecting, arrives in Cold Comfort Farm, *Orchard Theatre's lively adaption of Stella Gibbons's satire.*

Hitler's Whistle (1989)
JO ANDERSON

Edgar/Luigi **John Axon**
Jill **Henrietta Bess**
Jill now/Mrs Venn **Di Botcher**
Mr Venn **Carl Davies**
Mrs Matthews **Gill Nathanson**
Russell/The Polish Airman **Andrew Solomon**
Mrs Gant **Veda Warwick**

Design **Anne Curry**

Cold Comfort Farm was the last Orchard production to be sponsored by Prudential. *Hitler's Whistle*, a sensitive new play about a young girl in the South West trying to cope with both the war and growing up, was sponsored by British Telecom. The play also marked the directorial début for the Orchard of new artistic director Bill Buffery. Bill Buffery was appointed in February as successor to Nigel Bryant. He had worked for two years with the RSC, for which he had directed *Keeping Tom Nice* – among other plays. *Hitler's Whistle* opened in Plymouth on 17 May and toured the West Country until July.

Sound **Tom Nordon**
Director **Bill Buffery**

19. *Another new play for Orchard. Henrietta Bess as Jill Venn in argument with John Axon as Edgar in Jo Anderson's* Hitler's Whistle.

20. *Alan Cody, Lucy Maycock and Jonathan Milton – Leontes, Hermione and Polixenes in Orchard's production of* The Winter's Tale.

The Winter's Tale (1611)
WILLIAM SHAKESPEARE

An arduous tour began at Torrington on 6 September and ended at Cirencester on 18 November 1989. In the weeks in between, it took in 35 towns. Such commitment and energy is

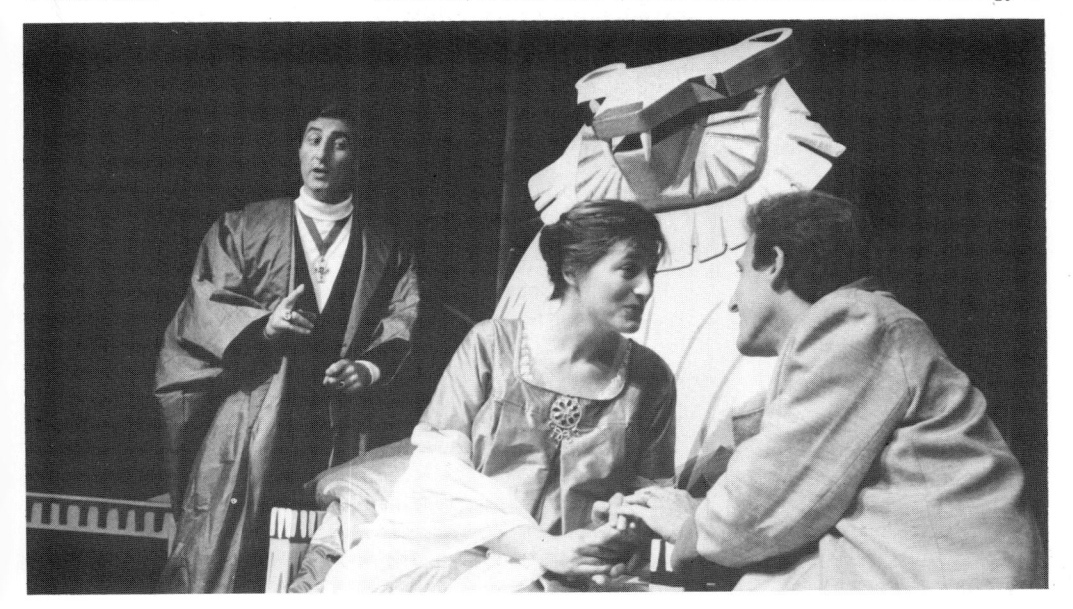

The Clown **John Axon**
Leontes/Autolycus **Alan Cody**
Camillo **Richard Copestake**
Florizel **Simon Elliott**
Polixenes **Jonathan Milton**
Antigonus/The Old Shepherd **Jared Morgan**
Perdita **Henrietta Bess**
Hermione **Lucy Maycock**
Paulina **Sarah Parks**

Design **Meg Surrey**
Music **Tom Mordon**
Director **Bill Buffery**

typical of the work that the Orchard Theatre has been doing for the past 20 years. Since 1969, Orchard Theatre has mounted more than 100 productions. It works in close harmony with the Theatre Royal, Plymouth, and with the Northcott Theatre, Exeter, and has a strong commitment to theatre in education. Orchard Theatre offers a variety of work from thrillers and plays with a West Country bias to Shakespeare and the classics, and it has pioneered much new work. The vitality of the company and the demands made on them can be seen from a glance at the cast list of *The Winter's Tale*, in which ex-RSC actor Alan Cody doubled in the roles of Leontes and Autolycus.

Orchard Theatre's future plans include a Christmas–New Year production of *The Snow Queen*, adapted by Karoline Leach, and a spring production of Caryl Churchill's *Fen*.

Oxford Stage Company

12 BEAUMONT STREET, OXFORD OX1 2LW
0865-723238

Artistic Director **John Retallack**

As You Like It (1599)
WILLIAM SHAKESPEARE

Oliver **Simon Kunz**
Orlando **John Kazek**
Adam/Sir Oliver Martext/Hymen **Richard Henry**
Duke Frederick/Senior **Stuart Richman**
Le Beau/Amiens/William **Clive Walton**
Charles/Corin **Brian Stephens**
Touchstone **Billy Hartman**
Rosalind **Deborah Findlay**
Celia **Carla Mendonça**

With the Playhouse closed, the Oxford Stage Company began their tour in The Rose in the Newman Rooms. This was new artistic director John Retallack's first production for the OSC, and it was greeted as a triumph. Michael Ratcliffe called it an exhilarating production, and Paul Taylor, in *The Independent*, spoke of it as 'a memorable and haunting production'.

Jaques **Michael Roberts**
Silvius **Raymond Greenaway**
Phebe **Matilda Ziegler**
Audrey **Saira Todd**

Design **Phil Swift**
Lighting **Chris Bond**
Music and Musical Director **Howard Goodall**
Director **John Retallack**

King Lear (1605)
WILLIAM SHAKESPEARE

King Lear **Philip Voss**
King of France/Fool **Raymond Greenaway**
Duke of Burgundy/Herald **Brian Stephens**
Duke of Cornwall/Doctor **Michael Roberts**
Duke of Albany **Clive Walton**
Earl of Kent **Billy Hartman**
Earl of Gloucester **Stuart Richman**
Edgar **Simon Kunz**
Edmund **John Kazek**
Curan **Saira Todd**
Oswald/Old Man **Richard Henry**
Goneril **Deborah Findlay**

A direct and economical production of *King Lear* was John Retallack's second offering in his new post, and once again the OSC's efforts were warmly applauded. The admirable Philip Voss gave a restrained and unfussy performance as Lear, falling into decline and madness before he realises what is happening to him.

Of the director, Charles Osborne wrote in *The Daily Telegraph*, 'He has managed to forge a team, and the success of "Lear" bodes well for a company which has had its share of hardship over recent years.'

Regan **Carla Mendonça**
Cordelia **Matilda Ziegler**

Design **Phil Swift**

Lighting **Chris Bond**
Music **Howard Goodall**
Director **John Retallack**

Red Shift Company

BATTERSEA ARTS CENTRE, LONDON SW11 5TF
01-223-3256, 01-223-6557

Artistic Director **Jonathan Holloway**

Timon of Athens (1608)
WILLIAM SHAKESPEARE

Poet/Lucullus/Bandit **Tony Bluto**
Jeweller/Sempronius/Debt Collector/Bandit/Timandra/Servant **Angela Bullock**
Timon of Athens **Kate Fenwick**
Apemantus/Flavius **Matthew Radford**
Painter/Lucius/Caphis/Phrynia/Bandit **Lucy Tregear**

Design **Charlotte Humpston**
Music **Adrian Johnston**
Director **Jonathan Holloway**

Jonathan Holloway's production of *Timon of Athens* aroused conflicting passions. The director chose to cut scenes drastically, juxtapose other scenes, rewrite, condense the whole into 80 minutes and recast Timon as a woman. One of Mr Holloway's reasons for casting Kate Fenwick in the part of Timon was his belief that there are far too few parts of substance for women in the classical repertoire. Few, however, were totally happy about the product. Andy Lavender in *City Limits* found much of it brilliant, but doubted if it was completely satisfying; while Michael Billington felt that this 'misconceived production' turned 'an ironic and bitter attack on the elevation of monetary above human values into a gaudy masque'.

Frida and Diego (1989)
GREG CULLEN

Diego Rivera **Nicholas Jeune**
Frida Kahlo **Anna Savva**
Senora Kahlo/Ella Wolfe/Christina/Jacqueline Breton **Phoebe Burridge**
Bertram Wolfe/Alejandro/Andre Breton/Arthur Niendorff/Musician **Jon Conrad**
Arturo Bustos/Newspaper Seller/Car Worker **Liam Grundy**

21. Anna Savva (Frida) and Nicholas Jeune (Diego) in Red Shift's vital and inventive Frida and Diego.

Red Shift toured *Timon of Athens* from February until June and then presented *Frida and Diego* at the Edinburgh Festival. Like Red Shift's *Misanthrope* in 1988, *Frida and Diego* took a top prize at the festival. The play tells the story of the turbulent lives of two Mexican artists, Diego Rivera and his wife Frida Kahlo. It covers a period of more than 20 years. It is hard to convey this wide expanse of time and place within the confines of 80 minutes, the restriction imposed by the festival requirements. Nevertheless, this is an exciting work. Diego, the communist, non-believer, divorcee is a wealthy muralist who is accepted by the Kahlo family because they need his money even if they are shocked by his morals and his beliefs. He courts skeletons and dances with them at the outset, for he has walked long with death and sees danger as vital to life. He lives with a passionate intensity that asserts itself in his

Senor Kahlo/Trotsky/Siqueiros/Dr Eloesser **Richard Hahlo**
Angelina Beloff/Lupe Marin/Helen Wills Moody/Natalia Trotsky **Kate Paul**

Design **Charlotte Humpston**
Lighting **Will England**
Music and Musical Directors **Adrian Johnston and Liam Grundy**
Director **Jonathan Holloway**

'complex sexual inclination'. He meets the famous of the period between the wars and is unwavering in his socialist beliefs and in the waging of the conflict between art and life, the one sustaining the other. He is the victim of sponsors who welcome the prestige of his work but shy away from its content.

Frida is an artist in her own right, equally passionate and surviving her own disasters. Their relationship is tempestuous but creative, artistically and politically, and when she dies and the whole Mexican revolution itself lays close to ruin we are still reminded that 'we need to dream a little'.

Perhaps Greg Cullen has chosen too wide a landscape, too big a subject for the confines of space and time allowed him. Nevertheless, he has still succeeded in creating a play which, in the hands of Jonathan Holloway and Charlotte Humpston, is visually exciting, poetically stimulating and politically and artistically provocative. As ever, the Red Shift Company work tirelessly. In the major roles, Anna Savva and Nicholas Jeune are totally convincing, passionately involved. The ensemble playing is excellent, and special mention should be made of Phoebe Burridge, who is vital and engaging in a multitude of roles.

There were plans to take the production to the United States early in 1990.

Index of Plays

A

Abingdon Square   183–5
Abolition   212
Absurd Person Singular   330–1
Across Oka   118
Admirable Crichton, the   298
Adventures of Brer Rabbit, the   342–3
After the Fall   204
Alchemist, the   242–3
Alexandra Kollontai   155
Alice in Wonderland   343–4
All Sewn Up   151–2
American Bagpipes   60
American Clock, the   286
Amongst Barbarians   278–9
And Then There Were None   250
Animal Island   307
Anything for a Quiet Life   130
Anything Goes   56–7
Apocalyptic Butterflies   148–9
Arms and the Man   260
Artist Descending a Staircase   18
Art of Success, the   309
Aspects of Love   57
Aspern Papers, the   240
Assignment, the   168–9
As You Like It   44–5, 121–2, 368
Awake and Sing!   319

B

Back Street Mammy   33
Back With a Vengeance   14–5
Baker's Wife, the   255–6
Bare Necessities   246
Bat the Father, Rabbit the Son   174
Beaux Stratagem, the   231–2
Be Bop a Lula   274
Bed   91
Belle of the Belfast City, the   205
Below the Belt   129, 182
Beyond Reasonable Doubt   350
Big Sweep, the   155
Billington, Michael (special article)   105–8
Bird of Prey   164
Birth of Merlin, the   283
Black Coffee   362
Black Comedy   193
Black Prince, the   5
Blithe Spirit   31
Blood   63
Blood Brothers   4
Blood Wedding   152
Blues for Mr Charlie   314
Boswell for the Defence   55
Bouncers   246, 360
Bourgeois Gentilhomme, the   172, 237
Branwen   283–4
Bread-Winner, the   332
Breaking the Code   299
Brighton Beach Memoirs   226, 230, 296, 328–9

C

Cabaret   257
Candida   239
Candide   36
Candle-Light   320–1
Captain Swing   264
Cardboard City   181
Carthaginians   154
Caste   201–2
Catastrophe   270–1
Cat in the Ghetto, a   190
Cats   35
Catwalk   360–1
Caving In   183–4
Chalk Garden, the   332
Charlie Gorilla   206
Chekhov's Women   29
Cherry Orchard, the   235
City Sugar   257
City Wives' Confederacy, the   149
Cleopatra and Antony   31
Cloud Nine   223
Cold Comfort Farm   365–6
Cold Turkey   133
Colony, the   142–3
Come and Make Eyes at Me   169
Comedians   204
Come For the Ride   150
Common Woman, a   151
Company   326–7
Complaisant Lover, the   240–1
Comus   159
Coriolanus   79–80
Corpse   248
Country Wife, the   262
Creditors   166–7

Crimes of the Heart   274
Cross Country   63
Crucible, the   244
Culture Vultures   222
Cymbeline   116

D

Dames at Sea   269
Damn Yankees   210
Dangerous Corner   363
Dangerous Obsession   230
Daughter-in-Law, the   213–4
Day in the Death of Joe Egg, a   310–1
Days of Cavafy   158–9
Dead of Night   275
Dear Brutus   304–5
Death of a Salesman   241–2, 336
Debutante Ball, the   153–4
Devil and Stepashka, the   168
Dial M For Murder   241
Dinner   194
Diplomatic Wives   319
Doctor Faustus   112, 174
Doctor of Honour, the   345–7
Doll's House, a   268
Dona Rosita   216–7
Don't You Know There's a War On   191
Douglas   243
Down Every Street   188
Driving Miss Daisy   255
Duchess of Malfi, the   277
Duet For One   161
Dust-Up In the Attic   240

E

Eartha Kitt in Concert   65
Edge   138
Educating Rita   285
Eighty-Four Charing Cross Road   202
Elsie and Norm's Macbeth   219
Entertaining Mr Sloane   233, 307
Epicoene   116–7
Equus   192, 253, 329
Evening With Queen Victoria, an   150
Exclusive   69–70

374   INDEX OF PLAYS

F

Factory Follies   194–5
Farewell to Sequins, a   30
Farrowland   31
Fashion   271
Fatherland, the   173–4
Fear and Misery of the Third Reich   273
Fears and Miseries of the Third Term   273
Feminine Singular   278
Fiddler on the Roof   249–50, 306
Fishy Tales   285
Fit To Bust   325
Flea in Her Ear, a   45–6
Fool For Love   277
Forbidden Broadway   19
Frankenstein   162
Frankie and Johnny in the Claire de Lune   12
Frida and Diego   370–1
From the Mississippi Delta   80–1
Fuente Ovejuna   84–7
Funeral Games   235

G

Gambler, the   291
Gargling with Jelly   355–6
Gaslight   295
Getting Nowhere – Again   144
Getting Out   282–3
Ghetto   83, 93–6
Ghosts   192, 237–8
Glass Menagerie, the   82, 229
Glen Hoddle, Glen Madeiros   169
Gods Are Not To Blame, the   178
Godspell   227
Golden Girls   296
Government Inspector, the   236
Grange Hill   247–8
Grapes of Wrath, the   98–9
Gulliver's Travels   197
Gypsy   361–2

H

Habeas Corpus   228, 265, 333
Hair   246–7
Hamlet   91–2, 110, 269–70
Happy Family   161
Hard Feeling   138–9
Harlot's Curse, the   195–6
Hawk Moon   143
Hay Fever   241
Heartlanders   211
Hedda Gabler   88–90
Heiress, the   221

Hello and Goodbye   292
Henceforward . . .   70
Henry IV, part one   37–8
Henry IV, part two   38
Henry V   38–9
Henry VI, parts one, two and three   39–41
Hero's Welcome   62
H.I.D. (Hess is Dead)   127
History of Tom Jones, the   318
Hitler's Whistle   366–7
House Guest   253–4
How The Other Half Loves   308, 341
Huis Clos   33

I

I Am of Ireland   174
Ice Cream   59–60
Ideal Husband, an   71–2
Idiot, the   277
Importance of Being Earnest, the   163, 208, 254, 286–7, 335
Improbabilities   179–80
Increased Difficulty of Concentration, the   170–1
Indigo   131
Infant, the   141
In His Name   182
In Lambeth   14
Inside Job   332
Inspector Calls, an   310, 324–5
In the Ruins   215
In the Talking Day   279
Intimate Exchanges   295
Island Life   193–4
Island of Slaves   142–3
Ivanov   68
I Wish I Wish   201

J

Jane Eyre   291
John Barleycorn   352–3
Judgement Day   170
Julius Caesar   276
June Moon   313
Juno and the Paycock   90
Jury Will Ignore That Last Remark, the   146
Just a Verse and Chorus   297
Just Frank   187
Just So   201

K

Kennedy's Children   163
King John   110–1

King Lear   42–4, 126, 369
King's General, the   307–8
Kirta, Sona and Ba   266
Kissing the Pope   126–7
Knickers   214
Krapp's Last Tape   271

L

Ladies in the Lift   181
Lady and the Clarinet, the   160
Lady Betty, the true story of   339, 347–8
Lady From the Sea, the   166
Lady Windermere's Fan   302
La Gran Scena Opera Co   133
Last of the Irish Indians, the   182
Last of the Red Hot Lovers, the   69
Last Waltz, the   148
Late Christopher Bean, the   340
Latin   166–7
Laughing Matters   13–4
Leaf Storm   186
Lend Me a Tenor   334
Leonardo's Last Supper   164
Les Liaisons Dangereux   6
Les Miserables   48–9
Les Parents Terribles   171
Lettice and Lovage   21–2
Lie of the Land, the   364
Little Foxes, the   263
Little Night Music, a   224–5
Little Women: The Tragedy   140
London Assurance   223
Long and the Short and the Tall, the   291
Long Day's Journey Into Night   289
Long Time Gone   30
Long Way Round, the   100
Look Back in Anger   27–8
Looking at You (Revised) Again   268–9
Lorca   13
Love Games   233
Love of the Nightingale, the   120–1
Low Level Panic   30
Low People   268

M

Macbeth   111–2, 242, 244, 364–5
Madhouse in Goa, a   7–8
Making History   84
Malcontent, the   162
Man at Yir Back, a   234
Man, Beast and Virtue   104
Man For All Seasons, a   298
Man of Mode, the   109–110

INDEX OF PLAYS

Man Who Came to Dinner,
   the 103, 117–8
Man Who Lost America, the 327
Man with Connections, a 59
March on Russia, the 92–3
Marshalling Yard, the 135–6
Mary and Lizzie 125–6
Master Builder, the 122–4
Master Harold and the Boys 276–7, 329–30
M. Butterfly 1, 66–7
Me and My Girl 2–3
Measure for Measure 77–9
Meatball 160–1
Mercedes 144–5
Merchant of Venice, the 52–3, 250–1
Metropolis 54
Midsummer Night's Dream, a 47, 109, 227–8
Misanthrope, the 212–3
Miss Julie 32
Miss Saigon 16–7
Moll Flanders 353
Month in the Country, a 264
Morticians' Tea Party, the 167
Mother Goose 293
Mother Poem 140
Mourning Becomes Electra 190
Mousetrap, the 64
Move Over Mrs Markham 333
Mozart and Salieri 131
Mrs Klein 6–7, 265
Mrs Warren's Profession 172–3
Much Ado About Nothing 68, 261
Murder on the Nile 363
Murder with Love 362
My Dearest Ivor 317–8
My Girl 187
My Mother Said I Never Should 59
My Wife Whatsername 362

N

Napoleon – the Untold American Story 53
Nearly Siberia 185
Northern Lights 356–7
Northern Mystery Plays, the 315–6
Noises Off 234, 288

O

O Architect 166
Odd Couple, the 280
Of Mice and Men 273–4
Old Bachelor, the 32
Old Country, the 238–9
Old Devils, the 282

Old Herbaceous 203
Oliver! 293
One Big Blow 336
One Careful Owner 245–6
One For the Road 232, 262
One-Sided Wall, the 134
On Golden Pond 287–8
On the Plastic 208
On the Road to Jerusalem 167
On the Verge 207
Orphans 322–4
Orpheus Descending 23–4
Othello 119–20, 148, 238, 260–1
Our Country's Good 61–2
Our Day Out 209–10
Our Ellen 208
Over My Dead Body 65
Overruled 191

P

Pack of Lies 200
Pale Performer 267–8
Parasol, the 280–1
Paris Match 21
Patchwork Girl of Oz, the 318
Pavane 189
Peace in Our Time 157–8
Pentecost 28–9
Pericles 121
Phantom of the Opera, the 25–6
Philanthropist, the 235–6
Pied Piper, the 365
Piers Plowman 175
Piggy Bank, the 149
Pin to See the Peep Show, a 239
Plague of Innocence 140
Plain Dealer, the 113
Playboy of the Western World, the 236–7
Playing Away 359
Play It Again, Sam 259
Play With Repeats 173
Plaza Suite 215–6
Pleasure Principle, the 165
Polygraph 131
Poor Nanny 156–7
Pornography of Performance, the 175
Prin 33
Private Lives 302–3
Punch and Judy the Real Story! 210
Purity Game, the 225–6
Put Some Clothes On, Clarisse! 18

Q

Queen of Spades and I, the 172

R

Ragged Child, the 290
Railway Children, the 337
Rat in the Skull 307
Recruiting Officer, the 61
Red Balloon, the 278
Redefining the Whore 182
Red Is the Colour of Night 151
Regeneration 152
Re: Joyce! 19, 71
Relatively Speaking 296
Reluctant Debutante, the 335
Restoration 108
Return to Dreams 267–8
Return to the Forbidden Planet 11
Revenger's Tragedy, the 312
Richard II 37, 50–1
Richard III 41–2, 51
Rissoles 167
Rivals, the 219
Riverman 189
Road 243–4
Rock-a-Bye Sailor 289
Rock In Water, a 62
Roll on Friday 321–2
Romeo and Juliet 108, 294
Room of One's Own, a 55
Rosie Blitz 290
Round and Round the Garden 317
Royal Baccarat Scandal, the 24
Royal Hunt of the Sun, the 351–2
Ruffian on the Stair 235
Run For Your Wife 72–3

S

Salt of the Earth 294
Screamers 9
Secret of Sherlock Holmes, the 74
Secret Rapture, the 96–7
September in the Rain 356
Serious Money 218–9
Seven Lears 316
Shades of the Jelly Woman 174
Shadowlands 309–10
Shadow of a Gunman, the 275
Shakers 161
Shaughraun, the 100
Sherlock Holmes – The Musical 10
She Stoops to Conquer 192, 236, 315, 336
Shirley Valentine 19, 274
Shoemaker's Holiday, the 263
Shout 354
Shylock 175–7
Siblings 29
Singin' in the Rain 50

INDEX OF PLAYS

Single Spies   58
Sitting Duck   252
Situation Vacant   171–2
Shock   317
Skin Deep   218
Slaughterhouse 5   272
Sleepie Nightie   198
Sleeping Beauty, the   311–2
Slice of Saturday Night, a   9–10
Sly Fox   305
Small Family Business, a   209
Some Americans Abroad   116–7
Song in the Night, a   32
Songs of Soweto   137
Sons of Bitumen   156
Speed-the-Plow   87–8
Spoils of War   265
Spokesong   205–6
Starlight Express   8–9
State of Play   180
Steaming   231
Steel Magnolias   27
Stepping Out   199, 252–3, 266, 324
Stiff Options   230
Strangers   168
Streetcar Named Desire, a   214
Struggle, the   147
Summerfolk   221
Swaggerer, the   48
Sweeney Todd   297–8
Sweet Shop Owner, the   196–7

T

Table Manners   251
Takeaway   341–2
Take Back What's Yours   195
Taking Steps   331
Tale of Two Cities, a   243, 288, 316
Talk of the Steamie   150
Taste of Honey, a   279
Tart and the Vicar's Wife, the   34
Tartuffe Today   206
Task, the   145–6
Teaser   143

Teechers   359
Tempest, the   113–5
Ten Times Table   333
They're Playing Our Song   257–9
Thoughts From a Very Private Diary   7
Three Guys Naked From the Waist Down   13
Threshold   205
Thunderbirds FAB   8
Thunder in the Air   142
Timon of Athens   369
To Kill a Mockingbird   34
Tom Thumb   245
Touched   233–4
Towards Zero   300, 349
Trafford Tanzi   311
Travels With My Aunt   244–5
Treasure Island   281–2
Triumph of Love, the   222–3
Trojan Women, the   272
Turn of the Screw, the   143
Twelfth Night   47–8, 211, 356–7
Two For The Seesaw   320
200% and Bloody Thirsty   155
Two-Way Mirror   74–6

U

Underwater Swimming   165
Unexpected Guest, the   228–9, 322
Up and Running   334
Up 'N' Under   218
Up on the Roof   306
Utopia   134

V

Valued Friends   153
Vera Baxter   146
Veronica's Room   292
Veteran's Day   24–5
Victory!   220–1
Village Wooing   191
Vinegar Works, the   130

Vision of Love Revealed in Sleep, a   139
Vortex, the   20
Voysay Inheritance, the   97–8, 280

W

Waiting for Godot   77, 204
Walk in the Woods, a   12
Warrior   222
Washday   138
Watchman, the   174
Water Engine, the   154
Waterland   353–4
Way of the World, the   340
Way South, the   134–5
Welcome Home   169
What Are You Afraid Of?   164
What is Seized   139
When I Was a Girl I Used to Scream and Shout   227, 261, 292, 309, 326
While the Sun Shines   304
Whistle in the Dark   61
White Liars   193
Who's Afraid of Virginia Woolf   207
Who's Left   170
Wicked Old Nellie   232–3
Wicked World of Bel Ami, the   188
Widowing of Mrs Holroyd, the   267
Will, the   105–8
William Tell   314–5
Wind in the Willows, the   261–2
Winding the Ball   281
Winter's Tale, the   367–8
Witness for the Prosecution   303
Wizard of Oz, the   284
Wodehouse on Broadway   309
Wolf at the Door   313
Woman in Black, the   20, 364
Women Beware Women   209
Wonder, the   147
World According to Me, the   55
Wush Way   183

Y

Yes and No But   267